THE ISLAND CHURCHES
OF THE SOUTH PACIFIC

The American Society of Missiology Series, in collaboration with Orbis Books, seeks to publish scholarly works of high merit and wide interest on numerous aspects of missiology—the study of mission. Able presentations on new and creative approaches to the practice and understanding of mission will receive close attention.

*Previously published in
the American Society of Missiology Series*

American Society of Missiology Series, No. 5

THE ISLAND CHURCHES OF THE SOUTH PACIFIC

Emergence in the Twentieth Century

Charles W. Forman

ORBIS BOOKS

Maryknoll, New York 10545

The Catholic Foreign Mission Society of America (Maryknoll) recruits and trains people for overseas missionary service. Through Orbis Books Maryknoll aims to foster the international dialogue that is essential to mission. The books published, however, reflect the opinions of their authors and are not meant to represent the official position of the society.

Published by Orbis Books, Maryknoll, NY 10545
in collaboration with the American Society of Missiology

Manuscript Editor: Lisa McGaw

Library of Congress Cataloging in Publication Data
Forman, Charles W.
    The island churches of the South Pacific.

    Bibliography: p.
    Includes index.
    1. Missions—Islands of the Pacific. 2. Islands
of the Pacific—Church history.   I. Title.
BV3670.F67   279   81-18666
ISBN 0-88344-218-3 (pbk.)   AACR2

To Jan

Contents

NORTH   PACI

MARIANA ISLANDS
•Saipan
ₒGuam

M   I   C   R   O   N   E   S   I

MARSHALL ISLANDS

ₒYap

Truk

ₒBelau

Ponapeₒ

Kosraeₒ

CAROLINE   ISLANDS

Tarawa
Abemama
Nauru   Ocean
             Island
                      KIRIBATI
                      Beru
                      Onotoa
                      Tamano
                      Arorae

M   E   New Hanover   L
         Kavieng   A
Manus
Aitape   BISMARCK
NEW   ARCHIPELAGO   N
GUINEA   Rabaul
         Madang   New
Telefomin Wabag   Britain   Buka
         Mt.Hagen   HUON PENINSULA   Bougainville
                    Lae   Choiseul
                    Shortland   E
                    Kolombangara   Isabel   SOLOMON
         PAPUA   Dobu Trobriand   ISLANDS
                    Port New Georgia Nggela Malaita
                    Moresby   Tulagi
TORRES STRAITS   Samarai   Guadalcanal   S
                              Bellonaₒ ₒRennell   Santa Cruz   I
                                                   Islands
                                                              Rotuma

                                        Banks Islands
                              Aoba
                    Espiritu Santo Aurora
                              Aore Pentecost   Vanua Levu
                         Malekula Ambrym   Ovalau
                              VANUATU   Viti Levu   Suva
                                                                  FIJI
                                        Erromanga
                              Ouvéa Tana
                    New Caledonia Lifou
                              Maré
                         Noumea

TUVALU

CORAL SEA

AUSTRALIA

SOUTH

Norfolk

HAWAII

CEAN

LINE ISLANDS

TOKELAU

MARQUESAS
ISLANDS

O   L   Y   N   E   S   I   A

Apia
Upolu   Manu'a
Tutuila
SAMOA

COOK ISLANDS

Bora Bora.
Leeward Islands
Raiatea
Moorea   Papeete
Tahiti
SOCIETY ISLANDS

TUAMOTU ARCHIPELAGO

u
GA   oNiue
pai
ofa
apu

Rarotonga o

Mangareva
Gambier Islands

Pitcairn.

AUSTRAL ISLANDS

CIFIC   OCEAN

Preface to the Series

The purpose of the ASM Series is to publish, without regard for disciplinary, national, or denominational boundaries, scholarly works of high quality and wide interest on missiological themes from the entire spectrum of scholarly pursuits, e.g., theology, history, anthropology, sociology, linguistics, health, education, art, political science, economics, and development, to articulate but a partial list. Always the focus will be on Christian mission.

By "mission" in this context is meant a cross-cultural passage over the boundary between faith in Jesus Christ and its absence. In this understanding of mission, the basic functions of Christian proclamation, dialogue, witness, service, fellowship, worship, and nurture are of special concern. How does the transition from one cultural context to another influence the shape and interaction of these dynamic functions?

Missiologists know that they need the other disciplines. And other disciplines, we dare to suggest, need missiology, perhaps more than they sometimes realize. Neither the insider's nor the outsider's view is complete in itself. The world Christian mission has through two millennia amassed a rich and well-documented body of experience to share with other disciplines.

Interaction will be the hallmark of this Series. It desires to be a channel for talking to one another instead of about one another. Secular scholars and church-related missiologists have too long engaged in a sterile venting of feelings about one another, often lacking in full evidence. Ignorance of and indifference to one another's work has been no less harmful to good scholarship.

We express our warm thanks to various mission agencies whose financial contributions enabled leaders of vision in the ASM to launch this new venture. The future of the ASM series will, we feel sure, fully justify their confidence and support.

William J. Danker, Chairperson,
ASM Series Editorial Committee

Acknowledgments

This book is based in part on archival research in the headquarters of the relevant missionary societies and churches. The author wishes to thank the following libraries and church and mission offices for permission to use their collections: the Council for World Mission, London; the United Society for the Propagation of the Gospel, London; the Société des Missions Evangéliques, Paris; the Padri Maristi, Rome; the Congregazione dei SS Cuori, Rome; the Neuendettelsau Mission, Neuendettelsau, Bavaria; the Division of World Missions, American Lutheran Church, Minneapolis; the Society of the Divine Word, Techny, Illinois; the Jesuit Missions Collection of Fordham University, New York; the United Church Board of World Ministries, New York; the Mitchell Library, Sydney; the former Australian Presbyterian Board of Missions, Sydney; the Australian Board of Missions, Stanmore, New South Wales; the Australian Council of Churches; the former mission boards of the New Zealand Presbyterian and Methodist churches, Auckland; the Houghton Library of Harvard University, Cambridge, Massachusetts; the Divinity Library of Yale University, New Haven, Connecticut; the Roman Catholic bishops of Port Moresby, Madang, Rabaul, Honiara, Port Vila, Noumea, Tarawa, Suva, Nuku'alofa, Apia, and Papeete; the Mormon headquarters in Nuku'alofa, Apia, and Papeete; the United Church of Papua New Guinea and the Solomon Islands; the Evangelical Lutheran Church of Papua New Guinea; the Anglican Province of Papua New Guinea; the Anglican Province of Melanesia; the Presbyterian Church of Vanuatu; the Kiribati Protestant Church; the Methodist Church of Fiji; the Free Wesleyan Church of Tonga; the Congregational Christian Church of Samoa; and the Evangelical Churches of New Caledonia and of Tahiti.

The following friends have assisted greatly by reading portions of the manuscript: Professor S. George Ellsworth, Reverend Cecil Gribble, Father Francis Hezel, Bishop John Kuder, Reverend R. H. Leenhardt, Reverend Elia Ta'ase, Reverend Bernard Thorogood, and Reverend Henri Vernier. They have reduced the number of mistakes in this volume; responsibility for any that remain rests with the author.

THE ISLAND CHURCHES
OF THE SOUTH PACIFIC

1
The Nineteenth-Century Background:
A Brief Survey

From the time of Captain James Cook's journeys in the mid-eighteenth century, the Pacific islands provided the world with the standard romantic image of primitive existence: happy, hospitable, uninhibited people, dwelling on lovely lagoons and beaches, with easily available food and shelter, and with simple wants. The picture had only a limited correspondence to reality among the peoples of the Pacific, and very little correspondence anywhere else.

In like manner the Pacific islands provided the world, from the early nineteenth century onward, with the standard romantic image of Christian missions, one which was somewhat appropriate in the islands, but almost only there. There was, as one element, the picture of the missionary being eaten by cannibals, an event scarcely known in Africa or Asia, but one which happened on quite a number of occasions in the Pacific. Especially because the cannibal feast was the final fate of men like John Williams and James Chalmers, already famous from their exploits and their writings, it became popularly associated with missionaries. It was in the Pacific also that missionaries were most often connected with the practice of putting clothes on people, that other stereotype of missionary work. Actually Pacific missionaries often questioned the values of full Western dress in a tropical climate, but it is true that the "Mother Hubbard," the most famous style of mission-inspired clothing, was developed in the Pacific. Critics of missionary practice in regard to clothing concentrated their attacks on the Pacific islands, claiming the gradual depopulation there as evidence of the evil effects of the practice.

Most important, it was in the Pacific that whole kingdoms were converted to Christianity by the missionaries, thus providing the nineteenth-century church with its principal images of great missionary success. The popular missionary hymns of that period referred to mass conversions:

> See heathen nations bending
> Before the God we love
> And thousand hearts ascending
> In gratitude above.

The kind of events pictured in such hymns took place, in reality, almost solely in the Pacific area. It is a surprising thing about the missionary movement of the past two centuries that scarcely anywhere outside the Pacific islands has it met with the unified national acceptance of Christianity that was typical of the conversion of Europe in the Middle Ages.

That pattern of acceptance in which the king led his subjects unitedly into the church might have been expected in Africa as much as in the Pacific. Both areas, like early medieval Europe, had nonliterary religious traditions, which have usually been the traditions most open to conversion. Both Africa and the Pacific also had religions that emphasized the place of ancestral spirits more than the place of any universal deity, and hence their religions were likely to seem limited in their range of experience and reference at a time when a wider world of contacts was opening up. But despite these similarities Africa did not make the kind of response to Christianity that was found in the Pacific and in Europe. For the most part African conversions were of individuals or family groups apart from their sociopolitical community. Where it happened that the ruler of the community became Christian, as in Buganda or Rwanda, he did not succeed in bringing his subjects with him as a unified body into his church. Only on a very rare occasion, as among the Ngwato of Botswana, did this kind of thing happen in Africa.[1] Yet it was the usual pattern in the islands of Polynesia.

The churches that developed in Polynesia tended, in consequence, to be all-embracing national churches like those of earlier days in Europe, rather than the divided, competing churches that were the rule in most African countries. Much competition was introduced in the Pacific, it is true, by the later arrival of new missions, but there was usually an initial establishment of one church that long continued to be the church of the rulers and of the great majority of the people. The Pacific, then, provided in many ways the archetype of nineteenth-century missionary activity and the stereotype of missions that has existed in the popular mind even during the twentieth century.

The intense and absorbing story of that nineteenth-century Christian activity has been often told. The original accounts of the work by the missionaries themselves were among the most popular books of their day and some of them have been recently republished.[2] Novelists of both the nineteenth and the twentieth centuries—Herman Melville, Somerset Maugham, James Michener—have painted the picture of the missionary in the islands for a still wider audience, much less flattering a picture than that found in the missionary autobiographies. There have also been a number of serious studies of the period, which have deepened our knowledge, though of course much remains to be understood.[3] Thanks to these various writers, but particularly to the work of the novelists and the early missionary authors, the story of the earliest missionary work in the Pacific is one of the most widely known segments of modern missionary history. It is certainly much better known than the more recent twentieth-century history of the development of the Pacific island churches. Once the excitement and glamour of the early pioneer period and its pivotal decisions passed, the island churches largely dropped out of the world's attention. Yet the pioneer achievements clearly cannot be understood or evaluated without some knowledge of the long-term results that flowed from them in the emergence of indigenous churches.

Before launching on the more recent developments, a brief reminder of the main sweep of events in the nineteenth century may be helpful. This should at least make clear how the various churches came to be located where they are, and the principal vicissitudes through which they passed that have colored their twentieth-century life.

The First Missionaries

The story begins in 1797 when thirty emissaries of the London Missionary Society (LMS) arrived in Tahiti. They were mostly artisans, with only four ordained ministers, and they had almost no knowledge of the people to whom they were going or of how to work among them. It was assumed that these people would have to be civilized before they could understand Christianity, which explains, in part, the large number of artisans. Being men of limited education, the missionaries were in no position to appreciate life outside their own cultural presuppositions. They reacted negatively to most of what they found and only a half-dozen of them stayed more than two years in Tahiti. Those who continued the work met indifference as far as their religious teachings were concerned; and when a revolt in 1808 drove the king, Pomare II, and his court to the small island of Moorea, only one man, Henry Nott, accompanied him, while the others embarked for Australia in a passing ship.

However, the reversals in politics had made King Pomare II more open to a new outlook, and when he reconquered Tahiti in 1815 he and his soldiers prayed to the God of the Christians before battle, and afterward led the way in the national acceptance of Christianity. Large churches were erected, schools were organized, the Bible was translated, and new "Christian" laws were enacted.

The transformation in Tahiti soon affected nearby islands. In 1820 Raïatéa, the most venerated holy spot of the Polynesians, along with some of the other Leeward Islands, adopted the "laws of Tahiti." Christianity seemed to be a rapidly spreading contagion. Natives of the Austral Islands driven to Raïatéa by contrary winds in that same year took Christian islanders home with them, and soon the Austral Islands were converted. The most famous missionary of that period, the redoubtable John Williams, made Raïatéa his headquarters but said, "I cannot content myself within the narrow limits of a single reef" and soon struck out to plant Polynesian missionaries in other groups of islands. His most impressive successes came in the Cook Islands, especially on Rarotonga, which he discovered in 1823 and where he left the teacher Papehia.

At about this time Congregational missionaries from the American Board of Commissioners for Foreign Missions in Boston arrived in Hawaii (1820) and met with a much more rapid acceptance of their teachings than Tahiti had afforded. In 1823 important members of the royal family were baptized, and this was followed by a mass movement into the church. Forty years later the American Board terminated its mission in the conviction that the essentially missionary task was completed; Hawaii had been Christianized.

The progression of missionary activity was, strangely enough, from east to west, that is from the areas most distant from Europe to those that were closer. This odd order of progression was due to the fact that Tahiti had received such early favorable notice from explorers and the fact that the nearer islands of Melanesia were reported to be inhabited by hostile and dangerous peoples. Accordingly the next islands to be entered after those around Tahiti and Hawaii were Tonga, Fiji, and Samoa. All were first approached by representatives of the English Methodists who came in the second wave following the Congregationalists from London and Boston. Tonga was entered on a long-term basis in 1826. The great champion of Methodism there proved to be Taufa'ahau Tupou, the principal chief of the outlying Haapai Islands, who was converted in 1830. At his baptism he took the name of George. He gradually extended his rule over the whole of Tonga, though not before Catholic missionaries established themselves among some chiefs opposed to him on the main island of Tongatabu. These chiefs then declared both their Catholicism and their independence of the central power in Tupou's hands. The result was a short civil war in 1852 when Tupou defeated his enemies and unified all of Tonga under his rule as a strongly Protestant kingdom.

From Tonga, Methodism spread to the large and populous islands of Fiji with their high culture and warlike traditions. Tongans had long been in touch with Fiji through trade and warfare, and Tongan missionaries accompanied the English Methodists, first to the smaller eastern islands and then to the main island of Viti Levu. Most famous was Joeli Bulu, who settled permanently in Fiji and became one of the most venerated figures of Fijian Methodism. At that time Fiji was coming under the sway of the fierce conqueror from Bau, Thakombau ("Evil pertaining to Bau"), and the English missionaries eventually ventured to take up residence at his court. In 1854 the most famous conversion in Pacific history, possibly excepting that of Pomare, took place when Thakombau, encouraged by King George of Tonga, publicly accepted the Lotu (Christianity). The following year there was a great victory of the Christian forces headed by Thakombau and aided by George. Methodism spread rapidly from that time, with the chiefs of each area giving the lead.

Samoa took to Christianity even faster. John Williams placed some Tahitian teachers there in 1830 and when he returned a short time later he found people far and wide calling themselves Christians and asking for missionaries. The London Missionary Society accordingly began work in 1836 and quickly found general acceptance. A rift developed in the new Christianity, however, because of work that had been done by an earlier group of Methodists from Tonga. Some chiefs, with the usual sense of rivalry to be found among Samoan leaders, adhered to the Methodist church against the Congregationalism of the majority. They asked for and received British missionaries from Tonga, but for only four years (1835–39). When the Methodist leaders in England received reports of the division they were supporting in Samoa, they ordered a withdrawal of their workers in favor of the London Mission. This action, however, did not alter the determination of the Samoan leaders, who continued in their Methodism and received some support from Tongans sent by King George. In 1857 the Australian Methodists finally agreed to help them out, and from that time the Methodists continued as a well-established minority in Samoa, though the great bulk of the population was in the Congregational church.

The Arrival of Roman Catholic Missions

The division introduced in this case was a minor matter compared to those that arose from the Roman Catholic missions when they arrived in the Pacific. A few Catholic missionaries had worked in the Marianas and western Carolines during the time of Spanish influence in the seventeenth and early eighteenth centuries and had been responsible for the Christianization of the Marianas. But those missions had disappeared, and when the new wave of missionary expansion reached the Pacific in the nineteenth century the Catholics were late on the scene, with the result that throughout the eastern and central islands their appearance produced dissension and division. In the eastern islands they were represented by the Congregation of the Sacred Hearts of Jesus and Mary, commonly known as the Fathers of the Sacred Hearts or the Picpus Fathers, and in the central region by the Society of Mary, or Marist Fathers, both orders being French. When the Picpus leaders arrived in Tahiti in 1836 they were faced with an expulsion order from the Protestant Queen, Pomare IV. Later they returned with a French warship, which cowed all opposition and secured their establishment. This action led to the French occupation. Again in Tonga, where the Marists under Pompallier arrived in 1837, there was resistance from the local rulers, and the Marists had to return (in 1842) with a French warship to gain a foothold. The Marists later moved on peaceably into Fiji and Samoa (1844 and 1845), although inevitably producing tension and division by their work.

The only large island in the central Pacific where the Catholics came first (1843) was New Caledonia, but disease and warfare caused them to withdraw. They came again in 1851, and two years later the French government, following in their wake, took control of the island. French rule provided them with effective backing but also created serious problems for them with the introduction of settlers (including many convicts) who appropriated large blocks of land despite mission objections and produced much hostility among the islanders. Even here the conflict with Protestantism was not entirely avoided because the London Missionary Society workers had been early established a short distance off the New Caledonian coast in the three Loyalty Islands. There were occasional attempts by each church to cross the channel dividing the islands. The French government also became involved. At one time French troops attacked the LMS mission station in the Loyalties, and, at another, French authorities deported the English missionary on a half-hour's notice.

In a few small island groups of the central and the east Pacific, however, the Roman Catholics came early and established undisputed sway. The very first field for the Fathers of the Sacred Hearts, before they approached Tahiti, was Mangareva, one of the Gambier Islands, and here they won the entire population and soon effectively ruled over them. Then, after their establishment in Tahiti, they moved into the Marquesas Islands to the north and succeeded in making those islands almost completely Catholic. The Tuamotu Archipelago south of the Marquesas was also to a large extent their domain as a few French priests worked in extreme isolation scattered over that vast expanse. In the central islands, where the Marists worked, the one Catholic preserve was the small island of Wallis with its companion, Futuna. Here the only canonized missionary of the Pacific, St. Pierre Chanel, labored and was martyred in 1841, and here a strong Catholic church arose, which was supported by the local royalty.

Protestant Expansion

While the Roman Catholics were entering these territories, the Protestants were also expanding their operations in the central Pacific. North, near the equator, a new kind of missionary initiative appeared. Kiribati and Tuvalu (then known as the Gilbert and Ellice Islands) and the Marshall and Caroline islands became the fields of work for the well-established churches of Samoa and Hawaii. Samoan pastors were sent by their church to convert and preside over the Ellice islanders and the southern Gilbertese. In the northern Gilberts and the Marshalls and Carolines the Hawaiian Evangelical Association launched a great endeavor in 1852, spreading across thousands of miles of ocean. In this latter case it was not just islanders who carried on the work but also American missionaries supported by the American Board in Boston, working in cooperation with them. Vanuatu (then known as the New Hebrides) was the one Pacific area where Presbyterian missions labored. It proved to be also the most difficult and dangerous Pacific area. On the island of Erromanga alone five missionaries were killed, one after the other, before the work began to take effect. There and elsewhere the progress was slow and halting. The missionaries, who began coming in 1848, represented a variety of Presbyterian churches in Australia, New Zealand, Canada, and Scotland. The most famous was the Scotsman John G. Paton, whose autobiography became one of the best-known missionary writings of the late nineteenth century.

The difficulties in Vanuatu were characteristic of the change of pace and style that came over the missions when they moved on to the western Pacific.

No more do we hear of whole island groups converted with their rulers, or of large, vigorous, missionary-minded churches appearing. Rather, we learn of slow, village-by-village work with only small gains.

The change was the result of the great difference between Melanesia and Polynesia. Melanesian social units were small, so that the conversion of one village did not lead naturally to the conversion of others, but might, because of long antagonisms, actually be a reason for resistance on the part of others. Each language covered only a small area rather than a whole archipelago as in Polynesia, making the first approach and the translation of materials more difficult. There were no kings or hereditary chiefs whom the whole society was accustomed to follow, but only "big men" in an independent and competitive society. The people, far from being hospitable and outgoing like the Polynesians, were usually withdrawn and suspicious of outsiders, which was one reason for their small groupings and separate languages. The conversion of Melanesia was therefore a slower business.

In the Solomons the Catholics arrived first in what became a disastrous effort in the 1845–52 period. They made no serious preparations and lost many of their men through disease and attacks before they gave up. Then the Melanesian Mission, an Anglican body, entered the field under the leadership of George Augustus Selwyn, the first Anglican bishop of New Zealand. Rather than stationing workers on the islands, Selwyn's procedure was to make annual voyages, stopping in the northern New Hebrides and the Banks and Santa Cruz islands as well as the Solomons, establishing friendships with the leaders and inviting them to send boys for training to his great central school located, for most of its history, on Norfolk Island. The method led to the beginnings of an Anglican church in the region, and a Diocese of Melanesia was established in 1861. The first bishop, John Coleridge Patteson, was killed in 1871 when he visited a small island from which some men had been carried off by white labor-recruiters. Other missions, both Protestant and Catholic, came at the turn of the century, but they can be better discussed later in connection with the twentieth-century history.

Adjacent to the North Solomons was the Bismarck Archipelago, and at its center lay the Gazelle Peninsula, the square protrusion at the northern end of New Britain. This became the center of the most rewarding mission work in all Melanesia as well as a center of great economic advancement and wealth. By the time mission work was started (1874), the churches of Australia were strong enough to begin to take their share, and it was the Australian Methodists who there launched their first missionary enterprise under the leadership of their pioneer and statesman, George Brown. The Methodists of Fiji and Samoa were also prepared to participate. The whole student body of the Fijian theological school volunteered to help with the endeavor despite warnings from the British governor of the dangers they would meet. Eight years behind them and a few miles away the Roman Catholics inaugurated a mission staffed by the Sacred Heart Fathers from Issoudun in France. Bishop Couppé was their leader and they soon developed a mission that came to be known as the "Pearl of the Pacific." Both they and the Methodists established flourishing churches with, as can be imagined, plenty of rivalry between them.

Mission Work in New Guinea

Finally we come to New Guinea, the greatest island of the Pacific and the last to be challenged by major missionary effort. The nineteenth century saw merely the beginnings of that challenge, with only the coastal fringes being touched. It was appropriate that the London Missionary Society was the pioneer here as it had been in the Pacific as a whole. In 1871 it opened work along the south coast, using pastors from the Loyalty Islands. In 1874 W. G. Lawes came from Niue to establish a headquarters at the newly discovered harbor of Port Moresby. Ten years later the Sacred Heart Fathers from France started their mission, making their headquarters in 1885 at Yule Island some seventy miles from Port Moresby. Both missions worked along the south coast, the LMS extending itself along the whole length of some eight hundred miles, while the Catholics were limited by government insistence to the strip near their headquarters and from there began to push into the rugged interior.

By this time British administration had been established (1884, protectorate;1888, annexation), and for the first time in Pacific history a colonial government took the initiative in bringing in missions.[4] The governor, Sir William MacGregor, who had been a good friend of the missions when he worked as a medical officer in Fiji, invited the Methodists and the Anglicans from Australia to add their forces to the field. A conference was held on his invitation in 1890, where the newcomers agreed with the LMS on a delimitation of territory. Response to all of these missions was fairly slow and scattered, but by the end of the century local churches were coming into being in numerous villages along the coast.

Meanwhile the northern part of the great island had been annexed by Germany (1884), and one Catholic and two Protestant mission societies from that land hastened to begin work. The two Protestant missions were very different in size and influence. The larger came from the obscure village of Neuendettelsau in Bavaria, but it became the largest Protestant body in Papua New Guinea. Its *point d'appui* was Finschafen, where work was begun by the resolute Johannes Flierl in 1886. The Rhenish Missionary Society, the largest society in continental Europe, came a year later and started work near Madang, but the mission was weak and suffered many reverses; and in the twentieth century, as we shall see, it finally withdrew from New Guinea. The Roman Catholics of Germany were represented through the Society of the Divine Word, which was established in 1875 and took on New Guinea at the request of the Vatican in 1895. Its work spread chiefly along the northern coast, west of the Protestants.

Obviously with these late beginnings there was little of a Christian church in New Guinea at the close of the nineteenth century. The situation was completely different from that in the eastern and central Pacific, which by then had old churches encompassing whole populations. The situation in the Solomons and in the Bismarck Archipelago was of an intermediate kind but closer to that of New Guinea than to that of islands further east. Thus while Christianity was indeed well planted in the Pacific by 1900, it showed very different stages of growth in the different areas.

Missions and Politics

We have thus far neglected the important subject of the relation of missions to governments. This showed as much difference between east and west as did the situation in relation to church growth. In the east and the central areas, where missions had early produced national churches for whole island groups, the missionaries played a large part in political developments. Colonial rule had not yet made its appearance. European traders, whalers, and adventurers were making their presence felt, but the island kings found in the missionaries a group of advisers who could be relied on more consistently than most of these other Europeans, even though they were not so helpful when it came to making war. The rulers also turned naturally to the missionaries for instruction as to the social and legal expectations of the new God they had accepted. The missionaries had definite ideas on this subject, which they were eager to communicate. These rulers were by no means the puppets of the missionaries. They decided what advice they would accept and what they would reject.[5] Furthermore, the missionary societies in Europe and America made it clear from the beginning that the men they sent out were not to enter into politics. It can be said that those who went so far as to take political office nearly always resigned their position with the mission. But because of the pressures of the situation, many who did not take office were nevertheless highly influential in political matters. Missionary-influenced kingdoms appeared in Tahiti, Mangareva, Hawaii, the Cook Islands, Tonga, Wallis, Fiji, and, on a smaller scale, in some of the villages and lesser islands of the New Hebrides. George Pritchard, the British consul and adviser to the queen in Tahiti; Honoré Laval, the priest-ruler of Mangareva; Grritt Judd and William Richards, the foreign minister and the educational minister in Hawaii; and Shirley Baker, the prime minister in Tonga, were the most famous examples of ex-missionary administrators (or, in Laval's case, missionary administrators) in the islands. The missionaries in Samoa also had a tremendous influence on social and legislative structures, although Samoan politics were too divisive for this influence to take shape in a single missionary-influenced kingdom.

The missionaries proposed new legal codes and constitutions. These emphasized the Ten Commandments, and especially the observance of the Sabbath. Punishments were lenient compared to previous island custom, capital punishment being avoided and labor on public works used as the penalty for most offenses. The constitutions, such as those of King Kamehameha III in

Hawaii and King George in Tonga, ended many privileges of the nobility and granted legal rights to the entire population. In practice the change in relations between aristocrats and commoners was not as great as the change on paper, but still there was a considerable transformation. The constitutions were explicitly Christian. That of Hawaii declared that "no law shall be enacted which is at variance with the word of the Lord Jehovah."

Because they feared the influence of irreligious Europeans, the missionaries were initially not inclined to favor European annexations in the Pacific. They changed their views only when the local governments proved unable to handle the white settlers or, more commonly, when they feared that the intrusion of a European power would champion a different form of Christianity from their own. Thus the LMS missionaries in Tahiti showed no interest in a British protectorate until Catholic France tried to assert its power and insert its missions. The Presbyterians in the New Hebrides tried to rouse the Australian government's interest in those islands only after French activity there became strong. The French missionaries in Tahiti and New Caledonia operated in concert with the French government, advancing its interests against the British influence already well established in Tahiti and threatening, they feared, in New Caledonia. In Fiji and Samoa the British missionaries gradually came to favor a European protectorate, though not necessarily a British one in the Samoan case, because of internal problems. However, in Hawaii, Micronesia, the Cook Islands, and Tonga the missionary influence was exercised for the most part in favor of independence. Only in the last of these was direct colonial rule avoided.

The political situation we have been describing was characteristic of the eastern and central Pacific, but, as has been noted, a very different situation prevailed in the western area. There no island kingdoms arose, no missionary prime ministers appeared, and no large churches or widespread acceptance of missionary leadership made possible a significant role for missions in relation to political affairs or colonial designs. In fact, as has been seen, in New Guinea the colonial power came in advance of the arrival of all but one of the missions.[6] In the Solomons, too, only one mission, the Melanesian, was present at the start of British rule. This does not mean that relations between the missions and colonial governments were more harmonious in the west. Problems aplenty appeared, as we shall have occasion to note. But the missions were in a different position vis-à-vis colonialism. They could not look back to a precolonial heyday when they had exercised fuller controls, nor had they been in a position to bring any influence to bear for or against the coming of the colonial powers.

The Island Churches

After this cursory survey of the events that brought Christianity to the Pacific and the establishment of the island churches, we may now turn our attention to the development of those churches, which took place in the twentieth century. Hawaii will have to drop out of our view at this time because, while it was a center for important Polynesian churches in the nineteenth century, with the advance of the twentieth century it became so overwhelmingly Oriental and American that it can no longer be classed with the other islands in terms of church life and development. New Zealand has not been included, even in this nineteenth-century survey, for similar reasons: the predominance of white settlers early gave to mission and church an entirely distinct set of problems and directions. The area of our attention in the twentieth century, therefore, will be that which has been more recently delimited as "South Pacific" by the intergovernmental South Pacific Commission, namely, the islands of the Pacific from Tahiti on the east to the Indonesian boundary in New Guinea on the west and from the Marianas in the north to the Cooks in the south.

The twentieth century in this area has seen both stability and change. The first half of the century (from 1900 to 1942) was a period of relative stability for the peoples and the churches of the islands. It was in some ways the high point in the life and influence of South Pacific Christianity. Competing influences from outside the area were still undeveloped. Colonial rule was present, it is true, so that the political influence of the churches in the east and the center was not what it once had been. But to balance this loss the missions in the west were now well started and were gaining new response and acceptance.

Yet within this stability, forces of change were at work. The time was still one of missionary leadership, but pressures toward the establishment of independent churches were beginning to be felt in some of the islands and the missionaries were having to deal with them. When World War II came, it forced radical changes on the church and mission situation. After the middle of the century there was a rapid transformation. Independent churches appeared everywhere. Independent countries came soon after. A new style of church life developed in relation to the new life of the Pacific, brought in by improved communication and education, economic development, and urban growth. By the beginning of the last quarter of the century it was clear that the island churches had emerged in their own right, free from missionary domination, and were together trying to undertake their responsibilities in Pacific society. To trace how all this occurred will be the burden of what follows.

NOTES

1. What might be thought of as another African example is the mass conversion of the Merina of Madagascar under the leadership of their queen and the subsequent creation of what was essentially an established church for that island. However, this Merina church was never accepted by the mass of non-Merina subjects, who were

hostile to it and later found their principal religious identity through other churches. The Merina, it may be added, were Malayo-Polynesian immigrants into the African scene.

2. John Davies, *The History of the Tahitian Mission, 1799-1830* (1961); James Wilson, *A Missionary Voyage to the Southern Pacific Ocean 1796-1798* (1965); Honoré Laval, *Mémoires pour servir à l'histoire de Mangareva, ère chrétienne 1834-1871* (1968); John G. Paton, *Thirty Years with South Sea Cannibals; Autobiography of John G. Paton* (rev. ed., 1964). The memoirs of a Polynesian missionary have also been published recently: R. G. and M. Crocombe, *The Works of Taunga: Records of a Polynesian Traveller in the South Seas*, 1833-1896 (1968); and the biography by Allen Birtwhistle, *In His Armour, the Life of John Hunt of Fiji* (1954), quotes extensively from the writings of that Methodist pioneer. Other famous original accounts, which have not been republished recently although they were widely read in earlier times, are William Ellis, *Polynesian Researches* (4 vols., 1831); John Williams, *A Narrative of Missionary Enterprises in the South Sea Islands* (1837); Rufus Anderson, *History of the Sandwich Islands Mission* (1870); Joseph Waterhouse, *The King and the People of Fiji* (1866), and George Brown's autobiography (1908).

3. The only scholarly monographs on the whole area are Rainer Jaspers, *Die missionarische Erschliessung Ozeaniens . . . bis 1855* (1972); Ralph Wiltgen, *The Founding of the Roman Catholic Church in Oceania 1825 to 1859* (1979); Niel Gunson, *Messengers of Grace. Evangelical Missionaries in the South Seas 1797-1860* (1978); and Aarne Koskinen, *Missionary Influence as a Political Factor in the Pacific Islands* (1953). Scholarly investigations of parts of the area include William Young, *Christianity and Civilization in the South Pacific: The Influence of Missionaries upon European Expansion* (1920); K. L. P. Martin. *Missionaries and Annexation in the Pacific* (1924); Georg Pilhofer. *Die Geschichte der Neuendettelsauer Mission in Neuguinea* (3 vols., 1961); André Dupeyrat, *Papouasie, Histoire de la Mission 1885-1935* (1935); Raymond H. Leenhardt, *Au Vent de la Grande Terre: Histoire des Iles Loyalty de 1840 à 1895* (1957); Hugh Larcy, *Marists and Melanesians: A History of Catholic Missions in the Solomon Islands* (1976); David Hilliard, *God's Gentlemen, a History of the Melanesian Mission 1849-1942* (1978); Sione Latukefu, *Church and State in Tonga . . . 1825-1875* (1974); and Noel Rutherford, *Shirley Baker and the King of Tonga* (1972). Important material on the earlier Pacific missions is also found in more general works such as Kenneth Scott Latourette, *History of the Expansion of Christianity,* vols. 5 and 7 (1943, 1945); Stephen Neill, *Colonialism and Christian Missions* (1965); W. P. Morrell, *Britain in the Pacific Islands* (1960); Ernest Beaglehole, *Social Change in the South Pacific, Rarotonga and Aitutaki* (1957); J. W. Davidson and D. Scarr, eds., *Pacific Islands Portraits* (1971); and Harold Whitman Bradley, *The American Frontier in Hawaii: The Pioneers 1798-1843* (1968). More popular accounts of the nineteenth-century missions are Louis B. Wright and Mary Fry, *Puritans in the South Seas* (1936); Bradford Smith, *Yankees in Paradise, the New England Impact on Hawaii* (1956); and Ian Shevill, *Pacific Conquest, the History of 150 Years of Missionary Progress in the South Pacific* (1949); the first of these (Wright and Fry) is marred by a constant effort to ridicule and the last (Sherill) by a considerable number of errors. Some serious, if not scholarly, histories have been written by the missionaries themselves including both nineteenth-century and later material: Joseph Blanc, *Les Iles Wallis* (1914) and *Histoire Religieuse de l'Archipel Fidjien* (2 vols., 1926); Victor Douceré, *La Mission Catholique aux Nouvelles Hébrides* (1934); Joseph Darnand, *Aux Iles Samoa: la Forêt qui s'illumine* (1939); Ernest Sabatier, *Sous*

l'Equateur du Pacifique: Les Iles Gilbert et la Mission Catholique (1939); and C.E. Fox, *Lord of the Southern Isles, being the story of the Anglican Mission in Melanesia 1849-1949* (1958). A number of other histories by missionaries do not deal to any extent with the nineteenth century. The following journals should be consulted for important articles on the early missions: *Journal of Pacific History; International Review of Mission;* and *Journal de la Société des Océanistes.* Three recent dissertations (which have not been published) throw much light on the early history, namely, Norman Douglas, "Latter-day Saints Missions and Missionaries in Polynesia 1844-1960," Australian National University (1974); A. W. Thornley, "Fiji Methodism, 1874-1945: The Energence of a National Church," Australian National University (1974); and P. A. Prendergast, "A History of the London Missionary Society in British New Guinea, 1871-1901," University of Hawaii (1968). A new work which provides a full treatment of the nineteenth century and forms a kind of complement to the present volume is John Garrett, *To Live Among the Stars. Christian Origins in Oceania* (1982).

4. At almost this same time (in 1887) the French government asked the Marist Mission to come into the New Hebrides.

5. Gunson 1969: 263-64.

6. The two missionaries of the LMS who were in Papua at the time of British annexation were both opposed to that step.

2
Missions and Churches 1900–1942: The Eastern and Central Islands

The twentieth century has been the time of the emergence of the indigenous churches of the Third World; it has also been the time of the largest missionary activity from the churches of the West and Australasia. In the Pacific this has been shown by the enormous growth in the number of foreign missionaries working in the islands. At the beginning of the century there were only 1,277 foreign missionaries in the Pacific. By 1930 this number had grown to 1,702. And by the 1960s it had shot up to 4,503. This was, in relation to the size of the population, the largest number of missionaries to be found anywhere in the world. Australia and New Zealand proved to be the greatest source for these increases, but Europe and America were still heavily represented. Roman Catholic missionaries comprised the largest group, greater than all the others put together.[1]

During the first half of the century missionaries held all the posts of highest command in the Christian community. It was the missions rather than the churches that the world could see and most people talked of *missions* in the Pacific rather than of *churches* in the Pacific. The churches were, so to speak, hidden under the missions, yet to come out into the light of day. Therefore any examination of the emergence of the island churches during this century must begin by looking at the churches as part of the missions. We start, then, by surveying the main developments of the missions with their subordinate churches, during the first forty years of the twentieth century. It should not surprise us if, in looking for the churches, we see in this period mostly the activities of missionaries.

French Polynesia

It is appropriate to commence with the oldest of the missions and churches, that of Tahiti. This church, started by the London Missionary Society at the beginning of the nineteenth century, came under the direction of the French Protestants, represented by the Paris Evangelical Missionary Society, in 1863. A small group of missionaries tried to maintain and to strengthen the position of the large Protestant Church, which contained the great bulk of the population.

14

At the beginning of the twentieth century this church in Tahiti had the distinction of being one of only three officially established Protestant churches outside the continent of Europe—the other two being the Dutch church in Indonesia and the Anglican church in India. It had received establishment by a decree of the French regime in 1884 whereby the government paid the salaries of the local pastors and of the Protestant missionaries assigned to church work. That France should make such an arrangement may seem incredible when we consider the way in which the French regime had come to Tahiti, primarily as the protector and promoter of the Catholic missions. Yet France was also concerned to maintain controls over the Protestant church, which commanded the allegiance of the people, and as early as 1851 and 1852 it passed laws for the surveillance of the church, hoping to eliminate the remaining influence of the English missionaries. The French Protestant missionaries, after their arrival, worked steadily to enlarge the liberties of the church, but once the establishment of 1884 had been decided upon by the government, they cooperated fully in its operation. The government required that every French missionary be given a place on the central church council and that each of the district councils be presided over by a French missionary. The government also had to approve all actions taken by the church councils, including all decisions regarding the location of pastors.[2] The missionaries sent out by the Paris Society were loyal French who had no difficulty in cooperating with the government and were even ready, when needed, to serve as government emissaries to secure the submission of rebellious groups.[3]

This establishment was under constant attack, in the press and in official circles, from its Catholic enemies, and in consequence the Protestant missionaries threw themselves into the political life of the country to protect their position. One of them, Charles Viénot, long-time president of the mission, was a member and vice-president of the legislature during the early years of this century. Another, Edouard Ahnne, served somewhat later as a member of the Administrative Council and President of the Council of Agriculture and, during World War II, was one of four men who took over the reins of government on behalf of the Free French forces. Another, Charles Vernier, became the first representative elected by Tahiti to serve in the French parliament.[4] The missionaries continued few in number– usually four or five in church work and a few more than that in the schools—but they were evidently persons of leadership and ability who made an impression in the colony. They saw their constant conflict with the Catholics primarily as a defense of the old Tahitian church against powerful intruders, but they were also ready to take the offensive. For example, they sent a Tahitian worker to start a mission in the Gambier Islands, which had always been a citadel of Catholicism from the time the first missionaries arrived, and they placed one of their members, Paul Vernier, for thirteen years in the heavily Catholic Marquesas Islands to revive and extend the work begun by Hawaiian pastors there in earlier generations.[5]

Despite all their efforts, government support for the church did not endure. The significant danger to it lay not in the local Catholic opposition but in the triumph of anticlericalism in France. At the beginning of the century the government failed for a time to keep up its payments for the salaries of the Tahitian pastors.[6] After the separation of church and state was achieved in France there was constant apprehension that the government would stop all its contributions to the church in Tahiti, including those for missionary salaries. That decision, however, did not come until 1927. Then, finally, the logic of the situation in France had its effects in Oceania, and the Tahitian church was deprived of all official contributions. There was a gain that went with this: government restrictions on church operations were greatly reduced.[7] The loss of government support might have been expected to be a great blow to such a church. Actually it did little harm. The church had already been sending sizable contributions to Paris for the work of the mission and those contributions continued to increase year by year, indicating that the added burden of the pastors' salaries had been assumed easily.

Another benefit of the change in 1927 was that the churches of the outlying islands, which had never participated with Tahiti and Moorea in the establishment, could be united with the central body in a single church. The Protestant churches in the Leeward Islands, the Austral Islands, the Gambier Islands, the Tuamotu Islands, and the Marquesas Islands were at last brought into a common organization. The most important of these were the churches of the Leeward Islands where the population, almost half as large as that of Tahiti, was, and is, almost solidly Protestant. These islands had continued to represent, almost to the beginning of the twentieth century, the church situation that had existed in Tahiti before the French occupation. The French rule had not been imposed on the Leeward group at the time it came to Tahiti, and the islands with their churches remained independent and maintained their London Missionary Society connection. When the French tried to establish their power they were met with armed resistance, which continued from 1887 to 1897. During that long period of warfare the people's homes were destroyed and many were forced to live in caves, church buildings were demolished, the last of the English missionaries left, and organized church life practically ceased. By the beginning of the new century, French power was established and gradually, with the return of peace and under the leadership of the French missionary Gaston Brunel, the congregations were formed again and the churches rebuilt.[8] Contributions to Paris were developed to an important level and a well-established group of churches was brought into the Tahitian body in 1927.[9] The central council in which all were represented then took responsibility for the island churches, which had been controlled by the missionary.

The most publicly appreciated operations of the Tahitian church were the large school for boys and the school for girls founded by Charles Viénot in Papeete. Actually they were missionary-operated institutions that had very little to do with the church. The old church schools taught by the pastors in the villages, using the Tahitian language, had disappeared in the nineteenth century under French pressures for French education. They lingered on in the Leeward Islands into the early part of the twentieth century. The new French schools in the capital provided a higher and more alien education for a select group. There was not a little dispute within the mission over the fundamental principles underlying this form of education. The missionaries in the schools were oriented toward meeting the examinations set in France for all proper French people and believed that this was the only direction to be taken by a church that would keep abreast of the new generation and its needs. The missionaries who worked with the church, on the other hand, became devoted to the old Tahitian culture and distinctively Tahitian ways of the church and felt that the schools were alienating young people from their own heritage and from the church that had produced them. The struggle resulted in a reassertion of some Tahitian values and the teaching of the Tahitian language in Protestant and other schools in the late 1920s and following, but in the long run the modernizing and Frenchifying tendencies were dominant. They also became increasingly dominant in the church because of the directions of the government and of the society as a whole. The Protestant schools went from strength to strength, more than doubling their size and the number of their missionary and local teachers during the first half of the twentieth century.[10]

The consideration of education leads us to the Roman Catholic church, which was preeminent among churches in that field. Recent reports show that one-third of the school children of Tahiti are in Catholic schools, while only 4 percent are in Protestant schools, the rest being in government institutions.[11] The Catholics began in the nineteenth century by operating the government schools, since they were able to provide the necessary French-speaking teachers required by the regime. The Brothers of Ploermel from Brittany and the Sisters of St. Joseph of Cluny were invited by the government to come to Tahiti to operate the schools. But at the beginning of the twentieth century the movement toward separation of church and state in France brought a complete change in the attitude of the government. The Brothers and Sisters who had lived in government buildings and received government salaries were ejected from their residences and from the schools in which they taught and the church had to take responsibility for their salaries. The final moves on this were taken in 1904. The results of the moves, however, were not exactly what the government had intended. The religious orders proceeded to set up new schools of their own and soon these were flourishing as a vigorous counterpart to the government system. The Brothers' school rapidly doubled its enrollment and became one of the outstanding schools of the Pacific area. These schools were unabashedly French in style and intention, and appealed particularly to the European and mixed elements of the population.[12]

The early years of the century brought the same turmoil to the Catholic church that they did to the Catholic schools. The anticlericalism imported from France resulted in police investigations and fears of expulsion among the clergy. Clerical leaders saw the new direction taken by the government as designed to please the Protestants and to increase Protestant influence. In

1906 the bishop, hearing that "a decree of spoliation" of church properties had been prepared, made a trip in haste to Honolulu. There he gave the church's properties to a quickly formed American corporation "composed of trustworthy men," thus placing them under the protection of the United States government. Despite this stratagem, litigation regarding church possessions was begun in the courts and continued for many years. Finally, just before World War II, fresh legislation allowed the Catholic church new property rights, making the American corporation unnecessary, and it was dissolved some years later.[13]

Despite these trials the church was prepared to take fresh initiatives. At the beginning of the century a new bishop, Athanase Hermel, who had been put out of his teaching post in France when the government closed his seminary, came to Tahiti and proved to be a dynamic leader. Great crowds came to hear him preach. He pushed the mission, against stubborn local resistance, into the Protestant strongholds of the Leeward Islands in 1906, and the Austral Islands in 1908. The priests he used for this pioneer work suffered greatly from deprivation and isolation in a hostile environment and some had to give up.[14] He and his successors received a steady flow of French clerics from the Fathers of the Sacred Hearts for the leadership of the parishes in Tahiti. Unlike the Protestants, who depended on Tahitian pastors for the operation of the local churches, the Catholics used only foreign priests and thus required a much larger missionary force. Their following was, understandably, drawn chiefly from the European and mixed elements of the population, whereas the Protestants were linked to the native Tahitian life and people. As French influence and modern culture gradually gained a stronger hold on the islands, Catholic numbers also grew slowly from less than a fifth of the population at the end of the nineteenth century to nearly a fourth by 1950—and over a fourth ten years later.[15]

The areas of major Catholic strength, however, lay east and north of Tahiti in the Gambier, the Tuamotu, and the Marquesas islands, areas governed from Tahiti but representing a much more traditional and conservative life with little of the cosmopolitan and modern influences associated with Tahitian existence. The Gambiers, with Mangareva as their principal island, were no longer the Catholic theocracy that they had been in the nineteenth century. By Catholics they had been seen as a Pacific counterpart to the one-time Jesuit republics of Paraguay, with cottage industries developed and run by the mission and government conducted under mission control. But the French regime had found this fiefdom intolerable and had finally deported the missionary, Honoré Laval, and closed down the industries. With the secularizing zeal of the early twentieth century it also closed down the mission schools. The subsequent history of the Gambiers has been little different from that of the larger Tuamotu Archipelago to which it is linked.

The Tuamotus, a huge area of low-lying atolls with a limited population and few communications, are famed principally for their pearl fisheries. They are the only part of the Pacific where the Reorganized Mormons, known locally as Sanitos, became an important part of the population. The larger part of the population, however, was Catholic. Each local church, whatever its denomination, was extremely isolated. For the Catholics five or six priests tried to make the rounds of the parishes, but with the poor facilities for transport most places were visited only once in two years.[16]

The Marquesas, high islands of the most rugged and picturesque type with a freedom-loving and pleasure-loving population, suffered far more than most island peoples from the European impact. They have attracted particular interest ever since Herman Melville stayed there and wrote his novel *Typee* about the area. The people have been described as demoralized and dispirited and the population declined drastically from 18,000 when Europeans arrived to 8,000 in 1900 and to 2,150 in 1926. After that it began to rise slowly.[17] The people were almost solidly Catholic. A small Protestant enclave continued as a result of the work of the early Hawaiian missionaries who came in 1854 and whose descendants are still to be found there. But the Fathers of the Sacred Hearts were the first European missionaries to establish continuing work, and they created what was essentially an enclosed Catholic world in those islands. They had a separate organization from their confreres in Tahiti with their own vicariate apostolic. As in Tahiti, the Fathers relied on foreign missionaries for the leadership of the church and though they did have a corps of strong local catechists for a time, they did not build these up, as was done in other parts of the Pacific, but allowed them to decline and then to disappear. Therefore the church made little progress toward indigenization, and nothing was done toward developing financial support from the people. In all their areas of work the Fathers of the Sacred Hearts did less toward developing indigenous leadership than did the other Catholic orders working in the Pacific. Yet the population in the Marquesas was very devout and nearly every home had a Bible or some biographies of the saints, which were the only books available.[18]

The destructive impact of the outside world was enhanced in the Marquesas by sudden shifts of direction on the part of the governing power, making adjustment to Western culture a continuously changing process. There had been two major shifts in the nineteenth century. Until 1862 the government joined the mission in a generally repressive stance toward the old culture. From then until 1888 it encouraged a revival of the old ways, which the mission reported as a return to cannibalism, human sacrifice, and licentiousness. After that there was a swing back toward greater restrictions and cooperation with the church, but with the opening of the new century the whole anticlerical struggle was imported from France and carried on more virulently here than anywhere else in the Pacific. Even the Chamber of Deputies in Paris heard attacks on the Marquesan mission. The schools of the mission were closed down and all the men teachers departed in 1904, and the properties of the church were ordered for confiscation.[19] The mission fought the expropriation in the courts, appealing the matter to Tahiti, and the case dragged on for twenty-five years before the government finally gave up. It gave up because by then there had been another change in direction and the regime was becoming more and more favorable to the mission. The mission school for girls was reopened in 1923, and boys' schools would have been allowed again but for many years the mission could not secure the necessary teachers.[20] The Marquesas hardly presented a satisfying picture from the perspective of the church or of the government, and least of all from the perspective of the people.

Easter and Pitcairn Islands

One other spot where the Fathers of the Sacred Hearts first converted the population was Easter Island, that isolated bit of land halfway between Tahiti and the South American coast, famous for its huge, monolithic statues. The history of a small, unprotected island of this type was one of endless neglect and exploitation. In the nineteenth century adventurers came. Some carried off the people as slaves. One stayed and terrorized the people with his gun and made them work for him. The priests did not preach resistance but when things seemed intolerable they finally tried to take the people to Mangareva. Only half the people could be accommodated on the ship and the rest were left without civil or religious leadership. Near the end of the century Chile annexed the island and the inhabitants were transferred to the ecclesiastical responsibility of Santiago. Exploitation and neglect continued. A Chilean company turned the people into debt slaves, and in 1914 a prophetess arose who demanded animal sacrifices, which led to thefts and then revolt against the Chilean representatives. The revolt was quelled by a warship, which brought the attention of the Chilean church to the island, and for a time annual visits were paid by a priest, but after 1923 these ceased.

A great change came in 1935 when a young German priest, Sebastian Englert, who had come to Chile as part of the German mission to the Araucanian Indians, became interested in the island and went there to work. He stayed thirty-five years and built up the parish life. The Vicariate Apostolic of Araucania soon took responsibility for the effort and sent some nuns who developed an educational program. So a modest improvement was maintained until Thor Heyerdahl brought the island to the world's attention and subsequent tourism brought a wave of prosperity and complete transformation.[21]

Of all the romances of Pacific history, none surpasses that of the beginnings of the church on Pitcairn Island. It was as if the story from the Garden of Eden had to be enacted all over again. The apparent paradise was turned into a scene of mutual killing until only one man and a few women and children were left. Then came the recognition of the realities of the human condition, the conversion and beginning of a church.[22] But that was all in the early days of European contact. The twentieth-century life of this church was as placid as its early life was tumultuous. Missionary visits from America in 1886 and 1890 led the people to accept the Seventh-day Adventist Church and they remained faithfully and unitedly in that body. Occasional missionaries from America and, later, more regular workers on two-year terms from Australia kept them in contact with that church and with the wider world beyond their narrow shores.

Cook Islands

Closely related to Tahiti ethnically and linguistically are the Cook Islands, yet they have followed a very different course because of their English rather than French attachments. The London Missionary Society, which began the church in both places, continued predominant in the Cooks. A missionary theocracy remained undisturbed through the nineteenth century and can be seen as almost an archetype for that form of government. The missionaries exercised a dominant influence over the chiefs and arranged for legislation which kept out other missions and preserved the land for the indigenous people. Islanders could not marry Europeans, which was one of the commonest ways by which land was alienated, or sell them land, and even leases were restricted.[23] Moral codes were also legislated and then enforced by the church deacons. But the mission-inspired regime was not strong enough to deal with the vigor and unruliness of white intruders, and the missionaries had finally to recognize the need for a British protectorate, which was established in 1890. In 1901 New Zealand took over the controls from Britain, and the Cook Islands were drawn more and more into the social and economic orbit of their southern neighbors and rulers.

The church lost not only its major influence on government, but also its role in education. Here where mission rule had continued longer than almost anywhere else, the retreat from church involvement in education took place earlier than anywhere else in the Pacific. This paradox can be explained only in terms of New Zealand's willingness to provide funds for its dependencies to an extent that European and Australian governments did not and the stronger tradition of secular education in that country. The London Missionary Society with its Congregational roots was also more amenable to the change than other missions might have been. Two years after New Zealand's entry into the islands, the mission proposed to the authorities that they take over its school buildings for government schools.[24] In 1915 the government finally began to do this and in a few years all the schools in the southern Cooks were in government hands. The northern Cooks were a different matter; they were extremely isolated and the government did not feel it could operate effectively there. Consequently the pastors continued to provide the schooling, and the government paid them for their educational work.[25]

The link with New Zealand resulted not only in secular education but also in great commercial development so that the Cook Islands came to have the highest per-capita export trade of any English-speaking islands of the Pacific. Along with this economic prosperity came a possibly related decline in the interest in religion. There were complaints of lethargy and worldliness in the church. Rarotonga, which was at the heart of the modern developments, gradually ceased to provide candidates for the ministry. It also ceased to provide foreign missionaries. The last Cook islander to go as a foreign missionary (except for one recent appointment) was sent out about 1910, bringing to a close a record of missionary activity that is unparalleled in any country of the world for the number of missionaries in relation to the size of the sending church.

The missionary force sent from England to the Cooks was reduced from four men at the beginning of the twentieth century to one man in most of the following years. However, the contributions that the Cooks sent to London to help pay for this work increased rather than declined, indicating that the prosperity was helpful at least in financial terms. The one English missionary continued to dominate the life of the church until the authorities in London insisted on independence, as we shall see in a later chapter. That independence for the church came a full twenty years before internal self-government was granted by New Zealand.

Other churches tried to develop in the Cook Islands, though without any great success. Alongside the one LMS missionary there were, by midcentury, thirteen Roman Catholic, four Seventh-day Adventist, and six Mormon missionaries. The Seventh-day Adventists had been there the longest, but the Catholics had the largest and most effective work. They came from Tahiti in 1894 after the British protectorate had put an end to the laws of the old kingdom prohibiting new missions. Their bishop announced that they were coming to undertake "the evangelization of the Cooks" and their most important contribution was through the schools they operated on Rarotonga. Unlike the London Missionary Society they did not abandon education to the government and eventually their secondary schools, operated by the Sisters of St. Joseph of Cluny, played a significant part in training national leadership for the Cooks. They separated from Tahiti to form their own prefecture in 1922. Bishop Hermel of Tahiti found by that time that a diocese which stretched from Easter Island to Rarotonga, a distance equal to the width of the Atlantic Ocean, was simply too much for one man to administer and so the division was created.[26]

Niue

The small and isolated island of Niue has been, like the Cook Islands, governed by New Zealand, but until the middle of the twentieth century it felt much less New Zealand influence. Outside contacts of any kind were few. The government started a small school in 1909, but did not take over the village schools from the pastors until 1941 and after.[27] In consequence there existed until midcentury a closed, sacred society on Niue built around the London Missionary Society church with its twelve congregations, the pastors being the leaders and the foreign missionary the highest authority. Village work was done cooperatively; everyone had land to cultivate, but no one could sell it; traditional ways were rigidly enforced; and the old men, the pastors, and the deacons kept a strict hand on the life of the island. They also kept themselves between the missionary and the rest of the people so that, although the power of initiative and final decision lay with the missionary, he could act effectively only when he cooperated with the other leaders to support and defend the traditional system.

In this situation the New Zealand government representatives felt constricted and resentful. They longed for other churches to come in to break the LMS monopoly and thus to create an opening through which their own power could expand. When Bishop Blanc, the great Roman Catholic bishop of Tonga and Wallis, stopped on the island in 1924, he was invited to stay with the New Zealand resident commissioner and invited by him to start a mission, even though outside the government house the people shouted "Popé, Popé" in hostility wherever Blanc went.[28] He had no personnel available at that time so nothing was done, but the government did not give up hope. The invitation was repeated. Finally in a later period there came a response. The Mormons started a mission in 1953, against local protest and threats, and the Catholics began a mission in 1955, both making small numbers of converts.[29] In that period communication with the outside world became much more frequent and many Niueans emigrated to New Zealand. The old religious uniformity was broken, the church assumed the more modest role that it has adopted elsewhere in modern times, and, in consequence, government relations with the LMS—or with the Ekalesia Niue, the independent church that arose out of the LMS mission—were much more cordial.[30]

Samoa

The Samoan church has been the largest and most vigorous in all Polynesia. It has been part of a most powerful and resilient social structure, quite the opposite, say, of that of the Marquesas. The Samoans are astute politicians and have been masters in handling the politics of church life. The missionaries who have worked among them have found it necessary to stay in line with Samoan ideas or they have found themselves gradually pushed out. The missionaries, particularly at the beginning of the century, were accorded great honor, but those who can bestow honor can also bestow "humiliation and discomfiture," as one group of missionaries pointed out when they bowed to certain Samoan wishes.[31] The case of the unfortunate J. W. Sibree, son of a famous missionary in Madagascar, shows the kind of pressure that could be brought. He gave an interview to the press while passing through the United States in 1920 in which he was critical of an American naval officer in the government of American Samoa, one who had been under a cloud and had been ordered to return to America for investigation of his financial operations. The interview gave rise to a rumor that Sibree had been critical of Samoa and in consequence the Elder Pastors of the London Missionary Society church demanded that he leave the islands immediately, although he had given faithful service for twenty-three years. His fellow missionaries tried to defend him and to point out the falseness of the rumors, but it was obvious that future effective work would be impossible for him and all had to agree reluctantly that he leave the country.[32]

Samoa entered the twentieth century in great turmoil. King Malietoa died in 1898. Most of the chiefs supported the selection of the high chief Mata'afa for the kingship, but others, backed by British and American interests, supported the old king's son. Civil war ensued, the last of many wars and rebellions that marked Samoan history in the nineteenth century. At one point Mata'afa's men captured the capital, Apia, and in reply British and American warships bombarded the town. Mata'afa happened to be a Catholic and the Catholic Cardinal Moran in Sydney claimed in a public statement that the Protestant missionaries "did everything in their power to oppose Mata'afa" and tried to get the warships to shell Apia's Catholic church. This accusation brought a storm of protest from Protestants in Australia. It also brought some full expositions from Protestant missionaries in Samoa of the ways in which their pastors had been instructed to stay out of all participation in politics, how they themselves had given no aid to either side, although some of Mata'afa's followers in distress had been cared for in their institutions. In light of the near anarchy that the country had experienced, the Protestant missionaries thought a protectorate by some imperial power or a strong advisor or governor backed by such powers would be desirable.[33]

What Samoa got was German rule over most of the country and American rule over the small islands in the east. The churches adjusted well to the new rulers, since complete religious freedom was maintained. The London Missionary Society was criticized by some German extremists who assumed that because it was English it was anti-German. But an official investigation exonerated the mission, and the government even urged the mission to prosecute for libel those who had made the charges, a step which the mission declined to take.[34] The extent of LMS readiness for cooperation with the Germans was shown in 1909 when the important chief Lauaki of Savai'i led a movement of resistance to the imperial rule. The missionaries first showed some appreciation for the movement, but when violence against the government was threatened, the leading LMS missionary, J. E. Newell, and some of his colleagues made their way to Lauaki's headquarters and convinced him to lay down his arms and accept exile by the authorities. Lauaki and nine other leaders, along with a large group of relatives and an LMS pastor to serve them, were sent to Saipan where they stayed until after New Zealand took possession of Samoa in 1914.[35]

The early years of New Zealand rule were beset by difficulties. The great influenza epidemic of 1918 struck Samoa—and also Tahiti—with devastating effect. Between one-fifth and one-fourth of the population of Samoa died; nearly half the pastors of the LMS were lost, including twenty-nine out of thirty in their Council of Elder Pastors. Church workers were particularly vulnerable because they were constantly visiting and helping the sick. Tahiti experienced a comparable loss from among its pastors and elders. The loss in Samoa was particularly damaging; during the following years the church and the society were plunged into a time of disruption and agitation when wise and experienced leadership was desperately needed but, because of the epidemic, was in short supply.

The agitation centered in the movement called the *Mau,* a name meaning "to stand firm." It was a nationalist movement originating largely in the part-European community of Samoa but soon winning the participation of the majority of the Samoans. It operated chiefly through agitation and non-cooperation; yet the threat of armed violence was great, and at one time violence was averted only when an LMS missionary, Reginald Bartlett, swam to the principal hideout of the Mau leaders to deliver a conciliatory message from the government and to urge negotiations.[36] For a time in 1927 and 1928 the movement succeeded in bringing the colonial government to a standstill.

The Mau did not affect the church directly until 1928 when one of the missionaries took the lead in presenting an address of appreciation to a departing governor. The governor had been one against whom the nationalists were struggling. The Mau leaders reacted by calling for reduced contributions to the missionaries, demanding the dismissal of certain church leaders, and bidding prayer meetings to be held on behalf of the national cause. These demands did not bring a great response from the church members, but the missionaries proceeded to stir up a tempest by forbidding the General Assembly of the LMS church from even discussing the demands. When the missionaries received from the assembly an assurance on this point, they regarded it as insincere, dismissed the assembly, closed all the church schools, and stopped all mission work. Their aim was to show the Samoans that they could not get along without foreign missionaries, but the result was a total impasse. London finally resolved it by sending out a deputation, which led to much greater independence on the part of the church. This development will be considered in a later chapter dealing with church independence.

Churches other than the LMS were not seriously affected by the Mau disturbances. They were smaller and did not have the position of a national church. The LMS during most of this century could count on the loyalty of somewhere between two-thirds and three-fourths of the Samoans. The rest of the population was divided fairly equally between the Methodists and the Catholics, together with small numbers of Mormons and Seventh-day Adventists. The division on religious matters was often a consequence of other divisions in Samoan society and it in turn exacerbated those divisions. A clan or a leader might express its opposition to others by joining a different church and then the church division made the opposition more permanently entrenched. It was in this way that the Methodist-LMS split first developed at the very beginning of Samoan Christianity. The Methodists found strength also in support from Tonga, which continued during the time that European help was withdrawn. Perhaps in consequence, Tongan ministers, along with European missionaries, were given positions of leadership above their Samoan colleagues in the Methodist church during the early years of the twentieth century.[37]

The Roman Catholic church, served by French Marist missionaries, had come much later than Methodism, but it grew more rapidly during the twentieth century. In recent years it has comprised 20 percent of the people, including many of the principal rulers. Its main development came through its schools and especially under the long episcopacy of Joseph Darnand (1919–53). The part-European population in particular was served by Catholic schools and also by Catholic recreational facilities. The majority of the part-Europeans became Catholics and, since many of them were leaders in the life of the islands, this enhanced Catholic strength in the national leadership.[38]

Schools were an important part of the work of all the missions. Particularly the LMS central schools—Malua for theological students, Leulumoega for youths, and Papauta for girls, and their smaller counterparts in American Samoa—became leading centers of education and the way to social prestige. Each of the other churches also had central schools at postprimary level. The lower schools, conducted by the pastors in the villages, were less satisfactory and were gradually replaced by government schooling. At first the pastors supplemented the government's instruction by giving lessons, particularly on religion, after school hours. But gradually the practice died out and the churches concentrated their efforts on postprimary education.

Kiribati and Tuvalu

The turn of the century was a troubled time for the churches of Kiribati and Tuvalu (then called the Gilbert and Ellice Islands). Christianity had first come to Kiribati in the mid-nineteenth century, as we noted earlier, through missionaries of the Hawaiian Evangelical Association and its parent body, the American Board. But the Hawaiian church was overextended in its Micronesian enterprises, and though American missionaries came for limited periods they did not survive and the work was left to Hawaiian pastors established on each island with only occasional American aid and supervision. The five southernmost islands and all of Tuvalu were left completely untouched, so the Samoan church came in 1870 and planted its pastors there. Samoa was much closer than Hawaii and every year English missionaries from Samoa made a tour of the work. Both Samoan and Hawaiian pastors established strict controls over the people, but their instruction in Christianity was not far developed. In 1886, in the last great massacre of the incessant Kiribati wars, the Christians on one island defeated the remaining pagans and proceeded to kill them all—at the urging, later Catholics said, of the Hawaiian pastor.[39]

Into this situation there came in 1888 Roman Catholic missionaries of the Sacred Heart from Issoudun in France. They went first to the area where the Hawaiian pastors were at work. Initially only a few came, but at the beginning of the new century Bishop Leray brought fifteen new recruits so that a missionary could be placed on every island. A dozen years later there were two on most of the islands. The Hawaiians proved to be no match for the French. They tried to defy the French, threatened them, and denounced any people who followed them. At times they led mobs who attacked the missionaries. But the vigor, determination, and persistence of the Catholics won. Where the foreign priest led in procession even a few followers, he cowed the crowds who were armed to attack. Catholicism became the majority religion of northern Kiribati and also developed significantly in the south.[40]

The Protestant response came from Samoa. The British government, which had just been established in the islands and was trying to restrict Catholic incursions in the interest of peace as well as trying to counteract the power of the Samoan pastors, urged that a British missionary be stationed there. In 1900 the Samoan LMS Mission, seriously concerned about a possible total collapse of Protestantism, sent W. E. Goward.[41] No one better could have been selected to master the situation and reverse the disintegration. Goward was a domineering, driving man of boundless energy. He established a central school on Beru Island, the old center of Kiribati political and cultural life, and there began to train the youth. To develop a residential school on one of these small, dry islands was no easy task. There was no land to grow food for outsiders, so each student had to receive on the annual or semi-annual visits of the mission ship enough supplies from home—coconuts, dried fish, coconut molasses, and pandanus fruit—to survive on until the next visit. Gradually soil was imported to build up the land for food production.

Goward also established strict discipline over the Samoan pastors working in Kiribati. The pastors did not take kindly to the imposition of a new master. They resisted his tight controls, and Goward had to answer charges that the pastors brought against him in the missionary meeting in Samoa. The missionaries, however, refused to judge the merits of the case because they did not want to encourage further possible Samoan unrest, and Goward was left as master of southern Kiribati. Even the British government could not command the obedience that he secured.[42] The Catholic advances in the south were stayed or even reversed.

Goward next turned his attention to the central and northern islands. The American Board's work there suffered a serious blow in 1909 when the one man whom they had been trying to keep in the field, Alfred Walkup, a former boxer turned missionary who for twenty years lived a lonely life on his little schooner touring the islands to keep in touch with the pastors, was lost with his ship during a storm in the Marshall Islands. Goward was pressing all along for the American Board to turn over its work to the LMS; the Americans had indicated their willingness, but the LMS was reluctant. For a time in 1911 a scheme of cooperation was worked out, but the American missionary who made the first attempt at cooperation, though he started out with much appreciation for Goward's abilities, soon discovered that Goward's "desire to dominate the whole situation" made impossible any true cooperation.[43] The American Board then offered to turn over all its work in Kiribati, including also Nauru, and even to pay the LMS annually for five years the amount that they had been spending on that work. This was agreeable and the transfer was completed at the end of 1917, just before Goward retired. The few remaining American Board pastors were gradually replaced by men whom Goward had trained.

From that time on the religious situation in the islands was stabilized with little movement from one denomination to another. Catholic and Protestant churches stressed inner strengthening, especially through education. Their pastors or catechists ran the local schools as well as their churches and the people thought of church and school as identical. The government did nothing for education beyond a miniscule grant to each of the missions for its work. Teacher training was part of the pastors' or catechists' training, given in the central school at Abemama for the Catholics and at Beru for the Protestants.

Protestants had a slight majority among the Kiribati people as a whole, but the Catholics were predominant in central and northern Kiribati. The two southernmost Kiribati Islands, Tamana and Arorae, and all Tuvalu were totally Protestant. Occasionally the Catholic bishop would attempt, against local opposition, to land a priest or catechist on one of those islands. An attempt was made in 1936 on Arorae; some of the people tried to block the way of the priest and only the intervention of the local pastor prevented a violent attack on him. Following this the government proclaimed the "Closed Islands Ordinance" whereby no outsider could land on Tamana or Arorae or in Tuvalu without official permission. The people of Tamana and Arorae erected large "covenant stones" in front of their churches declaring their perpetual covenant with the LMS.

One outbreak of violence between the churches has attracted much attention and investigation.[44] In 1930 on Onotoa Island there was an emotional revival among the Protestants, who comprised over 90 percent of the people. The leader of the movement, an LMS pastor, was called "the prophet" and "the Father of God." The people in their enthusiasm wanted to make a huge gift of copra to their mission. The headman of the island, who was a Catholic, tried to stop them, since it would leave them without enough coconuts for their food and taxes, but they went ahead and then demanded to be arrested for nonpayment of taxes. They were not arrested, but in the excitement of such possible martyrdom one of their women announced that the island would be destroyed by a great wave, and all would die except for those who gathered at a spot called the New Jerusalem. Nearly all the people gathered there, and when the wave did not come they blamed the Catholics for its failure and said they would be the destroying wave themselves. Two Catholics were killed, the headman was wounded, and the others were in flight when an LMS ship, the *John Williams*, hove into view. The English missionary, accompanied by a government officer, came ashore and, risking an attack on himself by the excited people, challenged their leaders, broke the spell, and quieted the situation. What might have become a separate Christian sect soon died down and disappeared. Brief though the outburst was, it revealed the emotional intensity that can lie below the often placid surface of Pacific Island Christianity.

The two phosphate islands, Ocean Island and Nauru, had a church history closely related to that of Kiribati. On both of them the church was first developed by American Board representatives partly supported by Hawaii, just as it was in Kiribati.

The first American Board missionary to Nauru arrived in 1899 and Christianity was quickly accepted by the Nauruans in the early years of the twentieth century.[45] When the LMS assumed responsibility for northern Kiribati it also took charge of the church on Ocean Island and Nauru. Ocean Island was in fact governed as part of the Kiribati group, and its church was part of that in Kiribati. Nauru continued to maintain a separate church and seldom had a European missionary after the LMS came in. Roman Catholics carried on a continuing work among the people but, having come a little later than the Protestants, had few adherents.[46]

Men from all over Kiribati came to the two islands to earn money in the phosphate diggings. They maintained strong churches for themselves, as distinct from the churches of the local people, and they sent large contributions back to their home churches in the various islands. The largest monetary income that the Kiribati churches received came from these contributions. Eventually when the phosphate was exhausted the outside workers ceased. The Ocean Island inhabitants (Banabans) moved to a new island, which they purchased in the Fiji group, and gradually, after receiving careful and considerate treatment, agreed to transfer their ties to Fijian Methodism. Nauruans decided against a change of location to an island that was offered them off the coast of Australia, and kept their church independent and wealthy from their past phosphate earnings.

Fiji

To move from Kiribati and Tuvalu to Fiji is to move from the isolated fringes of Pacific life to its very hub. It is to move from barren sandy strips that scarcely break the ocean surface to high mountains and lush vegetation. Fiji with its large population and central location has naturally become the center for South Pacific island affairs, as much in the church as in other fields of life.

The principal church of Fiji, the Methodist church, comprises nearly 90 percent of the Fijians. The Methodists have been deeply intertwined with traditional Fijian life. The British colonial government likewise believed in maintaining the traditional life and in governing through the traditional chiefs, although it forbade the ceremonies of traditional religion and sometimes jailed those convicted of practicing them.[47] So church and state tended to support the same leaders and the same religion and there was on the whole a good working relationship between them, although there was a tradition that the Methodist chairman had to be someone who would stand up to the government, and the government people sometimes exploded over missionary interference in government decisions and what they called "the system of espionage practiced by the Wesleyan religious authorities" through the pastors and teachers they had in every village.[48] The close relation that Methodism bore to the old system of government through the chiefs was shown in the fact that it was often referred to as "the chiefs' church" and that its headquarters until 1903 were maintained on the little island of Bau, which had been the seat of Thakombau, the highest chief. Only in 1903 did the church bow to the obvious pressures of modern requirements and move its headquarters to the capital city of Suva.[49]

The strongest challenge to the Methodists came, as might be expected, from the Marist missionaries of the Roman Catholic church. During most of the twentieth century the Catholics were staffed with two to four times the number of foreign missionaries that the Methodists possessed. Therefore it was possible for them to provide foreign priests for some of the more remote areas where the Methodists had only Fijian workers. Since the presence of a foreign missionary was a source of strength and a point of pride in any locality, there were occasional requests for Catholic missionaries from villages willing to join that church if they could have a foreign priest. The most famous case of this kind took place in Namosi in 1902, but there were similar developments in Namoli in 1922 and Navatusila in 1925.[50] These were fairly small accessions, however. The main area of Catholic strength continued to be on Taveuni and the adjacent part of Vanua Levu where the Catholics had preceded the Methodists in the nineteenth century.[51]

The greatest concern of both the Methodists and the Catholics was with their educational systems. The Methodists, during the early years of the century, had a complete system of education covering the whole country, rising from the network of village schools, to the circuit schools, to the central training institutions. The Catholics had fewer village schools, since they were established in fewer villages, but concentrated on central schools with European teachers and high standards. In 1909 there were 1,046 Methodist schools, 165 Roman Catholic schools, and three each of government, Seventh-day Adventist, and Anglican schools. In that year the government began to take a serious interest in schools and appointed its first commission on education, which led in 1916 to the first education ordinance. Under this the government was authorized to proceed to establish primary schools where needed and also to help mission primary schools that met its standards.[52] The standards included the teaching of English and, since the Methodist system had always been based on the Fijian language, few of its schools qualified for this aid at first. But improvements were made through widespread consolidation of weaker schools into stronger ones and through the reorganizing efforts of Reverend L. M. Thompson, who was education secretary for the mission from 1916 to 1931 and also a member of the government Board of Education. By 1925 he reported that the Methodists had 384 schools qualified for government aid. The aid system expanded from then on with the government paying the salaries, the village providing the land and building, and the mission supervising the operation of the school. From 1928 the government gave increased grants to the Methodist teacher-training institution at Davuilevu and used it to train its own Fijian teachers. There was a dispute with the mission board in Sydney over this. The board felt that there was too much possibility of government control over the institution at Davuilevu and withheld its approval. It also believed that the Fiji Mission had exceeded its powers in accepting the arrangement. After some altercations, however, the board gave in. The Catholics simultaneously began their own teacher-training center at Cawaci on Ovalau.[53]

The situation was not as satisfactory as it appeared on the surface, however. A government inspector reported that the Catholic schools with their European staffs were excellent, whereas the Methodist Fijian-staffed schools were poor. The government proceeded to take over Methodist schools without even consulting the mission. When the mission protested, the government pointed out that it was paying the salaries and the local people were providing the land and buildings, so the mission was legally powerless. In 1931 the Methodist Synod under these attacks informed the government that henceforth only those few schools that were under direct mission responsibility and on mission property would be regarded as Methodist schools.[54] The mission in succeeding years concentrated on improving these schools. But this was the end of the nationwide system of Methodist schools.

The apparently happy arrangement regarding teacher training also collapsed, although this development takes us beyond the time period covered in this chapter. In 1946 the government canceled all authorization for teacher training outside its own institution, which it proceeded to establish. This meant that the two mission institutions had to be closed down. The Methodists accepted this decision but the Catholics fought it and continually requested permission to renew their own training at a better level, for their institution had been admittedly a poor one. Finally in 1954 permission was granted and in 1958 they opened an impressive new training college in Suva. At the same time both missions concentrated on developing strong secondary schools and these became their major educational ventures. The government came forward with an offer of large financial aid to these schools in 1955. This was acceptable to the Methodists. The Catholic Mission as such opposed the acceptance of aid for fear of government influence. But two Catholic schools, which were operated by independent orders, went ahead and accepted the aid and soon the whole mission followed.[55]

It is evident from all this that the role of the churches in relation to education created more difficulties in Fiji than anywhere else in the Pacific. This is partly because the size and wealth of Fiji meant that there were greater resources for public education than in most other territories and therefore the government could take over the field more easily. It was also because, as the principal center of Pacific activity and communication, Fiji was more inclined to change with the world at large, so its churches had to struggle through their response to changes which, in most other islands, came later and which the churches in those other islands already expected and more easily accepted.

Before we leave Fiji there is one other church, besides the Methodist and Catholic, which demands attention, namely, the Anglican church. The Anglicans came to Fiji originally only to serve the Europeans who had settled in the islands. Later some Solomon islanders settled there in connection with labor on the plantations, and since they were originally Anglicans the church also served them and provided a school for them. But this represented no change in the principle of their work, which was to care for those of their communion, but not to reach out in a mission to others. In fact when their first priest arrived, in the nineteenth century, they made an agreement with the Methodists not to engage in proselytism among them.[56]

Just at the turn of the century, however, a different attitude appeared, which stood in continuing tension with the earlier ecumenical outlook. Bishop Alfred Willis, at that time bishop of Hawaii, believed that he had a divine mission to all the people of the islands in whatever church they might be found. He had a ready supporter in S. T. Nevill, the bishop of Dunedin, a stalwart advocate of Anglican expansion who had the hope, as he put it, that his "name should in some measure go down to posterity as the founder, or as instrumental in founding," a bishopric for Fiji and its neighbors.[57] Bishop Willis was forced to leave Honolulu in 1902 because Canterbury at that time transferred Hawaii to the American Episcopal church, and Willis' long anti-American stand made it impossible for him to work with the American bishops, men who were, in Nevill's opinion, "Americans first and churchmen afterwards."[58]

At the very time he was to leave Hawaii, Willis received a call from a significant group of Tongans who described themselves as Anglicans and desired his ministrations. This group had arisen, oddly enough, through the efforts of a former Methodist missionary, Shirley Baker, whom we shall meet again in the discussion of Tonga. Baker had for a time become the prime minister of Tonga and then had been dismissed from his high office and deported from the country. At the time with which we are here concerned, he had returned to the islands as an old man and had demanded a pension from the national church he had initiated during his days of power. He was summarily refused the pension and he declared that in retaliation for this rebuff he would start a competing church, the Church of Victoria (i.e., of the queen of England). He passed himself off as an Anglican priest and was able to get a lay reader's license from that Anglican expansionist, the bishop of Dunedin. He secured his largest following when one of the noble families of Tonga turned against the king, the leader of the national church. The young monarch had broken his engagement to the daughter of this family in order to marry a woman of lower social standing. The family, in retaliation, joined Baker's church. The young lady in question died, presumably of a broken heart. Baker insisted that he should conduct the funeral, but the government checked on his credentials and made public the fact that he was not an Anglican priest. When the leaders of the new church discovered that Baker was in fact no priest, they threw him out and it was then that they sent their appeal to Bishop Willis to come and help them. Willis came, though this was regarded as an act of dubious propriety by other Anglicans. He asked the bishops in New Zealand to make this a new diocese for him. His principal supporter was, not surprisingly, the Bishop of Dunedin who had convinced himself that the whole population of Tonga was ready to become Anglican, the king taking the lead.

The other bishops in New Zealand were angered by the whole affair. Willis' actions were an embarrassment to them, and they believed in maintaining the agreements to refrain from interference in the areas of other churches, agreements which the Bishop of Dunedin said the Methodists themselves did not honor and the Anglicans honored only when browbeaten by Methodist threats and blandishments in London. He believed that Willis should forthwith be put in charge of a new bishopric of Fiji, Tonga, and all Polynesia.[59] He continued to raise funds for Willis, although the other bishops refused to recognize him and referred the matter to England.

The church in England had been brought into the discussions from the beginning, since financial help would be required from there. The Archbishop of Canterbury was persuaded that the best way to deal with the situation was to establish the bishopric but to appoint as bishop a man with less grandiose intentions than Alfred Willis.[60] He pressed for funds so that the diocese might be established before fresh letters could come from New Zealand increasing the difficulty. Funds were raised and the Bishop of Dunedin agreed to withdraw his backing of Willis provided the bishopric were indeed established and some honorable post were provided for Willis.[61] Accordingly in 1908 the diocese was set up. Reverend T. C. Twitchell, an unassuming English clergyman, was made bishop in Polynesia, and shortly thereafter Willis was appointed as his assistant in Tonga. The diocese was to operate as a missionary diocese under the bishop of London and the archbishop of Canterbury, but in 1925 it was transferred, in accordance with a request of its members, to the Province of New Zealand. Its influential members were in large part Australians and New Zealanders. Its mentality was therefore heavily colonial until the volte-face of the 1960s, which we shall examine later.

The Fiji Indians: The greatest missionary responsibility of all the churches in Fiji was that to the Indian people who were pouring into the country during the last years of the nineteenth and first years of the twentieth century. They came as indentured laborers to work on the sugar-cane plantations. They lived for the most part in long barracks with minimal facilities and usually no family life, since the men came alone. Moral deterioration, health problems, and crime were among the results of this treatment.

The churches were singularly indifferent to this challenge. Though the public press had inveighed against the idea of bringing in Indian workers and predicted the social disruption it would produce, the missionaries and church members had nothing to say about it.[62] Once the laborers were in their midst some of the leading missionaries called on the Australian churches to send missionaries to them, and for three years the Fiji Methodists actually secured and paid for a Christian minister to come from India to work with them. But the Fiji missionaries and Fijians did not themselves become involved.[63] The Fijian people who were undertaking great missionary exploits in distant Pacific islands did not see the need of their closest neighbors. At first they looked down on the Indians as inferior and later they resented their presence and feared their growing power, but none of these attitudes could foster a missionary concern.

However, the Methodists in Australia began to awaken, and in 1897 they sent a missionary with experience in India, Miss Hannah Dudley, to start a program specifically for the Indians in Fiji. Five years later they sent the first minister for this work, Reverend J. W. Burton, who through his later writings and missionary statesmanship became one of the most famous missionaries of the Pacific.[64]

The Anglican church at this point began a small work also. Their first missionary was met by a prohibition imposed by the plantation owners, the Colonial Sugar Refining Co., against any preaching to the men on their plantations. The missionary lodged complaints about this with the local government and with the church authorities in England, and the company finally backed down. Though they relented, they evidently did not change their minds, since the company manager said in official testimony later: "In my opinion the knowledge of English and the profession of Christianity are certain signs of rascality."[65]

The small mission effort had important public consequences when Burton, in 1910, published a book (*The Fiji of Today*) in which he attacked the whole system of indentured labor and said that it should be ended. Most missionaries felt that there were indeed abuses in the indentured system but that these should be corrected rather than the system ended. Burton maintained that the power given to the plantation owners under the system was such as to make it unlikely that they would undertake significant improvements. The government of Fiji called on the chairman of the Methodist Mission to have Burton withdraw his charges, but the chairman replied that Burton would withdraw them only if they were disproved. The preponderance of missionary opinion gradually changed to condemnation of the system itself.[66] The concern spread to India and an official commission was sent out to Fiji, which presented only a favorable picture of the situation. Then an unofficial commission led by an Anglican missionary in India, C. F. Andrews, came and in its report castigated the system. This led to such an outcry in India that the Indian government stopped all permission for recruiting of indentured labor for Fiji—and so the system ended in 1917.[67]

In succeeding years the mission among Indians in Fiji moved more and more into the area of schools. The Catholics had no work specifically for the Indians until the 1960s, but their English-language schools served the Indian population along with others. The Anglicans, and much more the Methodists, had schools specifically for the Indians. Itinerant evangelism among the Indian people, which had been emphasized at first, declined in favor of the educational services. Perhaps because of this change the number of converts from among the Indians, which had never been large, slowed down and the small Indian-language church the Methodists had begun became fairly static. It had little sense of being a church rather than a number of mission stations and, living in the midst of the Indian community which was the most secularized in the Pacific of those days, it had little more than an ethical understanding of its faith.[68] The large Fijian church was separated from it by the language barrier and by the Fijian sense of superiority and exclusiveness. In the Catholic and Anglican churches the few Indian members were absorbed into the whole, which was possible in those communions because English was the common church language and they had no great Fijian church.

Tonga

The kingdom of Tonga has been as strongly a Methodist area as Fiji, but it has been throughout the twentieth century a divided Methodism rather than a united one. The divisions stemmed from the great struggle of 1885 when the first king of the country, George Tupou I, at the behest of his prime minister, the former Methodist missionary Shirley Baker, set up a new church, independent of the Australian missionaries. The king's new church was called the Free Church of Tonga and most of the people followed him into it. A small and stubborn remnant stayed with the missionaries in what was named the Wesleyan church and was in fact a district of Australian Methodism. The relations between these two churches and their successors have dominated much of the church history of Tonga during this century.

During the early years of the century the relations between them, which had been exceedingly bitter, were gradually sweetening. The Free Church was led by Jabez Watkin, another former Methodist missionary, who had cast his lot with the king when the church first began and had served as its head throughout its life. He was increasingly friendly with the young leader of the Wesleyan church, Rodger Page, a Methodist missionary who came out from Australia in 1908 and devoted himself with vigor and charm to improving relationships. An even more potent force for reconciliation, after the coronation in 1918, was the new queen, Salote, who wanted to end the division that afflicted her country and also to heal the religious rift in her family since she had married a Wesleyan.

In 1924 the queen drew the two parties together and secured their agreement to unite. But just when everything seemed ready for the union the plans misfired. Watkin announced that he was going back on his agreement and thousands of people assembled in the capital to petition the queen against taking such a step. She reacted vigorously, went to the Free Church Conference, and dismissed Watkin from his office. The union was then consummated forthwith under a new set of officers. But Watkin, with the cooperation of a high chief, Finau 'Ulukalala, led a large group who refused to go along and continued what they claimed was the Free Church. The division was as great or greater than ever because as many or more people followed Watkin out as there were people who came in from the Wesleyans.[69]

Worse was to follow. Watkin died eight months later and his followers proved unable to hold together. For a time they imported a New Zealand Presbyterian minister to serve as their president. But he was too tight-fisted with the church's money, and in 1928 Finau 'Ulukalala and about one-third of the church members revolted against his rule and left the church to found a new body, which they called the Church of Tonga. Such a second split would probably never have taken place if the Free Church had had the unifying strength of either the monarchy or the missionaries in its midst. Thus it was the effort at union that had, perversely, led to further division.

The two splinter churches, the Free Church and the Church of Tonga, led a durable, if ossified, existence. The united church, which took the omnibus name of Free Wesleyan Church of Tonga, continued as the major religious body of the country, flourishing under royal patronage and missionary assistance. Its ministers became the most highly educated indigenous church leaders in the Pacific. When in later times pan-Pacific church organizations and theological schools were established, Tongans from the Free Wesleyan church and the Roman Catholic church were the first islanders in the top offices of those bodies.

The close tie between the national church and the crown did not mean that that church or any other church received help with its educational program. Unlike the colonial domains around it, Tonga did not move toward government assistance for mission education. Under the first king some government schools had been established and the government found its limited resources strained to maintain even these schools. So the churches were left to operate their own educational systems unassisted. The majority of primary pupils were in church schools until 1948. After that the government began to build up its own primary education and the churches, one by one, proceeded to withdraw from that field. It was secondary education that then became, as in Fiji, the area of concentration for the churches, and the government left that field largely to them.[70]

From what has been said thus far the impression might be gained that there were only Methodists, of one stripe or another, in Tonga. This is not the whole truth. There were minority churches: the Roman Catholics, the Anglicans, the Seventh-day Adventists, and the Mormons. All of these we shall have occasion to examine. The Adventists and the Mormons we shall consider in later chapters. The story of Anglican beginnings we have already touched on when looking at Fiji. And the Roman Catholics we can appropriately turn to next when we are looking at Wallis.

Wallis

The island of Wallis (also known as Uvea) with its smaller neighbor Futuna is the most perfect example of a Catholic island in the Pacific. In fact it has been called the most Catholic place in the world.[71] Like Niue it was a small island, isolated from outside influences, and it developed a unified society around a single church, in this case the Catholic church. Until 1935 Wallis and Futuna were united with Tonga in a single diocese or vicariate with a single bishop, though the situation of the Catholics in Tonga was almost at the other extreme from that in Wallis. In Tonga Catholics were a struggling minority. It was not until the beginning of the twentieth century that the Catholic church was even allowed to establish itself in Tonga's capital. The first regular services began to be held in the capital in 1901. After that a school was permitted and the Marist Sisters did much educational work in the country, starting in 1924. But the church remained small.[72]

Wallis and Futuna, on the other hand, had a vigorous church, which included the entire population. The ancient social structures had been preserved and blessed by Christianity, except that warfare had been abolished and family life strengthened. The boys and young men still slept in special houses established for them, but now those houses were located in the mission compound and often visited by the priest. There were strong religious fraternities among the lay people and many vocations to the religious life. An indigenous priesthood appeared here sooner than anywhere else in the Pacific, and here alone the priesthood eventually became almost totally indigenous. The church always operated the schools, with financial assistance from the government.[73]

Church and government usually cooperated effectively, though there were times of tension and struggle between them. In 1910 the king of Wallis ordered the deportation of a French priest, and the people rose in rebellion, deposed the king, and put another in his place. The French governor tried to intervene, but to no avail. A new treaty with France was signed at that time, which excluded the missionaries from the government of Wallis. On Futuna, however, the Marist missionary continued to perform as the only delegate of the French government until 1957.[74] At times, as in 1929, this led to a revolt against the missionary, and the French power had to come to his support with a government ship.[75] But normally government was conducted by the traditional systems, and foreigners had little reason to intervene.

As in the case of Niue, this closed and static society was opened up recently by enormous emigration, this time to New Caledonia. There has been no religious diversity introduced since the French government, unlike that of

Niue, has made no effort in that direction. But modern currents have poured in and the church leaders who were once the bulwark of the old society have in many cases become advocates of the new.

Such was the story, during the first part of the twentieth century, of the churches in the eastern and central Pacific. These, as we have seen, were old and well-established churches. Only in Kiribati and Nauru were the churches still finding their feet at the beginning of the century and only in Fiji did they still have before them a missionary task among non-Christian people. In this respect the eastern and central islands were noticeably different from the islands to the west, where a considerable missionary task remained in nearly all the island groups. The western Pacific therefore merits separate consideration.

NOTES

1. For the basis of these figures and a fuller treatment of the work and outlook of the missionaries, see Forman 1978b.

2. *Église Évangélique:* 6.

3. *Église Évangélique:* 7. O'Reilly 1962: 478.

4. F. Vernier to Paris Mission, Feb. 27, 1903; E. Ahnne to Bianquis, Jan. 12, 1914, Paris Evangelical Missionary Society Archives, Paris. *Église Évangélique*: 7. *Journal des Missions Évangéliques* 95, pt. 1 (1920): 58–59. Langdon 1968: 250. *Le Christianisme au XX Siècle*, July 14, 1966, p. 345. O'Reilly 1962: 477.

5. *Nos Champs de Mission*, 39–40.

6. Minutes of missionaries' meeting, Dec. 13–20, 1900. L. de Pomaret to Paris Mission, June 4, 1901; F. Vernier to Paris Mission, Feb. 27, 1903. Paris Evangelical Missionary Society Archives, Paris.

7. *Journal des Missions Évangéliques* 80, pt. 1: 207–8; pt. 2: 278; 81, pt. 2: 265; 89, pt.1: 380. *Église Évangélique*, p. 11.

8. G. Brunel, L. de Pomaret to Paris Mission, Sept. 27, 1910. Notes to the Committee of the Paris Mission, Nov. 1901. Paris Evangelical Missionary Society Archives, Paris.

9. Ahnne 1931, p. 34.

10. de Pomaret to Bianquis, June 29, 1913, and E. Ahnne to Bianquis, April 3, 1914, Paris Evangelical Missionary Society Archives, Paris. Allégret 1928, Part 1: 50–51. Kessing 1945: 245. *Centenaire des Écoles Protestantes*, pp. 57, 66.

11. *Mission de l'Église* 18 (1973): 22.

12. Vicar Apostolic of Tahiti, Report to Society for the Propagation of the Faith, 1902, 1904. S.P.F. Archives, Paris. Lesourd 1931: 137.

13. Vicar Apostolic of Tahiti, Report to the Society for the Propagation of the Faith, 1900, 1901, 1902, 1906. S.P.F. Archives, Paris. Father Calixte Olivier, interview, June 1967.

14. A. Freitag 1952: 56. *Annales des Sacrés-Coeurs,* June 1932: 440–54.

15. *Horizons Blancs,* January 1967: 402.

16. A. Freitag 1952: 55.

17. A. Freitag 1952: 51.

18. *Horizons Blancs*, April 1963: 411, *Missions Catholiques* 39 (1907): 713–39; 59 (1927): 344–45.

19. Alazard 1905: 2. F. M. Bousquet of Picpus headquarters to Society for Propagation of the Faith, Feb. 14, 1905. Vicar Apostolic of the Marquesas to S.P.F., Sept. 30, 1904, S.P.F. Archives, Paris.

20. Vicar Apostolic of the Marquesas to Society for the Propagation of the Faith, Report for 1906. S.P.F. Archives, Paris. Bishop David Le Cadre to P. Alazard, July 1, 1920, and to P. Iledefonse, Feb. 1, 1931, File 47–9 in Sacred Hearts Archives, Rome. *Annales des Sacrés-Coeurs* 1938: 417–18. Lesourd 1931: 138. The boys' school reopened in 1960.

21. Englert 1964: 75–102. Mouly 1935: 147–59. *Worldmission* 16: 52–54. *Horizons Blancs*, October 1967, pp. 495, 502–7; October 1968, p. 117.

22. This is presented in semifictionalized treatment in Nordhoff and Hall 1934.

23. Gilson 1970: 142.

24. Larkin 1966: 40.

25. Viner et al. 1916: 43–45.

26. Since the Cooks were an English rather than a French area, the Dutch province of the Picpus Order in 1940 took over responsibility for the work. *LMS Chronicle* 1952: 124–126. *Horizons Blancs*, July 1964: 69. Freitag 1952: 57. Vicar Apostolic of Tahiti to Society for the Propagation of the Faith, June 4, 1894, S.P.F. Archives, Paris.

27. Viner et al. 1916:61. Harold Taylor, Annual Report from Niue, 1941. Council for World Mission Archives, London.

28. Blanc, Diary, July 29–30, 1924 Catholic Archives, Nuku'alofa.

29. *Pacific Islands Monthly 23* (February 1953): 128. Douglas 1974: 246–47. Therriault 1965.

30. Proposed Constitution for Ekalesia Niue, 1966. Council for World Mission Archives, London. Edwards 1971:24.

31. J. Marriott to R. W. Thompson, Oct. 11, 1902. Council for World Mission Archives, London.

32. Samoa District Committee, LMS, Minutes, December 1920, pp. 173–74. Church Archives, Apia.

33. Becke 1900: 220. Stephen and Hulme 1904: 15–17. General Committee, i.e., District Committee, of LMS, Minutes, August 1899, pp. 78–80. Church Archives, Apia. J. E. Newell, "Protestant Missionaries in the Samoan War," a lecture delivered March 11, 1903. Council for World Mission Archives, London. Statement presented to the International Commission, Apia, May 16, 1899. LMS Church Archives, Apia.

34. Keesing 1934: 77. Deekin 1901: 112–15. W. Hackett to R. W. Thompson, Sept. 9, 1901. Council for World Mission Archives, London. One restriction which the missions had to accept was that the only foreign language taught in their schools would be German. But even in this matter the LMS secured an exemption for those students who came from American Samoa or the Gilbert and Ellice Islands and therefore needed English as their second language. (Samoa District Committee, LMS. Minutes, May 1901, p. 224, Church Archives, Apia. W. Hackett to R. W. Thompson, Sept. 9. 1901. Council for World Mission Archives. London.)

35. Davidson 1967: 86–87. Keesing 1934: 96. The head of the Methodist Mission performed a like errand on behalf of the Germans at this time. Wood 1975: 315.

36. *LMS Chronicle* 95 (July 1930): 154–55.

37. Tamaali'i 1975: 8, 11-12. Wood 1975: 315.

38. Darnand 1934: 167-68. Davidson 1967: 198-99. Courtois and Bigault 1936:47.

39. Sabatier 1939: 112.

40. Sabatier 1939: 112, 255. *Missions Catholiques* 64, (1932): 574-77.

41. Samoa District Committee, August and December 1899. Church Archives, Apia. Sabatier 1939: 221-27, 257-58. Vicar Apostolic of Gilbert Islands to G. T. O'Brien, High Commissioner for the Western Pacific. March 1900. Society for Propagation of the Faith Archives, Paris.

42. Samoa District Committee, August 1899, pp. 88-89; August 1901, p. 250; August 1902, pp. 316-20, 324-28, 354. Church Archives, Apia. Grimble 1952: 217.

43. I. M. Channon to J. L. Barton, Oct. 12, 1913, Jan. 6, 1914. American Board Archives, Harvard University.

44. Cf. Maude 1967. Grimble 1952: 90-98. LMS *Chronicle* 96 (1931): 31-35. Sabatier 1939: 205.

45. P. Delaporte, Annual Report of Nauru, 1914. American Board Archives, Harvard University. *Missionary Herald* 98, no. 8 (August 1902): 334; LMS Annual Report 1963: 295-97.

46. Sabatier 1939: 172, 241. Linckens 1911: 76-77.

47. Adams 1930: 507. Destable and Sédès 1944: 172.

48. Reply of Magistrate Chalmers to accusations of Reverend J. C. Jennison, Aug. 19, 1899. Methodist Archives, Suva.

49. Burton 1910. Burton and Deane 1936.

50. Destable and Sédès 1944: 162-67, 171-76, 211-16. Vicariate Apostolic of Fiji and the South Solomons, circular letter to all Missionaries and Religious, Dec. 11, 1902. Archives of the Society for the Propagation of the Faith, Paris.

51. Blanc 1926.

52. Methodist Church of Australasia 1917: 6-7.

53. "Statement of the Fiji District Committee in the Matter of Grants in Aid from the Government," 1929. Methodist Archives, Suva.

54. Mann 1933: 3-4.

55. Blackett 1948: 7. L. A. Doherty, "Catholic Education in a Crown Colony." Catholic Archives, Suva. "Secondary Education in Fiji." Catholic Archives, Suva.

56. Morrell 1973: 206. Gunson 1973.

57. Nevill to Bishop of London, July 6, 1906. United Society for the Propagation of the Gospel Archives, London.

58. Nevill to Bishop Montgomery, secretary of SPG, Aug. 1, 1902. USPG Archives, London.

59. Nevill to Bishop of London, Dec. 7, 1904. USPG Archives, London.

60. Archbishop of Canterbury to Bishop Montgomery of SPG, April 22, 1907. USPG Archives, London.

61. Nevill to the Bishop of London, July 6, 1906. USPG Archives, London.

62. Russell 1969: 2-3.

63. Tippett 1964: 26-27.

64. Burton 1909. Burton 1949: 175-87.

65. T. C. Twitchell to Bishop Montgomery, Aug. 17, 1910. USPG Archives, London.

66. New Zealand Methodist Missionary Conference 1926: 80-81. Fullerton 1969: 210.

67. Fullerton 1969: 210-11.

68. Loy 1954: 83–84.

69. For fuller treatment of the union, see Forman 1978.

70. Sutton 1963.

71. Missi 27 (1961): 260.

72. Malia 1910: 313–17. Tremblay 1925: 86–98. Bigault 1939: 298.

73. Darmancier 1965: 26–37. Courtais and Bigault 1936: 80. Panoff 1963: 149. Blanc 1914. *Journal de la Société des Océanistes* 1969: 30–31.

74. O'Reilly 1963: 30, 43.

75. Blanc, Diary, Sept. 16, 1929; Nov. 1, 1929. Catholic Archives, Nuku'alofa.

3
Missions and Churches 1900–1942:
The Western Islands

The western Pacific south of the equator is the homeland of the Melanesians. The islands, which extend like peaks of a great submarine mountain chain, breaking the ocean waters in a long arc from New Guinea to New Caledonia and Fiji, are inhabited almost entirely by Melanesians. For the reasons that were discussed earlier, this area, with the exception of Fiji, responded to Christianity later than did the islands further east, which are Polynesian. Fiji, it should be noted, had a pattern of social organization more like that of Polynesia than like the rest of Melanesia, which helps to explain its different pattern of response.

North of the equator the western Pacific is dotted with the many small islands inhabited by Micronesians, a still different branch of Pacific peoples. Micronesia has had a separate church history from the South Pacific because its western areas were linked by missionary heritage to the Spanish churches of the Philippines and its eastern areas were linked by missionary heritage to the American churches of Hawaii. In the South Pacific, by contrast, the churches all had European or Australasian connections. Kiribati was the only part of Micronesia that was like the South Pacific in this respect, having been approached by European missions, both Protestant and Catholic, missions that were also operating further south. Yet even in Kiribati there was, as we have noted, an Hawaiian connection for a short time.

The area covered in this chapter, then, will be Melanesia west of Fiji and Micronesia west of Kiribati.

New Caledonia

The years around the turn of the century were pivotal for New Caledonian Christianity. Until that time the Roman Catholic church, in cordial cooperation with the French government, had been the only church on New Caledonia itself. On the nearby Loyalty Islands the London Missionary Society hung onto its work with one missionary, always under suspicion from the French rulers. The French did not allow settlers to go into the Loyalties, but they encouraged European settlement in New Caledonia. At the turn of the century in particular the governor was anxious to increase the number of

French colonists and drastically reduced the reserves for islanders on the main island. The government provided salaries for some of the Marist Fathers, the missionary order in the island, so that they would maintain religious services for these French. It also provided a house for the bishop and had built a fine cathedral for him, on which was inscribed: THE FIRST BISHOP OF NEW CALEDONIA HAS GIVEN THIS LAND TO GOD AND TO FRANCE.

But at the time of which we speak the cordial cooperation between government and mission was falling apart, and in the process Protestantism gained access to the island. Troubles between the Catholics and the state grew out of the missionaries' work with the indigenes. The local peoples who became Christian were expected to gather in settlements on mission stations and to work mission lands. The great majority of the Marist missionaries were employed in the work among these people rather than among the colonists. They provided the only education for the New Caledonians, since government education was for the colonists.

Some of the indigenous peoples refused to pay their head tax in 1896, and these, it turned out, were all closely related to the Catholic mission. A government inquiry into the causes of this action was initiated, and in the course of it various suspicions against the mission were made public. It was clear from the testimonies that the colonists felt, almost to a man, that the mission was antigovernment and anticolonist, and that it was keeping the New Caledonians from obeying the one and working for the other.[1] The mission denied the accusations and insisted that it had not stirred the people up against the government, that it had urged respect and submission, and that it had only stopped islanders from working for those colonists who did not pay their workers at all or paid them in alcoholic drinks.[2] Nevertheless, when the evidence is sifted it does appear that the mission had a desire to keep the islanders under its own control and to keep some of them serving on its lands, that it did restrain them from working for colonists of whom it disapproved as being too secular or having a pernicious influence,[3] and that it did regard the head tax as illegal.[4]

The governor, who was not only vigorously in favor of more colonization but also anticlerical in his sympathies, was infuriated by all this and proceeded to apply to the mission much of the antichurch legislation which had been enacted in France and which, as we have seen, had had effect in Tahiti and the Marquesas. In 1903 and 1904 mission schools, hospitals, and orphanages were laicized, the Fathers and Sisters were expelled from them, and the bishop's house was seized.[5]

Furthermore the government opened the way for the first time for the influx of Protestant pastors from the Loyalty Islands. The pastors from there had often come across in their small canoes to preach on the main island. Local officials continually tried to stop this with deportations and jailing and administrative warnings.[6] But in 1897 the pastors were encouraged by the governor to come across, and in 1911 they were granted special permission, unavailable to other indigenes, to move freely about the country.[7] As a result of their efforts Protestantism began to take hold among some of the non-Christian tribes.

The new church was given fresh strength by the arrival in 1902 of Maurice Leenhardt. He was the greatest ethnologist among Pacific missionaries and believed in creating a church that would live within the traditional culture and belong to the people rather than to the missionaries. He was sent by the Paris Evangelical Mission and worked alone on New Caledonia, although others of that mission were sent about this time to help the churches on the Loyalty Islands. He established his center at Houailou near the middle of the east coast among a people who had already begun to accept Protestantism because of the work of Loyalty pastors, particularly Pastor Mathaia from Ouvea. Leenhardt studied the language and culture thoroughly. He developed local leaders and helped the church to spread along the lines of the natural alliances of the people. The result was a rapid spread of Protestantism over the next two decades.[8] About one-fourth of the native New Caledonians came to be Protestants.

Leenhardt was an eager champion of the indigenous people, organizing them to stand up for themselves. He also developed schools to advance the people and to train new pastors and teachers.[9] The settlers were not happy about this and Protestants suffered under many attacks, particularly in connection with the so-called rebellion of 1917 with which they were falsely connected.[10] Leenhardt did not get along well with his fellow missionaries, partly because of his emphasis on developing the local people's initiatives. He also moved ahead on projects without awaiting the sometimes long-delayed approvals from Paris.[11] In 1926 he concluded his work in New Caledonia, but he had laid strong foundations there and he went on to a notable career as an ethnologist, linguist, and missionary theorist in France.[12]

It was evident that the Catholics had been left behind by Protestant development. They had been working for over a half-century with scores of missionaries but had still not reached people whom Leenhardt had reached almost singlehanded. Some of the Catholics took up Leenhardt's methods with good effect. François Luneau, for one, devoted himself to a more indigenous church and a better life for the people.[13] Also Edouard Bresson, who became bishop in 1937, made his main concern the development of an indigenous priesthood. By about 1930 all the indigenous groups had joined one or the other of the churches, and there was no great change in the relative size of the churches after that. Taking New Caledonia and the Loyalties together, the indigenous people were equally divided between Catholics and Protestants. The London Missionary Society finally withdrew from the Loyalty Islands in 1922 when their last missionary retired after forty-two years of service there. The Paris Evangelical Mission took full responsibility for that work from then on, although they, like London, seemed never to have more than two or three people in the area.

A later development in New Caledonia, though it falls beyond the time limit of this chapter, can best be described at this point. The kind of problem that Leenhardt had with his colleagues appeared again in the work of the mission.[14] Soon after World War II a young missionary was sent to New Caledonia who had studied under Leenhardt and had been much affected by him. This man, R. Charlemagne, made himself the champion of the indigenous people and became vigorously involved in local politics. He was one of the missionaries instrumental in the formation of the Union Calédonienne, a body representing the interests of the people in the islands over against the metropolitan power. His fellow missionaries supported him at first but then began to feel he was too deeply embroiled in politics. A leading Protestant chief in the Loyalties also began to oppose him.

The consequent trouble within the mission led Paris to send an investigator and eventually to try to move Charlemagne out from his central position as the head of the main school and teacher-training center of the church. Charlemagne refused to move and held the school for months until he was finally forced out. He then set up his own school nearby and attracted the bulk of his former pupils and, more importantly, the bulk of the teachers in the church schools. His challenging new ideas and political concerns made him a hero to the modern young men of the teaching corps, young men who chafed at the power of the conservative, ill-educated pastors. On May 10–12, 1958, soon after his departure from the main school, Charlemagne gathered together these followers and established a new church, the Free Church of New Caledonia and the Loyalty Islands.[15] Some 4,700 people threw in their lot with this movement, about half of the Protestants in New Caledonia, but only one-fourth of the total church membership, since few of the Loyalty Islanders joined.

Charlemagne kept strict control of everything in his own hands. He had few resources but he had enormous energy and ingenuity and he was able to keep the new church functioning. Its strength was in its schools, which were better than those of its parent body, but its weakness was in its churches. Few pastors came into it, so the congregations were largely in the hands of laity and were relatively inactive. At the end of 1959 Charlemagne in an astonishing reversal of his political stance joined the forces supporting the government. This opportunistic move won him certain favors, especially scholarships for his followers to study in France.[16] Various attempts were made to heal the rift and to reunite the churches, but it seemed that as long as Charlemagne lived this would not be a possibility. The initial élan declined but the new church continued.[17]

Vanuatu
(New Hebrides)

The religious scene in Vanuatu (known prior to independence as the New Hebrides) during the first half of the twentieth century was a complex one. For one thing, these islands constitute the first area we have encountered where the majority of the people, even as late as 1930, were outside the church, still adhering to their various traditional religions.[18] The Presbyterian denomination, though it presented more than half the Christians under a single name, was operating through five different mission agencies with little coordination. The Anglicans held to three islands in the north—Aoba, Pentecost, and Aurora, where they had been for many years. The Roman Catholics were newly arrived and rapidly spreading their missionaries. A new body on the scene, the Churches of Christ from Australia, added their efforts on Pentecost Island at the beginning of the century. The Seventh-day Adventists also were widely active, though small in numbers.

The Presbyterian missionaries epitomized the complexity. Though they met together as one mission every year, they were sent to the New Hebrides and given their locations by separate mission agencies in New Zealand, New South Wales, Victoria, and Tasmania, and also by an independent agency called the John G. Paton Fund. This last body operated on the basis of large monies raised in Britain just at the end of the nineteenth century by John G. Paton and his supporters, and it took responsibility for staffing five mission stations.[19] Paton, by his long work in the New Hebrides and his writing about them, had transformed this antipodean mission into one of the best-known missionary efforts in the world. In addition to these five bodies there were until the time of World War I two other Presbyterian churches, one from Canada and one from Scotland, which bore responsibility for certain islands; and for a period the Presbyterians of South Australia also had their own area. The situation was not one to foster concerted progress and, given the strong individualism of the missionaries, work was sometimes far from harmonious.[20]

Presbyterian efforts had begun in the southern islands and those islands, except for Tanna, were entirely Christian in the twentieth century. But their populations had dwindled and therefore they were, excepting Tanna, left without missionaries. The larger populations were in the north where there were three islands—Santo, Malekula, and Ambrym—with large groups still outside the church, and there the missionaries were concentrated. The concentrating of missionaries did not result in any rapid growth of the church, for the non-Christians lived in the inaccessible interior and they had great mistrust of foreigners, increased by the fact that they had known of the disease and decline of population that came through foreign contacts. Fred J. Paton, son of the great pioneer, worked for forty-nine years on Malekula, walking across or sailing around the island constantly, being the first white man to enter many areas of the interior, but no great response came to his efforts.[21] Doubtless one problem that made the Presbyterian work more difficult was their severe attitude toward the old customs of the people; Presbyterians would not permit their continuation in the church to the extent that other missions would. Presbyterian missionaries were often in trouble with the government for trying to control village life with their own system of government, their local courts and police, and their punishment of offenders by hard labor on the roads through the forests.[22]

The other denominations were smaller. In recent years the Anglicans and the Catholics have each had about 15 percent of the people and the Churches of Christ and the Seventh-day Adventists each about 5 percent, compared to the Presbyterians' 40 percent. The remaining 20 percent have held to their traditional beliefs or have been scattered in a variety of small churches.[23] The Catholics have had by far the greatest number of missionaries throughout this century, but they were not always free to locate their workers where they wanted among the island people, because they also had responsibilities for the care of French settlers who demanded their availability. The first Catholic missionaries had come in 1887 at the invitation of the French authorities who were acting on the basis of a request from the major French commercial company, and government and company each contributed to the missionaries' support. It was just at the beginning of this century, in 1901, that the Catholic mission became detached from New Caledonia and started to operate as a prefecture in its own right. Thus it had a late beginning and it was long regarded as one of the most distressed of Catholic missions.[24]

The Churches of Christ are remarkable for the way in which they started and grew. A man from Pentecost Island who had been working in the cane fields of Queensland, Australia—Toby Man Can—returned home in 1901 and began the church. Missionaries were sent to foster and advance his work a few years later. The main growth came in a solid block of villages on Pentecost between 1920 and 1940. Coconut planting brought prosperity to these people. The Churches of Christ are (appropriately for their location!) a Pentecostal body without a great deal of central organization; therefore the local churches were quite independent, and this body early became one in which the missionaries had second place to the New Hebrideans.[25]

None of the churches advanced education very far, but the Presbyterians did spread it widely. They had village schools, taught by the pastors and supported locally, all over the islands. The majority of the Presbyterians were able to read, and there was some literature printed for them in over thirty languages. The Anglicans also had a strong system of village schools. The Catholics worked more with district schools taught by their missionaries, a type of school of which the Presbyterians also had a few. But none of the schools was above the primary level and most of the teachers were untrained. The subject matter was heavily religious. The government was doing practically nothing in this field except maintaining a couple of primary schools chiefly for the benefit of its own personnel. In education the New Hebrides clearly lagged behind other parts of the Pacific.[26]

On the other hand, the New Hebrides are the first area we have come to where medical work was a major part of the Christian mission. Missionary medicine was not so necessary in the islands to the east because governments were more active. Fiji had a single missionary hospital built by the Methodist church in 1925 at Ba and a government leprosarium at Makogai operated by the Catholic Sisters and serving most of the central Pacific.[27] Tahiti had several dispensaries and two small hospitals carried on by the Catholics and a leprosarium operated by Protestants. New Caledonia had a few dispensaries and two leper asylums of the two churches.[28] But in the New Hebrides there was a whole system of local dispensaries and several mission hospitals. The Presbyterians were the pioneers in this, having at one time or another seven hospitals in the islands. The Anglicans maintained one major hospital plus a later minor one in the north, and the Churches of Christ and the Seventh-day Adventists each began one in later years after World War II. The Catholics provided missionary Sisters who served as the nurses for the three French-government hospitals. This heavy involvement by the missions in medical work was in part a reflection of the fact that the New Hebrides, without wealth or strong government, were less provided with public medical services than were the other islands.[29]

The greatest social involvement of the Protestant missions was not in medicine or education, but in the political struggle to keep France from taking over the islands and, if possible, to get Australia or Britain to assume control. The Presbyterians had carried on a great campaign for this purpose in the 1870s and 1880s, and the campaign was renewed in the twentieth century largely by that church. The conflict arose not so much because of opposition to French rule per se, though that may well have been subconsciously present, as because of the laxity of the French authorities in controlling the way their settlers treated the New Hebrideans. Lands were being secured through unscrupulous methods and workers were treated miserably. Appeals by the missionaries for legislation to protect the land rights of the indigenes were among the factors that led to the establishment of the Anglo-French Condominium in 1906, with its provisions for inspection of labor conditions and registration of land transfers.

The missionaries at first thought the condominium would secure islanders' rights, but the French authorities consistently failed to investigate labor conditions on French-owned plantations and insisted on registering French ownership of lands without investigating the validity of the deeds even when the missionaries reported their fraudulence. Hence, starting in 1912, the Presbyterians began a great campaign for British annexation. They were joined by the Anglicans in an inter-mission conference for this purpose in 1913. The campaign achieved some small government reforms in 1922, but still pressed for annexation. From 1924 to 1926 it reached its highest intensity, working primarily through Australia and New Zealand to put pressure on Britain. At one point the General Assembly of the Australian Presbyterian church made an appeal to the Australian government, and a petition with 40,000 signatures was presented in Canberra urging the end of the condominium. The chief coordinator of the campaign was Frank H. L. Paton, another son of the pioneer, who, after a period of service in Tanna, was working as mission secretary for the Presbyterian church of Victoria. The campaign did not achieve its major objective of removing France from the islands, but it did succeed at least in keeping Britain as a participant in the government.

Britain stayed because of Australian and New Zealand interest, and that, in turn, was primarily articulated by the churches.[30]

The vigorous participation of the missions in national issues at this time laid the foundations for even more vigorous participation by the churches when the independence issue arose at a later time.

Solomon Islands

The turn of the century was a turning point in many respects for the Solomon Islands. For one thing, British rule came into the South Solomons and German rule into the north just at the end of the nineteenth century. Then the Melanesian Mission, the Angelican body that had worked alone in the islands for a half-century, was joined by three new, competing missions and consequently changed its whole way of operation. The new missions filled in the untouched areas so that the islands were fairly well covered, but they also competed for some of the touched areas. Finally, starting in 1900, Australia repatriated all the islander laborers who had been employed on its plantations so that a contingent of widely experienced men, some of them partly educated and Christianized, were spread around the islands. The new century, then, began with a new scene.

The Melanesian Mission's approach to the islands had been a leisurely one. It kept its headquarters on Norfolk Island, a thousand miles from the Solomons. From there its ship, the *Southern Cross*, brought missionaries every year for a six-month stay at various stations. The ship, as noted earlier, also collected boys from the islands who went to Norfolk for training. In this fashion it was hoped to develop an indigenous church with indigenous leadership, avoiding the problems of white people settling in islands and controlling the church around them. But the method was a slow one and it trained the future leaders in a distant and foreign environment. When the other missions came in and placed their missionaries right in the Solomons they obviously got a speedier response from the people, and the Melanesian Mission had to change. With the beginning of the new century it started stationing its missionaries regularly in the Solomons on a year-round basis. Most of its workers believed that its central school and headquarters should also be transferred, but there was disagreement about that and not until 1919 was the facility at Norfolk finally dismantled and the headquarters moved to Siota on Nggela, near the center of the Solomons and near the seat of government at Tulagi.

The mission had its most solid adherence from the people of Nggela and Ysabel.[31] The island of Ysabel was practically an Anglican preserve, and in both areas the government, since it came in after the mission, had to exert itself to get its power recognized. On Ysabel this was not accomplished till the 1920s and 1930s when government headmen were appointed in each village. In general the personal relations between the missionaries of the Melanesian Mission and the colonial officials, who shared a common upper-class Angli-

can background, were cordial. But the government was so short-staffed and so lacking in contacts with the people that it was continuously afraid of being eclipsed by the mission and so avoided any significant joint projects with it.[32]

An important exception to the good relations between mission and government was provided by R. P. Fallowes, a missionary who was invalided home in 1935 after a mental breakdown, but returned four years later on his own to organize the people into a "parliament" where they could express their grievances against low wages and government policies. The movement attracted great enthusiasm, and three parliaments were held before Fallowes was summarily and without warning deported from the country. Most of the missionaries were as opposed to his activities as the government was.[33]

A remarkable outgrowth of the Melanesian Mission was the Melanesian Brotherhood, which was the largest and most effective religious order for men in all of the Pacific islands. This body was created in 1925 by a former policeman, Ini Kopuria, who felt called by God to take the Christian faith to all the villages to which he had gone to get prisoners. Ini was a vigorous leader and soon attracted 150 young men to join the order. They traveled, two by two, to villages throughout the Solomons and also to other parts of Melanesia, going to remote areas where the people were not Christian and offering to teach them the faith, receiving no salary but living on the donations of the people they taught. Their obvious dedication and their simple style of life opened doors for them and they became effective and influential missionaries. A steady flow of new recruits appeared and they have kept the order active through the years since Ini's death.

Of the missions that came to supplement the Anglicans, the first to arrive was the Roman Catholic. They came in two contingents, though both were Marist. One group came in 1898 from the Marists in Fiji and took over the South Solomons, moving thus from one British colony to another. The other group came from Somoa in 1899 and settled in the North Solomons, moving from one German colony to another. Both groups began their work on small islands where isolation produced safety, but later moved onto large islands where they could be more effective, the southern group onto Guadalcanal and the northern group onto Bougainville. The Anglicans were just getting started with a missionary on Guadalcanal when the Catholics arrived there, and the Catholic missionaries were so much more numerous than the Anglicans that they soon won the majority of the population. On Bougainville the Marists were the first in the field and eventually the overwhelming majority of its people became Catholic. The small Shortland Islands, where the northern contingent first began, were for a time officially closed to other missions and they also became heavily Catholic.[34]

North and south were established as separate vicariates. The greatest difference between them was the rate at which they developed local leaders. The South Solomons was one of the slowest vicariates in the whole Pacific in this respect. Its catechist training center was in frequent trouble and was closed twice. An indigenous priesthood was exceedingly slow in appearing. There

was much difficulty between the missionaries and the catechists who represented the church in the villages, and there was some bad faith shown by the
mission in relation to these workers and an outright rebellion against mission
authority in some districts in 1933–36.[35] In the north, on the other hand,
catechist training went forward vigorously, and before World War II there
were already two men in seminary who would become priests. The North
Solomons became the leading vicariate in the western Pacific in developing a
strong indigenous priesthood. This accomplishment is due most of all to one
man who laid the foundations for it, Bishop Thomas Wade, an American
who joined the mission in 1923 and served as bishop for nearly thirty years
(1930–59).[36]

The great rivals of the Catholics in the North Solomons were the Methodist
missionaries. Bougainville was an island which they entered late—in 1917
with their first local teachers and in 1922 with their first foreign missionary—
and they were consequently only a minority in relation to the Catholics there.
But there were other areas further south where the Methodists were the
pioneers—New Georgia, Vella Lavella, Kolombangara, and Choiseul—and
in this region, known generally as the Western Solomons, they eventually
encompassed three-fourths of the people.[37] The Methodists first came to this
region in 1902 and established their headquarters in the Roviana Lagoon of
New Georgia. The Melanesian Mission gave a grudging agreement to their
establishment, since it had done nothing in New Georgia and had no immediate expectations of doing anything.[38]

The head of the new mission was John F. Goldie, a slight and, at first sight,
an unimpressive young man from Queensland, Australia, but one who took
vigorous command and continued to do so for forty-nine years. He became
the dominant figure of the Western Solomons. He was persevering to a fault.
He endured all manner of hardships and deprivations unhesitatingly in pur-
suance of his task.[39] He was ardent in defense of the rights of the indigenous
people and of their lands, and was determined to represent these interests
before the government in order to be sure that the people were not hood-
winked or browbeaten into agreements. He believed in a very practical, non-
doctrinal Christianity and developed strong centers for industrial and technical training. The concentration on these centers meant that mission activity
was not so dispersed among the villages as it needed to be.[40]

Goldie often felt that local government officials were unfriendly to the
mission and he made his feelings known in high circles. At one time the British high commissioner wrote to Winston Churchill, then colonial secretary,
that Goldie would "go to any length to make things as unpleasant as possible
for the government and that he may instigate the natives, over whom he has
much power, in the same direction."[41] The government had to tread warily
where Goldie was concerned. At the same time it was not loath to press him
with regard to his personal ventures in trade and plantations, where he was
quite out of line with other Protestant missionaries in the Pacific. With the
kind of determined and dominant leadership that Goldie provided, the

Methodists showed great growth and strength as long as he was present, but they experienced the greatest schism of any church in the western Pacific after he retired.

The most unusual mission to come to the Solomons was that known as the South Sea Evangelical Mission. It was the first example in the Pacific islands of the nondenominational, evangelical type of mission that had been spreading in Asia and Africa and Latin America since the 1860s. This type of mission was usually founded by some outstanding individual; it drew support from people in many denominations, was very conservative in theological outlook, and inclined to emphasize evangelism rather than social services. All these characteristics fitted the South Sea Mission. It grew out of the work of a buoyant, indefatigable Australian woman, Florence S. H. Young, who started her mission among the Solomons laborers in Queensland. When the laborers were repatriated Florence Young and her cohorts followed them in 1904. Since the largest number of them came from Malaita, that heavily populated, rough, and ungoverned island, it was there that the mission made its main effort and eventually became the largest mission on the island.

The Queensland laborers were a great benefit to this mission in preparing the way and providing the first teachers for many villages. One of them, Peter Ambuofa, established a strong Christian center before the mission came and then became the most influential teacher in the mission. He began the system of taking converts out of their villages and establishing separate Christian villages, a practice not followed by the missions generally but one that the South Sea Mission made the rule. He eventually broke with the mission but was unable to take his followers with him. Many of the teachers were unhappy with the mission because of its policy of not paying them. It believed that the local church and its schools should be self-supporting from the start so that it could develop in its own indigenous way. The missionaries held to the narrow task of teaching the people the Bible and left it to them to decide what were the implications of the Bible for church life and community ethics. This meant that the missionaries were more aloof from the people than in other missions and, oddly enough, it produced a greater rejection of traditional customs than was found in most missions.[42]

One more important mission came to the Solomons, namely, the Seventh-day Adventists. This body had originated in America, but after 1906 its missions in the Pacific islands were the responsibility of its churches in Australasia. Its members were devoted to the cause of missions, and in both America and Australia they gave far more to missions in proportion to their size than any other denomination.[43] We have already seen this mission as it won the people of Pitcairn and entered the New Hebrides. In the latter years of the nineteenth and the early twentieth centuries it spread not only to the New Hebrides but also to Tahiti, the Cook Islands, Tonga, Samoa, and especially Fiji.[44] We have not noticed it in these areas because it was a minor church in all of them. Adventists had no hesitation about going to already Christianized lands because they believed that their special message about

Christ's Second Coming and their observance of Saturday and certain dietary rules were needed by Christians as well as by others. But just because they worked among Christian groups the responses they received were small and they did not reach anything like the size of the major churches. Their presence was also resented by the other churches.

In the Solomons they were the first mission to station workers in some areas, and consequently they were of greater importance here, though still much smaller than the four major churches. They arrived in 1914 and were invited by a trader and encouraged by the government to enter the Western Solomons as a counterpoise to the Methodists. Growing Methodist influence was resented by traders and administrators.[45] Given their beliefs, the Adventists had no hesitation about going where the Methodists had begun, but they found their main center in a section where Methodist influence was still scant, the Marovo Lagoon of New Georgia. There they became predominant. Elsewhere they spread out as a small minority. They believed firmly in creating separate, Christian villages and went further than any other mission in totally removing the people from their old life and creating a new way of living. Cleanliness, dietary regulations, health services, small businesses, and English education were emphasized.[46]

On two islands to which they spread—Rennell and Bellona, the Polynesian outliers to the Melanesian Solomons—the Adventists were much more than a small minority. During the 1930s the Adventists and the South Sea Evangelical Mission were both trying to reach the people of these islands. For a long time (1910-34) the government kept missions out of the islands because the first teachers sent there had been killed. Then it allowed a few people from the islands to go to central mission schools, but these people brought devastating epidemics with them when they returned home and the islands were closed again (1936-38) despite mission protests. Suddenly the people of Rennell, who had added to their traditional ceremonies some prayers to the Christian God, started acting wildly, quarreling, killing those with sores, destroying coconuts, and breaking sex taboos. When this phase had passed in a few days, they saw it as an angry reaction of their old gods, who had been in possession of them but who now had departed and left them free to become Christians.[47] Both islands then rapidly joined the Adventists or the South Sea Evangelical Mission, the latter group emerging with a slightly larger part of the population.

All the missions we have looked at in the Solomons were involved in education from the very beginning of their work. The level of education, however, was extremely low. In each village the pastor or catechist taught a small school, and there were district schools or central schools for somewhat more advanced work. Pawa, the central school of the Anglicans, and the Methodist central school were the most outstanding. The Methodists put more into education than any other body and were able to claim by 1926 that all the children in the Western Solomons could read and write. All the Melanesians who were employed in the civil service during the period before World War II were products of the Methodist schools.[48]

The government was far from satisfied with what the missions were doing. Education was only ancillary to religious instruction, and in most of the schools arithmetic was the only subject that was not a form of religious teaching. In 1930 the Resident Commissioner began to make proposals for improvements and for small government grants-in-aid. The missions, other than Seventh-day Adventists and possibly the Methodists, did not feel the minute grants would offset the disadvantages of government interference, and after a conference between government and missions in 1934, the proposals were dropped. The old system continued intact until after World War II.[49]

As in the New Hebrides, medical work was a significant part of the missions' operation in the Solomons, although it did not begin seriously until the 1920s and 1930s. There was an occasional doctor or dentist associated with the missions in the early years of the century,[50] and missionaries and their local assistants did much amateur treatment of illnesses. The Melanesian Mission started the first hospital in the territory in 1913, but it was closed three years later when the doctor went to war.[51] In the late 1920s the Melanesian Mission began another hospital, which was able to continue, and the Methodists began two of them with well-trained doctors. These doctors carried on considerable work in the surrounding areas as well as treating patients at their centers. In the 1930s the Catholics in Bougainville, fearful of the Methodist competition, started two small hospitals with only a nurse in each, supported by a newly formed organization in Australia, the Marist Medical Mission Society. Also the Seventh-day Adventists began a small hospital in 1926 and a larger one in 1937 but were not able to keep doctors at them.[52] The government gave some small help for this work, but also used the existence of these hospitals as a reason for doing almost nothing itself.[53] The very existence of the missions' small effort may thus have retarded the already backward medical development in the Solomons.

Papua

We come now to the giant among the South Pacific islands, the one great island, second largest in the world, which holds half the Pacific peoples— New Guinea. The first part of New Guinea to receive Christian missions was the southeast section of the island, which is known as Papua and which was taken by Great Britain in 1884.[54] The outline of the churches as they exist in Papua today were established firmly by agreements made in 1890, when the government called a conference of missions to decide in which area each would work.[55] The cordial relations that were established between the government and the missions at that time continued through the years. When Australia took over control of Papua from the British in 1906, the earlier British commitment to the promotion of "religion and education among the native inhabitants" and to "the suppression of barbarous customs" was reaffirmed.[56] The new governor, or lieutenant governor as he was officially called, was Sir Hubert Murray, who continued in that office until 1940 and built up a long tradition of cooperation between government and missions for the advancement of the people.

According to the agreement reached in 1890, the London Missionary Society, which had been longest in the territory, having antedated the British protectorate by twelve years, was to cover the whole south coast. It had a dozen mission stations, and the number of stations did not increase significantly in later years. This made for a rather tenuous occupation of so long an area. It also meant that there was little possibility of penetration into the interior. In only two spots did the LMS go inland: in the hinterland of Vatorate and Hula, east of Port Moresby, and in what was called the Moru Inland Mission developed by Ben Butcher in the 1930s in competition with the Catholics west of Port Moresby. The difficulty of the mission was enhanced by the enormous diversity of populations in the area. Some of the peoples were skillful and aggressive, some were backward and shy; some were warlike, some peaceful. Patterns of culture were varied and there was frequent hostility between groups. Thus it was exceedingly difficult to develop a common church life or to act in a coordinated way. The first stronghold of the mission was among the Motu people in the area of Port Moresby, and Motu was selected as the common language for education and church life. This proved a felicitous choice in some respects because the Motu were great traders, traveling in their double-sailed, high-decked canoes up and down the coast, so their language was widely known. The Motu were also a capable people, and they early took the lead in church life. The indigenous ministry was well established in their villages during the early years of the twentieth century when it was still in its infancy elsewhere.[57] Motu leaders continued predominant in the church all through the century. But other areas lagged, in part because the language of education and leadership was Motu.[58] Non-Motu people at times resented the predominance of this single group. The most backward regions by far were those in the west. There amid the meandering shallow streams and mudbanks the LMS was limited to a few coastal spots and developed little strength.[59] In 1913 the LMS withdrew from its westernmost location, the Torres Straits Islands, where its work had first begun. Since those islands had become a part of Australia and there were difficulties in traveling between them and New Guinea, it was deemed best to allow the Anglican Diocese of Carpentaria, which had been asking for those churches, to take them over.[60]

One LMS station developed into a separate mission. This was the station at Kwato in the extreme east. Under the vigorous leadership of Charles W. Abel, a cluster of industries, schools, orphanages, and plantations grew up. The people at the station were immersed in Western culture and separated from their own background much more than in other LMS centers, and the industrial and agricultural programs were more dominant and expensive. The dif-

ference in approach and the need for extra financing led to an agreement to
let Kwato organize its own mission, the Kwato Extension Association, in
1918 and to raise its own funds. Abel and, after his death in 1930, his sons
carried forward a program which foreshadowed the later development of
Papua in economic progress, modernization, equality and fraternization between races, and Western sports and recreation. They also accomplished a
highly successful, if also highly Westernizing, mission among the Keveri people in the mountains during the 1930s. The separation from the LMS work
continued until nearly the time of the death of Abel's younger son. Then, in
1964, Kwato again became a part of the church in which it had begun.[61]

The other two Protestant missions of Papua, the Anglican and the Methodist, arrived at the time of the government's invitation and, according to the
1890 agreement, established themselves, one along the northeast coast and
the other in the many islands to the east of Papua. The Anglicans constituted
a very distinctive type of mission and church. They entertained a romantic
view of traditional island life and they looked upon the ancient church of the
first four centuries as their ideal. Consequently they tried to preserve as much
as possible of Papuan culture inside the church and they adopted church
regulations similar to those in early Christianity. Following ancient patterns,
those who were preparing as catechumens for acceptance into the church
were required to sit in a special part of the church building and to leave before
the sacrament of the Eucharist. The Lord's Prayer and the Apostles Creed
were not repeated out loud in their presence or in the presence of non-
Christians, although the Lord's Prayer might be repeated silently. Church
discipline was rigorous, especially in cases of adultery, and those under excommunication were not allowed to step onto church or mission precincts or,
if they died, to be buried in the churchyards. These regulations seem to have
been readily acceptable and understandable to the Papuans.[62] The enormous
cathedral that the Anglicans built at their headquarters in Dogura between
1934 and 1939, using only the labor of their Papuan members with one missionary supervisor, seemed to belie the emphasis on indigenous culture because it followed early medieval architectural design, but its interior was dec-
orated with many indigenous motifs and the liturgy incorporated indigenous
elements.[63]

The Methodist church as it developed in the islands off the eastern end of
Papua was in fact similar to the Anglicans in acceptance of much traditional
life, although it did not adopt as clear a policy in that direction. It made its
center in the tiny island of Dobu, used Dobuan as its church language, and
followed the lines of former Dobuan military dominance and trade involvement in its spread. Its leading missionary, W. E. Bromilow, was inducted into
membership in the ring of exchanges in which Dobu participated. North of
Dobu in the Trobriand or Kiriwina Islands, the Methodists did very little to
change the old social structures and practices, joining with the government to
follow the recommendations of the anthropologist Bronislaw Malinowski,
who made that area famous through his studies.[64] Because of the strength of

the culture, membership in the Methodist church on Kiriwina was small for a long time but eventually burgeoned. The whole Methodist area remained backward and out of touch with modernizing developments for a long time. The Kiriwinans later came to resent their preservation as specimens of a strong traditional society because they found themselves unable to compete in the new national society that was emerging. The indigenous ministry did not develop in the Methodist-dominated islands at the rate it did elsewhere in Papua. The Anglicans in this matter showed a much better record in the early years even though they also encouraged the preservation of traditional life.[65]

In these three missions—LMS, Anglican, and Methodist—the majority of the missionaries were not white people from Australia or Britain but brown people from other parts of the Pacific. Because New Guinea was the last area of the Pacific entered by missions it could benefit from the earlier establishment of churches on other islands. Fiji, Somoa, Tonga, Rarotonga, the Solomons, and the New Hebrides all contributed missionaries to work in this one island, their missionary lodestar. Aside from the Methodist workers who went to help in the Solomons Methodist Mission, practically all the missionaries sent out by those various island territories were sent to Papua New Guinea: 220 people came to work with the LMS, 217 with the Methodists, and 48 with the Anglicans. These numbers include all who served up until 1970, but the overwhelming majority of them served before 1942. In fact, the largest numbers were at work in the first decade of the century. The figures also include workers in New Guinea Territory as well as Papua, but again the great bulk were in Papua. The only ones who went outside of Papua were the Methodists, who served in the New Britain area north of the Papuan islands.[66]

The Anglican contingent of islanders was different from the others. It was not sent by action of island churches, as the others were. It was made up solely of Melanesian laborers from the plantations in Queensland, who volunteered to go to New Guinea to help in the Anglican mission rather than return to their home islands at the time of the repatriation of indentured labor. These men usually came unmarried and settled permanently in their work in Papua, often marrying in the communities where they worked, while the other missions had workers who came for limited periods, being already married or later marrying someone from their home country. The Anglicans nearly all came between 1900 and 1907, only one arriving after that period, and consequently they had all died off before the late 1920s, while the other missions kept bringing in new workers, even though in reduced numbers. The Anglicans were noted for living closer to the people they served, being less inclined to lord it over the people or to impose their own cultural background than the other islander missionaries. But in consequence they made less of a cultural contribution than the others. The LMS and Methodist men and their wives did much to introduce new village arts and crafts, dances and sports, songs and agricultural methods, which the Anglican workers did not provide. The Anglicans also were taken less seriously by their white missionary leaders than the others were; they tended to be closer to the level of the Papuans, whereas the Methodists and the LMS workers were distinctly removed from the Papuans, being in an intermediate role between them and the whites.[67]

A fourth major church of Papua, the Roman Catholic, had a history separate from and different from the other three. It did not employ missionaries from other parts of the Pacific, as the Protestants did. This was due in part to the fact that it had so many more Europeans available, but it was also due to the fact that Catholics had not developed local leadership throughout the Pacific as much as the Protestants had.[68]

The Catholic mission had to struggle to assert its place in the territory. It refused to join in the conference of 1890 because it did not approve of the principle of that conference, which its bishop referred to as that "wretched piece of political Erastianism called 'spheres of influence'—which one is astonished to see exercising its narrow tyranny among a free, proud people like the English."[69]

The Catholics were confined by government policy to Yule Island and a tiny strip of adjacent coast between two LMS districts west of Port Moresby. Their work was chiefly among the unpromising Meko people on that coastal plain, a situation that the government recognized was exceptionally difficult for a mission.[70] They pushed into the LMS areas on either side, which caused considerable resistance and resentment. They also pressed inland, making contact with the inaccessible and widely scattered but more vigorous mountain peoples. It was a Herculean labor. They had to construct by hand three hundred miles of graded mule tracks through the mountains to connect their stations. They spread out behind the LMS stations on the coast and gradually advanced until they were reaching the headwaters of the rivers that flowed north to the other side of the island.[71]

Encroachments on the LMS and pressures on the government continued, and gradually under Sir Hubert Murray, who was a Catholic, restrictions against their expansion were softened.[72] In 1914 they began work in Port Moresby and in 1926 began a new mission in Samarai.[73] Here they were in the midst of long-established Protestant work, so the people they approached were already Christians. In Samarai they adopted the method of establishing schools, which they saw as the most effective way of working with such populations. They pressed strongly into the Methodist areas, eventually moving to establish a station a mile from Dobu itself. As they had much larger numbers of European staff than the Methodists, they were able to make some impact.[74]

New Guinea Territory

Over the boundary in the northern part of the island and in the Bismarck Archipelago, the Catholics were much stronger than they were in Papua. Here they were in territory that was German from 1884 to 1914 and then was taken over by Australia. They had two major areas of work, one in the Bismarck Archipelago, staffed by the same Sacred Heart Mission that operated in Papua, and the other along the north coast from Madang to the Dutch border, which was operated by the Divine Word Mission. These were both large and flourishing enterprises. The Sacred Heart Mission had a great center in Vunapope, near Rabaul. The Divine Word Mission likewise developed a major center, with many institutions and 150 buildings, at Alexishafen, near Madang. Both missions spread steadily, the Sacred Heart group throughout the Bismarck Archipelago as far as Manus, the Divine Word group along the north coast and then up the great Sepik River, the major river of New Guinea. Both were disturbingly close to Protestant work in certain areas, to the Methodists in the Rabaul area and to the Lutherans in the Madang area. The government at the beginning insisted on lines of division between their areas of operation, and these lines, while not enforced in later years, reduced the chances of friction considerably.

Both Catholic missions entered heavily into land purchases and built up large plantations, which eventually provided the major support for their operations. The German government in the early years was much more amenable to land acquisition by foreigners than was the British or Australian government of Papua, and in consequence these missions were able to become great landed proprietors. The Lutherans and the Methodists also acquired plantations, although not to so great an extent as the Catholics. One of the Catholics' principal ways of operation was to bring in men from new areas to work on their plantations and thus to make their initial contacts. They also trained catechists who went out to new areas of work, though they did not give anything like the responsibility for outreach to these people that the Protestants gave to their South Sea Island missionaries.[75]

Both Catholic missions were predominantly German in personnel. The Sacred Heart mission began with French missionaries coming from the Sacred Heart work in Papua. Its first leader, Bishop Louis Couppé, was French, but he presided over the gradual increase of German Sacred Heart workers, until by the end of his long episcopacy (1890–1923) the mission was heavily German. Both missions suffered severely after Australian rule was established because they were very short of staff and could not bring in any more Germans, while they were continually being threatened with the expulsion of those Germans they already had. The Lutheran missions of New Guinea, being likewise German, suffered the same problems in the 1920s.

The Lutheran church was established along the whole coast of New Guinea from the Catholic borders near Madang southeast to the Papuan border. It began, like the Catholics, at the close of the nineteenth century and, again like the Catholics, originated in the work of two missions, in this case the Neuendettelsau Mission and the Rhenish Mission, both from Germany. Much the stronger and more effective was the Neuendettelsau Mission, which centered in the Huon Peninsula. Its effectiveness was largely attributed to the carefully formulated mission method developed by one of its missionaries, Christian Keysser, who served from 1899 to 1921.

Keysser's method was based on a recognition of the integrity of the village or tribal community. The community should act as a whole, not seriatim in its individuals, when accepting Christianity. Its unity should be maintained and its culture, while purified at points, should be essentially preserved. The leaders of the congregation should be those who are leaders in the community, not trained and ordained ministers brought in from outside. There would, in fact, be no ordained ministry. A consciousness of missionary responsibility should develop within the congregation so that it would send out its most dedicated members to carry the Christian faith to other peoples and villages. Unlike the Polynesian and Melanesian missionaries in Papua, these men and women would not be responsible to the European missions but to their home congregations, which sent them forth. Keysser's method, it is evident, included elements from the experience and practice of other churches in the Pacific. There had been many places where Christianity had been accepted by whole communities under their traditional leaders. But Keysser carried through the implications of this communal solidarity more fully and effectively than anyone else. His ways can be most closely compared to those of Bruno Gutmann in Tanganyika (now Tanzania) and Roland Allen in China during this same period.[76] His immediate colleagues resisted his ideas at first, but before Keysser left the field they had been completely won over and the mission proceeded vigorously along these lines. The dispatch of thousands of missionaries by the congregations, particularly to the interior of the country, was the most impressive part of this work.

The weaker of the German Lutheran missions, the one from the Rhineland, eventually found that it could not maintain its work. This realization came after World War I. At that time both the Rhenish field and that of Neuendettelsau were administered by Australian and American Lutherans in accordance with requirements of the peace treaties. In 1927 the Germans were allowed to return but although Neuendettelsau was able to restore its mission, the Rhenish group soon found that its financial resources were inadequate and in 1932 it turned over its responsibilities and resources to the American Lutheran church, which had been assisting in its operations. The Australian Lutherans, a small body, withdrew at that time, though they continued to give valuable help to both the Germans and the Americans. Later, in 1936, one branch of Australian Lutheranism even took over responsibility for the work the Germans had been doing on the Siassi Islands northeast of New Guinea.[77] Meanwhile the American involvement increased rapidly and within a generation far outstripped the German.[78]

The oldest mission in New Guinea Territory has yet to be considered. It is the Methodist church located in the Bismarck Archipelago, and centered, like the Sacred Heart Mission, in the area around Rabaul. It began in 1875 with Australian workers joined by a large number of Fijians, Tongans, and Samoans. Like the Catholic church in that area, it was noted for its rapid development and prosperity, quite the opposite of the Methodist church in the Papuan islands, which developed slowly in a poor and backward area. The Gazelle Peninsula on which Rabaul was located was the most advanced economically in that part of the Pacific. The principal people of that peninsula, the Tolai, were the leaders of the Methodist church as well as of the Catholic church. They provided most of the early ministers and teachers of the Methodists and the catechists of the Catholics. Their language became the church language for the Methodist church throughout the Bismarck Archipelago. Both Methodist and Catholic churches were established before the German colonial power came in, but while the Catholics then changed from being French to being German, the Methodists continued to operate as an Australian mission with a few German workers added.[79]

Actually relations with the government were easier, even for the Australian missions, in the days of German rule than they were after Australia took command. The Germans seemed to feel that it was desirable to have missionaries, since they opened up new territory, while the Australians, perhaps because much territory had already been opened, felt themselves more in competition with the missions for influence among the people. High officials among the Australians were usually friendly, but lower ones were often in conflict with the missionaries. The kind of unified village life that grew up in connection with the Lutheran missions following Keysser's method was particularly galling and government personnel challenged it. In 1927, at a conference between missions and the administration at Rabaul, the missions tried to get the administration to recognize village congregations as the local government, but the administration refused. The tension continued until well after World War II, and only in recent years has the rapidly expanding power of government put an end to it.[80]

Micronesia

We come finally to the widely scattered islands of Micronesia—the Marshalls, the Carolines, and the Marianas. During the twentieth century the churches of these islands, more than any others in the Pacific, have been tossed about from one international connection to another and from one set of problems to another. The century has hardly been one for steady development.

At the beginning of the period, Spanish rule was in the process of giving way to German rule as Spain sold its interests. The old Spanish missions, which had established churches in the Marianas in the seventeenth century, and had been revived in the late nineteenth century, were on their way out. The new German administrators were willing for the Spanish to continue their work, but the German government at home wanted to have German missionaries on the scene. The German province of the Capuchins then offered to replace their Spanish brothers. So, with the pope's approval, they took over the work in the Carolines and the Marianas.[81] Only in Guam, which was held by the United States rather than by Germany, did Spanish workers continue.[82] Guam and the other Marianas had a traditional, Philippine-style Christianity, which went back to the seventeenth century. Many of the people were Philippine immigrants in fact. Of the former Micronesian inhabitants, large numbers had died off or been killed off and some of the remnant had intermarried with the immigrants.

Further east the Catholic church was less in evidence. The German Capuchins spread gradually through the Carolines. The first nuns came into the area in 1906, and schools were developed as well as churches, but it was slow work. The German government did not support the mission and did not require children to attend the mission school as the Spanish had done. In Yap all church life ceased and the mission's work collapsed when the Spanish governor, who had pressed the people to attend church and school, departed.[83] The Germans started work again on a different pattern, giving more attention to religious instruction and practical material improvements.[84]

In the eastern Carolines and the Marshalls, the Catholics had to contend with a long-established Protestantism, which provided more resistance. The first Catholic mission began in the Marshalls in 1899. The German trading company, which had been given a monopoly of the trade, wanted to bring in German missions to counteract the old American mission influence. It decided to invite the German Catholics because it found Protestants were a damper on trade, with their bans on smoking and drinking. It made approaches to Bishop Couppé in New Britain, and in 1899 he came to inaugurate the work. Thus there arose another Sacred Heart mission along with those in the Gilberts, Papua, and the Bismarck Archipelago. The German missionaries did solid work, building excellent schools and fine churches, translating religious literature and producing dictionaries, but the economic handicaps were great because there was no land for plantations like those of New Britain. Also there was very little response from the solidly Protestant people.[85]

The Protestants continued to be strongest in the Marshalls and the eastern Carolines, for they had been working there since 1852. Here, as has been mentioned, we meet an American mission, the Congregationalists coming out of Boston. They had suffered under the Spanish in Ponape, and their missionaries had been ejected from there during the latter years of Spanish rule, but in Kosrae (then known as Kusaie) and the Marshalls they had continued unmolested.[86] A local leader of high rank, Henry Nanpei, had been the pillar of their continuing strength in Ponape, paying the teachers after the American missionaries departed, and he continued as an important factor after their return until his death in 1928.[87] A semilocal person also proved to be their main continuing strength in the Marshalls. Carl Heine, a young Australian trader who came into the area and married a Micronesian woman, was converted to the church and began to work for it in 1902. He proved to be a major force in the work for forty years, and his children played important roles in the church and the society in later times.[88]

The German government was concerned about American influences. The people continued to celebrate July 4 instead of the Kaiser's birthday, despite the missionaries' efforts at change.[89] The government was looking for a Ger-

man Protestant mission, and finally, in 1907, an agreement was reached between the Americans and a German society, the Liebenzell Mission, for
cooperative work.[90] The first German helpers had already arrived by 1906,
and the Americans soon turned over to them Ponape, Truk, and the islands to
the west while they continued in Kosrae and the Marshalls.[91]

The Micronesian churches had to adjust to a whole new set of international
influences after World War I. Japan occupied the islands at the beginning of
that war and expelled all the German missionaries, Catholic and Protestant,
as soon as the war was over. But though it was hostile to the Germans, it was
not against Christianity. The League of Nations mandate, under which Japan
continued to hold the islands, called for the material and moral advancement
of the people, and, since Christianity was already well established, the government saw it as the religion most likely to assist in this effort. It turned to
the Christians of Japan, who were a tiny minority, half of 1 percent of the
population, for help. It went to the Roman Catholic church and to the Congregational church (as the form of Protestantism closest to that of the
islands) and asked them to take over the missions.[92]

The Catholics were unable to undertake such a responsibility, so the government sent Admiral Isoroku Yamamoto, a Catholic, to Rome to ask the
pope to find a mission to replace the Germans. After approaching twelve
orders the pope finally got agreement from the Jesuits of Spain, and in 1921
their mission began with twenty-two missionaries in the field.[93] These men
confirmed the church in the Marianas and extended it into new areas in the
Carolines, sometimes despite considerable resistance from Protestants. In
the Marshalls they found Protestantism too vigorous for them to have any
effect and they consequently made little effort. They were assisted after 1928
by the Mercedarian Sisters from Spain, who in 1936 began an upper elementary school for girls in Truk—a new step in indigenous education, although
the American Protestant school in Kosrae was sometimes called a high
school.[94]

The Protestants of Japan proved more responsive to government requests.
The Congregational, or Kumiai, church would not agree to undertaking the
mission, but when the government sent Admiral K. Yamanashi, a Bible student and friend of the principal Congregational leader, H. Kozaki, to talk
privately about the matter, Kozaki agreed to organize a missionary society of
his own with prominent Congregationalists on the board of directors. With
this the mission was begun. Four missionaries were sent to Ponape and Truk,
with the government providing the funds. Approaches were made to the
Marshall Islands, but the people there and in Kusaie preferred to keep the
American missionaries. After 1927 the German Protestants from Liebenzell
were allowed back to help the Japanese and to extend the work to Palau (now
Belau).[95] The churches were greatly developed under the Japanese leadership,
everything being well organized and under careful missionary control.
Church independence, however, was weakened. Even the pastors, who in
earlier days had been paid by their congregations, were now paid by the mis-

sionaries. Every summer fifty islanders went to visit the churches of Japan, and thus Japanese interest in the work grew. Soon Japanese churches were contributing as much as the government to the mission.[96]

In this period Christianity was spreading strongly in islands that had previously been untouched or unresponsive, such as parts of Belau and Yap.[97] The Japanese authorities were friendly and supportive, and the government made grants not only to the Congregationalists but also in smaller amounts to the Catholics.[98]

As the Japanese period drew to a close, however, the atmosphere changed completely. When Japan decided to fortify the islands, in defiance of mandate prohibitions, and to use the islanders for heavy labor, it was undesirable to have outside observers on hand. Missions therefore were constricted and attacked, and their property was seized. When missionaries tried to defend the people against abuses, they were made to suffer. The late 1930s and early 1940s were a time of extreme trial for Micronesian Christianity. People had to work on Sundays and families were broken up in order to staff labor battalions.[99] Later, after war began, the Japanese missionaries were repatriated and the Spanish ranks decimated by persecutions, as we shall see in a later chapter.

NOTES

1. "B.M." 1901.
2. Laurent 1900.
3. Saussol 1969:120.
4. Vicariate Apostolic of New Caledonia, Report to Society for Propagation of the Faith 1899. S.P.F. Archives, Paris.
5. Lesourd 1931:125. Bigault 1944:7.
6. The persecution continued until about 1914 despite the permissions given by the governor. Lengereau to Paris Evangelical Mission, Sept. 24, 25, 30, 1901. Mission Archives, Paris. Rey Lescure 1967: 23-25, 63. R. H. Leenhardt personal communication, Nov. 13, 1980.
7. Leenhardt 1922: 37-38. Rey Lescure 1967: 83-84. *Journal des Missions Evangéliques* 91 (1916): 165.
8. Allégret 1928: Part 3, 29-30.
9. Nerhon 1969.
10. Becker 1954. Guiart 1970.
11. Paris Evangelical Mission to the Mission of Maré—New Caledonia, July 28, 1910. Mission Archives, Paris. Guiart 1959:13-14.
12. Guiart 1959:17, 23-24.
13. Saussol 1969:122.
14. Leenhardt's nephew, Philippe Rey Lescure, who came to New Caledonia in 1922 and tried to work according to Leenhardt's method of close involvement with the people and maintenance of their rights and their culture, had trouble with his colleagues and after eleven years work was transferred to Tahiti. Rey Lescure was also the

one who began separate training of teachers for the church's schools, making teachers into a distinct corps from the pastors and thus laying the foundation for some of the troubles that came later. Guiart 1959: 18, 28. R. H. Leenhardt 1969: 394–95.

15. Schloesing 1952: 8. *Journal des Missions Evangéliques* 134 (1959): 127.

16. He was denounced as having deserted the people, but he maintained he was trying to help the ordinary villagers rather than the political sophisticates in the capital. *Le Journal Calédonien*, April 4, 1967, p. 8.

17. One evidence of a decline is the fact that at first the church was able, with government help, to maintain a mission in the New Hebrides, but in later years the necessary personnel for that work could not be found although the French government continued to be willing to pay the salaries. The fullest treatment of Charlemagne's movement is found in Guiart 1959: 65–87.

18. Burton 1930:48.

19. After 1954 the missionaries for those five stations were appointed by the Australian Presbyterian Board of Missions, the missionaries having been approved by the Fund Committee. Draft Memorandum adopted at the meeting in London, October 16, 1954. Presbyterian Board of Missions Archives, Sydney.

20. Paton 1913:6. Don 1927:247.

21. Don 1918. Nottage 1940. Parsonson 1956: 126–28. Paton 1945.

22. Scarr 1967: 236–37, 245–46.

23. Leymang 1969:240.

24. Douceré 1934:191, 236, 242–43, 293. Courtais and Bigault 1936: 55. Report of Governor of New Caledonia to Minister of Colonies, August 22, 1895, SPF Archives, Paris. Landes 1939:379–80. The prefecture was raised to a vicariate in 1904. Lesourd 1931:129.

25. Liu 1976. M. R. Allen 1968.

26. Derrick 1952:118. New Hebrides Presbyterian Mission, Report on Education 1952. Michelsen 1934:165.

27. Makogai was established in 1911 and the government first asked the Methodist mission to staff it, but when the Methodists had difficulty finding staff the Roman Catholics offered to do the work. McHugh 1965: 56–57. O'Reilly 1931:464.

28. Lesourd 1931: 137. Allégret 1928: Part 2, 22. Braam 1936: 251. *Missions Catholiques* 1954: 82.

29. Nottage 1940: 15, 19. Douceré 1934: 324, 359. Liu 1976: 30, 36. Patrick 1966: 12. Burton 1930: 47–48 speaks of there being one Catholic hospital, but he is doubtless referring to the French-government hospital in Vila, staffed by Catholic sisters, Catholic sources do not speak of any such hospital.

30. Forman 1972.

31. At the beginning of the century this mission had not yet entered the main island of Malaita, where half the population of the Solomons lived. It came in there in connection with the repatriation of workers who had gone to the Queensland plantations. A. I. Hopkins, who had labored for protective legislation for those workers, was the first missionary to travel around the new Christian villages, which workers established after their return. Hopkins was also able to settle on that island, in spite of government hesitations because of its dangers, in 1903. Hopkins n.d.: 27–37, 57, 90–95, 155–58.

32. Hilliard 1974: 109–11. Hilliard 1966: 110–13, 221–23. Hilliard 1978: 237–39, 262, 281. There was no one in the government service who proved able to write a

major anthropological study of the people, as the missionary R. H. Codrington did in his book *The Melanesians*, and probably no one who got as close to the people as C. E. Fox, the missionary who went through a ceremony of exchange of identities with a particular Melanesian. Fox lived as a part of this man's family and enlisted for plantation work like the other Melanesians.

33. Hilliard 1974: 112–15.

34. Hilliard 1966: 116, 121.

35. Larcy 1969: 230, 235.

36. Bigault 1946–47. Bigault 1943.

37. Luxton 1955. Hilliard 1966: 307–38, 343–45.

38. Hilliard 1966: 243–47. Tippett 1967: 54–55.

39. E.g., Luxton 1955: 104–06.

40. Latukefu 1969.

41. Oct. 12, 1921. Documents of Charges of the Methodist Mission against the Administration. CO 225, vol. 178. Public Record Office, London.

42. Hilliard 1969. For description of the Christian villages on Malaita and their relations to others, see Hogbin 1939, R. Keesing 1967.

43. Australian Council of Churches 1966: 26–29. Neill, Anderson, and Goodwin 1971: 6.

44. Their largest work by far in any of these six countries was that in Fiji. There were two or three times as many Adventists in Fiji as in any of the other islands in this list. Fiji also had twice as many Adventist ministers as all the others of these territories put together. Fiji was the location for the best Adventist educational institution, Fulton Missionary College. The largest growth in Fiji came from Methodist defections to the Sailosi movement mentioned in chapter 8. But even with the additions received from among Sailosi's followers there were less than a thousand Fijian Adventists by 1942. Thornley 1979:194–200. Hare 1969.

45. Boutilier 1978: 157. Hilliard 1966:416–19.

46. Cormack 1944.

47. Stewart 1956: 227–31. Hilliard 1973. Lambert 1941: 326. Monberg 1967. The people's story of how they changed is given in Monberg 1962.

48. New Zealand Methodist Foreign Mission Department Annual Report 1945: 2–3. Hilliard 1966: 334–47.

49. Boutilier 1978: 150–56. Laracy 1969: 253–55. Hilliard 1978: 262–63.

50. Dr. Henrey Welchman of the Melanesian Mission and Dr. Norman Deck, a dentist of the South Sea Mission were the best known.

51. Morrell 1960: 425, 433. Hilliard 1966: 148–49.

52. Hilliard 1966: 201–3, 320–23, 461–63. Artless 1936: 63–74. Luxton 1955: 143–45. Bigault 1947: 168. Marist Medical Mission Society, Reports 1935–39. Laracy 1969: 205–7. Cormack 1944: 243–51. The missions also maintained a few leper colonies, for leprosy was a serious problem in the Solomons.

53. Boutilier 1975: 19, 64–67.

54. We do not deal in this study with the western half of New Guinea which because of the extraneous factor of Dutch occupation has had a history—including a church history—more related to Southeast Asia than the Pacific.

55. Tomlin 1951: 13.

56. King 1905: 62.

57. Viner et al. 1916: 171, 190.

58. Chatterton 1968: 7.

59. Cocks 1950: 47.

60. King 1905: 51-58. Lenwood 1922: 494.

61. Wetherell 1973. Abel 1934. Barradale 1927: 76-77. Papua Ekalesia Church Assembly Minutes, 1964.

62. Sharp 1917: 11-17.

63. The Anglicans felt that there was no place for them, as the Church of England, in German New Guinea, but when that territory came under Australian rule and there were invitations from government people their view changed and they inaugurated a small mission in western New Britain in 1925. At first this was under the Diocese of Melanesia, but in 1949 it was transferred to the New Guinea Diocese. The work there remained small. Tomlin 1951: 195-98. "Report on New Guinea Mission Activities and Happenings 1950-1955," Australian Board of Missions Archives, Stanmore, New South Wales.

64. Malinowski 1922. Malinowski 1935. On the Bromilow legend, see Young 1977.

65. Bromilow 1929. Wetherell 1974: 231-32.

66. Forman 1970. Williams 1972: 139.

67. Wetherell 1974:144-66.

68. Three smaller Protestant missions which came to Papua in the years before 1942 should be mentioned before considering the Catholics. The largest and most important was the Seventh-day Adventist Mission which came in 1908, six years before it entered the Solomons, and found a gap between LMS stations where it established itself twenty-seven miles east of Port Moresby. It also spread inland behind Port Moresby and was a frequent thorn in the flesh of the LMS. Its greatest development grew out of a move it made in the 1930s into the eastern highlands. A smaller but significant body was the Unevangelized Fields Mission (UFM), which began work, by agreement with the LMS, on the Fly River in 1932. In its original efforts it worked only with the Gogodala people, and as late as 1967 all eighty ministers of the church it established, the Evangelical Church of Papua, were Gogodala. These men were also the missionary force of that church for its expansion into the southern highlands. A very small offshoot was the Bamu River Mission, commonly called the "mission in the mud" because of the tidal swamps in which it worked. It was created and staffed by one couple and did educational and medical as well as evangelistic work among a largely indifferent population. On the Bamu Mission, see *Pacific Islands Monthly* 18 (April 1948):65, and 26 (July 1956): 77-78. On the UFM, see its periodical, *Light and Life*, Horne 1962 and 1968, and Harris n.d. On the Seventh-day Adventist work, see Stewart 1956 and Maxwell 1966.

69. Bishop de Boismenu, quoted in Grimshaw 1915: 4.

70. British New Guinea, Annual Report 1900-01:xlviii.

71. Dupeyrat 1935: 291-338, 387, 496-99. Goyau 1938: 88-94. Dupeyrat 1948: 14-16, 95.

72. Dupeyrat 1935: 499-502, 513. Goyau 1938: 98-103.

73. The Samarai Mission was entrusted in 1929 to the Australian province of the same Sacred Heart order.

74. Dupeyrat 1935: 511-12. Goyau 1938: 110-11. *Weltmission* 40 (1959): 169. Methodist Church of Australasia, "Report of General Secretary's Visit to Papua 1947": 6-7. Methodist Mission Archives, Sydney. Vicar Apostolic of Samarai, "Report for 1959." Archives of Sacred Heart Mission, Rome.

75. Hüskes 1933: 36. "Michael" 1957: 15-16, 45-46. Laufer 1961. Wiltgen 1969: 329-54. Sterr 1950: 240. *Steyler Missionsbote* 61 (1933-34): 142.

76. Beyerhaus 1959: 97–99. Keysser, 1950: 60–61, 219. Grossart 1970: 375–377. Harrison 1975: 9–11. Braun and Sheatsley 1937: 96. Pilhofer 1961–63: vol. 2: 35–40.

77. Braun and Sheatsley 1937: 102–32. Kuder 1949. Pilhofer 1963: vol. 2: 105–11.

78. One other German Protestant mission in the territory was the Liebenzell Mission on Manus. It began in 1914 and was the outgrowth of the Christian concern of some German army officers. It was a small mission with two workers at first and seven by 1942, and was very conservative in matters of doctrine. The church that it established has always been a minority group on Manus in relation to the larger Roman Catholic body. Kraft 1965.

79. At one time the mission recommended to Sydney that the whole effort be turned over to the tiny Methodist church in Germany. Sydney answered by doubling the number of Australian workers. Methodist Church of Australasia 1912. New Britain District Synod Minutes 1910, 1912, 1913. W. H. Cox, who served as chairman of the Methodists during this period and up till 1934, recommended the transfer to Germany. He suffered from the antagonism of German settlers in October 1914 when he was whipped by some of them. Their leader was punished. *Missionary Review*, December 1914: 18; January 1915: 21. Methodist Church of Australasia, Board of Missions, Minutes, December 4, 1914. Methodist Archives, Sydney.

80. Harrison 1975: 216. Keysser 1950: 208–9. Kuder 1943: 3–6. Hogbin 1951: 234–35. Pilhofer 1963: vol. 2: 129–32.

81. The first German Capuchins arrived in 1903 and the area was entrusted to them by the pope in 1905. Lopinot 1964: 7–8. Hezel 1970: 222.

82. Sullivan 1957: 98–150. The last Spanish missionaries left in 1942 after the United States requested Rome to replace them with Americans.

83. Lopinot 1964: 9.

84. Though this was slow work, Kahn 1965: 274 has greatly overstated its slowness. He exaggerates the number of workers involved in Yap and has therefore implied more difficulty than actually existed. According to Kahn there were sixty priests in Yap during the German period. Lopinot 1964: 28–29 and Hezel 1970: 224 report only fifteen priests or thirty-three priests and Brothers in all the Carolines and Marianas.

85. Linckens 1911: 77–78, 102–4. Suárez 1921–22: 427.

86. Blakeslee 1921: 180–81. Jimmy 1972: 85. Under the German rule, in contrast to the Spanish, the Ponape Protestants were staunch defenders of the government. This was shown in the revolt of 1910–11. The Catholics at that time were accused of having contributed to the unrest. The official report on the revolt did not blame the Catholics, but the head of the Catholic mission was fined for slanderous statements about the government, which he made in the course of his efforts to withhold information that related some of his missionaries to the unrest. *Missionary Herald* 107 (1911): 227–28. Müller 1912. Fritz 1912. Lopinot 1964: 14–15.

87. J. Hoppin to W. Fairfield, May 20, 1933. American Board Archives, ABC 19.4, vol. 20. *Missionary Herald* 96 (1900): 147. For a time Nanpei was expelled from the church because of a scandal involving him. T. Gray to Govenor Berg, Sept. 27, 1904. American Board Archives, ABC 19.5, vol. 1, document 135.

88. C. Heine to H. E. Lacy, May 8, 1936. American Board Archives, ABC 19.4, vol. 20, document 279. *Missionary Herald* 131 (1935): 166–167. Kahn 1965:160. Heine 1974.

89. Blakeslee 1921: 183.

90. Braun and Sheatsley 1937: 37. American Board Report 1907: 147–49.

91. American Board Report 1906: 171; 1910: 187–92. The American Board made a

brief attempt—1901-10—to develop missions in Guam after the American govern-ment took over the island, but it could not provide the necessary personnel and funds and soon withdrew. In 1913 a small, conservative group, the General Baptist Foreign Missionary Society of Indiana, took over the work. Baptist efforts continue as a minority effort on Roman Catholic Guam to the present time. *Missionary Herald* 97 (1901): 231-33; 106 (1910): 520-21. American Board Report 1913: 186. Sullivan 1957: 114.

92. Clyde 1935: 121-22. Pedley 1925: 862. Pedley, document 35, ABC 19.4, vol. 19. American Board Archives.

93. Hernandez 1955: 18. Kennally 1946: 120. Lopinot 1964: 25.

94. Herrera 1921-22: 402-9. *España Misionera* 1946: 286-89. Berganza 1947: 70. Vicariate Apostolic of the Caroline and Marshall Islands 1955: 5. Larranaga 1961: 6-7. Black 1978 provides an account of the amazingly durable effects of a brief visit by one of these missionaries to an isolated island.

95. Pedley 1925: 862-64. Clyde 1935: 119-20. Heine to H. E. B. Case, Nov. 14, 1919, ABC 19.4, vol. 18, document 204, American Board Archives. Interview with M. Kozaki, April 1959. The American Board decided under financial pressure that it would close its mission in the Marshalls in 1932 and Kosrae in 1937, but when that time came it agreed to keep two missionaries on Kosrae for educational work and it continued support for Heine in the Marshalls, so the reduction in its staff was only one person. The Americans left at the time of World War II.

96. Jimmy 1972: 96-101. Interview with M. Kozaki, April 1959. *The Christian Movement in Japan, Korea and Formosa* 20 (1922): 56; 21 (1923): 71-81. *Japan Christian Yearbook* 35 (1937): 212-13. H. Kozaki 1933: 280-84.

97. Hernandez 1955: 22. Kennally 1946: 121. Ph. Delaporte to J. L. Barton, June 25, 1914, and C. R. Heine to N. G. Grasty, May 5, 1919, ABC 19.4, vol. 18, docu-ments 261 and 197, American Board Archives, Harvard University.

98. The usual annual amounts were 23,000 yen—$8,000—to the Congregationa-lists and 8,000 yen to the Catholics. Some much smaller grants were made to Buddhist missions, but these were primarily to serve Japanese immigrants. Japan 1925: 95; 1928: 65; 1933:57; 1937:54.

99. Berganza 1947: 70-72. Lopinot 1964: 24. John F. X. Condon, letter to author, May 4, 1975. Jimmy 1972: 102-3.

4
The Village Church,
Foundation for Independence

The large-scale activities of the churches prior to the mid-twentieth century were the activities of the foreign missionaries, as is evident by now. But this was not the whole story. The small-scale activities, the activities at the village level, were in the hands of island people. It was here in the many villages dotted across the island world that the foundations were laid for the eventual emergence of independent churches on the national and international scene. If this had not been the case, if the village churches had been lifeless copies of foreign originals, any formal independence at the higher levels could only be a façade. But if the local churches were firmly established with a distinctively Pacific kind of existence, then independent structures would only provide external recognition for what was basically already a reality.

An examination of the village churches will show that indeed they did constitute a distinctive type of church, indigenous to the Pacific. In some parts of the region these churches may have been old and well established by the beginning of the twentieth century, while in other parts they were just getting started. But the new sections proved to be remarkably similar to those that had been in existence for many years, so that it is possible to speak of a common style characterizing the church life of the islands. It was part of the relatively stable cultural amalgam that developed after the impact of the early traders, missionaries, and administrators had been absorbed and fitted into island ways of living and was at its height during the first forty years of this century.

The Village Church and Village Life

A visitor to the islands at any time in this period would have noticed Christianity first because of the church building erected in each village or group of villages. Located near the center of the village, surrounded by grass always closely cropped by the long knives of the people, it was invariably the largest building and usually the showpiece of the village. The building itself is not a bad place to begin an examination of the village church, for it has always meant much to the island people, who are more inclined to look on the concrete than the abstract side of things. Where the building was impressive, they found the religion impressive.

During the early part of the century church buildings began to show a significant change. The nineteenth-century churches had been constructed, for the most part, out of indigenous materials and according to indigenous styles. In some places the missionaries had encouraged the people to set up permanent structures made with coral lime. These followed Western architectural styles and were esthetically repulsive to visitors who prized the indigenous life and ways.[1] But the usual churches were constructed in the island style of poles and thatch, matting or leaves. Sometimes they reached enormous proportions, as in those put up by the kings of Tahiti and Tonga. Even when they were simple they had much beauty in the intricate tracery of the poles holding up the ceiling or the patterns of the mats that made walls or floors. Their disadvantage was that they required frequent repair and could not survive much more than five years without replacement of roof or walls. They also lacked the exotic appeal and prestige of Western-style structures made of sawn timber or cement blocks. In consequence the islanders were more than willing to save and struggle in order to become the proud possessors of the imported style of church. In 1907 Fijians generally were beginning to put up wooden churches with galvanized tin roofs, and ten years later they had largely given up constructing the traditional style of church. The change, missionaries said, "detracted from the picturesque appearance of the villages but provided much more stability and comfort."[2] A commission from the London Missionary Society, visiting the islands in 1916, reported that a fine old church in Niue had lost its thatched roof during a hurricane the previous year and that unfortunately few of the picturesque old churches of the islands were left. The western islands in this as in other matters changed somewhat later. The largest Protestant body in New Guinea reported its first village church made of boards shortly before 1927, and following that it was decided all churches would be made in this way.[3]

The work of the Brothers who came with the Roman Catholic missions contributed substantially to the change. These men were often skilled builders who managed, with local help, to put up large churches reflecting what they had known and loved in Brittany or some other European province. These structures were much admired and were a point of pride. The first stone structure in the Solomons was the Catholic church at Visale, completed in 1910, an effective answer to Anglican pride in the possession of a steamboat. In the Gilbert Islands by the 1930s, thanks to the work of the Brothers, the Catholics had fine European structures on island after island while the Protestants still used the traditional, open-sided *maneaba*.[4] But the new style spread. In Samoa, after the Catholics put up their large cathedral in Apia, its dimensions were known in every corner of the country and others set out to equal or to surpass it.[5] Quite apart from this incentive, Samoa became the great area for large, even mammoth, church buildings constructed with cement in a bewildering variety of Western styles. Each village, as a matter of pride and often in rivalry with other villages, erected its own impressive church building. Sometimes the structures were so large that, though the whole population of the village attended service, the building was only half full. At one point the government of American Samoa felt it necessary to issue regulations against excessive church building.[6] Samoa continues to be the showplace of the Pacific as far as impressive churches are concerned.

The Westerners in the church did not always encourage this Westernization. Bishop John Steward of the Anglican church in the Solomons, convinced that Westernization meant death for Melanesia, stood firmly for indigenous structures and had as his chief joy a large leaf-and-thatch cathedral, which lasted until the attacks of World War II. His counterpart in New Guinea, Bishop Gerald Sharp, maintained that the island style was "far more beautiful and far more suitable than our European built churches," and Catholics in Rabaul also encouraged the local style.[7] But the advantages of more permanent construction proved overwhelming and at the present time only the more isolated or impoverished areas display churches of the traditional type.[8]

The opening of a new church was always the occasion for great festivities. Guests were invited from far and wide, and feasting and special programs marked the occasion. In Tahiti the people customarily included the costs of the festivities as a major item in the initial calculations of the cost of a building. And well they might. At one church opening in Samoa, 5,000 guests devoured 400 pigs and 80 head of cattle, while at another close to $16,000 was spent for food and presents, which was half as much as the building itself had cost. Part of the expense was always defrayed by contributions from the guests. In Samoa choirs from neighboring churches which were invited to sing at the opening would often donate large amounts and be given places of importance in the program commensurate with their donation.[9]

The central location of the church building was symbolic of the place of the church in village society. It was the "focus for kinship groups, social life and social ambition."[10] Often it was the center for the announcement and discussions of village and government news.[11] The whole life of the village was permeated by religion; prayers were offered in connection with every sort of activity. If something needed to be done for the church, it would be announced to the village as a whole and the whole population would carry through the project, often treating it as a social occasion with much laughing, singing and even dancing combined with the work. Church rules were often enforced by the village government, and European government administrators had a thankless and sometimes hopeless task in trying to prevent this and trying to keep local government decisions out of church hands. European missionaries, conversely, often had a hopeless task trying to keep decisions on the life of the church, such as the selection of a new minister, from being taken by the whole village rather than by the church members. The people had always known a unified society in which no lines were drawn between its religious operation and its other operations and they saw no reason to introduce such divisions because the religion was now Christianity.[12]

The traditional headmen or chiefs, as the natural leaders of the village, played an important role in the life of the local church. It was not usually an officially recognized role, for official church structures seldom made any mention of them. Only occasionally, as in the Loyalty Islands up to about 1915, did the chief have the official right to name the pastor.[13] Sometimes the church would call on the chief to supplement its own discipline by the punishment of offenders.[14] From the other direction, the church at times played a large role in the naming of the chief; and ceremonies of investiture, as, for example, in the case of the high chiefs in the Cook Islands, were carried out by the church.[15] But the headmen's roles in the church were more often informal ones. In their meetings they would keep an open Bible at the center of their circle and would discuss church affairs routinely in the course of their discussion of village affairs. They did not sit on the church councils ex officio but they were quite likely to have a place in those councils because of the importance of their opinions. In Tonga, Fiji, and some other areas they were often given a special raised seat at the front of the church sanctuary, and their presence had much to do with the universal attendance at church services.[16] The church did not sanctify their position to the extent that the traditional religions had done, but it did provide much of the cement for the social structure in which their paramount position was recognized. In those places where the French colonial policy deprived chiefs of their political power, the church became the principal arena where their traditional authority had some acknowledgment and their wishes were frequently consulted.[17]

But though the church was intertwined with the village and village leadership, it also had its own officers and dignitaries. The local pastor or catechist was the most obvious of these. He was usually an outsider, assigned to the village by the missionaries who managed the central church structures. Protestant churches normally had a plethora of pastors. On the average there was a pastor for every 175 people, which gave the Pacific islands one of the highest proportionate numbers of pastors in any part of the world. Samoa had one for every eighty-five people, which meant that half of them could not possibly be assigned to congregations and were counted as "resting pastors." The pastors' prestige was as high as their numbers. They were the chief representatives of the new life and new learning that had come in with Christianity. They normally sat on the village council or were consulted by the chiefs. They were usually the leaders in proposing improvements in village life. They had more formal education than others and their children were the first to enter secondary and tertiary educational institutions when those began to appear and thus later formed a large part of the educated elite of the islands. In more isolated areas where government and mission contacts were weak, the pastor sometimes became a dictator in the village. This situation was reported from Niue, the Ellice Islands, and some of the outlying islands of the Solomons.

In general Roman Catholic catechists did not have as much prestige or influence as the Protestant pastors. This was chiefly because there were so many more Catholic foreign missionaries in the islands available to visit the villages and to hold the prestige and power. It was also because the catechists did not have ordination, which meant that they could not preside at the sacraments of a highly sacramental church. The little island of Wallis was the only place where a significant number of local Catholics became priests, starting with the first ordination in 1886. Even there indigenous priests were not given full parish responsibilities but were always paired with foreigners. It should be recognized in this connection that some Protestant churches were also very slow about ordaining the people who took pastoral responsibilities in the villages. Before the middle of the twentieth century such ordinations were almost unknown among the New Hebrides Presbyterians, the Solomons Methodists, and the New Guinea Lutherans.[18]

Alongside the pastor were a number of strictly local officials who were called by different names in different denominations but whose roles were very much the same. In Congregational areas (including the Protestant churches of New Caledonia, the Loyalties, and French Polynesia) they were deacons. They were the principal men of the church, sometimes calling themselves the "policemen of the church." They organized the congregation to do what the pastor said the church needed to have done. Often they visited in the homes and even, as in Tahiti, had the pastoral responsibility for the sections of the congregation, each with its own meetinghouse where they conducted services during the week. Sometimes they, or certain ones among them, had exclusive rights to prepare the elements for the Communion service, and in Samoa this became a matter of great solemnity and pride with a special room or small house built for their specific use in this task.[19] Once elected they served for life and as a result they were usually far more numerous than necessary.[20] With the pastor they constituted a kind of governing board of the church subordinate to the congregational meeting.

In Presbyterian and Lutheran areas (the New Hebrides and northeast New Guinea) elders likewise made up a governing board. In point of fact they often had more authority than the Congregational deacons because neither Presbyterians nor Lutherans developed a significant number of ordained ministers until after World War II. Even then their ministers were often supervising a number of villages rather than giving full attention to one. So the elders led in worship and preached as well as overseeing the congregation. In the Lutheran areas they were almost always the long-established headmen of the village, and among the Presbyterians there was much overlapping between the group of elders and the council of chiefs on an island. The elders, because of their direct access to a European missionary, often had the greater actual authority.

The Methodist villages had a larger variety of local officers with stewards, class leaders, prayer-meeting leaders, and local preachers. Together these made up the leaders' meeting of the local church. The stewards took care of the collection of funds and kept order in the services. In New Britain they did this with the aid of long poles, which they used to tap any disorderly or somnolent worshipers. Class leaders were meant to take charge of the traditional Methodist class meeting, which was held once a week. They also were to be concerned for the spiritual growth of the class members, though sometimes stewards had this type of responsibility for a group of the people. The local preachers were expected to be ready to preach when called upon, but they were so numerous that, if all of them had preached, the very air could not have contained their words. The office of local preacher and probably also that of class leader was more widely esteemed and more frequently held in these islands, in proportion to their size, than anywhere else in the world of Methodism. In Tonga about half the male members of the church were local preachers and in recent years their ranks have included the king himself. Any man who took his religion seriously would aspire to become a local preacher. Many who took their social position seriously had like aspirations. In Fiji it was recognized that although according to the rule there should be examinations of prospective local preachers by each local preachers' meeting, in many cases this was not done.

Anglican and Roman Catholic areas could not boast such church offices for the local village people. Being more sacramental in orientation, these churches lodged the official responsibility for the local church with the European priest or with the catechist who worked under the supervision of the priest. But unofficially there was likely to be a council of older laity who did not lag far behind their Protestant counterparts in managing local church affairs.[21]

Considerations of rank and status in the village permeated the actual operation of these many church offices. The islanders appropriated offices that had been created in the churches of the West and proceeded to emphasize the element of status in those positions far more than was true in the churches from which the offices had come. This was something to be expected in Polynesia with its long tradition of aristocracy and in those parts of Melanesia that had a tradition of graded societies for the men. Micronesian society also ranked each person as higher or lower than each other person; Ponape Protestants had nine ranks for church members.[22] Sometimes the offices simply conveyed status without involving any duties. This became true, for example, of "Senior Members" (*Duase ni siga*) and women class leaders in Fiji and must have been true of most local preachers in Tonga. Tonga also had a grade of women called *Akonaki,* or "Those Who Can Teach." Their office doubtless carried some responsibility originally, but it soon became only a badge of honor. The members were privileged to wear a peculiar kind of hat of which they were very proud. Today they wear a red scarf, and, with 4,262 members, they include most of the active female membership of the church. For the women of the Congregational churches there has been a like honorable status in the position of "Deacon's Wife." These women are deferred to as the leading women of the congregation, and they also carry some responsibilities. They look after the furnishing of the pastor's house and they care for village guests, who are always entertained in the pastor's house.

Church membership itself became something of a badge of honor in many cases. Because Christianity was usually accepted as the religion of the community long before all the people could be given training or accepted for baptism, it was inevitable that for a long time the baptized would be only a small proportion of the "Christians." On New Britain in the 1930s they were only 5 percent in a population that was already overwhelmingly Catholic or Methodist.[23] In this kind of situation the baptized tended to have more prestige and to exercise more influence than their neighbors in both church and village affairs.[24] The government officer on Tanna, New Hebrides, in 1913 even felt that he had to protect any man who was not baptized because he was treated by the church people "as a son of perdition and many indignities and no little injustice were meted out to him privately and . . . also officially by the courts."[25] One church, the Anglican in New Guinea, would not let the unbaptized into the church building until they had undergone two years of preparation for baptism and further ruled that there could be no outside porch or place where they might stand to hear the service. "Christian services are for Christian people" was the motto.[26] Lutheran churches would not permit unbaptized people in their regular services, but held special services for them.[27] In most places, however, the unbaptized were welcome and were even expected to attend church when they were part of the Christian community.[28]

After the churches had been longer established, baptism took place in infancy, and, since all were baptized, there was no room for the invidious distinctions of the past. But then a new source of separation and superiority appeared in some churches: between those who, baptized as infants, went on at an age of discretion to become full communicant members of the church, and those who did not. The problem appeared chiefly in the older Protestant churches. Catholics, apparently satisfied with a rather low level of discretion, gave confirmation at an early age, about seven years in many areas. The Lutherans also confirmed those who were quite young. But other Protestants expected a more mature decision and therefore waited until people were fifteen or sixteen or older.[29] Many of these delayed their decision indefinitely. This was not because they had trouble accepting the Christian doctrines. In fact the doctrines were so taken for granted that some churches asked for no statement of beliefs at the time of accepting new members.[30] But people held back nevertheless because of the standard of conduct that was expected of them and the trial period through which they were expected to pass.

Sometimes these very group-oriented people shied away from the public self-assertion required in becoming a member, as in New Caledonia where they had to step out before the congregation, seize a stick planted in the ground, and raise it up while announcing their decision for church membership. This act many of them delayed until the inspiration and enthusiasm of the annual church convention would, they hoped, take them over their fear. As a result of these things full communicant members of the church were a minority, and sometimes a small minority, of the population in Samoa, Tahiti, Fiji, the New Hebrides, and other older, predominantly Protestant areas.[31] In some places this resulted in a sense of superiority among members and not a little resentment among nonmembers. Members expected to be given some priority when anything was to be done for the church and did not like to see the pastor approach nonmembers ahead of them. They also felt that they represented a higher standard of Christian conduct, an opinion that nonmembers were prone to ridicule.

Divisions and ranks were also fostered by the disciplinary practices of the church. Nothing about the Pacific island churches has been so noticeable as their systems of discipline. Sometimes these have been attributed to the Puritan background of the missionaries from the London Missionary Society who first introduced Christianity to the region. But though that was doubtless a factor in those islands where the London Mission had an early monopoly, the important role of church discipline spread far beyond those islands. Lutherans, Anglicans, and Catholics, who had little enough of the Puritan streak, still made much of their discipline.[32] There was evidently much in the island situation itself that accented the disciplinary side of Christianity. Probably the fact that the people lived, and in many ways needed to live, in tightly knit communities holding closely together to meet the demands or dangers of their situation, and had by consequence a keen sense of responsibility for each other, was the most important reason for a strong discipline. Especially when the old tribal coherence was gone and the new governmental controls had not been firmly established, the discipline of the church served to maintain the coherence of the community. We must also recognize that where Christianity had been accepted as a communal act with little of personal decision involved, it was natural for the people to look to communal regulations rather than to personal conviction as the way to maintain the Christian life.

It may be also that the islanders had a tendency greater than that among most people to be carried away by the emotion or enthusiasm of the moment and therefore were in greater need of external discipline. The experience with the game of cricket at the turn of the century suggests that this may be true. In both Samoa and Tonga cricket became such a craze that men played for weeks on end and food production was seriously affected. The church finally made cricket playing a disciplinary offense, and the governments felt they had to limit playing to one day a week in Samoa and two days a week in Tonga with stiff fines for those who played at other times.[33]

For reasons such as these, codes of discipline, either written or customary, were developed by the churches. They were administered by priest or congregation, depending on the constitutional structure of the church.[34] An offender was usually excluded from church activities, especially the Communion service, for a period of three months to a year, though in more serious cases the person would be dropped from the church roles altogether. In a society where church life pervaded the whole of common life this could be a traumatic experience and the culprit would sometimes depart to live in the bush for the period of chastening.[35] However, when the disciplining involved only exclusion from the Communion service in a situation where communicant members were a minority group anyway, the effects were less impressive. Those who had been excluded often preferred to stay excluded from the inner circle and to continue to participate in the common church services and activities. Sometimes a significant proportion of the Christians were continuing under discipline in this way, although this tended to be less true as time went on.[36]

In application of the code the churches tended to be strict, preferring to follow the letter of the law than to consider circumstances. This was apparently true of both the more priestly and the more lay-oriented churches. The Roman Catholic bishop Joseph Blanc felt that the Catholics on Futuna were too inclined to use church discipline as a kind of external government, sometimes even refusing absolution, rather than regarding it as an encouragement to reform.[37] And in the Gilbert Islands Protestant church a pastor once complained of the way his congregation pressed for the permanent excommunication of a man who had committed the relatively minor offense of sending contributions to a wedding of the traditional Gilbertese type, which does not have church approval. Such application of the rules tended to make them more a barrier than a support to church membership and to maintain division rather than to unite the community.

Prayer and Worship

The divisions, however, were much less important than the unity which underlay them and which came to expression in the worship of the church. The frequency and regularity with which the islanders worshiped always impressed outsiders. Henry Adams at the end of the nineteenth century told how Cook islanders went to church five times on Sundays and how in Fiji "when the night has fallen . . . lugubrious music is heard all about, near and far, announced by the wooden drums which resounded over the whole country, from every village, at prayer time morning and evening."[38]

Morning and evening prayers, either in the home or at the local church,[39] were universally observed in the islands. A bell or drum sounding at dawn and at dusk to call the people together or to remind them that it was time to assemble for prayers at home was one of the familiar sounds of village life. In some areas, especially Samoa and its ecclesiastical fiefs, the Tokelau, Ellice, and southern Gilbert islands, proctors were appointed to patrol the village to see that everyone was at prayers, and the village government was ready to levy fines on those who failed. An outsider passing through the village would be told to stop in at the nearest house to join the devotions there rather than continuing on his way. Papuan Methodists organized "messenger bands" to go out to all the houses in the village and up into the hills around to gather the people for worship times.[40] Even today in a modern municipality like Pago Pago some neighborhoods observe the traditional prayer time and the young men take pride in ringing the bell and keeping the streets clear during that half-hour. By the 1930s, however, the universal character of this custom was disappearing in some areas, and more recently the morning prayers in particular have fallen into desuetude.[41]

Sunday services were great community affairs with all the people of the village in attendance. White was the favorite color for Sunday attire and in many of the central and eastern islands of the Pacific white dress was de rigueur. The crowds of people in white assembling on the green grass around the church or under the shade of the palms on the atolls made an attractive sight. Most of the day on Sunday was devoted to services. Tahitian Protestants set a high standard with a service at 7:00 in the morning, another at 11:00 and a third one following, sometimes without a break, at 1:30 or 2:00. Then came a free period, and the evening service ended the day.[42] Other areas did not provide quite so abundant a supply of times for worship. Three on a Sunday and a special service at midweek was the more usual fare. Even this number tended to be reduced as the years passed.[43]

The forms of worship used by the people were those learned from the missionaries and they followed the customary patterns of the various denominations. There was more of routine observance than of life-giving inspiration in most of these services. Sometimes, however, in one of the services, such as on Sunday evening, the denominational formality was dropped for a freer island atmosphere in which all could express themselves in singing, praying, and appeals and admonitions. One departure from denominational and even Christian tradition that shocked many outside observers was the substitution of island food and drink for the bread and wine of the Communion service. Coconut juice and taro or yams were used as the elements of Holy Communion. But this was only where the Free Church tradition prevailed; the Catholic-influenced groups would have nothing to do with such innovations.[44]

Sermons were usually an important part of the service and were often well delivered, for islanders are commonly eloquent and many of their cultures emphasized oratory. But eloquence tended to overwhelm thought. "I know your folk are fluent," said a European mission leader, "and anything you can do to avoid fluency will be so much pure gain."[45] Strenuous exhortation and simple exposition of Bible stories were the staples of the homiletic diet. In only one area did there appear a striking new form of presentation designed to make the message real and compelling to the people. This was among the Lutherans of New Guinea where the practice grew up of creating a dramatization or demonstration of the biblical text worked out in advance by a group and presented to the congregation as part of the service. The need for unity in the church, for example, might be expressed by showing the failure of individuals in an effort to move a heavy log and then the triumphant success of the same individuals when they pulled together. This kind of "preaching" meant much to those people of New Guinea who were accustomed to speaking in parables all the time and who always left it to the hearer to interpret their parables.[46]

What a different matter was the music of the service! In this everyone came to life. True, nineteenth-century Western music made up the bulk of the congregational singing—the old French tunes brought by the Marist Fathers, or, more often, the Moody and Sankey gospel hymns from America—but these were tremendously popular with the islanders and, they rapidly spread even to villages where Christianity was still unknown.[47] Church choirs became a passion in many islands during the first part of the twentieth century and this passion has continued. Fijian choirs were renowned for their powerful male voices. Samoan choirs, which first added women's voices to the men's about 1930,[48] developed the practice of producing a new composition from each choir each year. Tongan choirs were the most famous of all, performing extensive and difficult pieces of European music learned entirely by ear. Competition among choirs was (and is) keen, and a good choir could greatly enhance a village's reputation. Some saw in this a sublimation of the old warfare between villages.[49] When preparations were under way for an important choir competition in Tonga, the people, according to one colonial official, "filled the whole country with music as practice went on day after day and night after night."[50]

All these choirs sang in the European style. But from French Polynesia and the related Cook Islands came choirs—and congregations—with a style of singing both original and unique. In Tahiti it was called the *himene*, and its origins went back to the early years of that church. Words have never succeeded in conveying the impression made by this music. Some have said that it was like an ocean wave, coming in with growing strength as the voices increased in intensity, breaking and rolling and bounding and then dying down and disappearing in a long, sustained note. The women's voices carried the melody while the men provided a deep, rhythmic counterpoint, one of them with a great voice sometimes throwing out cries and appeals. All the people rocked back and forth as they sang, many with their eyes shut, entirely lost in the music.[51] Rarotonga, the Austral Islands, Tahiti, the Leeward Islands—each had its distinctive style within this common type of singing.

Rarotongan missionaries carried this music to the south coast of Papua and during the early years of the twentieth century it took root there, spreading along the whole length of the coast as translations were made into one language after another. The Papuans called these songs *peroveta*, the Motu form of "prophet," because there, as in their home islands, the songs were used to tell the Bible stories, and they became a continuing feature of Papuan church life. This Rarotongan and Tahitian music was also adopted in Samoa during the early days of Christianity, but there it did not continue.[52] It was even beginning to disappear from some of its home areas during the 1930s[53] and has lost more ground since then.

The other great example of indigenous Christian music was the *same* (psalm) in Fiji. It was an entirely different genre, a high-pitched chant ranging over two or three notes with one voice taking the lead and the others coming in in succession. It was the only music in Fijian churches till the late nineteenth century, when it was dropped by the young people in their eagerness for Western melodies. In the twentieth century it has been maintained only by the older women who have made it a practice to recite pages from the catechism in a similar type of chant before each church service. Again modern European music almost pushed it out for a time, although Fijian nationalism has given it something of a revival since then.[54]

Festivals and Associations

As if the services on Sunday and during the week were not enough for the people, they loved to celebrate great festivals in connection with the life of the church. In the days before the arrival of Christianity, the festivals had been a main feature of their life. In New Guinea the people of one village or another were constantly holding a festival and inviting neighboring villages to join them in dancing and eating for days on end. The regular Christian worship seemed a tame affair compared to this kind of thing, and consequently Christian festivals blossomed and flourished. Protestants and Catholics differed little in this regard even though the Catholics could draw on their background for more saints' days and feast days for celebration, while the Protestant heritage for the most part was inclined to be critical of any celebration of special days. Yet whatever the church, on the great days of the year the people would assemble from over a wide area to feast and worship, to sing and often to dance together.[55] The Protestants of all Tahiti and Moorea used to have a great gathering at Christmastime lasting for over a week, when they would live in temporary shelters and spend their time in special services and especially in Bible discussions. This great national gathering disappeared during the years after the worldwide influenza epidemic of 1918 when the bulk of the older leadership of the church was lost. The Catholics of New Britain celebrated Christmas with adaptations from their indigenous festival of the firstborn, which included announcement on horns of musselshell, decoration of the birth-hut, and presents to mother and child. On Ash Wednesday they would place before the church door a small house such as was used on the grave of a chief.[56]

It was not just the usual Christian festivals that were celebrated. The people created new ones out of their own past or their present needs. The traditional new-yam festival of many Melanesian groups was adopted by the Presbyterians of the New Hebrides and the Catholics of New Caledonia. In the New Hebrides, following the old pattern, no one could eat yams until the service of thanksgiving was held and then everyone would cook and eat them all day. Yams were brought as offerings to the church and then distributed by the church to important people and institutions. The Cook Islands had their great festivals of biblical dramas presented by the Sunday schools of all the villages to the assembled population of an entire island. The dramas and music took a full day and were presented with much ingenuity and magnificence, making them quite the most exciting event on the island calendar. Children in Samoa had their special Sunday, which came in October and required long preparation and new white clothes. The parents waited on the children, instead of vice versa, and much money was spent for the occasion.

In youthful eyes it ranked second only to Christmas in importance.[57] And in the Caroline Islands the Catholics loved to organize huge *muitch*, with people from different islands assembling for High Mass followed by a meeting marked by religious songs and speeches.[58]

The most widely celebrated indigenous Christian festival was the May (or Me). This was found in the island groups all the way from Tahiti to New Guinea with the exception of a few areas such as the New Hebrides and the Solomons. Sometimes it appeared to be a great national festival, continuing for four or five days and ending with a preaching and Communion service and involving the gifts of the people for the work of the church. "Nothing could replace this feast in the people's life," wrote one observer.[59] The odd thing about it was that it had its source in neither the normal church calendar nor the traditions of the people. It derived from the old May meetings that were held in London by the various philanthropic and missionary societies connected with the British evangelical movement during the early part of the nineteenth century. The London Mission representatives imported the practice in their first area of work, Tahiti, and from thence it spread as a common feature of Pacific Christianity though its origins were little known, and it was often not even held in May.

The May or some festival like it was at the center of the financial operations of the church. The commonest way of raising money for the churches was not to take up a collection at the Sunday service, but to hold a great annual festival for which the people would save up their funds or their produce through the year and at which they would come forward individually or as families and make their contributions. The amount of the contribution would be announced publicly to the assembly, which would often respond with loudly expressed appreciation. In some territories opportunity would then be given for friends to come forward and augment the family's contribution by additional offerings to be put down as part of the family's gift. As might be expected, there was much competition among families within the village, and then among the different villages, as to the size of the total offering collected. Great excitement was aroused by these annual festivals. In the majority of the Protestant churches of the eastern and central islands the funds collected in this way were sent to the headquarters of the mission society in Europe or Australia as a contribution from the Pacific for the general operations of that society.

One type of special meeting for which the Pacific churches were formerly famous is little seen in the twentieth century, namely, the great revival meeting. In the nineteenth century great emotional revivals used to break out, with long series of meetings marked by intense preaching and conviction of sin and release, often expressed through abnormal physical manifestations. Tonga and Hawaii experienced particularly famous revivals in the first half of the century at a time when the same sort of thing was also well known in the West. But with the twentieth century this kind of phenomenon declined in Western churches and, probably as a consequence, largely disappeared from the Pacific. There were only two movements that might be characterized as major revivals in the Pacific churches. One was the emotional outburst, taking the familiar forms of earlier days, that occurred in Tonga during the centennial year for Christian missions, 1926. One who was there tells of seeing groups of people, especially boys, being carried out of church after fainting during the prayer period at the end of the service, and of uncontrollable weeping during the "testimony meetings," which were the main occasion for the revival in each locality. These meetings continued through subsequent years although with much less emotion.[60] The other major revival was the Eemasang movement, a much quieter and smaller thing and yet one with greater long-term effects, which began among the Kate people in the Lutheran part of New Guinea in 1927. It grew out of the change of heart experienced by the dominant man in the Kate churches, one who had manipulated the church for his own benefit but who then with some companions began to go into villages where the church was in a moribund state and to engage in prayer and song for its revival. The result was a deepening of church life, which spread all through the Kate and the Hube country.[61]

But if revivals decreased, the interest in forming pious associations of one kind or another noticeably increased as the years passed. Catholics in particular boasted a growing number of these—the Third Order of Mary, the Sodality of Our Lady, the Children of Mary, and especially the Apostleship of Prayer, whose members met for prayer and for a month at a time meditated on particular mysteries of the faith. For those who were more truly activists, there came later the Legion of Mary and Catholic Action. Methodists had their class meetings, which were held once a week, providing occasion for individual members to witness to their faith or to express their thanksgiving or joy or penitence. A similar gathering, which was popular in the New Hebrides (now Vanuatu), was the "exercise meeting" where each one might lead in a hymn or prayer or biblical exposition. Christian Endeavor was also established in the New Hebrides, as well as in Samoa, Micronesia and other islands. Samoa had its own society in the Watchers' Prayer Union, which met on Sundays at 5:00 A.M. and held a great rally once each year, early in the morning, as part of the annual church synod. The growth of these associations in the church can be seen as evidence of the intensifying of Christian faith among the people and to a certain extent it was that. But, as the names reveal, these organizations were based primarily on Western models. They were introduced by Western missionaries. For the most part we must look beyond them to discover what Christianity meant to the islanders.

NOTES

1. Beaglehole 1957: 124.
2. Methodist Missionary Society of Australasia, 1917: 34.
3. Wagner 1964: 72.

4. Laracy 1969: 83–84. Sabatier 1939: 151–52, 192. A study made in 1964 found that the Protestants still usually preferred to use the *maneaba*, though many of them had half-finished structures of concrete. Lundsgaarde 1968: 42.

5. Professor J. W. Davidson in interview, January 1967.

6. Keesing 1934: 403.

7. M. R. Newbolt in Steward 1939: 7–8. Sharp 1917: 28. Costantini 1949: 423. J. R. Metcalfe, the Methodist pioneer on Choiseul in the Solomons, also encouraged the people to maintain their traditional skills, and some elegant churches were built under his supervision. Luxton 1955: 49, 121–122.

8. The Ulithi Islands in Micronesia, for example, still have churches built, like the local houses, with doors so low that one must crawl through them. But whenever a hurricane destroys such a church it is replaced with one having a more conventional doorway. William J. Walter in *Jesuit Missions*, September 1965, p. 13.

9. *Pacific Islands Monthly* 8 (May 1938): 7. J. H. Hoadley, Annual Report for 1949. Council for World Mission Archives, London.

10. West 1961: 120, describing the contemporary situation in Tahiti.

11. Burnett 1911: 61, describing the Cook Islands.

12. Viner et al. 1916: 32–33, 35–36. Rowley 1966: 142, quoting a report of 1917 on the practice of government representatives in the Huon Gulf area of New Guinea using their courts to enforce church law. Pilhofer 1961: vol. 1: 45. Reverend Brian Ranford of Funafuti, Tuvalu, in interview, March 1967, told how in those islands the village elders still make the arrangements for church repairs and how church officers feel they must consult the village elders in selecting a new pastor. A report from New Guinea as recently as 1964 told of a local government council with a Christian majority trying to forbid some of the old religious cults. *Not in Vain*, December 1964: 7.

13. Viner et al. 1916: 15. The New Britain District Synod of the Methodist Church recommended in 1908 that "chiefs or other prominent men . . . be appointed as stewards." Fullerton 1969: 241.

14. In the New Hebrides the presbytery of South Santo stated in an official report as recently as 1959 that it referred troublemakers to the chief for punishment, and when one of its pastors was involved in adultery it was proposed in presbytery that the chief be asked to impose a punishment on him. Expatriate missionaries dissuaded the presbytery from such action on the foreign conception that secular punishments are not the business of the church. Presbytery of South Santo, 1959 Assembly Business and Presbytery Minutes, April 24, 1959.

15. Fullerton 1969: 81–82. William Camden of Tangoa, Vanuatu, in an interview, May 1967, told of a recent case where a local church session decided to remove a chief and had a new selection made by the village.

16. In the great new Wesleyan church in Nuku'alofa there is a thronelike seat at one side of the platform for the King and raised tiers of seats on the opposite side for the other important persons. R. Crocombe 1972.

17. Allégret 1926: Part 1: 46. West 1961: 97. This was the situation in Tahiti. In French areas, like the solidly Catholic island of Futuna, where the chiefly authority was not under such attack from the government, the church preserved the position of the chiefs as part of its effort to resist outside influences. Panoff 1963: 149.

18. For a fuller exposition of the pastor and his style of work, see Forman 1974.

19. The great influence of Samoan missionaries on the Loyalty Islands is shown in the continuing practice there of having a small building outside the church where the deacons prepare the elements and in the jealously guarded prerogatives of the deacons

in this responsibility. A recent action by a pastor in permitting nondeacons to prepare the elements when the deacons were absent or sick produced a great outcry.

20. A survey made in 1958 in Samoa showed one deacon to every six or seven members, whereas one for fifteen members would have been enough. Samoan Church 1958: 46.

21. See, for example, the description of the group of old men known as *mwaresea* in the Melanesian Mission churches of Aoba. M. Allen 1968: 42. In 1968 the Jesuit missionary conference in the Caroline and Marshall islands called for the establishment of councils of laity in all parishes to serve as advisers to the priests and to assist in the implementation of plans. There were always pious associations of lay people which played a large role in parish life, though not technically in church government. Caroline and Marshall Islands Mission 1968: 88.

22. Jimmy 1972: 106-7. Where there had been graded societies, the church offices in many ways corresponded to and were treated like those grades. Among Presbyterians in the New Hebrides the offices of teacher, elder and pastor corresponded to the three traditional grades, and the phrase used in connection with promotion to any of these offices, "getting a new name," was that used for the old grades. Interview with W. Camden of South Santo, May 1967. Michael Allen 1968: 42, reports that the three grades of officers found in the small Churches of Christ mission on Aoba again are counterparts of the three grades of men in traditional society.

23. Valentine 1958: 214, 218.

24. E.g., among the Sinasina in New Guinea. C. V. Turner 1964: 179-80.

25. W. Wilkes, quoted in Scarr 1967: 244.

26. G. Sharp 1917: 11-12. Diocese of New Guinea, n.d.:1. *Responsibility in New Guinea* 1965: 39.

27. This practice, however, has not survived in the expansion of the church to the newer areas of the highlands, and in the older areas of the church the unbaptized have largely disappeared. Pilhofer 1961: vol. 1: 221.

28. In Kiribati the official church name for them was "pagans beneath the law of the church," and they attended all church services and contributed to the church buildings and programs and had a full part in all church decisions, although continuing to worship the old gods privately, and not having their children baptized. There continue to be such in Kiribati today, though they are disappearing.

29. Samoan Congregational churches have often allowed the age for communicant membership to drop as low as ten or twelve, but the church leadership has tried to hold it at sixteen. Samoan Church 1958: 22. New Guinea Lutherans have coined the term "children of blessing" for those being confirmed, indicating the tender age at which this rite takes place. Pilhofer 1961-1963: vol. 3: 49.

30. This was the practice in the Protestant church in Kiribati, although instruction in the faith for the period of a year was expected to precede membership. Letter from Reverend G. H. Eastman to author, April 25, 1967. This instruction period, commonly and probably more appropriately referred to as a probation period, was later reduced to six months and even to three months and now one month. Interview with Church Secretary Kamariki, April 1967. In the Cook Islands a six months' training period was standard. H. Bond James, report for 1932, Council for World Mission Archives, London. Among Protestants of New Caledonia and the Loyalties the length of training has depended on the decision of the pastor, but two to four years has been common. In New Guinea the Congregationalists require a year in the "seekers' class," the Anglicans require two years, and the Lutherans two to three years of the same kind

of instruction. *Responsibility in New Guinea* 1965: 39. In the Methodist churches in Fiji and the Solomons there has been little insistence on instruction prior to membership. Cf. Tippett 1967: 312, on the Solomons. And though the Methodists in Papua have required a year as a catechumen, this has been seen as a time for participation in church life and attendance at services more than as a time of instruction. Papua Methodist District By-Laws 1962. But cf. *Responsibility in New Guinea* 1965: 59 for emphasis on instruction. The Methodists everywhere have used a period of trial membership following the catechumenate, extending sometimes over many years and emphasizing the probationary character of the training period.

31. In Tahiti the church members in recent years have been about 4,000 in number out of 38,000 Protestants. G. Preiss 1957: 401–9. In the New Hebrides in 1906 there were 3,500 out of 20,000 converts. G. J. Paton in Pierson 1906: 138–39. In Fiji in 1967 there were 36,645 out of 149,054 Methodists. Interview with J. Robson, June 1967. In the Gilberts in 1919 there were 3,200 out of 10,598 Protestants. LMS Islands Committee Minutes, March 23, 1949, p. 127. In Tonga in 1910 the Free Church reported 6,169 active members out of a total membership of 15,470. Free Church of Tonga Conference 1910 Minutes: 123. Church Archives, Nuku'alofa. In Samoa in 1903 the LMS had 8,387 members and 29,086 adherents. Samoa General Committee Minutes, May 1904. Church Archives, Apia.

32. Cf. Pilhofer 1961: vol. 1: 243–44; Hilliard 1966: 535–38; and Dupeyrat 1935: 367–74, on the need for careful regulations and discipline in these three churches. The Anglicans in the Solomons established a series of minute disciplinary regulations in 1921.

33. Lovett 1895: vol. 2: 398–400. W. E. Goward to Frank Lenwood, Dec. 30, 1918, Congregational Church Archives, Apia.

34. Catholics and Anglicans entrusted discipline to the priest, or, for the most serious matters, to the bishop. Hilliard 1966: 536. Lutherans handled discipline through the elders with final action taken by the congregation. Mager 1937: 40. In Congregational areas the matter was always carried to the congregation. Among the Presbyterians, until a full church structure was established in 1948, discipline was essentially in the hands of the local white missionary. Methodists, in varying situations, handled cases through the missionary, through the local leaders' meeting, or through the Quarterly Meeting.

35. Hogbin 1951: 166. Hogbin 1939: 178.

36. About 10 percent of each congregation in Samoa was put under discipline each year. Lovett 1895: vol. 2: 398–400. The New Guinea Methodists over a seventeen-year period put half as many people under discipline as they took in as new members. New Guinea District Report 1960. More recently most island churches report a very small proportion under discipline, though a Catholic priest in Tahiti has stated that over a third of the Catholics in the Tuamotu Islands are under discipline and that the situation in Tahiti is not much better. Interview with Father Oliver Calixte, June 1967.

37. Blanc, Joseph, Diary, Dec. 12, 1916. Catholic Archives, Nuku'alofa.

38. Adams 1930: 490, 496.

39. Tahiti, Samoa, and Gilbert and Ellice Islands Protestants and also Samoan Catholics followed the practice of family prayers in the home morning and night. Most of the others, including Fiji, the Solomons, and New Guinea, including both Protestants and Catholics, held morning and evening prayers in the church. In Tonga, the Cooks, and the New Hebrides much was made of the daybreak prayer services held one, two, or three times a week and still continuing today. These services consist,

in Tonga, of the women first praying all together out loud and then the men who wish leading in prayer individually, the more important men coming toward the end, and finally, the pastor concluding. A considerable sense of mystery is created by the murmur of the women's voices in the half-light of early dawn. Thorogood 1960: 14; Nottage 1940: 31.

40. A. Ballantyne to Benjamin Danks, Feb. 10, 1911, Methodist Mission Archives, Sydney.

41. Interview with C. E. Fox on the Solomons, January 1967. Interview with Aisake Raratabu of Lakemba, Fiji, May 1967.

42. Interview with H. Vernier, June 1967.

43. E. g., in Suva the Methodists gave up the Sunday afternoon service some time after 1903. McHugh 1965: 50.

44. Occasionally tea replaced wine, and for bread the solid center of the sprouting coconut was employed. Substitution of Communion elements occurred in all of the areas where the London Missionary Society was at work, among the Protestants of New Caledonia and the Loyalties, where the LMS traditions still were dominant, and in the South Sea Evangelical Mission in the Solomons. The frequency of the service of Holy Communion followed the usual patterns of each denomination. Roman Catholics and Anglicans, who emphasized the importance of attendance at this service, reported extraordinarily regular participation by all their communicants. E.g., Pearce 1963: 23; Hüskes 1933: 207; Martin 1960: 26. The only exceptions to this were in the early years of the century where church life had not been fully established. Dupeyrat 1935: 377; Hilliard 1966: 530. Lutherans in New Guinea normally had Communion once a year preceded by private confession to the minister or elder or, in some cases, public confession in prayer. Hogbin 1947: 14; Mager 1937: 41; Pilhofer 1961: vol. 1: 174-175, 280-82. The Catholics and Anglicans also practiced private confession, but Methodists, Congregationalists, and especially the South Sea Evangelical Mission included the use of public confession. Sabatier 1939: 152. Hogbin 1939: 194, 197. The Methodists in the Solomons, under Goldie's lead and continued insistence, departed sharply from usual Methodist practice with regard to the Communion service, in that they celebrated it only at their annual synod when few islanders were present, and thus they deliberately deprived the island people of this sacrament, believing that they would not understand it. Hilliard 1966: 531.

45. Frank Lenwood to H. Bond James, July 9, 1919. Council for World Mission Archives, London.

46. Freytag 1940: 45.

47. Luxton 1955: 45. Kent 1966.

48. *LMS Chronicle* 96 (1931): 147.

49. Keesing 1945: 194.

50. Neill 1955: 45. The particular competition described here took place in connection with the visit of Queen Elizabeth II and the Duke of Edinburgh to Tonga, but much of the same intensity characterized earlier competitions.

51. Lebeau 1911: 239-40.

52. Falatoese 1961: 85-86.

53. Challis 1940: 24.

54. There have been efforts to develop indigenous church music among a number of churches that had never had any. The Catholics in the Bismarck Archipelago, after an initial period of ignoring indigenous tunes, began in the 1930s to encourage the writing of hymn tunes modeled on the old *lili* sung by women at funeral wakes. This

88   THE VILLAGE CHURCH

met some opposition but also an enthusiastic response from the people. The Lutherans in New Guinea about the same time made the same change and produced a gradually increasing number of hymns to Melanesian tunes taken over from pre-Christian times. The Kate language hymns are about half of this type. Mager 1937: 34. Frerichs 1957: 139. Inselmann 1944: 38; 1948: 18. These changes were evidently part of the general emphasis on indigenization that was sweeping through Christian missions in every part of the world in the 1930s in response to the rising nationalism in Asia. The results of such efforts have been considerably less impressive than the music that has been maintained by churches like those of Fiji and Tahiti, who kept indigenous music from the beginning of their Christian period. The Catholic church in Tonga has recently tried liturgical music following the traditional style used in the presentation of bananas and yams to a chief, but this has been dropped as the people laughed and said they could think only of bananas and yams. Interview with Bishop J. H. M. Rodgers of Tonga, April 1967. Some Lutheran areas, it should be noted, had been producing a large number of hymns in the local style well before 1930. Lehner 1921: 215. On Fijian changes cf. Thornley 1979: 111.

55. Tippett 1967: 67, has pointed out that in the Western Solomons the gathering of people from a wide area at the mission station resulted in the substitution of the station for the village as the center of religious life. There were no adequate substitutes for the old village festivals, and village life was impoverished and weakened thereby. As Tippett recognizes, in other parts of Oceania there was often more place for village festivals.

56. Laufer 1961: 91.

57. Individual Samoan villages also often have their local festivals celebrating some significant event in their history.

58. *Caroline and Marshall Islands Missionary Bulletin*, February 1951. Catholics in Kiribati have made it a practice to have gatherings, called *kapana,* bringing together all of their number from an entire atoll for three or four days of celebration and discussion four or five times in a year. Interview with Bishop Pierre Guichet, April 1967.

59. Delord 1905: 12–13. The odd thing is that it was in this very church of New Caledonia and the Loyalties that a later missionary, Dolfuss, about 1940, convinced the church that it should drop this celebration. However, it returned to popularity and general use. *La Vie Protestante,* Nov. 3, 1963. Another great annual occasion in this church has long been the "Convention," a time used for stirring up the faith and for announcing decisions for Christian commitment, church service, or moral reform, especially abstinence from alcohol. It is held annually on each of the Loyalty Islands and moves through the parishes on New Caledonia.

60. A. H. Wood in interview, January 1967. Cf. his article in *The Missionary Review* 36, no. 1 (July 5, 1926): 8.

61. Leonhard Flierl 1931. Pilhofer 1963: vol. 2: 160–61. Other areas had similar revivals. The Methodists in the Solomons reported one that spread to all parts of their district between 1910 and 1912. Solomon Islands District Synod Minutes, 1912. The Gilbert Islands Protestant church conducted open-air revival meetings with boys' bands and processions of students to mark its fiftieth anniversary in 1920, and considerable improvement in church life resulted. LMS 1920: 2–3. The South Sea Evangelical Mission, coming from a very conservative type of Christianity in Australia, was constantly holding revival meetings in its area of the central Solomons. Cf. *Not in Vain,* June 1965, p. 6; December 1965, 6.

5
The Indigenous View of Christianity

Officially, that is to say superficially, the island churches have had the same understanding of Christianity as Christian churches in other parts of the world. During the first third of the twentieth century they did not produce much in the way of official statements of their faith. Such statements came later, when autonomous church structures began to be established after 1945. When such statements were produced or when catechisms were prepared for the instruction of new Christians, whether in the earlier time or later, they generally repeated standard Christian doctrines about God and humankind, sin and salvation, Christ and the church that could as well have been written in Rome or Geneva as in Rabaul or Nuku'alofa.[1] This was partly because European missionaries usually had a hand in the formulation of the statements, though it was also because official statements always tend to emphasize what is standard and universal rather than what is specific and local. Yet for all this official orthodoxy, outside observers have consistently remarked in the island churches a particular emphasis and selection within the broad spectrum of Christian beliefs. And since islanders themselves have not been inclined to write out statements of their beliefs other than the recent official ones,[2] we must follow the observations of the outsiders if we are to get at all below the crust of standard doctrines. Needless to say a considerable degree of tentativeness must attach to whatever is said here, for the possibilities of misunderstanding by outsiders are always great.

The islanders' initial understanding of Christianity naturally began to take shape before they themselves became Christians. When they first encountered the Christian religion, as many of them were still doing in the Solomons and New Hebrides until the 1920s and in New Guinea until the 1960s, they saw it primarily as the sacred lore of the white people.[3]

Since the islanders were convinced that sacred ritual and knowledge were essential to all effective action, they were ready to see Christianity as a very practical key to European achievements. From this perspective, it was not the beliefs so much as the ritual that stood out as important. Traditional religion never had sharply defined beliefs; it conveyed its benefits not through believing certain things but through doing certain things. Truth lay in the act, and Christian acts were regarded more than Christian beliefs. The Christian way, it is true, appeared rather poor in ritual acts compared to the traditional practice of the islands. Catholics offered more in this line than Protestants,

89

for they had the blessing of medals, the use of holy water and of rosary beads, and the observance of saints' days. These were generally appreciated and even Protestants were known to ask for them on occasion. But all churches had their weekly service of worship, normally held on Sunday, and this was naturally seized upon as something crucial. George Brown told (1903) how in villages of New Britain where Christian preaching had never taken place the people assembled every Sunday morning, with loincloths on in the Christian fashion, and sat in silence for a respectable period of time. At the end they stood up, removed their loincloths, and returned to their work.[4]

Another common and highly visible practice was that of reading and writing. To the islander there was something mysterious about conveying sounds and ideas through marks on a page, and at the same time the church showed such interest in reading and writing as to suggest that these might be part of its sacred mysteries. Almost the first thing that a mission representative would do upon becoming established in a village was to begin a school. The reading-and-writing ritual was to be mastered, as always, for the gain that it would bring. As Johann Flierl said about the first boys who came to him: "The real reason to enter the station school was surely not the desire for instruction but for acquiring European goods." And a later Lutheran worker repeated, "The expectation of material advantages seems to be the main background of the friendly attitude the heathen demonstrate."[5]

But though a ritual for material gain may have been the first picture of Christianity, there was soon another rather deeper view of it. As the old religion had provided the framework and rationale for the traditional way of life, so Christianity was seen as a new framework within which there could be a rationale for the new way of life that was appearing. The old religion had not been designed to account for the great changes that were taking place with the European impact. In consequence it lost vitality and its great ceremonies decayed, while the Christian religion commended itself as a way of accounting for the new. It was taken as a source of social cohesion and new vitality in communities threatened by death. The astonishingly rapid collapse of the old beliefs and their replacement by Christianity was described by New Guineans in their usual figurative language: "A giant Jamaza tree . . . stood in the forest from ancient times and defied the storms. Then appeared Anutu [the Christian God] and breathed lightly on it. Thereupon the giant tottered and came crashing to the ground."[6]

The Christian faith provided a new source of shade to protect society. It also could be seen in quite an opposite way as offering new freedom for the members of that society. The conversion of the Manus people was described by Margaret Mead as a reaction against the pressures and fears of the old system with its built-in animosities and the envisioning of a greater freedom in Christianity. Young men especially were likely to see Christian life as one of freedom from domination by the elders and as a quick road to prestige without waiting for it to be conferred by wealth and age.[7]

A few specifics of Christian belief filtered through to the animist islanders and formed part of their picture of the new religion. They noted that this religion had much to say about eternal life and dealt with it in more explicit terms than did the traditional religion. People inquiring about Christianity were very likely to ask about this feature, and one anthropologist residing on Malaita in the 1930s was convinced that the promise of eternal life was, apart from education, the chief attraction of Christianity.[8] Closely related to this was sometimes a vague acquaintance with the millenarian expectations of Christianity, the belief that with the second coming of Christ the wrongs of this world would be righted and human society would become what it should be. This, of course, fitted easily into the indigenous desire to use Christianity as the mystical key to all European wealth, and it therefore brought forth a ready response from the islanders, though it is questionable whether it can be singled out as the primary reason for conversions, as some have done.[9] On a more obvious level Christianity was recognized as a religion without a system of sacrifices. Christian propagandists made much of this. "You have to buy and kill more and more pigs as sacrifices," they said, "till all your money is gone and you are poor men. We do not have to 'buy' our God like that. His son has paid for us, once for all, at Calvary. Now we do not have to be making sacrifices of pigs."[10]

It was a limited picture that the non-Christian had of Christianity and yet it was because of such a view, as well as because of considerations related to European power, that the inhabitants of the western islands were coming into the Christian fold during the early years of the twentieth century. After all, since they were not Christians they could hardly be expected to change their religion for what might be regarded as particularly Christian reasons. Being, rather, what would be called animists, they had to become Christians for animist reasons.[11] This does not mean that there were not real struggles involved in the transfer of spiritual loyalties. There were everywhere dramatic acts of destroying the old abodes of deities, burying the revered skulls of ancestors, burning magic paraphernalia, and casting out social practices not tolerated by "the new law."[12] An enormous change in the style of life was involved and both animists and Christians recognized this. But the dramatic rejection of the visible forms of the old might not carry with it any more than an external appropriation of the new. The pragmatic and utilitarian outlook that encouraged the adoption of Christianity in the first place tended to survive within it and became the very thing that made any real change in religious outlook very difficult to achieve. New things were often done within the perspective of, and for the purposes of, the old.

To combat this danger the churches almost universally required of the new converts that they undergo a considerable period (varying from six months to three years) of instruction before they could be accepted for baptism.[13] The attitudes of those who finally reached the baptismal rite show both the possibilities and the difficulties of change. Baptism was seen as a critical point in life and was taken with great seriousness as a washing away of the powers of evil. The first group of adults baptized at the Lutheran center of Sattelberg in

New Guinea reported that as they approached the baptismal place their knees were shaking and they could hardly stand up. "When the water touched our heads it was as if a stream had poured over us," they said.[14] But at the same time there could be a very utilitarian attitude toward this great event, as is witnessed by the more recent case of a man who tucked a tuft of grass under his belt before his immersion and later squeezed it out onto his pig and his garden to ensure fertility.[15] Even the period of instruction, which was designed to provide a better understanding of the meaning of baptism, could be subjected to the same misunderstanding, as one member of the Melanesian mission indicated in his report that the people were quite ready to accept his requirement of two years' instruction and of learning the catechism because these were the necessary charms to enable them to get the magical benefit of baptism.[16]

Once such people had entered into the church, the church's understanding of Christianity presented what is to the Westerner a strange and yet understandable and very biblical combination of views. It had simultaneously a worldly view of religion and a religious view of the world. This was true not only of the newer churches of the western islands, which were made up largely of the first-generation Christians we have been describing, but also of the older churches of the central and eastern islands. It was due to the fact that most of these Christians, like many nonliterate peoples, were not inclined to make the sharp distinctions to which sophisticated Europeans are accustomed between the material and the spiritual or the natural and the supernatural. The two categories flowed back and forth into each other. Therefore at one point the outside observers of island Christianity remarked on the deep piety of the people and at another point they remarked on their gross materialism. Some noted, for example, that the island Christians identified heaven with the city of Sydney, thus keeping it well within the geographical sphere, while others observed that the islanders fancied Jerusalem and other biblical spots to be not on this earth but in heaven, thus etherealizing the geographical reality.[17] The two views, which seemed so different, were in fact deeply connected in the sense of unity between the spiritual and the material. Heaven and hell, wherever they might be located, were always depicted by the people in the most glowing terms (though in different senses of the word).

As in earlier times the islands had recognized *mana,* the spiritual energy pervading the world and coming to powerful and even dangerous focus in certain people and things, so now they saw God's power in and over everything. They were not ready to accept a God who dealt with only part of life or who was remote from their existence. They lived with a strong consciousness of the divine presence, and their common life was constantly being referred to God. "We are all here, men, women, children, pigs and dogs, before you," ran a village prayer. Acts of piety came naturally in this atmosphere. Catholic villagers in Papua erected small shrines to the Virgin at the entrance to their villages and gave an "Ave" to these as they departed or returned.[18] Earthly actions, as in other "ontocratic" societies, mirrored heavenly realities.[19] Some

Lutheran pastors in more recent years have stoutly resisted removing the names of uninterested catechumens from their class lists because this might mean the removal of their names from the Book of Life in heaven. Physical reality was alive with the spiritual. Theological students were known to believe that if they stole fruit it was not just because of their own weakness but also because an evil spirit surrounding the fruit kept calling, "Steal me."

But the necessary counterpart of all this was their sturdily materialistic emphasis in relation to spiritual things. People who changed their religion had little compunction about attributing the change to prospects of material gain. Prayers were used to secure success in fishing or other endeavors and for protection against natural enemies like the rhinoceros beetles that destroyed coconuts. The efficacy of prayer for material ends was undoubted even by those most indifferent to their church. Sin, as the islanders understood it, was a matter of external disobedience to the rules of custom, the kind of thing that could be set right by the payment of a fine, rather than an internal attitude of placing oneself ahead of God.[20] The punishment for sin also came in visible form. Every misfortune implied a sin, perhaps an unrecognized one, perhaps one committed by a close relative, but always providing a logical antecedent. Once when there was a drought on Niue, the church elders demanded that there be an island meeting to discover the "Jonah" responsible for the trouble, but the local missionary, knowing that the lot would likely fall on him or some leading pastor, avoided calling the meeting out of self-defense.[21]

The pre-Christian concept of taboo continued to operate in this ambient, although with a range of application much reduced from that of pre-Christian times. Many taboos were broken in the process of conversion; in fact, this was one of the most startling and most offensive things about Christianity. But there was a carryover of the circumspect handling of those objects and occasions closely related to the divine. There was often great hestitation about tearing down old church buildings and some were left to be overgrown and to decay rather than being removed. The service of Holy Communion was sometimes preceded and followed by a period of sexual abstinence on the part of church members. Holy Communion became particularly taboo in those churches where there were few islanders ordained and its celebration was consequently a prerogative of the foreign missionaries. It was obvious in these churches—the Catholics and Lutherans, the Anglicans of New Guinea and the Methodists in the Solomons—that while many people were permitted to preach and teach the faith, celebration of Communion was reserved for a few, and the implications with regard to possible taboos and magical powers were easily drawn. New Britain Methodists took to calling Communion "the secret meeting" by analogy to the secret meetings of men in the old society. On one occasion catechumens in the Lutheran church refused further instruction from a missionary until those who had already been baptized were provided with Holy Communion so that the new powers or wealth it might bring could be seen.[22]

The view of God's nature that prevailed in such churches was what has

sometimes unjustly been called an "Old Testament view." Actually it followed more the view of the spirits and gods that had existed in the traditional
religions than any full-orbed Old Testament view, though certain elements in
it are supported by the Old Testament. God was seen as the one who created
and sustained the natural world and the human community and who
punished any transgression of the limits he set in these spheres. As in ancient
Greece, those who pushed too hard against the divinely ordained limits were
expected to meet their nemesis. God's retributive role was his main way of
relating to people; his love and forgiveness were much less evident.[23] Consequently fear of the Lord much more than love of the Lord was the principal
operating force in popular belief. When twenty-six Fijians reported their reasons for joining the church, all but two said it was because of some frightening experience or a frightening sermon.[24] In accordance with this the place of
Jesus Christ, when it was even considered, was chiefly that of the one who
overcomes the evil powers and the fear of them. Christ was the great hero and
the final judge rather than the suffering servant and the savior from sin.[25]

   If these views seem to reflect something less than the whole outlook of the
Bible, this was not because the Bible was unknown or unused in the islands.
In all the older Protestant churches, at least, the Bible was the one great book
of the people. If its perspective did not predominate it was because the Bible
was read through traditional spectacles rather than because people did not
read the book. In fact, in those areas where a full translation of the scriptures
had long been available, biblical knowledge was phenomenal. Every tortuous
detail and obscure point in the entire book seemed to be common knowledge.
European administrators learning an island language were sometimes
warned that they might not get the point of much that was said by the people
because of the frequent biblical allusions in popular speech. Even where
translations had not been made or where church tradition placed little emphasis on Bible study, there was a surprising degree of familiarity with the
main outlines of the Bible story. Many churches maintained regular weekly
periods for Bible study. In Tahiti and the Cook Islands these were the most
popular of all church functions, when a passage would be raised for comment
or a clever question raised for discussion by the pastor, and the people would
vie with each other for hours on end, sometimes the whole night long, in
providing commentary or suggestions. Behind this enthusiasm for the book
there was doubtless often a semimagical view of it, and there was also the fact
that invariably it was the first large book available in the language of the
people.

   As a result of the popular knowledge of the Bible story, the people had very
widely appropriated the whole salvation-history of Christianity as their own
history. Telling their beliefs meant repeating that history, and even those who
in later years started new religious movements tended continually to repeat
the biblical story.[26] It began with creation, how there were not different
makers of different parts of the world but one maker of the whole, who made
it good. It went on to the story of humankind's fall, the stories of Israel's

heroes, and finally to the coming of Christ with power to overcome the evil in which people were ensnared. All these were often conceived of in terms of the local situation, with God's struggle against Satan likened to the warfare of local headmen against scheming usurpers and the authorities who crucified Jesus likened to the colonial officials. Sometimes the people's own ancestors were identified with the Bible story, their tribe having presumably gone through it all and later migrated to their present abode. A large stone would be said to have come from the tower of Babel, or local spots might be pointed out that were identified with biblical events or were regarded as entrances to heaven or hell—these latter doubtless being spots that had once been thought of as the entrances to the abode of ancestral spirits. The cosmic conflict between the good God and the powers of evil was seen as one that caught up and included the village life and individual decisions.[27]

This incorporation of Christian memories into island life did not necessarily mean the banishment of the old deities to the realm of unreality. Many people continued to recognize the existence of the old spirits, although believing them to be inferior to God. This was not so true in the older churches of Polynesia. Tahitian and Cook Island Christians claimed, in spite of some contrary evidence, that they had little or no interest in the old beliefs.[28] But in Melanesia and Micronesia there was clearly a continuing undercurrent of belief in the old deities. Catholics of Yap practiced traditional and Christian rituals side by side. In Fiji, where the old beliefs lingered longest, the people who continued the ceremonies for the spirits were also present in the Methodist church on Sundays, for God and the spirits were both in their pantheon. Fijian households might still invoke their ancestral spirits as well as have family prayers in the Christian style. In Vanuatu, after the great volcanic eruption on Ambrim, sacrifices to the old gods were renewed, since they had obviously caused this devastation; the Christian God would do nothing like that.[29] In most of the area, however, there was not so much a continuation of active rituals for the former gods as simply a continuing belief in their subordinate power, particularly for evil, and a recognition that their power might impinge on life at critical points.[30] Sudden encounters with ancestral spirits could still result in the death of a person. Magic formulae for fishing or gardening continued in use, often without clear recognition that they embodied appeals to the spirits. Harking back to totemic beliefs, animals were regarded as bringing messages from the spirit world, as when a pastor in Tahiti was told not to accept a call to a neighboring island because a turtle had been seen moving away from, rather than toward, that island. At times people were thought to be transformed into animals by eating certain types of fruit.

Where evil spirits were recognized, sorcery could be expected. The sorcerer was the antisocial person, the one who secretly cut himself off from the wholesome, divinely sanctioned community—once animist, now Christian but still divinely sanctioned—and who engaged in a kind of counterreligion employing the evil powers of the spirits. The Melanesian churches were much more subject to this practice than churches in other areas were: in some Melanesian societies sorcery had been an obsession in earlier days, and there it continued most strongly. But it was a problem everywhere. A 1915 report tells of a Christian in Tonga threatening to place one of his banana stalks in the church in order to cause the death of the person who had been stealing his bananas, and Samoan pastors of the 1930s were known to consult witch-doctors when ill because they believed that evil spirits were responsible for their sickness.[31] New Caledonian and New Hebridean Christians seemed to be particularly susceptible to the fear of sorcery. The churches saw this as a sign of their weakness but there was no agreed method of dealing with it.

European missionaries normally denied any reality to sorcery,[32] but this was not the reaction of the indigenous Christians. Sometimes they took disci-plinary action, as in the case of church elders in New Guinea who would search the baggage of young men returning from labor on plantations or in mines to confiscate any tools of sorcery that might be found.[33] Sometimes prayer was used to ask God's protection, or, in the case of those less Chris-tianized, to bring suffering on the evildoer.[34] In Roman Catholic and Angli-can churches there were rituals for countering sorcery and demon possession. These churches calculated, with reason, that actions as well as words were needed to announce the sovereignty of God over the spirits. Their priests would undertake the exorcising of haunted spots. One Catholic teacher in New Guinea distributed holy water to known sorcerers and made them drink it to neutralize their evil power.[35] However, there is no clear evidence that this ritualistic approach was more effective than that of the nonritualistic churches in overcoming the fear of sorcery. There was certainly much evi-dence from both types of churches of a gradual decrease in sorcery and the fear thereof,[36] but it was a slow process and any time of calamity could arrest or reverse the advance.

The intermingling of traditional views and Christian teaching in the actual beliefs of the people is perfectly apparent in all this. Which of the two was predominant it would be foolhardy to estimate. When regarded from the perspective of the Western observer, the traditional elements are more strik-ing and some observers have consequently concluded that Christianity in-volved little or no change in the popular religious outlook.[37] *Mana*, taboo, and the emphasis on fear were all carried over. The churches continued to be characterized by an absorption in the externals of religious observances without much regard for the inner meanings, suggesting that the traditional religious outlook, which made much of proper acts and rituals but worried little about beliefs, was still very present. "When people speak of their faith it is only in formal terms and there is little content," wrote a Methodist mis-sionary in New Britain. "If we cannot produce a more robust Christianity than we see now, then the huge cost at which this work is carried on is not justified."[38] A Catholic in Tonga described the people as "formalists and literalists," and a LMS commission said that the Cook Islands church had little interest in spiritual things.[39] The problem was accentuated in the second and third generations, for then the memory of the struggle over conversion and the contrast with the old ways had passed away and everywhere there were complaints about the listlessness of church life and the dull routine into which it had settled.[40]

But if much of the old religion remained inside the new, as would naturally have to be if Christianity were to be truly appropriated by the island peoples, there were also genuinely new elements slowly making themselves felt in the old life, and these were doubtless more noticeable to the islanders than to outsiders. Fear may still have had the primary emphasis in religion but it had a more limited scope, resulting in a greater range of freedom for people. The recognition of one creator God through whom all people were bound together was a major change, bringing consequences of peace and cooperation in intergroup and interracial relations and a sense of meaning in the more-than-tribal world that had opened up. More profound was the nascent sense of responsibility to that one God, who was ever faithful and loving and in whose holy will lay humankind's greatest good. This can be glimpsed breaking through in the prayer of an old Fijian pastor: "I have come a long way and sometimes my going has been too slow, but now I have come to the ending of the way and I see my resting place. I thank Thee, my God, for the long life Thou has given me, Thy unprofitable servant. I rejoice in it because it has enabled me to serve Thee, and to do a long work in the field that is Thine."[41] The attitude that breathes through such a prayer is far removed from the traditional attitude shown in the first encounters with Christianity.

For certain people there was even an individual faith, which would have been unthinkable under the old dispensation. Most Christians, it is true, continued simply to identify with and rely upon the public religious practice as they would have in pre-Christian days. Private prayer and study did not fit into their existence. But religion was becoming more individual, and for some it became an intensely personal matter. Osea Ligeremaluoga of New Britain writes of the change that came to him at a time of crisis:

In August of 1920 a primus stove exploded and burnt me. Whew! The pain was excruciating and I nearly died. . . . In this accident I have seen the hand of God. . . . It is true I was in the work of God right from the time I had gone to church and I was in his schools. I had heard many good sermons and I had preached myself. But I didn't really *know* Jesus or *feel* his love in my heart. . . . But when this accident with the primus happened to me, I really saw God, and realized he didn't want sin.[42]

Though it should not be suggested that the islanders' view of Christianity corresponded to modern Western views of personal salvation and regeneration, it had, for all its formalism and legalism, possibilities of depth and development of its own kind. The Pacific islands were developing their own form of Christian faith, though the time had not yet come when the wider world would be willing to pay attention to it or to learn from it.

NOTES

1. E.g., *The Constitution of the Presbyterian Church of the New Hebrides*, 1; Moritzen 1974; Melanesian Mission, *A Confirmation Notebook*; catechism printed at the end of the Fijian Methodist hymnbook; Evangelical Lutheran Church of New Guinea, *Church Order*, 1, which simply refers to the inspiration, inerrancy, and authority of the Scriptures and accepts the Apostles' Creed and Luther's Smaller Catechism as expressing the faith of the church; *Statut de l'Église Evangélique en Nouvelle-Calédonie et aux Iles Loyauté*, which again accepts the Apostles' Creed and the "Confessions of Faith of the Reformation"; Gilbert Islands Protestant Church, *Second Draft of the Constitution of the Church*, 2–4; *The Faith of the Church. Lessons in the Faith for Junior Schools in the Diocese of Melanesia*. Winthuis 1929 gives an unusual example of lessons for training in the faith, which take much account of the Melanesian environment, but it is clear that the environment has been used only for illustrations and not in any way to modify what is taught.

2. Only occasionally have the statements of belief by islanders extended to more than a brief quotation in the work of a European. Osea Ligeremaluoga's autobiography gives the fullest presentation by a twentieth-century Christian. Laracy 1969 contains as an appendix, pp. 431–39, an islander's statement on "The Teaching of the Catholic Church," which arose in connection with Marching Rule in the Solomons in 1947, but the teachings are, significantly, all on morality and the fines levied for breaches thereof, rather than on doctrine. Keysser 1921, is filled with statements by indigenes of what they are thinking, though the whole work runs only twenty-two pages. The two long chapters on "Native Christianity" in Ian Hogbin's two books, *Experiments in Civilization* and *Transformation Scene*, the one describing the Solomons and the other New Guinea, provide a wealth of comment by islanders themselves on what they believe; and Vicedom 1957 is an article on indigenous theology in New Guinea. See also Havea 1977, Misso 1977 and 1978.

3. For an examination of the islanders' initial understanding of Christianity during the early period of Christian contact in the nineteenth century, see Koskinen 1957. What the inhabitants of the eastern and central Pacific saw in that period parallels closely what the people of the western Pacific saw in the twentieth century. Cf. Firth 1970: 313–378; Ahrens and Hollenweger 1977: 32–72.

4. Brown 1903: 14. Wigg 1912: 43–44, reports how a Papuan worker returning from Queensland established a system of Sunday observance with worship services and hymns over a whole district on the northeast coast and used force to make people conform, although they had no idea what they were conforming to and their hymns were in English words unknown to them, in one case only repeating the days of the week.

5. J. Flierl and F. Hoehne, quoted in Wagner 1964: 65.

6. Keysser 1929: 65. The view of Christianity as a framework for new life and social cohesion has been identified by Guiart 1962, and also by Rowley 1966: 140–41, by Hilliard 1966: 480, and earlier by Keesing 1934: 412.

7. Mead 1956: 27, 31, 34, 92, 93–95. Hogbin 1939: 180–81. Hilliard 1966: 476.

8. Hogbin 1939: 181.

9. Guiart 1962: 122–38.

10. *Not in Vain*, 1919–20: 7, quoted in Hilliard 1966: 478.

11. Cf. R. N. G. Bulmer and R. M. Berndt, dealing in a more recent period with two peoples of the New Guinea highlands, in Lawrence and Meggitt 1965: 102–3, 158–59, and Laracy 1969: 12, dealing with the Solomons. Given the original materialistic orientation, which continued through the religious change, it is hardly appropriate to state, as does Peter Buck 1939: 64, that the people "deserted their gods and sold them for a mess of pottage." Buck, it must be recognized, is speaking of Polynesia, while the conversions to Christianity that came in the twentieth century were almost entirely in Melanesia. However, in Polynesia also, as Buck indicates, there was a wide range of deities and it was customary to adopt new ones while forgetting old ones when this seemed advantageous.

12. E.g., Philhofer 1961: vol. 1: 179–81. Vicedom 1961: 17–22. Tippett 1967: 101–8.

13. The most carefully developed program of instruction was that of the Sacred Heart Mission in New Britain, which normally required three years training for catechumens and, in the text of Winthuis 1929, has produced a model for use in such training. The Anglicans on New Guinea also produced a detailed program of instruction covering two years on Bible stories, the Ten Commandments, the life and teachings of Jesus, and contemporary elements of the Christian life. This had to be preceded by a period of two years in new areas and six months in areas where the church is longer established, during which a person was enrolled as a "hearer." (Diocese of New Guinea, *Hearers and Catechumens*: 1–6.) The neighboring Anglican Diocese of Melanesia in 1911 required two years, and recently one year, of instruction, and the Diocese of Polynesia one to two years. (Hilliard 1966: 489–90, *Canons of Discipline of the Diocese of Melanesia . . . 1962*. Interview with the Bishop in Polynesia, May 1967.) Other churches in the Solomons have left the amount of instruction given to adults to the discretion of the priest or minister involved. (Hilliard 1966: 490. Laracy 1969: 156–57.) The Sacred Heart Mission in Papua had no program for adult catechetical training at all until 1908 when a one-year period of instruction was introduced. (Dupeyrat 1935: 375–76. Cf. Grimshaw 1915: 8–9.) Lutherans in New Guinea have had a two- to three-year period, Methodists in the same territory require six months, and the Papua Ekalesia one year. (*Responsbility in New Guinea*: 39.) In the islands with older churches, adult instruction prior to baptism has disappeared as Christians are baptized in infancy.

14. Pilhofer 1961: vol. 1: 135–36; Lehner 1921: 220. Black 1978 reports the same belief in baptism as the cure of evil among the Tobi islanders in Micronesia.

15. Turner 1964: 179–80.

16. Hopkins n.d.: 75–76.

17. Lawrence and Meggitt 1965: 212. Laracy 1969: 181. Leenhardt 1947: 48. Hopkins, n.d.: 12. The present author was informed by a Roman Catholic theological student from New Britain that his home villagers when he spoke to them were most surprised by his statement that biblical places were actually on this earth just like places in New Britain. A recent attack (Leymang 1969: 250–51) on Christianity's effort to separate body and soul, the earthly and the heavenly, does not recognize how largely that effort has failed.

18. Dupeyrat 1958: 218. Andersson 1968: 148–58 reveals how many of the same attitudes characterize African Christians.

19. Cf. the description of such societies in Arend Th. van Leeuwen 1964.

20. Lehner 1921: 216. Freytag 1940: 40–41. Levy 1969: 131–34. Metais 1953: 200.

21. Harold Taylor, "Report from Niue, 1942." Council for World Mission Archives, London.

22. Wagner 1964: 154.

23. A recent study by Robert I. Levy (1969: 133) confirms that this way of thinking about God predominates in present-day Tahiti as it was found by students such as Hogbin (1939: 189–91) to predominate in other areas in the earlier years of this century. Levy maintains that the Tahitian view of God corresponds to the qualities which Tahitian parents show toward their children, leaving them alone as long as they do not break any important rules but intervening strongly if they go beyond the established limits, showing no deep and abiding personal concern, which are important elements in Western family life and in the Western Christian view of God. On the islanders' view of God, see further Lawrence and Meggitt 1965: 24; Vicedom 1957; Lehner 1921: 217. The relevance of Old Testament views is brought out in Keysser, 1934. Firth 1970:371 maintains that Christian Tikopians saw no anger or malevolence in God, but rather the ultimate in goodwill.

24. Deane 1921: 25 (also Davis 1935: 221). Cadoux 1953: 264–65 reports the same attitude among Papuan Catholics.

25. Lehner 1921: 217–18. The same understanding of Jesus Christ has been reported from the African Churches by W. T. Harris and E. G. Parrinder 1960: 60–61. It certainly stands as one element in the New Testament picture of Christ.

26. E.g., the leaders of the Paliau movement on Manus as reported in Schwartz 1962: 252–56.

27. Hogbin in his three accounts from the Solomons and New Guinea (1939: 185–87; 1947: 8–12; 1951: 240–45), gives the fullest statement of the indigenous Christian mythology. See also Sterr 1950: 128; Pilhofer 1961, vol. 1: 223; and Vicedom 1961: 64–66. The identification of local places with biblical events and the entrance to heaven and hell is reported in Gifford, n.d.: 287 and, for Vanuatu by J. G. Miller, General Letter 1943/1, Presbyterian Mission Archives, Auckland.

28. Lebeau 1911: 255. Keesing 1945: 73. But Thorogood 1960: 42–44 indicates that the disclaimers should be doubted in the Cooks, and Levy 1969: 128–31 indicates the same in the Society Islands. Cf. Gifford, n.d.: 288. Lehner 1922: 367 says that Christians never return to spirit worship, but this was written before cargo cults in his area showed the contrary.

29. Cato 1947: 156; 1956: 102–4. H. Davis 1935: 220. Hogbin 1951: 267–71. Coulter 1957: 231, 241.

30. Lawrence and Meggitt 1965: 162, 221, 277–78. Lawrence 1955: 16; 1956: 82. Hogbin 1939: 203–4. Hilliard 1966: 525. Coulter 1957: 231, 241. Hogbin 1947: 28–33. David 1899: 181. This was the same pattern as in much of African Christianity. Anderson 1968: 133–37. Debrunner 1959.

31. Gifford, n.d.: 340. Raymond Firth, in Williamson 1937: xiv. *Pacific Islands Monthly* 21 (June 1952): 33. W. Deane 1910: 9. E. Bergeret 1935: 370. Grimble 1952: 114. Keesing 1945: 2.

32. There were occasional exceptions. Cf. Cormack 1944: 162.

33. Pilhofer 1963: vol. 2: 140, 176–77. The Constitution of the Diocese of Melanesia prescribed the lesser excommunication for those possessing charms to harm others, and the punishment of those trying to cause serious harm in this way to be the same as if they had caused it (p. 13).

34. Tippett 1967: 273–74, 278, 284. Lawrence and Meggitt 1965: 24.

35. Dobson 1963: 7–8. Laracy 1969: 391–92. J. K. Vasethe in *Melanesian Messenger,* Easter 1966: 19–20.

36. Hogbin 1939: 217. Dobson 1963: 14–15. Pilhofer 1963: vol. 2: 176–77. Rivers 1914: vol. 2: 406.

37. Henry Adams 1930: 429. Hilliard 1966: 547. Beaglehole 1957: 194–99.

38. W. H. Cox, "The Spiritual Life of the Local Church," Methodist Mission Archives, Sydney.

39. Malia 1910: 288. Viner et al. 1916: 33. The same indictment is made regarding Tahiti and Maré in Schloesing 1952: 22–23 and *Journal des Missions Evangéliques* 122 (1947): 136–39.

40. Paton 1913: 125–28. Dupeyrat 1935: 378–88. Hilliard 1966: 534. Keysser 1929: 303–5. J. M. Alexander, in Pierson 1906: 103. Morpeth Conference, Questionnaire on Indigenous Church, New Hebrides Reply, p. 3, Archives of Australian Council of Churches, Sydney. Joseph Darnand, Diary, Nov. 19, 1921, Marist Archives, Apia. Joseph Blanc, Diary, Dec. 12, 1916, Catholic Archives, Nuku'alofa. Ba-Rau Division Report, 1948, Methodist Archives, Suva.

41. Quoted in Heighway 1932: 235.

42. Ligeremaluoga 1932: 21. Cf. Davidson 1967: 37 and, on increasing individual sense of religion, Fiji District of Methodist Church, Chairman's Report, 1932, Methodist Archives, Suva, and Firth 1970: 356.

6
Christian Ethics in a South Sea Setting

Nothing in Christianity has been of such interest to the islanders as its ethical prescriptions. And, as islanders have had their own way of understanding Christian doctrine and church life, so have they had their own views of Christian morality. Independence in this realm was a limited but growing reality in the years before 1942 and was another aspect of that distinctive self-identity that formed the background for official church independence.

Christian Morality and Islander Culture

The importance accorded to moral codes in Oceania fits well with the tendency, noted in the previous chapter, to emphasize ritual more than doctrine. The islanders were practical people and saw actions, whether ritual or ethical, as the touchstone of religion. In their pre-Christian traditions they had had clear codes of conduct and well-defined human relationships, which were linked with religious beliefs.[1] Christianity now had to provide the same kind of linkage. The physical situation of small groups of people isolated in vast expanses of water engendered a great concern about conduct. Their isolation made the people watch each other closely and discuss each other endlessly. The horizons of a small island are physically the widest in the world, but socially the narrowest. There is even some evidence that the smaller the island, the more precise the moral regulations.[2] And narrow horizons meant that discussions tended to be on the minutiae of behavior instead of on broader ethical questions. Church councils in southern Kiribati, for example, struggled at length with the question whether if a man were out fishing at midnight on Saturday and found that wind and tide prevented his return to the shore he might continue fishing or had to remain unoccupied in his boat. Such narrowness was not limited to the church. A well-known government officer in southern Kiribati remarked in 1930 on the fact that in matters of self-government the islanders "appear to administer the law in a mechanical and unintelligent manner."[3]

Though in earlier days the content of the church law had been largely dictated by the foreign missionaries, this dictation was increasingly balanced by the influence of indigenous church members. In some areas, particularly the eastern islands where Christianity was longer established, this change was a natural result of the passage of time, which brought more emphasis on the actual situation of the people. The pastors in most of the older churches were paid by the local congregations, and therefore in the long run local views tended to take precedence over the views of the missionary at the headquarters of the organization. Slow and uncertain transportation between headquarters and the local village also tended to emphasize the importance of local factors, and the more isolated islands that could be reached only once a year or once in two or three years had minimal outside interference in their church regulations. Sometimes the increasing role of the indigenous church was a matter of conscious policy. This was particularly true in the newer churches of the western islands where more modern missionary ideas about the indigenization of Christianity could take effect early in the life of a church. The Lutherans of New Guinea were noted for the policy, linked with the name of Christian Keysser, by which the people of the congregation decided in long discussions what their ethical norms should be.[4]

Even where mission policy moved toward noninterference, however, the indigenous church naturally carried on many of the attitudes taught by foreigners in the past, and it continued to treat the ethical prescriptions of missionaries with great respect.[5] Roman Catholics everywhere continued to leave the decisions on ethical teachings with their foreign personnel, though these were usually more tolerant of traditional views then Protestant foreigners were.[6] Foreign dictation among Protestants was most marked and least chastened in the New Hebrides. A Fijian working in the New Hebrides in recent years remarked that he had heard New Hebridean pastors complain about the way in which missionary dictation had destroyed their old way of life, a complaint he had never heard from Fijian pastors.[7]

The Christian ethic that came out of this process was, as might be expected, an amalgam of foreign missionary teaching and traditional island practice. The two became a united whole and it was difficult to think of one without the other. The church stood as the guardian of this amalgam, protecting what remained from pre-Christian practices just as staunchly as it supported the newer Christian ethics. The recognition of the church as the guardian of the pre-Christian tradition was evidenced when the French administrator of the Leeward Islands set out in the 1920s to codify the traditional law and found that he had to turn to the pastors and deacons of the church for the information he needed, or again when the traditional lore regarding Samoan genealogies, titles, and precedence—the famous *fa'alupega*—needed to be compiled and published and the Samoan Church (LMS) was the body that took responsibility for the task.[8] "Traditions are walking side by side with Christian teaching," is the way a high Tongan official described the situation. Where the church had fullest sway, as for example in the isolated Catholic island of Futuna, it froze most thoroughly its modified version of the old society and tried, until recently, to keep it from any further change.[9] Everywhere in the Pacific there appeared a "folk church" representing the society and reflecting its standards rather than a prophetic church ranged over against the society.[10]

In some ways the new amalgam was made easily because much of the old morality of the islands fitted well, even if superficially, into Christian teaching. The islanders' traditional emphasis on generosity is the most notable example. It was similar to the Christian teaching regarding love for neighbors and giving to one who asks of you. There have probably never been any people who fulfilled the Christian commandments about giving more completely than the Pacific islanders. In most of the societies of the Pacific the way to make an impression and to be recognized as important was not to own a lot but to give a lot. Guests were loaded with gifts beyond what they could carry away. Great feasts were presented by the "big men," and in Melanesian graded societies these feasts provided the way to advancement. Samoa had its massive distributions of fine mats and other goods whenever political offices were being sought or important marriages arranged. Fiji had its unbreakable rules of *kerekere* according to which a relative had to be given anything he requested. The Gilberts had the same custom, called *bubuti*.

These practices are far from extinguished even yet and it is easy to see how they have fitted into the teaching of the church. Actually they are often far from compatible with New Testament thought because they operate only within a clearly defined circle of relationships and obligations, and the marvelous generosity that they show may vanish altogether in situations where no obligation prevails. Also, these practices are usually aimed more at gaining prestige than at expressing love, which raises some questions about their Christian quality. But these questions were largely unrecognized by the islanders.[11]

In the same way, the islanders adopted easily the Christian teaching about honesty. "Thou shalt not steal" was repeated along with the rest of the Ten Commandments in the churches. But stealing was easy to condemn simply because it was almost nonexistent in Pacific societies. The Christian code fitted neatly with the traditional one. Sometimes, it is true, people were known to steal things from outsiders and therefore they got a reputation among the Europeans for thievery, but within their own societies such action was usually unknown. It came as a relatively late European importation and was applied first to European articles that they had acquired. But though direct theft was quickly condemned there were other forms of dishonesty, which the islanders found it very hard to recognize and which the church was largely unable to stop. This was the case with the practice of giving away, with typical island generosity, funds that did not belong to the giver. In church after church the problem recurred. Funds disappeared not because the pastor or treasurer in whose keeping they had been placed was making off with them but because in good spirit he was giving them out to people, usually relatives, who came asking for them.[12]

The same moderate honesty applied in the case of telling the truth. Island churches, like many islanders, were not inclined to push truthfulness as a virtue regardless of the effect it would have on people. They preferred to be considerate of people's feelings and tell them what they would like to hear.

Sometimes this was done with kindly intentions and sometimes it was done diplomatically to gain an end, with the assumption that if anyone believed what was said it was the person's own fault. But this attitude toward the truth, as can be imagined, caused many problems in the churches. The Roman Catholics in Samoa during the first half of the twentieth century almost never granted dispensations for their members to marry Protestants on the basis of promises made to raise the children as Catholics, because the promises were taken so lightly.

Industriousness was another virtue that the churches had a hard time with, or at least the missionaries had a hard time inculcating. It does not appear that the island churches, as distinct from the missionaries, were eager to make their members industrious. Christian Keysser, who wrote so much about his indigenizing of the church in New Guinea, claimed to have fashioned a Christian village where everyone worked steadily according to a schedule under the direction of the chief[13]—a rather Germanic idea of indigenization it would seem. But this harmonious, industrious community did not long survive his departure, and elsewhere the teaching of steady work habits seems to have been limited to the missionary-run institutions. Missionaries made much of it. "We must not only teach the natives religion, but make them industrious, too. The Gospel goes well with work and they should not be separated," said the Australian Methodist mission secretary in 1908.[14] But islanders continued to work hard only when immediate necessity required, and otherwise to enjoy the leisure time that an abundant nature allowed them.[15] The so-called Protestant ethic of honesty, industriousness, frugality, and thrift, although it was brought to the Pacific by many of the Protestant missionaries, was obviously not congenial to the island way of living and simply did not become a living part of the ethic of the island churches whether Catholic or Protestant.

Island Warfare

But if the churches largely adapted to island practice in these matters, there was another ethical question, that of warfare, where island practice was strikingly changed. It was not a clear and total change at first. In the nineteenth century Christianity played a peculiar role in relation to island warfare. Despite missionary admonitions against fighting, the divisions between Christians and non-Christians at times got mixed into the political reasons for war. This happened in connection with the emergence of Christian rulers in Tahiti, Tonga, and Fiji, and in Samoa warfare between parties of Christians continued to flare up sporadically, regardless of the churches' distress over it, until colonial rule was established in 1900.

In the twentieth century Christianity was less ambiguous and more successful in its opposition to warfare. The church was spreading in areas where colonial rule had already been imposed, so its peacemaking efforts could be backed up by the peacekeeping program of the imperial power. But there were also many examples of Christians establishing peace in areas where the colonial writ did not run, showing that the church was independently effective in this work. The efforts of Amos Tozaka, a Methodist leader on Choiseul, illustrates this. He made two dangerous trips into the very heart of enemy territory in 1919 to bring an end to the wars of the famous chief, Liliboe. Completely unarmed, he was able to climb the enemy's stockades by night and to slip safely into their headquarters with his offers of peace before anyone was aware of him, and this itself was taken by the enemy as a sign of divine sanction and support for his mission.[16]

Within the villages, too, Christianity acted as a pacifying force. Old ideals of fighting and revenge became no longer admirable. The Fijian no longer shaved half his head to remind himself vividly of the wrong he must avenge. Homicidal emblems, once worn with pride by young killers in Keveri villages of Papua, began to disappear from view. Young men of Manus could grow up as friends rather than being channeled into bitter rivalries. Traditional exogamous divisions in New Britain were regarded by indigenous Christians as a weakness to be overcome through Christian love.[17] There is no doubt that the abolition of old rivalries and warfare caused much damage to the social structure, which had in many ways been built around those activities; but where the new church life was vigorous, the damage was well repaired by the development of fresh interests around which social structures could grow.

Secret Societies

Most island customs did not meet with either the wholehearted endorsement given to traditional generosity or the condemnation meted out to warfare. As they were related to the new "Christian" morality, they were given a more conditional approval or condemnation, as the case might be, and the judgment on them changed from place to place and time to time. The secret societies for men in Melanesia provided a case in point. These societies were the stepping stones by which men rose in rank and respect until they became the leaders of their communities. By killing many pigs, providing great feasts and dances with much grandeur, a man would rise through these graded societies. They had their secret ceremonies as well as their public functions and in their secretly made costumes the members would often pose as spirits and terrorize their fellow villagers into making payments to them. These societies were seen by some as providing the necessary schooling for future leaders, training men in patience and initiative. Others saw them as a tool of domination and of exploitation exercised by the older men over the younger men and the women. Both aspects were present, though it would seem that with the development of new interests and experiences for Melanesian villagers the more valuable role of the societies declined and the exploitative and "money-grubbing" side predominated. On the whole the churches were unhappy about the societies. The Presbyterians in the New Hebrides, with the exception of the old Scandinavian missionary Oscar Michelsen, forbade them and their feasts. On New Britain, Protestants and Catholics alike put a ban on the Duk-Duk Society, which became notorious for making its members rich at the expense of the gullible villagers. But there were also those, particularly among the Anglicans, who had a more appreciative attitude and who believed in allowing the continuation of the societies as long as they maintained their vitality. Eventually their strength disappeared as other avenues of advancement and influence, including the avenues provided by the church, took their place.[18]

Attitudes Toward Dancing

The variations, not to say vagaries, in judgment regarding island tradition were most extreme in relation to the traditional dancing. South Pacific dances have long fascinated the world. Whether it be the more individualistic dancing of Tahiti and Samoa with its grace and charm or the more organized group dances of Melanesia with their power and vigor, they represent one of the main cultural achievements of these peoples. They also represent their principal form of entertainment, their own form of sports, and have traditionally played a large role in their religious life. Because of this last quality and also because of sexual references in some of them, they aroused the wrath of the early missionaries and were generally forbidden by the churches. The common verdict was that they were "lewd and indecent and led to licentiousness." Most churches tried to stop them altogether, but the Roman Catholics and Anglicans, true to their more Catholic orientation, usually forbade only those dances that were obviously related to the old worship or to sex. In Tahiti and the Gilberts however, the Catholics at first followed the more common practice of prohibition, and individual Catholic priests took the same stand in other areas such as the Marquesas.[19]

The prohibitions had only limited success. Tahitians kept bursting out with their love for the dance, especially in connection with the French celebration of July 14 when political enthusiasms seemed stronger than ecclesiastical. In Port Moresby the highly respected William Lawes found that he had to quell "outbreaks" of dancing in the villages around after the prohibition had been put into effect. Some more zealous missionaries pursued the demon when it appeared in new guises. William Goward reported from the southern Gilberts in 1902 that the pastors were leading the schoolchildren in "swinging, waving and posturing" till they worked themselves up to a frenzy. "We decided to stop the whole thing," he said, and added in self-justification, "I believe that this was a relief to the pastors because they found it was getting out of hand." In the Marshall Islands the American Board representative at that time even indicated that the reason for a continued supervision of the church by missionaries was the tendency to introduce dancing under the guise of marches in the Christmas plays.[20]

But this kind of rigorism could hardly last. It was suppressing too much in the life of the people. Some government officials argued that "where there is

least dancing there is most thieving and vice."[21] The missionary attitudes began to be affected in this as in other matters by the advance of more liberal
theology and of anthropological studies. The islanders, it must be recognized, showed an ambivalent attitude. Sometimes, where the missionaries
were less restrictive, the islanders abandoned the dancing of their own accord
because it seemed too pagan and reminiscent of the old style of life.[22] But
other groups of them were ready to maintain it in modified form or to return
to it when it was again permitted. Before the end of the nineteenth century the
change was begun. Tongan Christianity allowed dancing by 1890. In Samoa
in 1890 it was reported that for the first time a missionary attended one of the
indigenous dances.[23] A distinction began to be made between the uproarious
Samoan "night madness" and the more usual type of dancing. The Samoan
LMS approved the latter type of dance early in the twentieth century; the
Samoan Methodists moved more slowly and have only recently begun to allow dancing in the daytime under pastoral supervision. In the Gilberts the
government began to press the missions for a relaxation of their ban on dancing, and in 1920 the LMS Church Council agreed to this provided that the
government would arrange committees of control to maintain standards of
decency.[24]

The churches also began to make use of dancing in their own activities. The
Anglicans and Methodists in Melanesia had traditional dances as part of their
church festivals. Catholics in Bougainville celebrated Christmas with all-
night dancing, and in Papua when the Catholic bishop visited the moun-
tainous area of his diocese on one occasion he was greeted by thousands of
villagers advancing in village groups, each group running in, howling at the
top of their lungs, the men in front in long rows approaching and retreating
like great waves, the women following singing in high voices. All this was
followed with a long period of dancing.[25] In both the Cooks and Samoa the
churches took to organizing dancing bands, which put on performances, in-
terspersed with prayers and hymns, in neighboring villages. In Samoa this
became at times such a popular way to raise money that villages had to make
announcements that they would accept no more visiting dancers because they
were completely drained of cash and food.[26]

Bible stories often provided the subject matter for these dancers. Perhaps
the fullest development of dancing to biblical themes took place in the Ellice
Islands. There in marvelously graceful and intricate group dances the young
people performed the stories of the Hebrew patriarchs or of the birth in
Bethlehem or of later church experiences in their own area. This was carried
on week by week under the critical eyes of the village elders who commended
and commented on each performance in order to improve the quality of the
art. Dance as a part of the liturgy was not known in those days but has more
recently begun to make its appearance among Fijian Roman Catholics.[27]

The last stronghold of the old repressive attitudes among the major
churches was among Protestants of New Caledonia and the New Hebrides. In
the New Hebrides the Presbyterian Synod repeatedly banned all kinds of

dancing and urged the people to be on their guard against this sort of thing, which "savours of heathenism." Some of the Catholic priests followed the same course and the old dances were largely lost as the older generation died off. Not until 1956, long after the change was effected in other island groups, did a crack appear in the wall of prohibition. In that year under prompting from the newer, more liberal missionaries, the synod voted to allow whatever rules there might be about dancing to be made locally, since it believed that in places where the church was strong and Christian life well established dances could now be held without creating trouble. Opposition to the change came primarily from the New Hebridean pastors along with a few missionaries who insisted that "we should try to block all kinds of dancing in our villages."[28] But as a result of the new permission, some villages made a serious effort to revive the old dance forms under church auspices and before long the meetings of the General Assembly itself were regularly ended with big traditional dances. Thus in recent years one finds that only the New Caledonian Protestants and the Marshall Islands church along with some of the smaller churches like the Seventh-day Adventists, the Church of Christ on Aoba, and the South Sea Evangelical Church have continued the old restrictive regulation.[29] In general, dancing has returned unquestioned among the island churches and the people are quite unaware of the former restrictions. The problem now lies with the breakup of village life and the influx of new styles that make the old dances passé. In many places the church, which tried so long to prohibit traditional dancing, is one place in society where it is fostered and preserved.[30]

Marriage and Sexual Traditions

Marriage is another and far more important element of traditional culture with which the churches had to deal, and here they showed much more consistency than in their approach to dancing. The island societies had long traditions regarding the way marriage should be carried out and the restrictions that should be placed upon it. Usually the church was willing to recognize the traditional marriage as valid for non-Christians and even as indissoluble for those who later joined the church. Often it added a ceremony of Christian blessing of the earlier marriage. After the people were all Christian, the old forms were usually continued as a kind of adjunct or supplement to the church wedding. Before the pastor would proceed with the ceremony he would make sure that the traditional formalities and gift exchanges between the families had been observed. Without them it was feared the marriage would be unstable. Thus the church often became so closely linked to the old traditions and so insistent upon their observance that the younger generation arising toward the middle of the century resisted church marriages because they did not like the pre-Christian practices that went with them.[31]

The practice to which they most often objected was that of parents and relatives arranging the marriage. Ideas of individual freedom of choice were creeping in from the "Christian" West, but they were having little effect on the church. Everywhere the church, following island traditions, assumed that parents would make the decisions and the arrangements for their children's marriages and might even negotiate marriages between young people who did not know each other.[32] Missionaries were known to object to this latter extreme, and churches usually would not proceed with a marriage if the bride or groom were unwilling. W. V. Milne tells of lecturing a village against an attempt at a forced marriage, after which "the disappointed groom got up and bolted." Yet missionaries and new-style youth notwithstanding, the churches on the whole continued to honor the parents' wishes in regard to marriage and refused to marry any young people whose parents were opposed.[33] In solidly Catholic Wallis the church actually stood *in loco parentis* and handled the arrangements. On one day a year the young men gathered in the priests' compound and the young women in the Sisters'. A chosen messenger was then sent from the men to inquire through the Sisters about a desired marriage. If the girl agreed, the good news was announced by the firing of a gun. The process was repeated for others and all the marriages for the year were celebrated forthwith. No more could be held till the following year. In 1928 Bishop Blanc put an end to this custom, despite local pleas, in order to be "like the rest of the world."[34]

The church also came to terms fairly generally with the old custom known to Westerners as "bride price." This was the practice, common in Melanesia though unknown elsewhere in the Pacific islands, according to which the clan of the groom made a payment to the clan of the bride. The payment expressed the involvement of the whole family in the relationship and had a stabilizing effect on the marriage. It could, however, be regarded as a purchase of the woman, especially when, as in some cases in the Anglican area of Papua, the price was tatooed on her arm! Occasionally a zealous missionary or a congregation under his influence tried to put a stop to it.[35] But efforts were usually ineffective and the churches normally contented themselves with trying to keep the price within reasonable limits and emphasizing the commitment it represented as opposed to the commercial element it included. In the New Hebrides the Presbyterians eventually, after trying to oppose the system, set a £10 limit on payments, and payments of about that amount were common elsewhere. The Catholics in New Britain, in order to be sure that everything was done properly, required that the money be given to the priest at the time of the betrothal and that he pass it on to the bride's family at the wedding. In more recent years, with the rise in some areas of financial interests and larger wealth, it has been hard to hold to any limits. Old Christian families in the Port Moresby area, in a full-blown commercialism, have been reported to require over $10,000 for a daughter in marriage, and New Caledonians have been known to ask similar amounts. But these situations are exceptional and in general it can be said that bride price has not been the large problem in the Pacific churches that it certainly has been in Africa.[36]

The same is true with regard to polygamy. While the African churches have found polygamy to be a constant obstacle limiting their growth and producing dissident sects, the Pacific churches have been little troubled by it, at least in the years prior to World War II. Only in the Trobriand Islands where, as in many African societies, polygamy and political life were tightly intertwined, did it seriously limit the acceptability of the church. After the war when the New Guinea highlands opened up, the churches entered another area where polygamy was important and there the problem was serious. Problem or no, the traditional Christian stand of refusing baptism to anyone who had more than one spouse has been almost universally and unquestioningly maintained. Even the Mormons, who suffered so much for their polygamist doctrines in their early years in America, did not bring those doctrines with them to the Pacific; and the great Christian Keysser, who advocated so vigorously the right of the people to have their own version of Christianity, imposed his own Western ideas at this point.[37] Only after the war did a few New Guinea churches of the more strongly Protestant type begin to question the traditional stand. This was largely a result of anthropological training given to the newer missionaries. Among the Methodists and the Missouri Synod Lutherans there developed a clear cleavage on this point between the new generation of missionaries and the indigenous church leaders, the latter abiding firmly by the standards inculcated by earlier missionaries and saying it was unfair "to past members who had been won at great cost to admit to membership any who were not willing to follow the same path."[38] In the few places where any change was made it was only to allow those who were already polygamous to be baptized without breaking their existing marriage ties. There was no thought of permitting established Christians to become polygamists.

But if polygamy with its public commitments and responsibilities was largely stopped, adultery and fornication, though lacking those positive features, spread and flourished. Pacific societies before the coming of Christianity had varied from the quite permissive to the extremely restrictive in sex relations. The permissive ones created a legend but the restrictive may well have been more usual—rules for the death or mutilation of men and women involved in adultery and the killing of children born out of wedlock were common in Melanesia and Micronesia. But the breakdown of old cultures under Western impact led to a general loosening of the restrictive societies and more permissiveness in the others. Colonial governments would not allow executions for adultery and so removed some of the deterrence, although they often did provide milder penalties for sexual offenses. The church also put a stop to the more extreme penalties and thus had on the whole a loosening effect even though it imposed many rules.

Initially many churches tried to deal with this situation by appointing lay officers who kept a close watch on community morals and beat the bushes at night to find offenders. This kind of action was particularly associated with the LMS churches in the smaller islands but was also used elsewhere, as in the Anglican island of Ysabel in the Solomons.[39] The growth of effective colonial power with its own police and its jealousy of any alter-government from the church largely put an end to this sort of church police in the twentieth century, though in more isolated areas the new government's powers continued to be used in the old church ways. A British official in the southern Gilberts reported in 1930 that most jailings were still for adultery and a man might be hauled before the local island court on vague charges of "being in love with someone not his wife."[40]

Church discipline almost everywhere continued to be primarily concerned with sexual offenses, and missionary reports made constant reference to the low level of morality. Not only lay people were disciplined, but pastors were frequently removed from their work because of adultery. Church visitors from Europe were distressed by the lack of any great concern among most people over these offenses, but given their frequency the unconcern should hardly have been surprising. In the Polynesian islands it was commonly accepted that sex relations might take place before marriage, and marriage was postponed until later in life when people were ready to settle down or was even postponed indefinitely. The Catholic island of Wallis reported in 1965 that between one-fourth and one-third of all births were illegitimate, and at the beginning of the century a ten-year study of the graduates of the finest Congregational girls' school in Samoa revealed that close to one-third of its graduates were living with men to whom they were not married.[41] Fiji, Tonga, and most Melanesian and Micronesian lands had much stricter rules than this, but the violations of their standards seemed constant. Only the New Hebrides and New Caledonia found their codes fairly well observed.

Reports after the middle of the century offer considerable evidence to suggest the development of more disciplined sex relations at least among pastors and church leaders. Observers in Samoa, Tonga, and Fiji have reported independently that there were few cases of discipline for sex offenses among the clergy and theological students after about 1950. Samoan pastors also reported that more people were getting married before living together.[42] This change may be the result of higher educational standards and the growth of Western influence. But Western influence also brought the breakdown of traditional controls and a new permissiveness and marital instability, so the picture is a mixed one. The churches that had never done anything but regulate and discipline began at last, under European inspiration, to try to educate. A number of seminars on marriage were held in different areas, starting in 1969 with the help of the World Council of Churches, and hundreds of people were trained and some thousands reached in this way.[43] A strong taboo against all discussion of sex became apparent throughout the islands in this connection, and some pastors maintained that it was shameful for the church to be involved in discussing such things. But tremendous interest was aroused everywhere and young people were eager to join in the new thinking.

Stimulants and Intoxicants

Another whole area of Christian ethical prescriptions of great importance in the Pacific churches is the area of stimulants and intoxicants. The Pacific, like other regions, has both its own traditional forms and its foreign forms of drugs taken for the sake of relaxation or stimulation. And, as is true elsewhere, there has grown up in the course of time an intricate pattern of church regulation in this field, a pattern which has shown variations from island to island and which has changed markedly through the years. Four products are involved here: betel and kava, which are indigenous, and tobacco and alcohol, which have been introduced. One might expect that because Christianity came to the Pacific in the person of European missionaries it would have maintained rather friendly relations with those stimulants and intoxicants that came from a European background and would have entered into continuous warfare with those indigenous to the Pacific. The lines, however, did not form in that way. Nor can it be claimed that the opposite situation prevailed, that because of the indigenization of Christianity as the religion of the islanders it easily accepted the indigenous drugs and fought the foreign ones. No, if any pattern can be seen in the Christian reaction to drugs it is that those that caused little evident damage to the people were little opposed and those that caused greater obvious damage were more opposed.

Tobacco, though foreign in origin, met the least resistance from the islanders in their church organizations. Only two or three churches maintained any serious opposition to it, and they were either of American provenance (the Micronesian Protestants and the Seventh-day Adventists) reflecting an attitude toward tobacco that had developed in the American churches in the nineteenth century, or were of an extremely pietistic type (the South Sea Evangelical Mission) reflecting general distrust of worldly pleasures. One of the famous Baldwin sisters who spent a lifetime in an isolated spot in Micronesia could maintain that "smoking is proving a means of downfall to many of the boys and young men."[44] She could well say this because smoking was taken as adequate ground for exclusion from the church. The same policy characterized the other two antitobacco churches and was the source of frequent tribulation in them as in Micronesia. But the more usual attitude was one of tolerance and even, in some places, of symbiosis between Christianity and tobacco. In the western islands, where whites arrived later than in the east, tobacco rolled and pasted together in sticks served until very recently as the commonest medium of exchange, and missions often could not secure the land or goods they needed until the people had a desire for tobacco and would exchange these things for it. The faith and the tobacco trade went together.[45]

Betel (i.e., the chewing of the combination of areca nut, lime, and the leaf or bean of the betel vine) attracted little, if any, more opposition than tobacco, although the one was indigenous and the other imported. Betel was used only in the area of the Solomons and New Guinea and there it was banned only by the more pietistic bodies—such as the South Sea Evangelical Mission (SSEM) and the Manus Evangelical Mission. The Methodists were the one large church in the New Guinea area that tried to discourage the use of betel by teaching against it, but an effort to make Methodist pastors an example in this respect by forbidding them to use it had to be given up because of the important men who continued its use. The reasoning of the SSEM in the matter is peculiar: "We know," said one of their leaders, that smoking and chewing betel-nut lead Christians to tell lies and steal, and therefore "many men and women who have trusted the Lord cannot be baptized until they are prepared to give up these two things." [46]

Kava drinking is found in those parts of the Pacific where betel is not used. The drink is made by grinding the root of the kava plant and mixing it with water. Neither kava nor betel has any very obvious effect on the user, though both of them produce a mild sense of relaxation and, in the case of some people, they become psychologically necessary. Most churches made no issue out of kava drinking, and some, particularly in Samoa, incorporated the ceremonial drinking of kava and even kava libations into their Christian ceremonies. It was the practice in welcoming guests to pour a little kava on the earth as had been done in offerings to the ancient gods and then to say a prayer of Christian thanksgiving before drinking together. But some churches—rather more than were opposed to betel chewing—tried to put a stop to kava drinking. The Presbyterians in the New Hebrides and the Methodists in Fiji were the only large churches of this type. The Presbyterian opposition was more persistent and rigorous. Abstinence was made a condition for church membership and sometimes bands were organized to go about pulling up the kava plant. [47] The Fijian opposition was more sporadic. Early in the century it was the practice to raise the question at every monthly meeting of the Methodist sections as to how many people had taken the pledge to abstain from kava (or yanggona, as it is known locally) and tobacco. In 1918 the Fiji Methodist Synod took a further step when all its members pledged abstinence from kava. But this dramatic move did not prove effective, and gradually the Methodists retreated to the point where they asked only that ministers limit themselves to strictly ceremonial drinking, whereas ordinary church members could do as they wished. One of the leading Methodist missionaries finally came to the conclusion that the attempts at kava prohibition had been a serious mistake. [48]

But it was on alcohol, a European importation, that the churches concentrated their major effort. Year in and year out they treated alcohol as the greatest social evil that they had to fight. Protestant churches often made abstinence from liquor a rule of church membership. [49]

In most areas their struggle was made fairly easy by strict government regulations against the sale or gift of alcoholic beverages to the island peoples. Where the churches had found themselves so often at odds with the government, on this point at least they were in agreement. It was a mark of enlightened colonial policy at the turn of the century, when the humanitarian possibilities of empires were recognized more than ever before (or since), to prohibit the liquor traffic with the islanders. The Brussels conferences of the imperial powers (1890, 1896, 1907) had established a policy of either prohibition or high import taxes for liquor in the African domains. The Pacific

islands were able to profit by the new emphasis more than Africa could because imperial rule had come so recently to most of the Pacific that no long-
term pattern of support for colonial administration through liquor revenue
had been established. Both Britain and Germany (and later Japan) adhered
to the prohibition policy. Even the weak condominium of the New Hebrides
had laws against the trade, although the Presbyterians there were forever
complaining that French settlers violated the law flagrantly and with impu-
nity.[50]

After World War I, when prohibition sentiment was running high in many
parts of the world, there developed a strong move in some of the churches to
stop the sale of liquor to white people as well as indigenous peoples in the
Pacific. The Methodists of Fiji were the most active in this, as they were in the
campaign against kava at the same time. The provision for total prohibition
in Samoa (for Europeans and Samoans) when New Zealand took over that
area from Germany encouraged them. In 1919 and 1920 they made appeals to
London for action. A dozen years later, in 1932, they were approaching the
Colonial Office again and this time were joined by leading Hindu, Sikh, and
Muslim organizations of the Fiji Indian community, those religions having
strong teaching against alcohol. But even these combined efforts failed to
move London, and white people in Fiji continued to enjoy the privilege of
alcoholic drinks.[51]

The one exception to the "enlightened colonial policy" was the French
regime in Tahiti, New Caledonia, and the Loyalties. France did forbid alcohol for the islanders of the Leeward and Tuamotu islands where indigenous
society was most intact, and they put varying restrictions on it in the Marquesas and Wallis.[52] But in the larger and more populous domains there were
no limitations. This meant that if there were to be any effort against alcohol it
would have to come from the churches. The Catholics with their own liberal
French background in these matters bestirred themselves very little. The
Protestants, on the other hand, were endlessly active. Their concern can
hardly be attributed to a different background, since it was the missionaries
from France who took the lead, rather than the local people, and the activity
was just as great in New Caledonia, where there had never been any English
Protestant work, as it was in Tahiti and the Loyalties, where British legacies
remained.

The people were in fact, like many other preliterate groups in contact with
European cultures, demoralized by drink, and it was this that stirred the
Protestant concern. Henry Adams, no friend of the missions, wrote, "Rum is
the only amusement which civilization and religion have left them [the Tahi-
tians], and they drink—drink—drink, and more and more every year, while
cultivation declines, the plantations go to ruin and disease undermines the
race."[53] Maurice Leenhardt, the missionary anthropologist, believed that the
New Caledonians, faced with the destruction of their old culture, were com-
mitting suicide with alcohol. A temperance society, the Croix Bleu, was established and given every encouragement by the mission, and in New Caledo-

nia abstinence was made a condition—in fact the most clearly recognized condition—of church membership. Leenhardt carried on a vigorous campaign for legislation, and finally in 1917 the sale of alcohol to indigenous peoples was officially forbidden in New Caledonia and the Loyalties.[54] Notices of the prohibition were affixed to the walls of bars where they may still be seen in some of the smaller French settlements, although the law they proclaim has long since been repealed.

Repeal came in a later period than that covered in this chapter. It came not only in New Caledonia, but in all the Pacific islands. The apparently firm structure of legislation that had been established everywhere except Tahiti proved very shaky in the storms of World War II. The dislocations during the war, combined with the wide distribution of troops who drank heavily, spread the use of alcohol among the people. After the war it was hard to reassert the old restrictions, and the argument was advanced that discrimination between Europeans and islanders in regard to drinking rights was unfair. In a period when nationalism was rising all over the colonial world this argument struck a sensitive spot, and certainly concessions could be made to incipient nationalism more easily in regard to alcohol than almost anything else. Accordingly the governments proceeded one by one during the first twenty years following the war to remove all discriminatory legislation on drinking.[55] The churches reacted variously. Methodists, Congregationalists, and Presbyterians, along with smaller bodies like the Seventh-day Adventists, fought the change vigorously, while Lutherans, Anglicans, and Roman Catholics, the churches that have all through their history been more liberal about alcohol, supported the repeal.[56]

The consequences of the change have not been catastrophic, although certainly island society now has a serious problem, especially in the cities, which it did not have before. It could be argued that the relatively sober way in which the islanders have adjusted to alcohol indicates that the earlier fears and restrictions were not necessary and that the churches were long fighting an imaginary enemy. This may well be, though it can never be proved that if the change had come earlier, in the days when population was declining and islanders were dispirited, it would not have proved extremely damaging. The example of Tahiti at the beginning of this century could be cited to illustrate the dangers, but then Tahiti is not in every way typical of the Pacific islands.

Sunday Observance

Finally among the many elements of Christian ethics we turn to the most visible and universally recognized of them all, the observance of Sunday. We have already noticed the part that Sunday worship played as the distinguishing mark of Christians, but Sunday worship was only part of the day's observance. Most of the early missionaries were strong sabbatarians, believing that on the Lord's Day there should be neither work nor play. The island Christians responded much more enthusiastically to this limitation than they did to the various limitations on drugs, sex relations, and dancing. The recognition of a sacred time, a taboo day, fitted with their older ideas about religion. It provided something of a substitute for the festivals associated with their earlier religion and it gave some outward demonstration of the power of Christianity.

The islander missionaries were noticeably stricter than European missionaries about Sunday observance,[57] and the kingdom of Tonga, as the one independent government in the area, had, and still has, the fullest recognition of Sunday. Its constitution said "the Sabbath day shall be sacred in Tonga forever."[58] British rulers who succeeded such independent governments recognized the sacred day but moderated the restrictions. In the Gilbert and Ellice Islands cooking and bathing on Sundays were permitted when the British came, and church attendance was no longer required, but it was announced that such work as "canoe-building, carrying coconut leaves and cord-making will not be countenanced on Sunday."[59] French rule was much more permissive but the church regulations still dominated Tahitian life, and the church by its constitution required the disciplining of any member who went so far as merely to loan something to a person who was going out on a Sunday.[60] In Fiji, church authorities even pressed for recognition of the day by those who were not Christians. They were able to stop Sunday motion pictures for Indians in Fiji until 1938, when it was said that the "Indian influence has become too strong."[61]

Of course all churches were not equally strict. Roman Catholics were quite free about allowing organized recreation on Sunday. They maintained a prohibition of regular work, though one of their priests remarked wryly that he was not much impressed when a man said he did not work on Sunday because, given the islanders' proclivity to relaxation, he could as well have added Monday and Tuesday.[62] Seventh-day Adventists were the most strict of all the churches, but of course with regard to Saturday rather than Sunday. One happy bit of confusion enabled the Adventists to fit in with majority patterns in Tonga. The international dateline makes what is to them an unrecognized jog to the east around Tonga. So what other people call Sunday they, ascribing divine warrant to the 180th meridian as the true dateline, call Saturday, and all can comfortably worship on the same day. The same harmonious arrangement prevailed in the Cook Islands until the calendar there was changed in 1898, after Roman Catholic appeals, to fit with their actual position east of the dateline.[63]

The variations among the churches made it possible that on occasion some urgent Sunday work like the loading and unloading of ships could be done by one group or another. But this was feasible only in islands where there was a large or religiously varied population. In smaller islands, especially where the main church had come out of a Calvinist tradition and there was no second church of significant size, there was no way to arrange for the working of ships on Sunday. In the Marshalls and the southern Gilberts and even more in the Cooks and Niue this became the great bone of contention between the government, representing the shipping interests, and the church. The local government tried to press the people into working, threatening that ships would no longer call if they were not worked on Sunday and even, in one case, shutting off the water supply to enforce cooperation. Appeals went from the churches to higher authorities in New Zealand regarding government actions in the Cooks and Niue, and at one point the New Zealand prime minister gave a commitment that the wishes of the people on this matter would be respected.[64]

The way in which the observance of Sunday was carried out is revealing of the whole nature of Christian ethics in the islands. There was much more emphasis on the negative than the positive elements. Some positive things were emphasized—generosity, peacefulness in village relations, mutual support in marriage relations—but the greater emphasis was on the prohibitions. Furthermore, the negative elements were often marked by a certain mistrust of celebration and joyous expression. Sobriety was the obvious intention. The rules about dancing and kava and alcohol and Sunday observance all had this quality. The extent to which Christianity did away with the great feasts of the New Guinea villages provides another example. In many areas of New Guinea the main interest of the villagers used to be in preparing and holding great feasts to which they invited neighboring villages. The churches for the most part tried to stop these feasts because of the debauchery, license, and quarreling that were often connected with them, a process of destroying rather than purifying an institution that meant a lot to the people.

It is difficult to judge a primarily negative ethic in any but negative terms. Fortunately the joyousness and enthusiasm of the peoples have come through largely unscathed and have given the actual life of their churches a far happier atmosphere than this long list of prohibitions would suggest.

NOTES

1. It should be recognized, however, that the ancient gods were sometimes regarded as being uninvolved with the specifics of social conduct. They provided, rather, a sacred background for the social system as a whole. Cf. Williamson 1937: 234, on Tahiti. Firth 1970: 25, 111, 370 indicates that rather than supporting any general morality, the gods on Tikopia were seen as supporting those who worshiped them.

2. Lundsgaarde 1966: 52–53 finds this tendency in comparing two islands in Kiribati. Allégret 1928: Part 1: 1 notes the absence of wider concerns in the churches of the smaller islands and their consequent proclivity to constant discussion of themselves and their own small scene.

3. H. E. Maude (District Officer in Beru), "General Report of the Island of Beru," Aug. 22, 1930, in Gilbert and Ellice Islands Administrative Reports, Public Record Office, London.

4. Keysser 1921: 21. Cf. Freytag 1940: 47; Wigg 1912: 50. The Melanesian Mission also reported that it believed in allowing the local church to decide ethical questions

regarding customs. Morpeth Conference, Commission II Report, p. 14.

5. As for example in the Kwato Mission where there was a policy of noninterference in the indigenous culture, yet the people were taught from the beginning that certain of their customs were wrong. *Oceania* 15 (1944–45): 128ff. In an area not far from Kwato a missionary in the 1930s trying to leave the way open for a fuller acceptance of traditional customs found the church people rigorously against them because of the earlier teaching they had received. Hurst 1937: 28.

6. The more discriminating attitude of Roman Catholic missionaries is shown in Samoa by Deekin 1901: 108, and in the contrast between them and the Church of Christ on Pentecost Island in the New Hebrides by R. B. Lane, in Lawrence and Meggitt 1965: 277. That Roman Catholic missionaries could also be constantly attacking "the bad practices of the heathen ancestors" who thought all day on evil and "spoke no true word, all was only lies" can be seen in Winthuis 1929: 152–57. The previous bishop of Kiribati has said in conversation that the early Catholic missionaries in those islands were also against the traditional culture and believed in keeping old customs out of the church.

7. Missionary dictation in Vanuatu (New Hebrides) Presbyterianism in the early part of the twentieth century is reported in Scarr 1967: 235, 237, and Carmichael 1967: 41, 49.

8. Allégret 1928: Part 1: 47. "The church and the world are but one," said the missionaries of the Paris Society in the French Establishments in Oceania at their meeting, Dec. 13–20, 1900. On the *fa'alupega*, see Davidson 1967: 17. Davidson has said in conversation that the church first undertook the compilation of the *fa'alupega* at the end of the nineteenth century, and the first publication took place about 1910. A recent edition is *O le Tusi Faalupega o Samoa*, published by the Samoan Church (LMS) Press at Malua in 1958.

9. Panoff 1963: 149.

10. Fullerton 1969: 77–78. For a complete and judicious treatment of the relation of Christian ethics to social structures in the British islands and the gradual process of secularization that has been taking place there, see Fullerton's entire work.

11. It should be noted that a recent study in the Leeward Islands emphasizes the general social condemnation of ambition and pride, although it is not clear that this would extend to these qualities when expressed through generosity. Levy 1969: 131. The LMS deputation to Papua in 1916 pointed out that Papuans were nowhere near as generous as the Polynesians, which is no doubt true. But Hogbin found the emphasis on generosity as a primary virtue, along with the unconcern about pride and the desire for prestige, was characteristic of New Guinea and Solomon Island churches. Hogbin 1939: 183, 215; 1951: 252–58. Vincr et al. 1916: 201. Cf. Keesing 1934: 326–27. Stanner 1953: 177. West 1961: 10.

12. David 1899: 183–87. Keesing 1934: 326. Cato 1956: 106. Coulter 1957: 361–62. Hogbin 1947: 17.

13. Keysser, 1950: 69–70; 1921:16.

14. Benjamin Danks, quoted in Fullerton 1969:186.

15. Burnett 1911: 59. Wigg 1912:39. Keesing 1934: 328–29. Beaglehole 1957: 156–59. Lenwood 1925: 9. Leenhardt 1922: 81–82. Ahnne 1931: 23–24. But it should be noted that some missionaries, such as the Anglican Chignell in Papua, valued the work patterns of the people. Tomlin 1951: 75. The same fruitless attempt of most missionaries to change the work habits in an otherwise unchanged economic situation has been reported about the Protestant missionaries among the North American In-

dians in the nineteenth century. Berkhofer 1965: 70–88.

16. Luxton 1955: 80, 86–88. White 1979 shows how some big men of Ysabel Island in the Solomons increased their power by becoming champions of peacemaking through the church.

17. Williams 1944–45: 101. Mead 1956: 31. Laufer 1962: 114. Guiart 1958: 206 shows that though Christians on Santo refused to attack Europeans, as non-Christians did, they may have been secretly supportive of the attacks. They certainly had the most to gain from them. Evidence of any Christian complicity in the attacks, however, is only indirect and circumstantial.

18. Allen 1968: 39 shows the opposite attitudes of Anglicans and the Church of Christ on Aoba in the New Hebrides. The Roman Catholics in New Britain modified their opposition to secret societies in 1966 when it became apparent that the society could no longer exercise control over the people through their superstitions as it once did. (Bishop's circular letter no. 13 of 1966. Dec. 7, 1966.) Cf. Artless 1936: 77–78. Durrad 1920: 20–21. Danks 1933: 282–83. Laufer 1949.

19. Among the coastal people of Papua the Catholics reversed the usual trend by starting out with a permissive policy and then, in the 1930s, trying to put an end to dancing. Dupeyrat 1935: 368–69. Cf. Sabatier 1939: 151–52.

20. J. King 1905: 63. Goward 1900–02: 8. *Missionary Herald* 98, no. 8 (August 1902): 333.

21. A. F. Grimble in Sydney *Morning Herald*, Dec. 29, 1921.

22. The Methodist mission in the Solomons, which began in the twentieth century, allowed most of the old dances, as did the Anglicans in the Solomons, but both found their people giving them up. Hilliard 1966:510–12.

23. Adams 1930: 445.

24. Keesing 1934: 411. Barradale 1927: 50–51. The Lutherans on New Guinea usually did not allow dancing because of its religious implications, though it is said that the missionaries recognized the need for it in the culture. In 1923 both the Jabem and Madang areas of the church legislated against it, and the Sattelberg area had already prohibited it. But in more recent years the ban has been lifted. Pilhofer 1963: vol. 2: 143–44. Hanneman 1935: 30–34, 40. Mager 1937: 34. Keysser 1950: 70. Hogbin 1951: 254.

25. Bigault 1947: 142. Dupeyrat 1948: 116–22.

26. Beaglehole 1957: 172–73.

27. Kent 1966: 28–29.

28. Presbyterian Church of the New Hebrides, General Assembly *Proceedings* 1956, Minute 94 and 94b. Presbyterian Mission Synod (New Hebrides), June 15, 1920.

29. Hilliard 1966: 510–12. Allen 1968: 39. Kahn 1965: 266.

30. An equally striking change could be ascribed to the churches' position on clothing. In the nineteenth century in most areas church members and particularly church leaders were expected to dress in European clothing or adaptations of European styles. But in the twentieth century adaptations to island styles, such as the lavalava or sulu, have been adopted by the churches generally—except for the Micronesian Protestants, who have continued to use Western dress. In Tonga it was the European missionaries who convinced the ministers of the Free Wesleyan church in the 1930s to change from black coat and trousers to the national dress. Ministers of the more isolated Tongan churches—the Free Church and the Church of Tonga—still use the old European style of dress. Today with the influx of modern and Western

ideas and styles it is the church members and the ministers who are often the main supporters and examples of the old island style of clothing. In the Western islands this often means the continuation of just skirts for the women and girls at a time when modernization is bringing in blouses for them as well. Thus the church has been cast in the role of the chief defender of seminudity. Hilliard 1966: 519–20. Laracy 1969: 153. Winthuis 1929: 129. Hölter 1946: 43–55.

31. Keesing 1934: 412. Beaglehole 1957: 176–79. Sharp 1917: 17–18. The combination of traditional and Christian practices and the recognition of traditional marriage as valid have been reported in these sources and also orally from New Caledonia Protestants, New Hebrides Catholics, and New Britain Methodists. H. J. P. Short of Samoa in his report for 1946 (Council for World Mission Archives, London) stated that the missionaries discouraged European marriage customs and encouraged the preservation of the indigenous nuptials. The New Hebrides Presbyterians did not adopt an order for blessing traditional marriages till the 1950s, and there "custom marriage" disappeared even for non-Christians. (Presbyterian Church of New Hebrides General Assembly *Proceedings* 1956, Appendix 4.) The Anglicans in the Solomons always recognized traditional marriage, but in 1921 they declared that Christians marrying by the traditional ceremonies rather than the Christian service would be temporarily excommunicated. Their 1962 Discipline seemed to be less severe, stating merely that Christians married without the Christian service must have their marriage blessed. (Hilliard 1966: 505. Diocese of Melanesia 1962.) A much stricter attitude has been maintained by the Catholics in Kiribati. Any Catholic even attending a traditional marriage, or the feast after it, is put out of communion for three months.

32. Beaglehole 1957: 176. Tippett 1965: 88–90. *Pacific Journal of Theology* 19–20 (June–September 1966): 24–25, 28, 54.

33. L. L. Linggood, "Some Aspects of Marriage and Divorce in the Raluana Circuit of New Britain about 1935," Methodist Mission Archives, Sydney. Dobson 1963: 23–24. W. V. Milne to W. Mawson, Jan. 9, 1931, New Zealand Prebyterian Mission Archives, Auckland. A Roman Catholic informant from New Caledonia reports that his church has always been ready to marry young people whether the parents agreed or not, but this is not common and is quite the contrary of Protestant practice in New Caledonia and the Loyalties. The Presbyterians of Vanuatu decided in 1960 that the church should hear appeals from young people who were prevented from marrying by the objections of their parents or relatives. Presbyterian Church of New Hebrides, General Assembly *Proceedings* 1960: 27.

34. Blanc, Diary, Jan. 6, 1928, Catholic Archives, Nuku'alofa. Bishop John H. Rodgers to author, May 6, 1967.

35. E.g., Benjamin Danks of the Methodists in New Britain in the early part of this century (Reed 1943: 111) and some of the Lutheran congregations in New Guinea under the earlier missionaries. Pilhofer 1961: vol: 1: 231. The Seventh-day Adventists in the Solomons forbade the practice among their members, and the Solomons Methodists officially opposed it, although it continued among them. Hilliard 1966: 506–7. Cf. Hogbin 1939: 211–13.

36. Henao and Perry 1964: 20–25 decry the commercialism coming into marriage arrangements in the LMS section of Papua. In the Presbyterian Church of the New Hebrides, the General Assembly in 1951 (action 21) and 1960 (p. 27) took a stand against the practice as a whole, but the first assembly allowed a limited payment, which has been the common practice, although many more conservative elements in

the church have wanted to remove the limitation. South Santo Presbytery Meeting Minutes, April 22, 1959. For varying Anglican attitudes, see Steward 1926: 19–21; Bishop of New Guinea to mission staff, Aug. 15, 1957, and 1964, in Australian Board of Mission Archives, Stanmore, New South Wales; Hilliard 1966: 110; Tippett 1967: 176. Laufer 1962: 118, tells of the arrangement through the Roman Catholic priest. Cf. Montauban 1948: 10–11. Marie Reay, in Fisk 1966: 168–69.

37. Ellsworth 1959: 21. Keysser 1950: 122–23. Keysser tries to veil the imposed quality of the decision for monogamy, but it is a thin veil. The imposition may be responsible for the fact that recently there has been some recrudescence of polygamy among Lutherans, with eighty cases reported in his old district. Kate District Report, 1967, Mission Archives Neuendettelsau.

38. Wyllie 1951: 141 and passim. The Papua Ekalesia voted in 1965 to baptize bigamists (Church Assembly Minutes, pp. 5, 57) and the Unevangelized Fields Mission made the same decision at an earlier date (Wyllie 1951: 143–44). A surprising thing is that the Roman Catholics on the Papuan coast had allowed for this during their very early years but then moved away from it to the standard Catholic position when the more rigorous Bishop de Boismenu took charge in 1908. Later they went back to their earlier stand in 1929. Dupeyrat 1935: 369–70. Goyau 1938: 109. For the usual monogamist stand of the churches, see Davidson 1967: 119: *Statement of Doctrine of the Samoan Church* 1958: 12; Luxton 1955: 103; Hilliard 1966: 509; Sharp 1917; 19; Pilhofer 1961: vol. 1:229–31; Territory of Papua and New Guinea 1947: 3; *Steyler Missionsbote* 61 (1933–34): 276.

39. "Annual Report of Ysabel District, 1932," Public Record Office, London. Cf. Beaglehole 1957 for the regulative and investigatory activities of deacons in the Cook Islands.

40. H. E. Maude, General Report of the Island of Beru, Aug. 22, 1930. In Gilbert and Ellice Islands Administration Reports, Public Record Office, London.

41. Darmancier 1965: 39. V. Schultze, "Decennial Report on Women's Work in German Samoa, 1900–1910," Congregational Church Archives, Apia. The Wallis figures are recent but the situation in the early part of the century would have been no stricter. Cf. Le Cadre to Bousquet, Jan. 19, 1908 (S.P.F. Archives, Paris), reporting how Marquesan Catholics lived in concubinage and adultery.

42. Samoan Church (LMS) 1958: 12–13.

43. *Sex, Marriage and the Family in the Pacific,* 1969.

44. Elizabeth Baldwin to E. F. Bell, April 4, 1913. American Board Archives, ABC: 19.4, vol. 18, document 15.

45. Braam 1936:244–45.

46. *Not in Vain,* December 1965: 2.

47. In some areas of Vanuatu the opposition was not so persistent; the rule regarding church membership fell into abeyance. This was because Vanuatu Presbyterian practices were very largely determined by the convictions of the local missionary, and certain missionaries were not strong proponents of the church's stand. Morpeth Conference, Commission II Report, p. 13. Michelsen 1934: 113. Gunn 1924: 121–22.

48. Burton 1949: 46. District Synod Minutes, 1918, Methodist Archives, Suva. Methodist Church of Australasia 1907: 5. Heighway 1932: 101.

49. As, for example, the LMS In Samoa, the Gilberts, and the Cooks; the American Board in Micronesia; and the Methodists in Tonga and Fiji (though the few Fijians who held government permits for liquor were excepted; *Fiji Times,* April 25, 1906).

The Tahitian Protestants regarded themselves as taking this stand, though their official discipline called for suspension from membership only of those who drank often. *Ture Haapaoraa na te mau Ekalesia Tahiti* 1882: 16.

50. *Missionary Herald* 96 (April 1900): 147–48. Burnett 1911: 51. Lenwood 1925: 14. Morpeth Conference, Commission 10 Report, p. 12. Hanneman 1942: 26. Beaglehole 1957: 107. Lundsgaarde 1966: 202. Scarr 1967: 190–91.

51. Fiji District Synod Minutes, 1920: 20. "Petition to the Right Honorable Sir Philip Culnliffe Lister, K.B.E., M.C., M.P., Secretary of State for the Colonies, 8 January 1932." Methodist Mission Archives, Sydney. In New Guinea the Methodists made a similar request for prohibition in 1924 and 1925. New Britain District Synod Minutes, 1925: 14. Many times the Fiji Methodists also made strong representations to the government in favor of stricter enforcement of the existing ban against liquor for islanders.

52. Lubach 1929: 24. *Journal de la Société des Océanistes* 19 (1963): 32–33. G. Brunel, "Notes présentées au comité des Missions de Paris," November 1901, Archives, Société des Missions Evangélique de Paris.

53. Adams 1930: 467. Cf. Burnett 1911: 28–29.

54. Leenhardt 1922: 112 and passim. Delord, 1905: 14. *Journal des Missions Evangéliques* 124 (1949): 7–12.

55. Samoa and Tonga never had discriminatory provisions in their laws but they had forbidden alcohol to all except those who secured government permits. Consequently they did not change their basic statutes, but issued permits on a wider basis than they had previously.

56. Only a few of the churches have maintained abstinence from alcohol as a rule for membership. The Samoan Methodists, the New Caledonian Evangelicals, and the South Sea Evangelical Church are the main ones of this type. Seventh-day Adventists and Mormons have always been strict on alcohol and continue to be.

57. Hilliard 1966: 288.

58. Luke 1962: 65.

59. Statement of Resident Commissioner, Sept. 12, 1903, in Vicariate Apostolique des Iles Gilberts. Memorandum . . . 1904. Catholic Archives, Tarawa. David 1899: 199. American Board of Commissioners for Foreign Missions, *Report* 1900: 131.

60. *Ture Haapaoraa na te mau Ekalesia Tahiti* 1882: 16. This constitution continued in effect until 1972.

61. C. O. Lelean to William Green, Feb. 17, 1938. Methodist Archives, Suva. Cf. Report of Commission to Fiji, August 1938, Methodist Mission Archives, Sydney, where further action was called for because the limitation to Indian pictures was not being observed.

62. Herrera 1921–22: 396.

63. *Horizons Blancs,* July 1964, p. 71.

64. Samoa District Committee of LMS October 1928, Congregational Church Archives, Apia. W. G. Murphy in Cook Islands Decennial Report, 1941–51, addendum; G. E. Phillips, LMS secretary, to H. Bond James in Rarotonga, March 2, 1931; Emlyn Jones of Gilbert Islands, Report for 1959; all three in Council for World Mission Archives, London. W. Price, quoted in Van Dusen 1945: 77.

7

The Beginnings of Church Independence

It is by now abundantly evident that during the first half of the twentieth century the Pacific churches had their own character and a distinctive life, which they themselves had created. They had their own understanding of the Christian faith and their own moral codes, which though they were derived from missionary teaching were much influenced by local attitudes in the way they were carried out. In these respects the churches had much of what is meant by the word "independence." They were largely living their own life in their own way.

They were also independent in another significant way—they were for the most part financially self-supporting. In this respect they differed from the majority of the churches of Asia and Africa. On those continents the usual pattern was for foreign missions to provide the financial support for the local churches, and the twentieth century has seen a long struggle by the churches to break away from that enervating arrangement. In the Pacific such a struggle was normally unnecessary because the local churches were self-supporting from the start. They constructed their own church buildings and provided the salaries for their pastors. In most islands, to be sure, the pastors grew their own food, so there was no need for much salary. But what was needed, the local people provided. In Samoa and a few other places people even provided the food, bringing it from their own gardens so the pastor would be relieved from gardening work.

There were some important exceptions to this general picture of self-support. The biggest exception was the Roman Catholic church. It was not the custom of Roman Catholic parishioners to give to the church. The priests were normally foreigners who provided for their own financial needs, either through gifts from abroad or through local plantations and industries. The catechists, who served under the priests and were the people usually in charge of the local churches, raised their own food, as most Protestant ministers did, and received whatever they needed beyond that from the foreign missionaries. They were usually poorer than the Protestant pastors. Sometimes all they received was a new loincloth each year and a little kerosene and some tools, given them by the missionary. In consequence their dependence on outside sources was not great.

The Anglicans also, in Papua and the Solomons, and the Seventh-day Adventists, wherever they worked, likewise provided support from outside. But of the other churches, most were locally self-supporting from the start and the remainder became so without difficulty. Self-supporting from the start were the Lutherans, the South Sea Evangelical Mission, the French Reformed, and the London Missionary Society (except in Papua where the early use of Polynesian missionaries as pastors set a continuing pattern of outside support). Of the remaining churches, the Presbyterians had been largely self-supporting from early days and became completely so during the first years of the twentieth century. The Methodists made the transition gradually, dropping all foreign help for their churches in Tonga in 1875, in Samoa by 1915 and Fiji by the late 1920s, in New Britain by 1937, and in Papua and the Solomons after 1950. The American Board in Micronesia continued to give help for a long time, but by 1926 all its churches in the Marshall Islands were self-supporting and the churches in the Carolines became so gradually after the Japanese withdrew, along with their subsidies, in 1945. Thus in finances as well as in way of life and faith, most though not all Pacific churches could be said to be independent in the period before World War II.[1]

Still, in the most obvious sense these churches were not independent. Foreign missionaries held the positions of overall leadership and decision-making and, in many places, the church structure was constitutionally subordinate to a mission structure. A break from that situation had to be made if the churches were going to be recognizably independent.

Three countries took the lead in making this break. They were Tonga, Samoa and Fiji, the three lands which were most often the spearhead for new developments in the Pacific. In these islands alone did action for independence take place before World War II. Elsewhere such action came after the war (and hence belongs in a later chapter).

Tonga

Tonga was the pioneer of church independence, as it was of national independence. It was the one country in the Pacific to maintain at least a nominal freedom from colonial rule all through the nineteenth and twentieth centuries. It was also the first country to establish a much more than nominal independence for its church. The ecclesiastical independence began, as we have already had occasion to note, in 1885 when King George Tupou I, and his prime minister, the ex-missionary Shirley Baker, set up the Free Church of Tonga in opposition to the Wesleyan missionaries from Australia and gathered most of the people of the country into their new fold. This may be claimed as the first and almost the only occasion when Pacific islanders revolted against foreign tutelage in the church and established their own independent church structure. But the truth is not quite as simple as that. The Tongans were impelled to this action by a former missionary who had a grudge against some of his previous colleagues and it is doubtful whether without his instigation the Free Church would have come into being. The king had, indeed, a desire for greater independence of the church from Ausralian controls. He was angered by the decision of the Australian church, against his express wish, to recall Shirley Baker at a time when Baker was still a missionary, and the refusal of that church to recall Baker's rival, J. E. Moulton, when the king demanded he be withdrawn. In his anger at the Australian church's decision against Baker, he demanded that Tonga become a financially independent district of the Australian church equal with the other districts of Australian Methodism. This wish was granted by Australia and the king expressed his satisfaction. But it was Baker who was not satisfied, who wanted to strike back at those who censured him. He created a new, totally independent church, and he took king and country with him.[2]

The result was a truly "Free Church." It worked entirely without reference to outside churches and supported its own ministry and erected its own buildings. The only trace of foreign influence in this church was the fact that it used a former Methodist missionary, Jabez Watkin, as its president.

In 1924, as we have seen, a union was brought about between the national church and the small remnant of Wesleyans faithful to the missionaries. Two years later the newly united church, the Free Wesleyan Church as it was named, associated itself with the General Conference of the Methodist Church of Australasia. This had been agreed to at the time of reunion and was probably the kind of association that the old king had had in mind at the beginning. The Tongan church entered the General Conference as an autonomous and equal member with the Methodist churches of the various states of Australia. The General Conference had jurisdiction over its members only in terms of doctrine and ministerial training. So the subordination was minimal.

It was, however a small backward step in terms of church independence. There were also, as limitations on independence, the fact that the theological education of the Tongan church was handled by foreign missionaries and that the church continually elected a foreign missionary as its president. The foreign missionaries were, until 1934, all paid for by Tongan funds, for this church was completely self-supporting, as its predecessor had been, so there was no financial dependence. After 1934 Australia paid the salaries of the missionaries it sent in order to make them a gift rather than a burden for the Tongan church, but since they were few, the dependence they represented was still not great.[3] Also, the succession of missionary presidents did finally come to an end. The Methodist Mission Board in Sydney in the 1950s began pressing for an end to these foreign presidencies but the Tongans continued to prefer them until finally, in 1971, they felt that they were ready for their own leader and elected Sione 'Amanaki Havea as president.

Six years later, in 1977, Tonga dropped out of the General Conference in Australia. More precisely, the General Conference dropped out of existence, so Tonga could no longer be part of it. The Methodists in Australia decided at that time to join with the Australian Presbyterians and Congregationalists in organizing a new national body called the Uniting Church of Australia. Churches in other countries could not very well participate in such a national union. So Tongan Methodism ceased to be a part of any outside General Conference and became fully and completely an independent church. Thus the situation of the Free Church prior to 1924 was restored, although now Australian missionaries continued to come at Tongan request to help with particular parts of the church's work.

Between 1924 and 1977 the only fully independent churches were the two splinter groups made up of those who refused to go into the union, namely, the Free Church of Tonga and the Church of Tonga. They were the first churches in the Pacific to operate without missionary leadership, for the old national church, known also as the Free Church, still had Watkin as its head. The two smaller churches, after a brief trial of foreign leadership, elected members of their own ministry as their leaders.

These two churches, it must be admitted, did not give an encouraging picture of what could be done by an independent church. There was financial irresponsibility at the highest level. Theological education was almost non-existent, and men were often ordained on the basis of favoritism or financial contributions rather than on the basis of competence. They were very conservative in matters of liturgy, doctrine, and dress, less prepared to undertake indigenizing innovations than their foreign-related counterparts were. They showed no vigorous outreach into the society around them or into foreign realms. In short, in those matters where the missionaries feared an indigenously led church would be deficient, that is, in financial responsibility and theological education, they were indeed deficient, and in those matters where an independent church might have been expected to be outstanding, that is, in fresh thought and action along indigenous lines, in adaptation to indigenous forms of worship and dress, and in dynamic outreach into the wider society and the world, they were notably lacking.[4] They proved, to be sure, that independent churches could survive and hold their members through many vicissitudes, but their poor performance beyond mere survival placed a question and challenge before the other churches of the Pacific as they came to independence.

The Tongan experience cannot serve as an adequate guide to the understanding of the forces that led to church independence in the Pacific, because the factors at play there were often such personal ones, and independence came early, far ahead of other countries, when the churches had not had time to develop the various sides of their life. There is more understanding to be gained from the other two pioneering territories, Samoa and Fiji.

Samoa

In Samoa the basic structure for an independent national church organization began very early in the major church, that of the LMS. In the 1860s the LMS directors in London began to press for the formation of independent congregations. Most missionaries did not accept this, but some of the younger ones sided with London and finally secured agreement to ordain a number of pastor-teachers. Once this was conceded to some, the others demanded it too, and in 1875 the missionaries gave in to this demand.[5] In that same year, 1875, the missionaries first called together a general assembly of all the pastors to give advice on church matters. The assembly was named, in Samoan, Fono Tele ("big meeting"), and it gradually assumed powers of decision as well as of advice. It took responsibility for ordination and for the settlement of difficulties referred to it from the districts. From 1893 laity were added to its membership. After German rule was established in the country at the end of the century, this assembly became the only body that had something of the nature of a national congress. It met for three weeks every May, and its sessions were the high point of church life, having the character of religious conventions and festivals as well as of deliberative assemblies. So the first steps toward church independence had been taken. But the major power in the church continued to lie, not with this assembly but with the Samoa District Committee made up of the foreign missionaries.

The pressure for giving more power to the Samoans came during the early part of the twentieth century from the directors of the London Missionary Society in England. The LMS missionaries in Samoa exerted little pressure in this direction, and the Samoans themselves were largely passive on the matter. The directors in London clearly shared the long-established policies of the major British missions, which called for turning power over to the indigenous church and moving the missionaries on to new areas. They wrote in these terms to Samoa. The policy had been put into effect in a limited way by the American Congregationalists in Hawaii in 1865, and since the LMS represented the English Congregationalists they could not but be aware of that. Furthermore, there was a shortage of funds in the LMS, which made a reduction in its commitments desirable.[6]

The LMS missionaries in Samoa obviously did not hold such strong convictions about the importance of turning over power. The missionaries were usually reluctant to institute the changes that London proposed. They carried through the changes but with certain caveats. The situation never arose of the missionaries proposing changes that the directors in London regarded as risky and in connection with which they advised caution. Things were nearly always the other way around, with London suggesting transfers of power and the missionaries issuing warnings. They "received with anxiety" the proposal that missionaries be decreased in number and Samoans be made district superintendents. They were convinced that they must not give control of funds or of educational work to Samoans, although London was suggesting limited moves in that direction. Such action "would be the ruin" of their "splendid work" in Samoa. They also feared that the overweening influence of the chiefs might destroy the freedom and spirituality of the church.[7]

It was hard to tell at that time whether the LMS saw the real possibilities for advance while the missionaries were unable to rise above the concern for their own power and position or whether the LMS was visionary and unrealistic and the missionaries had their feet firmly on the Samoan ground and knew what was feasible. The only experiment they could both look to was the Free

Church of Tonga, which the missionaries, with some justice, regarded as a disappointment in its financial and institutional operations.[8] The Hawaiian experiment provided no model because it had never gone very far in turning over control to the Hawaiians even though the American mission board had terminated its connection. The American missionaries who stayed on as pastors continued to be in charge.

Despite the missionaries' hesitations, Samoa did move and the missionaries participated fully in the changes that were adopted. On London's urging the church was given its first constitution. The congregations, which had been grouped together only in large districts supervised by missionaries, were now associated together in subdistricts established in 1906. On the suggestion of a missionary, these subdistricts proceeded to elect elder pastors, who formed a national council called the Au Toeaina. This body gave prior consideration and advice on all matters coming before the General Assembly and gradually it became the weightiest body of the church. Its members supervised the work of pastors in their subdistricts and recommended appointments and dismissals. They became very much like bishops and began to be seen as successors to the first apostles.[9] Ten years later London sent out a deputation, which recommended that Samoa should raise all the funds necessary for its own churches and schools and even for the maintenance of the missionaries sent to it. This challenge to complete self-support was accepted by the Samoans and immediately met, so that Samoa became the only country in the world where the foreign missionaries were entirely supported by local funds. If any church could have been said to have "earned" the right to complete self-government it was the church of Samoa. But when, at the same time, the LMS proposed that Samoans be associated with missionaries in the management of all Christian institutions including the central schools, the missionaries rejected the proposal as premature. The Samoan church representatives agreed with the rejection—as they had agreed in rejecting the suggestion that Samoans be put in charge of some large districts supervised by the missionaries.[10]

The attitude of the Samoans through all this is surprising. Evidently they had little desire to advance in self-government in the church and were willing to let the missionaries continue to dominate. Nationalism had not yet developed among them to such an extent as to make the foreign control seem onerous. But the situation changed rapidly during the 1920s. Then, as we have seen, the nationalist movement swept over the country and with it a different atmosphere appeared in the church. The missionaries were stunned by the change and remarked on how the happy and cooperative atmosphere of the past had been replaced by "a new spirit of opposition."[11] They were surprised that Samoans began to challenge their financial decisions and to claim that since they paid for the missionaries they should also have a part in deciding what the missionaries should do. The deputation of 1916, which had originally proposed local support of the missionaries, had expected just this result, so the surprise was scarcely justified.[12]

When the confrontation with the Mau movement led to the impasse between missionaries and Samoans that we have already noted, it became clear to London that the missionaries' power would have to be reduced. The board sent out a deputation from England in 1928, which recommended that the organization of the missionaries, the Samoa District Committee, which had been the final locus of decision since 1836, should cease to exist. Its final meeting was held in November 1928. In its place was created a Mission Council made up of all the missionaries and a number of Samoans—at first a minority but within a few years a decided majority.[13] The institutions of the church, including all the schools, were put under the control of this body. So was the work of the missionaries.[14] A Samoan treasurer was appointed to handle funds with the European treasurer, and capable Samoans were regularly found for this work.[15] One point of past missionary unhappiness was met by the provision that the elder pastors would no longer be elected for life, as they had been under the constitution of 1906, but for five-year terms. The missionaries had been increasingly unhappy at the growing power of these leaders in their own subdistricts and in the church at large.[16]

The crisis of 1928 resulted in the creation of an almost fully self-governing church in Samoa at about the same time that the almost fully self-governing Free Wesleyan church was set up in Tonga. The gradual increase in the proportion of Samoans on the Mission Council and the eventual absorption of that body in 1942 as an executive committee of the General Assembly completed the process.[17]

The provision of full financial support for foreign missionaries was increasingly seen as a heavy obligation. It was known as the London Bill and was the source of some hard feelings in the church. As a result the LMS took the initiative in 1961 to change this arrangement with Samoa. Whatever funds were sent to London were to be free-will offerings to the society, not a prearranged sum for the payment of missionaries. This gave the Samoan church a much greater sense of freedom in its finances. At the same time the decision was made to draw up a new constitution, the constitution of 1962, which incorporated the changes made over the years and which finally dropped the foreign mission connection from the name of the church. What had been originally the "LMS" and then the "Samoan Church (LMS)" became the "Congregational Christian Church in Samoa." Even this change was made only after ten years of urging by London.[18]

One may say that the whole constitutional development toward self-government was the work of the London Missionary Society, rather than of the missionaries or the Samoans. The troubles of 1928 offer some exception to this generalization, but even they showed only particular complaints from the Samoans and intransigence from the missionaries. The efforts from London proposed and produced a move toward self-government out of that crisis.

With regard to Samoan Methodism it must suffice here to say that in broad outline it followed the developments in Fiji (see below). Synods that included indigenous ministers began in the first year of the twentieth century, at the

same time they were starting in Fiji. The church became financially independent, paying even the salaries of its Australian missionaries from 1915 till
1934. Control of the funds, however, was kept in the hands of the missionaries for longer here than in Fiji or in the Samoan LMS. An autonomous
Annual Conference was established in 1964, the same year as in Fiji. And the
final break from Australia's General Conference came at the same time as
Fiji's.

Fiji

The third of the pioneers of independence was Fiji. The basic forces in
operation in Fiji were similar to those in Samoa, but the structures in which
they operated were different, since the Fijian church was Methodist. The
Methodist system did not provide for a large, indigenous body such as the
Samoan General Assembly to which increasing powers could be transferred
from the mission. Rather, there was a smaller group in control, the District
Synod, made up originally of missionaries, but on which Fijians could gain
increasing numbers of seats until they gradually assumed control. At first—
1863—the Fijian clergy were allowed only to form a group to give advice to
the District Synod. Then later, in 1875, there was a debate in the mission as to
whether or not the indigenous ministers should be made members of the
synod, as had just been done in Tonga. The decision was to allow one indigenous minister from each circuit to join the ministerial session of the synod
where matters of doctrine and ministerial training and discipline were considered, but not the main session of the synod, known as the representative or
financial session, where the main business was transacted. With the beginning of the twentieth century it was time to give the Fijians a greater part in
their own church, and the move to do so came from the mission headquarters
in Sydney.

At that time George Brown, the most famous Methodist missionary leader
of the Pacific, was rounding out his career by serving as the general secretary
for Australian Methodist missions. In 1901 he proposed fundamental
changes for the Fiji District. This was not because any dissatisfaction about
existing constitutional arrangements was being expressed by the Fijians, for
while there had been some agitation for higher salaries and status on the part
of Fijian ministers, there was little or no pressure for greater independence.[19]
But Brown was very much aware of what had happened in Tonga twenty
years earlier and he wanted to remove the grounds for any such explosion in
Fiji. Five years later, in fact, there did appear a small separatist church in
Nadroga and also even a "Free Church," modeled on that of Tonga and using
a Tongan minister, in one of the Lau islands. Nothing came of these movements but Brown believed they were evidence of the need for a greater voice
for chiefs and people in the church.[20]

One of the chief complaints in Tonga had been about the sending of church
collections to Sydney. This was still the practice in Fiji in regard to the collec-

tions made once a year for work above the parish level. Brown suggested that only one-half of this money be sent to Sydney and that it be used only for the payment of the Australian missionaries working in Fiji. It would cover about one-third of the cost of those missionaries. The other half should be kept in Fiji and used for the operating costs of the church there. This proposal was readily accepted by the Australian authorities and the Fiji District in 1902, although later (1923) it was modified so that most of the money was kept in Fiji and whatever went to Sydney was used as support for missions in other lands rather than as support for the Australians in Fiji. Local support for foreign missionaries proved to be a policy susceptible to the same problems in Fiji that it had been in Samoa—the invidious comparison with the lower level of local church salaries and the feeling of a burden placed on the church from abroad—so it was not an arrangement that endured in either country.[21]

Brown's other proposal created more of a storm. His suggestion was that the Fijian ministers already in the ministerial session of synod should now enter the financial session and also that representative laity be included in those sessions. The ministers would equal the number of missionaries; the laity would produce a heavy islander majority. This was accepted by the General Conference in Australia, but the missionaries, who saw that they would be completely outvoted by this group, raised a great protest. They were willing to accept the ministers but not the laity. A group of younger men, including John Burton, C. O. Lelean, and others who later distinguished themselves, protested that the Fijians were not experienced enough in financial matters to be given this power. Ten out of the sixteen missionaries asked to be withdrawn from Fiji because they could not conscientiously cooperate with the new constitution.[22] The result was that the provision in the new constitution for lay representation was held up. Some of the older missionaries, however, warned against the dangers inherent in the situation as it was then developing. Australia was seen as offering something to the Fijians that the missionaries were blocking. A commission was sent from Sydney to explore the terrain. It met with a group of Fijian ministers who strongly supported the proposed inclusion of the laity. Finally the missionaries gave in after the 1907 General Conference in Australia reaffirmed its decision for the new constitution. But they still expressed misgivings and declined "to take any responsibility whatsoever for any disastrous results which may follow."[23]

No disastrous results followed. In fact, the financial experience gained in the District Synod led on, after a period of years, to the establishment of financial independence in the circuits, the groups of churches which made up the district. The first circuit to try this got into trouble, but thereafter it was handled successfully and gave great satisfaction to the Fijian church. In the 1930s some Fijian ministers began to be put in charge of the circuits.[24]

The progress toward independence did receive one serious setback as a result of the mission work among the Indians. The Indians and the workers among them wanted their own synod and after much delay and some resistance from the Fijians, it was finally agreed in 1926 to have two parallel synods, one Indian and one Fijian, with a third, European Synod, over them both. The arrangement was cumbersome and designed to arouse resentment, for when the Fijian Synod, which had become accustomed to making decisions, had to see those decisions reviewed by the Europeans and possibly delayed or set aside by them, or by the Mission Board in Australia as happened with the plans for a girls' school in 1933, the Fijian chiefs and ministers felt great shame and loss of authority.[25] Here was one source for Fijian desire for church independence.

Another source was among some of the more individualistic, entrepreneurial Fijians who were appearing on the scene. A group called the Toko Farmers, who were of this type, took the lead in asking for an independent church. The Fijian Synod was far from independent. It was not only subordinate to the European Synod, but that body in turn was subordinate to the New South Wales Annual Conference. Fiji Methodism had been a district of that conference from its earliest days and the question of its becoming a conference in its own right was now raised by the Toko Farmers. They were men who came from the village of Toko in Ba District where an unusual missionary, A. D. Lelean, had started some new experiments. Lelean was a charismatic figure and it was said that he had more influence on the people than government or business did. He had little carefulness in financial matters and finally left Fiji after only about five years in the field because of the financial confusion of his work. He later became noted for his powers as a healer, serving a parish church in Australia. But in Fiji his great effort was to get the Fijians into individual agricultural enterprises, particularly sugarcane production, and at Toko a group of young men began working in this way under the leadership of the chief, Ratu Nacaniele Rawaidramu.

In 1936 the Toko Farmers commenced collecting 100 whale teeth and £500 for a purpose that they said they would not announce for five years, but which was evidently related to church independence. In 1941 they appeared before the Fijian Synod and presented 118 whale teeth and the full amount of the money. The purpose they then announced was to make Fijian Methodism an autonomous conference instead of a district of the New South Wales Conference. The whale teeth were to be ceremonially presented to the chiefs of Fiji in order to win their support. According to immemorial custom the acceptance of a whale tooth by a chief bound him to support the cause of the donor. The money was to be used to help launch the new conference on its way.[26]

The synod was far from ready for such a proposal. The rank and file of Fijian Methodists had little interest in independence and the senior ministers who led the synod were afraid of any loss of support from Autralia and nervous about the possibility of having to work with the Indians if they were independent. The Toko Farmers' offering was accepted for possible future use but nothing further was done.[27]

Some missionaries, however, were convinced that moves toward a separate conference should be made. Also in the next few years shortages of foreign personnel due to the war made clear the need to advance local leadership.[28]

They worked to convince those Fijians who had doubts, and in 1944 an important step was taken. The missionaries in a venture of faith quite contrary to the attitudes of 1907 voted in favor of abolishing the European Synod and placing the control of their work fully in the hands of the local bodies. A new United Synod made up of the elected representatives of the Indian and Fijian synods was created. Principal church matters were to be handled in the separate synods; educational and public issues were to be handled in the united body and it was hoped that the two groups would thus learn to work together effectively. At the same time Fijians were put in charge of more circuits, which were reduced to a manageable size.[29]

The Toko Farmers were still concerned and they sent a letter and appeared before the synod to press their cause. Their original leader died and his successors were not always clear on the exact formulation of their cause, saying to the synod simply that it was whatever was written in the original appeal. But their devotion did not flag. The synod delayed the matter, however, saying that time would be needed to grow toward independence and though it made a request for independence in 1950 it assumed that five to fifteen years would be needed to reach that state.[30]

So matters were allowed to stand, and although missionaries spoke about fuller autonomy no further steps were taken. The missionary chairman of the synod said that when he pushed for independence he felt he was whipping a dead horse because of Fijian indifference. Fear among Fijians of the growing power of Indians in the land was largely responsible for their doubts about an independent church in which the two communities would be united. The Mission Board in Australia, however, was not willing to allow the drift and, as it had been at the beginning of the century, so again it became the prime force for change. In 1958 it called upon Fiji to work out a plan for independence. A year later it expressed disappointment at the lack of progress and in 1960 sent its general secretary to visit the islands and push the matter. He gave categorical assurances that there would be no reduction in Australian assistance because of independence. The missionary chairman of the United Synod worked with him in persuading the people. As a result of this pressure, in 1960 the United Synod voted to establish a Fiji Conference as an autonomous church, yet also a member of the General Conference of the Methodist Church of Australasia. The time had come at last to distribute the whale teeth to the chiefs in order to receive their approval of the new autonomy. This was done and in 1964 the conference was inaugurated. At the suggestion of the former missionary chairman a Fijian, Setareki Tuilovoni, was elected the first president.[31]

The fact that the Fiji Conference continued to be a member of the General Conference in Australia did not mean any important limitation on Fijian autonomy. The General Conference, as we have noted in the case of Tonga, met only quadrennially and had power over its constituent bodies only in matters of doctrine and ministerial training. The time soon came, however, when even this last official link was severed. When the Methodist Church in

Australia decided to join in the newly organized Uniting Church it was clear that the Methodists of Fiji, like those of Tonga, would have to go their own way. So in 1977, when the General Conference ceased to exist, Fiji Methodism became completely independent. The Australians continued to send and maintain missionary helpers, but this fraternal relationship carried no limitations on autonomy.

Such has been the story of church independence in Tonga, Samoa, and Fiji. These were the only areas in the Pacific where there was any considerable element of struggle in the achievement of independence. This is because their independence was largely achieved in the period before World War II, although obviously the completion of Fiji's story has taken us into a later time. In those earlier years there was some resistance on the part of the missionaries who held the controls and hence there was an element of struggle. In the later years that resistance disappeared and independence then swept in easily. This was one of the consequences of the radical changes in Pacific life and missionary attitude that followed World War II. The war and its aftermath must, therefore, first be examined.

NOTES

1. Reports on the extent of financial self-support in the various Protestant churches may be found in the following sources. For the Anglicans, in McCall 1957: 15, in Tippett 1967: 90–91, and in Tomlin 1951:110. For the churches connected with the London Missionary Society, in the minutes of the Islands Committee of the Society, June 25, 1945, p. 26 (Council for World Mission Archives, London); in Lenwood 1925: 18, 21, and in *Responsibility in New Guinea* 1965: 64, and Challis 1940: 11. For the South Sea Evangelical Mission, in Hogbin 1939: 178. For the churches connected with the French Reformed missions, in Allégret 1928: Part 2: 21. For the New Hebrides Presbyterians, in Nottage 1940: 17, and in letter from F. H. L. Paton to John Burton printed in Methodist Church of Australasia 1923: 27. For the various Methodist areas in the *Missionary Review* 35, no. 10 (April 5, 1926): 3; in Methodist Missionary Society of Australasia, Report for 1908: 22; in Thornley 1979: 264, 270; in Williams 1972:145; in Methodist Church of Australasia, 1907: 8; in New Guinea District Methodist Church, Synod Minutes 1925: 14; in New Guinea District Methodist Church, Chairman's Report, 1936; and in Papua District Methodist Church, Chairman's Report, 1939 (Methodist Mission Archives, Sydney). For the churches related to the American Board in Micronesia, in *Missionary Herald* 120, no. 8 (August 1924): 346, and in the report "Regarding American Board Work in the Marshall Islands," Dec. 7, 1926, ABC: 19.4, vol. 19 (American Board Archives, Harvard University). The Catholic catechists in Fiji and New Caledonia have, in recent years, served as volunteers, receiving no payment from the mission or from their congregations. Snijders 1971: 25.

2. Wood 1975: vol. 1: 167.

3. Wood 1975: vol. 1: 229.

4. For fuller treatment, see Forman 1978: 15–19. Ministerial salaries in these churches have been extremely low, requiring much sacrifice by the ministers. Mafi 1978.

5. Gilson 1970: 134–135.

6. R. Wardlaw Thompson to J. W. Hills, June 17, 1905, September 30, 1905. Council for World Mission Archives, London.

7. Samoa District Committee Minutes, May 1905: 514–18. Congregational Church Archives, Apia. James E. Newell to R. Wardlaw Thompson, February 12, 1909; March 12, 1909; June 3, 1907. R. W. Thompson to J. W. Hills, March 4, 1909. Council on World Mission Archives, London. Viner et al. 1916: 84.

8. James E. Newell to R. Wardlaw Thompson, March 12, 1909. Council for World Mission Archives, London.

9. Falatoese 1961: 80–81. *Constitution of the Congregational Christian Church in Samoa,* 1962: 8, 35–36.

10. Goodall 1954: 370.

11. Samoa District Committee Minutes, May 1920: 173–174. Congregational Church Archives, Apia.

12. Viner et al. 1916: 82. Samoa District Committee Minutes, May 1927: 152–153. Church Archives, Apia. Samoa District Committee to V. A. Barradale, May 28, 1928. Council for World Mission Archives, London.

13. V. A. Barradale, May 28, 1928. Council for World Mission Archives, London. *Constitution of the Samoan Church,* 1928: 9. Goodall 1940: 28–30. It should be noted that Goodall 1954: 372 says that the Samoans had a slight majority even at the first, but this does not seem likely since the constitution provided for only five Samoans on the Mission Council and there were normally seven missionaries in the country. Later, however, as Goodall 1940: 28–30 mentions, the number on the council increased till by 1940 there was a total of eighteen, with all the additions being Samoan.

14. There was also a committee of missionaries to exercise discipline over their own number. *Constitution of the Samoan Church,* 1928: 21.

15. Morpeth Conference Commission 3:7.

16. Hough and Parker 1928: 12. Samoa District Committee to V. A. Barradale, May 28, 1928. Council for World Mission Archives, London. *Constitution of the Samoan Church*, 1928: 13. This provision, which satisfied the missionaries, was the only point at which the Samoans were dubious about the new constitution. In succeeding years the elders did not cease to dominate the scene. They controlled the ordination and discipline of all pastors and continued to press for life tenure for themselves. In this effort, however, they failed because of London's opposition. London Missionary Society, Southern Committee, Minutes Nov. 15, 1937: 27–28. *Constitution of the Congregational Christian Church in Samoa,* 1962: 35–36.

17. Goodall 1954: 372.

18. Craig 1961: 4–5.

19. Methodist Church of Australasia, 1907: 15, 18; 1923: 7. McHugh 1965: 45. Thornley 1979: 56–66.

20. Brown to A. J. Small, April 30, 1906; April 2, 1907; Oct. 11, 1907. B. Danks to Small, June 11, 1906; Aug. 7, 1906. Methodist Mission Archives, Suva.

21. Methodist Church of Australasia, 1917: 40; 1923: 7, 8, 10. *Missionary Review* 33, no. 4 (September 1923): 5.

22. Methodist Church of Australasia, 1907: 12–16. *Fiji Times,* April 7, 1906. B. Danks to A. J. Small, Aug. 7, 1906. Methodist Archives, Suva.

23. Methodist Church of Australasia, 1907: 10–15. Fiji District Synod Minutes, 1907. Methodist Mission Archives, Sydney.

24. Methodist Church of Australasia 1923: 9–10. Fiji District Chairman's Reports, 1934, 1935. Methodist Mission Archives, Sydney. Burton and Deane 1936: 92.

25. Methodist Church of Australasia, Report of General Secretary's Visit to Fiji, May 1933. Mission Board Minutes, Feb. 7–10, 1933. Methodist Mission Archives, Sydney. Tippett 1964: 30.

26. Fiji District Chairman's Report with Appendix, 1942. Methodist Mission Archives, Sydney. Correspondence between A. D. Lelean and District Chairman, 1931–35. Methodist Archives, Suva.

27. M. G. Wilmshurst, Fiji District Chairman, to Methodist Mission Board, Sept. 12, 1949. Methodist Mission Archives, Sydney. "Report to Mission Board on Discussions on an Independent Conference," Methodist Board of Missions Minutes, Feb. 7–10, 1950. Methodist Mission Archives, Sydney.

28. Fiji District Chairman's Report, 1942. Methodist Mission Archives, Sydney. Interview with A. R. Tippett, June 1967.

29. Tuilovoni 1948:78. A. R. Tippett in *Souvenir of the First Fiji Methodist Conference*, 1964: 30–31. *Missionary Review* 52, no. 9 (March 1944): 11. Interview with Stanley Cowled, Dec. 1966.

30. M. G. Wilmshurst, Fiji District Chairman, to Methodist Mission Board, Sept. 12, 1949. Methodist Mission Archives, Sydney. "Report to Mission Board on Discussions on an Independent Conference," Methodist Board of Missions Minutes, Feb. 7–10, 1950. Methodist Mission Archives, Sydney. Interview with Stanley Cowled, Dec. 1966.

31. Report of General Secretary's Visit to the Pacific Districts 1960. Methodist Mission Archives, Sydney. Fiji United Synod Minutes, July 23, 1960. Methodist Mission Archives, Sydney. Interviews with S. Tuilovoni, May 1967 and Douglas Fullerton, March 1968.

8
Church Identity Through War and Its Aftermath

The War Experience

The Pacific war of 1942–45 swept over the islands like a tropical hurricane, uprooting and destroying. In the islands toward the east and south it was an uprooting power. In those to the west and north it was also a destroying power.

Samoa, Tonga, Fiji, the New Hebrides, and New Caledonia were overwhelmed with foreign troops, mostly Americans. Tahiti was spared this inundation, but only at the price of opening Bora Bora in the Leeward Islands to it. In all these places the troops brought a new way of life—contacts with new ideas, quantities of easy money, a breakdown of social restrictions, and a weakening of social structures. In some places they also brought an awakening of anticolonialism. The considerable equality that black troops enjoyed with their white cohorts made many islanders resent the subordinate place in which they were held by colonial regimes. The excitement that came with new contacts, the wealth that poured in for the islanders to share, the new possibilities for employment and recreation that opened up made the war period seem like a golden time to many people who were remote from the combat zones.

The churches experienced many of these same problems and benefits. The widespread indifference to religion among the troops had some negative effect on the churches. But the increasing wealth brought a doubling of contributions to the churches in some places. The troops, it is true, took over a few mission institutions for their own use, but they usually paid well for them and also collected large amounts of money for church activities and church buildings. Their chaplains often led in the worship services of the island churches.[1] The breakdown in morality and in social structures troubled the church people greatly, but it also gave to their more experienced leaders a new sense of the importance of Christian faith and showed them that the faith could be distinguished from traditional island life.[2] Some of the new desire for emancipation from foreigners appeared also in the churches.[3] In these ways the war produced, even in the noncombat zones, some sense of the identity of the Pacific island church over against the Pacific island society and over against the foreign missions.

138

Change was much more pronounced in the churches of the combat zones. The most evident and most immediate change was the termination of the work of foreign missionaries. In the Gilberts one LMS missionary, the young Alfred Sadd, tried to stay but was soon apprehended and beheaded by the Japanese. The Roman Catholic bishop of the Gilberts was put in detention and the priest on Ocean Island executed, although other Catholic missionaries, being mostly nationals of nonenemy states, were allowed by the Japanese to continue at their posts.[4]

In the Japanese mandated Territory of Micronesia the Catholics did not fare so well. Though the missionaries were Spanish and hence from a friendly country, the mission was destroyed. Nine missionaries were executed and six others died from malnutrition and exposure; twenty-one survived, although unable to do their work.[5] On Guam the foreign priests were removed and only the two indigenous priests were allowed to remain, one of them being killed later.[6] In the Protestant churches the American missionaries were ordered out by their home office as war threatened and the German missionaries were interned and moved from place to place.

The Solomons were, like the Gilberts, partly in the combat zone and partly out of it. The South Sea Evangelical Mission's work, being mostly on Malaita, was largely unaffected by the fighting. The Melanesian Mission was in both zones, with its headquarters under Japanese occupation. Most of its missionaries stayed at their posts and its head, Bishop Baddeley, moving about the unoccupied area, became a central figure in encouraging the missionaries and the government personnel to stay at their posts. The Methodists were entirely in Japanese-occupied territory. All but four of their missionaries got away at the last minute in a small launch, which they were able to navigate despite many mishaps and uncertainties, all the way to Australia. The four who stayed behind worked secretly in different spots in the interiors of the islands. One was captured and died but the others were either evacuated or survived until the war ended.[7]

The Roman Catholics suffered heavier losses. In the south, on Guadalcanal, four of their missionaries were killed by the Japanese while they were trying to stay at their posts. In the north, in Bougainville and Buka, most of them moved up into the inaccessible mountains, as many of the islanders did, and tried to move about secretly and strengthen the churches. Food and clothing were scarce and a fourth or more of the population died. At one point ten of the missionaries who happened to be together set out to find their bishop, Thomas Wade, to get instructions on their work. After seven days of walking and inquiring they finally found him, weak from sickness, in a small village. He saw the uselessness of their position and some months later was able to get away with them on a submarine. Those who did not get away were mostly held in internment centers or survived with difficulty in the bush, but two died of deprivation and ten were killed through erratic decisions of individual Japanese commanders.[8]

In New Guinea, the south coast and its adjoining islands were untouched by combat, but the LMS and Methodist missionaries who covered that area left for a year or two, on government orders, which in the event proved quite unnecessary. The Anglican bishop, whose area of work was on the east coast where the danger was real, refused to obey the orders and kept his missionaries at their posts. But the Japanese overran his more northerly stations, from which the missionaries then tried to escape over the high, uncharted mountains. Seven of them, including both men and women, were captured and killed and an eighth was held in prison camp.[9]

Further north, in the mandated Territory of New Guinea, the Lutherans and Catholics experienced even greater losses. The Lutherans were in trouble as soon as the war started in Europe because Australia was fighting Germany and the whole staff of the Neuendettelsau Mission was German. A number of these missionaries had formed an organization to support the Nazis, even though the Nazi party would not allow missionaries to join it. Their oldest leader had praised Hitler as a gift of God and as one who had unveiled the machinations of the Jews.[10] These actions cast suspicion on the entire mission and consequently nearly all the German men were removed from their homes and work and were interned in Australia at the war's beginning. The American Lutheran Mission, centered around Madang, then stretched itself to the breaking point by sending its own personnel to try to cover the abandoned work of the Germans. Everyone was overloaded as a result. When war began in the Pacific some of these men and all of the women were evacuated by the authorities. The men who chose to stay behind to try to maintain their work were all either interned or killed by the Japanese.[11]

The Catholic missionaries likewise were rounded up by the Japanese and interned under hard conditions of heavy labor and little food. Some were killed. Their greatest losses, however, came on evacuation ships. When the Japanese began to be hard pressed by their enemies, they decided to evacuate all the interned missionaries from the Madang area on a ship going to Hollandia in western New Guinea. Most of these missionaries were Catholics, although some were the interned Lutherans. When a group of American planes attacked the ship, the missionaries were kept on deck presumably with the thought that their clerical habits would deter the attackers. They proved no deterrent, however, and in fifteen minutes sixty-one missionaries were dead or dying on the deck, including the Catholic leader, Bishop Wolf. Those who survived in Hollandia had further miseries to endure. The Catholics around Wewak were evacuated earlier on a ship bound for Rabaul and with them were taken some Protestant Liebenzell missionaries from Manus. Orders were received by the captain in a sealed packet delivered to him when the ship paused at Kavieng, to execute them all, so between Kavieng and Rabaul sixty-two men, women, and children in rapid succession were shot and their bodies thrown into the sea. All but eight of these were of the missionary party, including Bishop Loerks.[12]

If this last group had reached Rabaul, they would have joined the largest missionary internment center in the Pacific. Most of the missionary force of the great Rabaul Catholic Mission was concentrated in a large camp near Vunapope, the Catholic headquarters. Here nearly two hundred missionaries lived for three years eking out an existence from the soil. A few who remained outside were killed for one reason or another. In the camp five were killed in American bombings and twenty-four died for lack of food and medicine. Bishop Scharmach managed through a constant battle of wits with his captors to avoid even larger losses. The other main mission in the Rabaul area, the Methodist, suffered a greater disaster in relation to its size. The ten men of the mission sent the women and children to Australia when the Japanese were approaching and themselves withdrew into the hills, hoping to return and continue their work when the Japanese authority was firmly established. They were led by their chairman, the outstanding educationalist L. A. McArthur. When they returned, instead of being allowed to work they were all interned, and then put on a ship bound for Japan. The ship was torpedoed off the Philippines and thus the entire male staff of the mission was lost.[13]

So it was that all through the combat zone of the Pacific the churches were suddenly and completely deprived of the missionaries who had been their founders and leaders. This meant that church operations above the village level almost entirely ceased to exist in the combat zones, for those higher church structures had been in the hands of the missionaries. What was left was the local village church, and the continuation of Pacific Christianity in the areas of warfare depended on those village churches.

Village life generally was subjected to great pressures, which inevitably affected the local churches. The old structures of living together were weakened as people saw unbelievable new things happening in connection with the great military activity all around them and as they were drawn into totally new experiences. Tens of thousands of able-bodied men were conscripted to serve as burden-bearers and to assist the troops. This was done primarily by the Allied forces in Papua and by the Japanese in certain Micronesian islands such as Ponape and Nauru. Over one-third of the Nauruans died in the process. Papuan villages became mostly settlements of women and children. On Bougainville the coastal villages were subject to threats and demands from Japanese troops so the villagers, as we have noted, withdrew into the high mountains of the interior and suffered great losses. On New Britain in the latter part of the war it became almost impossible for the villagers to work in their gardens or to light fires to cook their food because of the danger of being spotted and bombed by the Allied planes. Common church life was well nigh impossible to maintain under such circumstances.

Furthermore, the Japanese at times forbade the holding of church meetings and sessions of the village schools taught by the pastors. In New Britain and in the Marshalls they confiscated prayerbooks and other Christian books and issued orders against the possession of such literature.[14] In Micronesia all the Catholic mission houses and churches were occupied by the military and fifty Protestant churches were destroyed in the fighting.[15] Quite a number of the Catholic catechists in the area around Rabaul were imprisoned, beaten, or killed. One young man there who used to slip into the internment camp to bring news to the missionaries and to take the sacrament from them to sick people, was imprisoned for engaging in religious activities when they had been forbidden and died two weeks later.[16] The great local leader of the Marshallese Protestants, Carl Heine, was killed for fear he might help the Americans, and his son and daughter-in-law vanished, presumably killed also.[17] On the Duke of York Islands the Japanese found traces of an American landing and suspected the Methodist church leaders of complicity. Fifty or more of them, including all twelve pastors, were taken away and never heard of again.

Under such pressures some village churches gave way entirely. The old religion reasserted itself with some of its ceremonies and dances, and the church services were discontinued on the assumption that the missionaries' capture or departure showed the weakness of the Christians' God. The village of Kaiapit in the Markham Valley of New Guinea was a well-known example of this, although it should be noted that a government officer there claimed the people of Kaiapit had never had any real interest in Christianity so that the change was more superficial than real.[18] North, along the New Guinea coast near Aitape, people began to put sacred carvings on their canoes again in order to secure the protection of the spirits when the protection of the Christian God was gone.[19] In Kiriwina churches fell into disrepair and the observance of Sunday declined as long as 25,000 troops there worked seven days a week. And along the east coast of Papua some of the people looted the abandoned Anglican mission stations and were hostile to the church leaders.[20]

The most serious disaffection took place on the island of Buka just north of Bougainville. There was a large concentration of Japanese soldiers on this island. They treated the people well and announced that from then on the people would be their own masters, freed from the European yoke. They restricted the operation of the churches, mostly Catholic on this island, and sponsored in their stead a cult of ancestor worship. Each village was encouraged to open a center where the ancestors would be venerated with special ceremonies taught by the Japanese. These were generally accepted and people began wearing around their necks little packets with ancestral remains. In the latter stages of the war a Japanese soldier was stationed in each village to make sure that the people provided regular food for the troops and to bring the people together morning and evening for ceremonies in honor of the dead.[21] In places such as this it began to appear that Christianity was largely an affair of the foreign missionaries, something that came and went with the missionary presence but had no deep roots in the life of the people. But it must be noted that places like this were exceptional.

The common response of the churches to the war situation throughout the combat zone was to keep village church life in operation even though there was no missionary leadership. As long as villages were not under actual attack the regular worship services were held and sometimes the village schools were also continued. In some places regular offerings were taken and kept intact until the end of the war. Things that the missionaries had left behind were carefully preserved and in certain places where missionaries had been killed they were buried and their graves lovingly tended. When villages were in danger and the people fled into the forests, it was more difficult to maintain religious life, but even here church operations were often maintained. One congregation on Choiseul continued to meet every week under a large tree from which they could look down on their old village and church, and they considered it a mark of divine providence that only once in the entire war period was there such a rainfall as to keep them from worshiping.

The forty-five indigenous Sisters of the Catholic church in New Britain held together even though the Japanese drove them out of their house and the bishop told them they could doff their habits and return to their individual villages. They stayed together without shelter in a banana grove until some students took pity on them and built them some houses. Then they continued to say their prayers together and to grow their own food until the end of the war. They also took food to the missionaries in the internment camp and were undeterred even though at one point they were all arrested and tortured.[22] Soldiers from the contending armies often had reason to be thankful to the Christian villagers who rescued them and cared for them after their airplanes had been shot down or their boats sunk. The most famous such rescued person was John F. Kennedy, who was helped by people from three different denominations.[23]

Strong local leadership emerged in many churches because of the difficulties and because of the absence of the former foreign leaders. In the Gilberts a local committee was formed to take over operations at the LMS headquarters island of Beru, a committee that tried to continue its responsibilities after the war and made difficulties for the LMS in the process. It was eventually abolished. On Choiseul two local catechists were put in charge of the Methodist work for the whole island and continued in their duties after the war. A number of Polynesian missionaries were at work for the Methodists in the Solomons and Papua, and they took over much responsibility when the white personnel left or were imprisoned.

An outstanding example was Isikeli Hau'ofa of Tonga who became the main power for continuing social organization on Misima Island off Papua. Nine hundred workers imported to the island to dig in its gold mines were abandoned by their fleeing white employers and they proceeded immediately to loot stores and homes. They began to fight against the local people for scarce food supplies and Hau'ofa stood between their battle lines all one night and succeeded in stopping the fight. Two remaining white miners who had guns then instituted a reign of terror, killing whom they willed and seizing great quantities of stores. Hau'ofa's efforts could not stop them. One of them, however, began to fear that someday government would return and so he loaded his goods on a boat and left the island. In a fog he suddenly found himself close to a Japanese ship, and was captured, tortured, and killed. The other terrorist then made peace with the people and Hau'ofa continued as the central person maintaining the common life.[24]

On the whole, then, the war experience, especially in the combat zones, served to strengthen the sense of identity and independence of the Pacific island churches. Though the people nearly everywhere were hoping for the missionaries to return, and welcomed them with joyous arms when they came, they had learned that they could get along without them. They had kept their churches in operation as their own institutions. They had found their own leadership strong enough to carry on and found it strengthened in the process. They had learned what strength there was in their faith and, as some of them said, had learned the truth of the psalmist's words, "What time I am afraid, I will trust in Thee."[25]

Postwar Developments

The aftermath of the war was a totally different time for the churches, especially in the combat zones. The missionaries came back in larger numbers than ever, foreign funds came forth in larger quantities and self-reliance was less necessary. Though the commitment of the missions was more explicitly to the development of the independent indigenous church, the immediate aftermath of the war brought an increase in dependency.

The reasons for the great new influx of outside resources were many. This period was one when foreign missions from Europe, America, and Australia were growing tremendously in every part of the world and reaching their peak in numbers. The war experience had shown how closely the world was tied together for good or for ill, and therefore those who wanted to strengthen the forces for good poured out their efforts on a worldwide scale as never before. Australia in particular had been made very aware of its close relationship to the Pacific islands as the bulwarks of its own security. Australians devoted themselves to foreign missions on a scale hitherto unknown. Over 2,000 Australian Protestants were soon working as foreign misssionaries and two-thirds of these were in the Pacific islands. Australian Catholics, who hitherto had been absorbed in establishing themselves in their own land, likewise turned their attention outward. At the end of the war they had 278 foreign missionaries, a decade later over six hundred, and two decades later over a thousand, of whom three-fourths were serving in Oceania.[26]

Missions from America also increased more rapidly than ever before and showed a new interest in Oceania. American troops had been heavily involved in the Pacific war, and this made American churches more aware of that part of the world. The American government also assumed much wider responsibilities in the area at the end of the war by taking over the Japanese mandated islands, and this stirred interest in Micronesia among both American Protestants and American Catholics.[27] The American Board, the Congregational body that had maintained a small and decreasing force in Micronesia during the prewar years came back with renewed commitment. Its workers gradually grew in numbers till there were 16 missionaries in the area instead of the three or four of the pre-war years.[28] They still divided the field with their German colleagues, the Liebenzell missionaries who had kept a precarious foothold in the islands during the war. Liebenzell worked in Belau, Yap, and the western half of Truk, while the American Board covered the islands to the east. The German mission, however, became more American. It developed a branch in America and gradually transferred most of the responsibility for its Micronesian work to its American office.[29]

On the Catholic side also Americans became involved in Micronesia. The Spanish Jesuit responsibilities were transferred by the Vatican to the American Jesuits for work in the Caroline and Marshall islands and to the American Capuchins for work in the Marianas. The old Spanish missionaries who had managed to survive the war lingered on to help, but they gradually retired or died and the Americans replaced them rapidly. Where in prewar years thirty-six Spanish missionaries had tried to maintain the work, there were eventually 180 American missionaries to handle it.[30] These missionaries were equipped, as one of the oldtimers said, with "facilities the like of which we Spaniards would have never dreamed."[31] The Jesuit mission encompassed all aspects of island life and was praised by many government officials as "the most productive, thoughtful, energetic, and modern-minded work" being done in the Territory.[32] The Jesuits were assisted by Maryknoll Sisters, another American order, and by the Mercedarian Sisters, who had come in previous years from Spain but who now also developed an organization in America and sent out missionaries from there.

With these enlarged missionary groups the church in Micronesia moved forward rapidly. The postwar years saw the last groups of non-Christians, mostly in the western Carolines and on isolated atolls, finally accept Christianity. Micronesia was an important area for foreign-mission expansion during this period.[33]

The other area into which new missionaries came in large numbers was New Guinea. Here the Australian work was largely concentrated, but many Americans came too. The reason lay not only in the new Australian and American awareness of New Guinea's geographic importance. It lay also in the discovery of great numbers of unknown people on that island. The interior highlands of New Guinea with their broad, heavily populated valleys, had been slightly explored just before the war, but they had not been opened up to the world until the postwar years and it was then that the new missionaries and new missions poured in.

In the prewar period missionaries had played a large part in the initial exploration of the highlands. As early as 1919 and 1920 Lutheran missionaries from the Neuendettelsau Mission began to penetrate the eastern highlands. They were the first white people ever seen there and the islanders often regarded them as spirits and sometimes thought their horses were their ancestors, since they carried the men on their backs as fathers carry their children.[34] In 1922 the first local evangelists began to work in the area. These evangelists were volunteers sent by the older Lutheran churches in the Kate-speaking district. They carried the explorations still further and it was their leader, Gape'nuo', who discovered the traditonal trade route leading across the mountains into the Purari basin. They settled in the newfound villages, planted their own gardens, learned the languages, entered into the common life, and then began to preach the gospel and to open schools. Schools and church life were conducted in Kate, which now became the church language for all the Lutheran parts of the highlands. By 1930 there were forty evangelists at work in the eastern highlands.

Soon the western highlands were entered, not only by Lutherans but also by Catholics. The young Lutheran missionary, W. Bergmann, was the first to establish his residence in the Chimbu Valley, located between the eastern and western highlands. This was in 1934. Already, in the year before that, the explorers J. Taylor and the Leahy brothers had gone on up into the western highlands, to the Wahgi Valley and Mount Hagen. Michael Leahy wrote to his friends in the Catholic mission and urged them to come up to the region, and in November 1933 the first Catholic missionaries visited the Wahgi Valley. In early 1934 they sent another expedition up through the Chimbu Valley and as far as Mount Hagen and then dropped back to establish a residential station at Mingende. In midyear they began work at Mount Hagen. Also in 1934 the Lutheran missionaries established residences at Kerowagi and Mount Hagen in the western highlands and within a year had twenty-four evangelists in villages of that area and seventy in the Chimbu Valley.

There seemed to be a ready response from the people, and prospects were hopeful when an unexpected blow fell. Two Catholic missionaries in close succession were killed by war parties of the local people. The government, which was coming into the highlands on the heels of the missions, took fright and forbade any more foreigners to come into the highlands and required those already there to stay in their stations. The next year, 1936, a further order required indigenous evangelists to live in the same stations as the missionaries.

The highlanders expressed great grief at the withdrawal of the evangelists, many cutting off fingers and others cutting off ears. In the eastern highlands a great movement of penitence began. The leader of one village declared that in expression of their distress at the departure of the evangelists they should all finally do what the evangelists had been urging, namely, to make peace between all the villages. Large gatherings were held and peace cermonies were enacted. Thousands of people gave their implements of war and sorcery to be carried to the government headquarters and burned thère. The government officials were so impressed that they prevailed on the central administration to modify its restriction on the evangelists, and in 1937 they were allowed back, not into the western highlands but at least into the eastern highlands villages. The peace made in this emotional outburst was not easy to maintain after the long generations of warfare, but with only small exceptions it held.[35]

Then came the time when the peacemakers themselves were involved in war. Foreign missionary work came to a standstill while New Guinea was engulfed in the worldwide conflict. Yet, as soon as that was passed, in 1947, the restrictions were removed and missions were allowed to enter. The government made sure that this time its authority went first and that missions were not allowed to get ahead of it in entering new territory. The initial introduction of modern services, a cash economy, and administration thus came through the government, while missions had to play a less dominant role than they had in the early history of other parts of the country. But once the place of government was established, the administration was ready to welcome missions with their educational and medical work and their message of peace.[36]

Lutherans and Catholics came back in strength; the Kate-speaking Lutheran congregations soon had ninety-one evangelists back in their former circuits. The Catholic missionaries of the Divine Word returned and were supplemented by other Catholic orders that came to help. The Seventh-day Adventists were one other mission that had begun work in the highlands before the war and that came back greatly expanded. They had started in one station in the eastern highlands in 1934 and had assigned two families to the work. After the war they had as many as sixty-four missionaries established in a chain of missions across the whole length of the highlands.[37]

The Methodists came into the southern highlands. Some of their workers were from Australia and New Zealand but more were Pacific islanders. As Papua, New Britain, and the Solomons had in earlier days been the great missionary challenge to the Methodists of Fiji and Tonga, so now the highlands were the great missionary challenge to the Methodists of Papua, New Britian, and the Solomons. Many of them volunteered for service.[38] Anglicans too, from their base in Papua, spread into the new lands using mostly indigenous workers from the Melanesian Brotherhood and their Papuan churches.[39]

All the churches grew with amazing speed. Those highlanders who had received some Christian instruction in the prewar mission stations had been spreading their beliefs in the intervening years, and large numbers had become interested. Even from still closed areas appeals came for teachers and evangelists over the mountains,[40] and some indigenous evangelists, ignoring the law, walked over the mountains into distant places beyond government control.[41] The receptiveness of the people was doubtless related to the fact that they had been comparatively well treated by the white people. They also had put less emphasis on their old religion than did the coastal peoples, making them readier to change it; and their religion was said to be more closely linked to morality, thus bringing it closer to Christianity.[42] The growth of the Catholic church in the western highlands district shows the rapidity of the change. In 1943 there were 470 baptized Catholics, while twenty-five years later there were 70,000, making this the third largest Catholic mission in Oceania.

It was not only the old missions that expanded into the highlands. There were also new missionary bodies in Australia, America, and elsewhere that heard of the exciting prospects in that area and came pouring in. The government, following the war and the acceptance of the country as a Trust Territory under the United Nations, had given up all thought of regulating the location of missions as a way to keep them out of each other's territory. The United Nations frowned on such restrictions and some missions opposed them.[43] So new and old missions crowded in upon each other and competition was rife. The older missions, such as the Lutherans, were spread thinly and new bodies inserted themselves in between their stations.

By 1953 there were eight new missions in the country in addition to the five that had been there so long, and a decade later an additional nineteen had begun work. By that time there were 422 foreign missionaries working for the new missions, and all of these were in the highlands or in the Sepik district, another area with newly opened tracts. Most of the newcomers represented small, recently established missions and churches of a strongly evangelical outlook, quite different from the older missions, which all represented more traditional forms of Christianity. They were scattered all through the highlands so that this part of the country showed a variety of churches within a small area and often even within a village, quite different from the one-church pattern that prevailed in other parts of the Territory. Group conversion also gave way to individual conversions as competition forced churches to adopt early baptism for each convert.[44]

Mormon Growth in the Pacific Islands

Beyond Micronesia and the highlands, any consideration of the postwar increase of foreign influence in the churches must pay attention to the enormous growth of Mormon influence. Mormons were growing strongly in many parts of the world in this period and were sending out increasing numbers of missionaries. They had been intermittently active in Polynesia since the mid-nineteenth century. In fact this was their first foreign mission field. But prior to World War II they had not been of great importance. This was partly because they had come into Polynesia after other churches had been accepted and established there, making conversions very difficult, and they had never gone on to Melanesia where there were untouched areas of greater promise. They did not admit black-skinned people to the priesthood or the higher ordinances of their temple.[45] It is understandable, therefore, that they were not drawn to *Mela*nesia, the "*black* islands."

They worked according to a very distinctive pattern of mission operations. Any male member could be called by the church to go into missions. Usually young men of college age were called, and young Mormon men normally expected to spend two or three years in missionary work before completing their education or getting married. Their families had to pay their expenses, and in prewar days they were often poor and ill provided-for during their work. They had only minimal training; most of them were raw country youths coming from a limited farming background so they were not prepared to handle Pacific islanders with skill or understanding. They walked in twos from village to village talking with people. Their poverty, constant turnover of personnel, poor attire, lack of good church buildings or good schools all caused people to look down on them.[46] They tried to make up for these disadvantages by sheer persistence in work. They worked every waking minute and put great store on the number of people they could speak to. They were expected to submit weekly reports on the number of hours worked and the results achieved, which were then compared with past performance and the performance of others and with the mission norm which in more recent years was set at eighty-four hours of work per week.

The island governments were chary about admitting Mormons in numbers. Their persistent proselytizing stirred animosities among the people and at times gave rise to disorderly incidents, which created concern in government circles even though the disorder was not from the Mormons but from those who were provoked by their presence. Tahiti, Samoa, and Tonga all restricted Mormon workers to small numbers. In fact Tonga passed legislation in 1922 forbidding their missionaries entirely because, as the Tongan premier stated, "They can hardly be looked on as Christians and therefore religious liberty would not apply to them."[47] This extreme limitation was withdrawn in 1924,[48] but restrictions continued with only five of their American missionaries being allowed in the country at a time.[49] Samoa made a short experiment in the 1950s of removing any limitation, but the number of Mormons coming into the country shot up from fifteen to 120, and this brought complaints from other churches. So in 1958 quotas were again imposed.[50]

Despite the fact that the number of American missionaries continued to be limited, the Mormon missions did grow enormously in their impact during the years after World War II. They advanced through a variety of means. The church in America was increasing greatly in wealth. The young people coming out on missions were now dressed in standardized neat, fresh, attractive dress rather than the often slovenly or threadbare clothes of the past. Their work was more carefully organized and, instead of being left to engage spontaneously in discussions with others, they now memorized conversations, which they repeated with all who would admit them.[51]

More importantly, an enormous building program was undertaken with American funds, which transformed the image of a transient, impoverished church into one of permanence and affluence. All over Samoa, Tahiti, and Tonga, and in new missions in the Cook Islands and Niue, impressive church buildings were erected according to a uniform pattern in village after village. These were not meant so much to serve existing congregations as to attract new people. They provided a useful assembly hall for village functions and a recreation area for village youth, including nearly always a court for the American game of basketball. They were erected by a small number of American and New Zealand Mormon builders who were assisted by larger numbers of island Mormon youth, who thereby learned valuable trades.[52] With these new facilities the Mormons could turn to advantage the youthfulness of their missionaries, which had hitherto been a handicap. They provided entertainment and recreation for the Polynesian young people, whom the older churches had handled only with controls, and many youths responded to them.

The Mormons also provided new educational opportunities for young people. New schools were built along with the new churches. Whereas previously their schools had been of poor quality, taught by untrained local people or the ever transient missionaries, they now brought in professional teachers who were paid professional salaries from America rather than being supported by their families. After 1957 the schools were removed from mission control and put directly under a Mormon Board of Education in America in order to improve their quality. Government quotas on missionaries did not apply to the teachers in these schools. In addition to their primary schools, large secondary schools were erected in Tonga, Western Samoa, and American Samoa, and French permission for a primary school in Tahiti was secured by recruiting Mormons from France. From the secondary schools students could get assistance to go on to Mormon colleges abroad, especially the college in Hawaii, and this was an important added attraction for membership in the church. Youths who finished there or found they were not able to finish for academic reasons, often returned and gave a period of missionary service in their homelands, thus increasing greatly the number of missionaries who were actually functioning in the country over the limited number allowed from abroad.[53]

These new efforts brought a considerable response. During the twenty years following the war Mormons increased by their own count from two thousand to eleven thousand in Tonga and from five thousand to eighteen thousand in Samoa.[54] They also reached out to new territories, to the Cook Islands and Niue as has been mentioned, and to Fiji and New Caledonia.

The mission was started in Fiji with a fine new building begun in 1956 and with government permission for missionaries to enter.[55] This move is surprising in light of the Mormons' previous avoidance of Melanesia and their statements that Fijians were negroid. But in 1955 they changed this position and announced that they did not see Fijians as Negroes but as among the children of Israel.[56] A dozen years later their missionaries were allowed into New Caledonia and they began a small work there.[57] There was no statement about the race of the New Caledonians. Given the Mormons' traditional outlook on racial matters, it is not surprising that these missions appealed primarily to the Indians and Polynesians in Fiji and to the French and Tahitian settlers in New Caledonia.

The increasing number of Mormons was one of the causes for an increasing number of other missionaries in the South Pacific. Wherever there was a group with foreign leadership challenging the existing churches, those churches were eager to keep foreign leaders of their own. In this way they achieved greater prestige and presumably greater strength in resisting any challenge. Foreign leaders were also useful to them in dealing with the Europeans who made up the colonial regimes. So while in other parts of the world foreign missionaries were beginning to be regarded with some hesitation by the indigenous churches, in the Pacific they were warmly welcomed. Their numbers, as previously mentioned, went up to over 4,500 during the 1960s compared to 1,700 before the war.[58]

Foreign expenditures on behalf of the churches increased comparably. In the spurt of new educational and medical service that followed the war, church institutions of service grew rapidly and foreign support for them increased, as we shall see in a following chapter. All this would make it appear that foreign influence and control were enhanced by the aftermath of World War II. This was true—yet it was not the whole story. It was also during this period, as we shall see, that the churches moved most rapidly to take over control from their missionary mentors and established themselves as independent or semi-independent bodies.

NOTES

1. See Van Dusen 1945.

2. Tuilovoni 1948. Burton 1949: 61–72.

3. *Journal des Missions Evangéliques* 121 (1946): 283. Emlyn Jones, Report for 1944–46, Council for World Mission Archives, London.

4. *Pacific Islands Monthly* 15 (June 1945):12; 18 (August 1947): 44. Bitton 1947. Bigault 1946: 67. Sabatier 1946.

5. Hernandez 1955: 1. Palma 1946. V. I. Kennally 1946 says that seven missionaries were killed.

6. Sullivan 1957: 154–68.

7. *Not in Vain*, March, July, September 1943; September, December 1944. Morrel 1973: 204–5. Artless 1965: 40–43. Fullerton 1969: 141–42. Luxton 1955: 170–82.

8. O'Reilly and Sédès 1949: 83–105, 120–26, 153–65. Bigault 1947: 174–82.

9. Fullerton 1969: 140. Hughes and Tomkins 1969: 31–75. Bell 1946: 3–4. Benson 1957. Tomlin 1951: 172–90.

10. Eppelein 1934: 34.

11. Frerichs 1957: 66–80. Pilhofer 1963: vol. 2: 250–54. Hogbin 1951: 234–35. Wagner 1964: 6–7, 80–83. The German Roman Catholic missionaries were also accused of Nazi teachings. *Pacific Islands Monthly* 7 (May 1937): 6; 11(Oct. 1940): 42.

12. Sterr 1950: 200–40. Wiltgen 1965: 379–82. Kraft 1964: 38.

13. *Pacific Islands Monthly* 16 (June 1946): 5. *Missionsleiden* . . . 1947: 24–25. Scharmach 1960: 188–99.

14. Luxton 1955: 179. Jimmy 1972: 103. Van Dusen 1945: 80–81. Laufer 1948.

15. V. I. Kennally 1946. Hackett 1947: 51.

16. Scharmach 1960: 242. Laufer 1950: 106–9.

17. Cormack 1956: 30.

18. Hogbin 1947: 113–15. Wyllie 1951: 109.

19. Dobson 1963: 14–15.

20. Shotton 1947: 12. Gill 1954: 94–98. Bell 1946: 15–17.

21. O'Reilly and Sédès 1949: 166–67, 181–90.

22. Scharmach 1960: 244–48. Strong 1947: 75–76. Fricke 1947: 18–24. Gill 1954: 49. Hogbin 1947: 5–6. Threlfall 1975: 169.

23. Utt 1963: 154–55. James Michener 1950: 390 says: "The government remembers that during the war only mission boys betrayed Allied airmen to the Japs." Although this may have been true in a few cases, the common and repeated experience was just the opposite. Cf. Van Dusen 1945. Government memory in New Guinea after the war may have been affected by the fact that at that time government officals were trying to weaken mission influence in the villages and to replace it with governmental power.

24. Hau'ofa 1944. Metcalfe, n.d. Luxton 1955: 179. Choiseul Circuit Report, 1946, Methodist Mission Archives, Sydney. *Missionary Review* 79, no. 3 (Autumn 1971): 14. *Not in Vain*, March 1944: 4–5.

25. Luxton 1955: 184.

26. Forman 1978b: 39–40.

27. Van Dusen 1945, a popular book in the American churches at that time, gave clear evidence of this new awareness.

28. United Church Board for World Ministries, Report, 1973 p. 28. In 1960 the American Board became, as the result of a denominational merger, the United Church Board for World Ministries.

29. *PCC News*, December 1978, p.8. Käser 1972. Another American mission that began work in the islands immediately after the war was the General Baptist Mission, which established itself on Saipan and Guam. The indigenous people of these islands, however, continued to be solidly Roman Catholic. Hemphill 1971.

30. Japan 1937: 54. *United States Catholics Overseas 1970:* 77–78.

31. Hernandez 1955:25.

32. *New York Times*, Feb. 12, 1962, p. 14.

33. Yanaihara 1939: 234 reports how the proportion of Christians in Micronesia rose from 53 percent in 1926 to 78 percent in 1936. Clyde 1935: 120 reports nearly the same figures for 1935. By the late 1950s the proportion of Christians was nearly 100 percent, according to Trumbull 1959: 109.

34. Frerichs 1957: 109–10.

35. Radford 1977. Ross 1969. Reitz 1975.

36. Rowley 1966: 129–30. Strong 1947: 38. Luxton 1955: 203–4. Territory of Papua and New Guinea 1947. Some scientists who were interested in keeping the highland peoples untouched urged the government to prohibit missionary entrance, but the government, being itself involved in touching them, took the opposite view. Keesing 1945: 81.

37. Stewart 1956: 193–94. Territory of New Guinea, *Report for 1964–65.*

38. Methodist Church of Australia, Highlands District, Report for 1960. Methodist Mission Archives, Sydney.

39. Anglican effort was partly in the eastern highlands, but strongest in the western.

40. Pilhofer 1963: vol. 2: 263–66. David Tuff, Report on Wonenar Circuit 1964, Neuendettelsau Mission Archives.

41. Berndt 1965: 100.

42. Lawrence and Meggitt 1965: 19–20.

43. At a meeting in 1956 with the long-established missions the government said it would welcome a policy of separation of missions, but the Roman Catholics said

they could not agree. Methodist Board of Missions Minutes, Oct. 12, 1956. Methodist Mission Archives, Sydney. Territory of Papua and New Guinea 1947: 55–68.

44. The most prominent of the new churches were the Missouri Synod Lutherans in the Wabag area, the Apostolic Church in the western highlands, the Australian Baptists in Baiyer River and Telefomin, the Church of the Nazarene and the Swiss Evangelical Mission Brotherhood both around Minj, the Assemblies of God primarily in the Sepik area, the Christian Missions in Many Lands also in the Sepik, the Four Square Gospel Mission and the New Tribes Mission in the eastern highlands, and the Salvation Army and the Wycliffe Translators, both widely scattered. Territory of New Guinea, *Report for 1963–64*: 306–7.

45. Brewer 1968: 519. This limitation on blacks was ended in 1978.

46. Dubois 1928: 379.

47. Premier Tuivakano to I. McOwan, British Agent and Consul, April 6, 1921. CO 225, vol. 177, document 279. Public Record Office, London.

48. Douglas 1974: 241.

49. Douglas 1974: 305 states that in 1946 and 1947 they were making monthly applications to double the size of their American force, but they had to be content with only the five they were allowed. Presumably then this was about the number that had been permitted after the prohibition was withdrawn.

50. The new quota was one missionary for every two hundred adherents and it applied equally to all missions. In effect, however, it was a restriction on the Mormons, since other churches were not bringing in missionaries at a higher rate than that. *Samoa Bulletin*, May 30, 1958. In Tahiti in these same years the quota for their missionaries varied between eight and sixteen. Douglas 1974: 306.

51. Britsch 1979: 23.

52. Cummings 1961.

53. Nix 1967. Sutton 1963: 20–21, 46. Sutton states that the Mormons in Tonga were able to send more of their students overseas than the government and all other churches combined could do.

54. These figures are taken from charts in their Samoan and Tongan offices and from *The Improvement Era* 69 (1966): 374. Tongan census figures are considerably lower, giving their 1966 membership as about 5,500, but this is still a considerable increase and represents 7 percent of the population as compared with 5 percent ten years earlier.

55. *Improvement Era* 61 (1958): 726. Cummings 1961: 198. These sources indicate that the government gave permission for seven missionaries. Douglas 1974: 373–75 states that permission was granted for only two.

56. Douglas 1974: 376–77.

57. Douglas 1974: 379 gives the starting date for their mission branch in New Caledonia as 1961, the mission being established to take care of Tahitian immigrants. There were indeed occasional visits made to the Tahitian settlers from 1961 on, but it was not until 1967 that a mission was decided on and 1968 that the first missionaries arrived for work in that territory, "Noumea-New Caledonia," undated document, Mormon Church Archives, Papeete.

58. Forman 1969b. Forman 1979: 36.

9

Meeting the Challenge
of Adjustment Movements

An unexpected challenge shook the churches of Melanesia in the World War II and postwar years, a challenge for which they were little prepared. This was the explosion of new religious movements, known variously as cargo cults, revitalization movements, or adjustment movements. These movements had been present on a smaller scale before the war. A number had been known in nineteenth-century Polynesia and Micronesia.[1] More had appeared in Melanesia in the late nineteenth and earlier part of the twentieth centuries. But it was in Melanesia in the war and postwar years that they became a phenomenon of major importance and a continuous problem to the churches.

The movements usually arose among Christian congregations. Occasionally such a movement appeared among people who had not been converted to Christianity, but in general adjustment movements were a post-Christian phenomenon. They arose out of strong feelings of deprivation and frustration, where people had seen the power and wealth of the Europeans and had made some initial, unsuccessful attempts to share in that power and wealth. Typically then a prophet emerged among the people bearing a supernatural message and supernatural power, calling upon the people to reorganize their life *in toto* and to follow his new way to a better world. Community life was reintegrated; religious, social, and political operations were unified as they had been before the foreign intrusions. Strict rules of life were adopted, and careful ceremonial was enacted. Many of the traditional beliefs and practices were revived along with some Christian ideas that were maintained.

Nearly always there was the promise that as a result of this reorganized life and these ceremonies there would come a total transformation of the conditions of existence. Large quantities of goods, such as the white people enjoyed, would be brought by ships or airplanes or would emerge from the ground as gifts from the ancestors for the people to enjoy. The white people would depart or would become the servants of the Melanesians.

The movements were usually hostile to the foreigners who had taken control of religious and political life. Government authority was often rejected and the missionary church was abandoned. Missionaries were seen as having

154

kept hidden the ritual secrets of European wealth and as having conveyed only part of their religion. Sometimes the people stayed in the church just to carry out some of the ceremonial of the new movement, which had incorporated Christian elements. This purpose would be kept secret from the missionary and perhaps even from the local Melanesian pastor, who could guess what was going on only by the strange intensity and unity of the people in the performance of some church ceremonies. But usually the break with the church was made public before very long and the people threw themselves openly into the rituals and regulations of the new cult. In the new life there was great excitement and a sense of release from the frustration of the past. In consequence the emotional pitch was high and total commitment was required. Only those who joined in the movement would share in the blessings it promised and if any held aloof they might, by breaking the unity of the community, delay the fulfillment of those promises. Hence there were strong reasons for all doubters to come in; it was to their own interest as well as to the interest of the group, and few could resist this combination of attraction and pressure.

The reasons why these movements were concentrated in Melanesia, and even in certain parts of Melanesia, are not clear. They are obviously part of the wider phenomenon of adjustment movements, which has been known in Africa and North America as well as Oceania.[2] But the phenomenon is not equally evident everywhere. In Oceania it has been concentrated in Melanesia and most heavily concentrated in Papua New Guinea. One reason for this, it has been suggested, is that Melanesians regard religious ritual as an essential element in human productivity, and their previous religious life, whether traditional or Christian, put great emphasis on ritual behavior linked to material blessing. Therefore it is understandable that new movements to secure material goods and a new place in the world should take a religious form. This is doubtless part of the explanation, but in these respects Melanesians were little different from Polynesians who had, by comparison, few of these movements. It may be that the great Melanesian emphasis on acquired wealth, as contrasted with the Polynesian emphasis on hereditary rank, moved the Melanesians in this direction and that the greater color consciousness between whites and Melanesians, as contrasted to that between whites and Polynesians, produced a greater sense of deprivation and frustration and consequently more adjustment movements among Melanesians. But these factors would not explain the differences within Melanesia.

Some have thought that those areas in Melanesia that suffered more from the seizing of laborers and lands were more prone to the creation of these movements, and while this does seem to account for some differences within Melanesia, it certainly does not fit the majority of cases. Papua New Guinea's predominance in adjustment movements does not mean that that country suffered more from labor traffic or land seizure than the Solomons or the New Hebrides. In fact, it did not. Nor does another theory, which links the utopian expectations of these movements to the millennial preaching given by

Christian missionaries,[3] fit with the time and place of the movements, for millennial preaching was more in evidence among the earlier missionaries to Polynesia than the later ones to Melanesia and was almost unknown among Roman Catholic missionaries and the liberal Protestant missionaries who established the major churches of Papua New Guinea and the Solomons. Yet Melanesia, and more specifically Papua New Guinea, had the bulk of the movements and the Catholic and liberal Protestant churches were heavily involved.

Possibly the best explanation comes from those observers who note that within Melanesia the greatest tendency toward cargo cults occurred within those societies that had the greatest emphasis on the ceremonial exchange of material wealth.[4] Wealth, seen as the chief mark of prestige, recognized through ceremonial exchanges and related to supernatural powers, would have predisposed a society to engage in new wealth-creating religious movements when they came in contact with Europeans. A number of the Melanesian societies that had these characteristics did produce cargo cults. But it must be recognized that by no means all of them did so, and this explanation, therefore, cannot be taken as final. No fully adequate understanding of the source of these movements seems to be available. It is not strange, therefore, that the churches were surprised and confused as they were confronted by this new phenomenon.

The phenomenon, though primarily Melanesian, had one significant example in Micronesia during this century. In Belau, starting in 1916, a new religious movement, called Modekngei, spread widely and became a serious challenge to the Japanese regime. It was based on new revelations from the ancient gods, but it concentrated its attention chiefly on healing and on commercial enterprises. It reached a climax under the Japanese about 1937, but in the American period when there was not so much governmental pressure causing resistance among the people, it began to crumble. Its leaders then adopted Christian symbols and tried to make links with the established churches, maintaining that they were all serving the same God.[5]

But Melanesia was the real center for adjustment movements, and they arose first in Fiji, which might be expected because Fiji was the first part of Melanesia to accept Christianity. Already in the late nineteenth century there appeared the Tuka movement and a movement called Water Babies, so named because of the garden spirits it worshiped. The twentieth century saw first a movement started by Sailosi in 1918 and then one led by Apolosi about 1930. Both these movements combined some Christian teaching with parts of the old worship and ceremonies. Both rejected the government and were crushed by it. They drew people away from the Methodist church but did not keep them long. Because of the strong Methodist condemnation meted out to them, a good number of Sailosi's followers ended up in the Seventh-day Adventist church. Apolosi's people were treated more gently and returned to their original flocks where they were welcomed back.[6] Since then there have been a few smaller movements organizing people collectively for farming or commerce and perhaps separating them from the church. But they have not been of sufficient size to affect the life of the church.[7] At no time were these movements the predominant challenge to Christianity in Fiji that they were in Papua New Guinea.

Papua reported its first adjustment movement in 1893 and German New Guinea its first in 1913. Papua had several more, including notably the Vailala Madness (1919–23) in the Gulf District and several smaller ones in the Northern District. The Catholic Mission near Yule Island was attacked by the ex-Catholic followers of such a movement and the French priest was beaten.[8] Northward in what had been German New Guinea the emotional revival in the Lutheran church, called Eemasung, which we have already noted, was followed by a cult movement in the Sattelberg area starting in 1929 and another in the Kalasa area (1933–35). These both emphasized, in consonance with their revivalist background, continuous prayer as the way to riches. In the latter movement the local pastor's garden was plundered and his helper was beaten for opposing the new ideas.[9] Further west around and beyond Madang were two important movements in the years before World War II, known as Mambu and Letub, one primarily among Catholics and the other among Lutherans, with ex-catechists taking a leading part.[10] Buka Island at the north end of Bougainville was the other great breeding ground for these movements. It had one in 1913 and another starting in 1932, which emphasized both Christian worship and instruction and also prayers to the ancestors, much care being bestowed on graveyards.[11] There were other similar movements in addition to these more important ones before World War II, but the great number arose during and after the war.

War conditions were perfectly suited for the production of such adjustment movements. They displayed such quantities of material wealth and power as would overawe any people. The desire to find the secrets of this wealth was therefore raised to fever pitch. The old structures of social life were broken down by the war and therefore the need was accentuated for new structures which might come with the reorganization of everything by a cult leader. A new cultural identity was necessary and could be found in a leader coming from among the people themselves much better than with leaders appointed by foreigners. Finally, the European overlords who had been the objects of hostility in so many of these movements were shown by the war to be vulnerable. From many of their centers in the western Pacific they fled in headlong retreat. And even though they came back they could no longer play the role of unquestioned, invincible masters. For all these reasons the war years and the two decades thereafter showed the greatest exuberance of new movements. As in the case of the prewar movements, we can look at only the most important of them.

The area of mandated New Guinea including its smaller islands continued to be the chief hotbed. Papua experienced a number of small ones. There were also a few in the New Guinea highlands, although the highlands people did not seem inclined to move in this way, perhaps because they had a less manipulative type of religion and perhaps because they were in better economic condition. But in parts of mandated New Guinea church work became almost impossible. Especially around Madang and further north around Aitape old movements revived and new ones were born, which kept Catholics and Lutherans in turmoil. The Mambu and the Letub cults continued for a time, turning more anti-European with the advent of the Japanese. About 1950 an even more powerful new movement was started by a man named Yali, who attracted both Catholics and Lutherans. The movement was revived in 1968 when Yali ran for the national legislature and has not disappeared yet, although Yali has since died.[12] In the Hube area a strong movement tried to operate within the Lutheran church following the pattern of the Buka Catholics in demanding very strict observance of church attendance and church morality but combining this with traditional elements such as prayer meetings in graveyards and in pools of water, and the spilling of pigs' blood in certain places and calling on the ancestors to bring the cargo.[13]

In the New Guinea islands it was Manus that saw the most firmly established movement, that of Paliau Maloat. The people were organized by Paliau to deal with modern life and economic opportunities, though for a time they also expected a ship with cargo. They established their own church, which was a simplified Catholicism. They regarded themselves as Catholics still, but would have nothing to do with the Catholic mission. They believed the true Bible had been revealed by Jesus to their leader and that the missionaries had only a falsified version. The Paliau movement has been one of a very few that showed for some time the possibility of being a continuing church rather than a sudden excitement that is soon evaporated.[14] On New Britain there were several short-lived movements: one at Nakanai near the center of the island, where a Catholic priest and catechist were attacked; another among the Bainings, the mountain folk near the eastern end of the island, where a Methodist who refused to join the movement was killed; a very brief one among the Tolai of the Gazelle Peninsula; and most recently one called the Story Cult among the Kaliai near the western end of the island.[15] On New Hanover there was a strong movement in the mid-1960s to bring in American rule, making President Lyndon Johnson the expected savior who would provide for all the needs of the people.

Buka Island continued its turbulent story. The movement that had put every stress on Catholic observance before the war turned strongly against the church and the missionaries after the Japanese came. An attempt to sacrifice a man in order to secure cargo led the Japanese to suppress the movement and to behead its chief leaders. But after the war it broke out more strongly than ever and three thousand Catholics as well as nine hundred of the thousand Methodists of the island left their churches to join what was now known as the Hahalis Welfare Society. It was led by two former teachers of the Catholic mission and was devoted to economic advances as well as traditional rituals. It introduced "Baby Gardens" where women could be visited indiscriminately by men and the children would belong to the society. It became involved in bloody confrontation with the government in 1962, and the leaders were then put in jail. The movement continued despite these problems and secured from the government some of the economic benefits for which it had been working. More recently, however, it has seemed to be disintegrating as a religious movement.[16]

A most striking thing about the war and postwar adjustment movements is that they appeared at last in the New Hebrides and the Solomons, parts of Melanesia that had seen very little of such activity previously. Earlier in the century the New Hebrides had had one or two small movements on Santo, but the main developments came during and after the war when strong cargo movements developed not only on Santo but also on Malekula, Ambrym, and, most important, Tanna.[17] The others all died down after a time but the Tanna movement, called John Frum, is still in existence. John Frum was the name of the mythical hero who was expected to return to Tanna with new money to end the European rule and to provide the Tannese with houses like those of the Europeans. The movement began at the end of 1940, and in a few years it had brought the administration to a halt and had swept the Presbyterian church almost completely out of this island that had once been one of its strongholds. The leaders of the movement were deported, but later allowed to return and the movement continued. It made its peace with the government, but not with the church. It secured some government help for schools of its own to replace those of the mission and so began to provide some of the advantages it had promised. Its strength was gradually drained, however, as people tired of waiting for all that was to come, and large numbers started to return to the church.

The two principal movements to appear in the Solomon Islands[18] were very untypical of Melanesian adjustment movements. One had far less of religious elements than these movements usually had, and the other retained much more of its Christian heritage than was usual. The first was called Marching Rule and was largely a phenomenon of the island of Malaita. It organized people in new towns along the coast where its leaders took over political control and where community life was well regulated according to many traditional ideas and also some new conceptions. It refused submission to the British and looked to the possibility of a return of American troops with all their wealth. Most of its leaders were former teachers of the South Sea Evangelical Mission (SSEM) and the movement emphasized the teaching of human brotherhood in a way derived from the Bible. Its leaders rejected the SSEM missionaries, but it was not explicitly antichurch. In fact the Roman Catholic missionaries worked with it quite effectively and found in its new towns a ready field for evangelism. This cooperativeness decreased as the movement tried to revise Catholic discipline. By 1951 government arrests of the leaders and the failure of the millennial hopes brought the movement to an end.[19]

The other movement was really a split in the Methodist church of the western Solomons. It took place in 1960 under the leadership of the catechist,

Silas Eto. Eto had gone through ecstatic experiences and led his local church in the direction of such experiences. These ecstasies and strange visions became more common in the disturbed days following the war and in the uncertainties following the retirement of J. F. Goldie, who had been the dominating head of the mission through all its existence. Missionary leaders gave no importance to these experiences and tended to discount their place in the life of the church, or even to denounce them as the work of the evil spirit, rather than of the Holy Spirit as Eto and his followers claimed. The opposing interpretations of the trances, dances, and shaking led the people to reject the mission leaders, although they claimed loyalty to Goldie's heritage and to true Methodism. Some older men who had been given recognition by Goldie and by former government officers, but who now felt they were unrecognized, were also interested in seeing a separate church created where their influence would continue. The break came in 1960, and 3,500 people left the Methodist fold. The group was named the Christian Fellowship Church. Eto was recognized as its head. It completely reorganized village life and developed new agricultural and commercial enterprises. In these respects it was like some other adjustment movements, but it had little of the millenarian outlook that they usually included. It was not expecting cargo to arrive. Consequently it did not suffer the disappointment and decline that most of them went through and it has proved to be remarkably stable.[20] It is the one movement in the Pacific that can appropriately be classified with the independent churches of Africa. Those too are adjustment movements but far more durable and more like the usual Christian churches than are the Melanesian adjustment movements with the exception of the Christian Fellowship Church.

The adjustment movements of the Pacific, except for Eto's and possibly John Frum and Modekngei, seem now to be on the way out, at least as religiously oriented movements with which the churches have to deal. They have created much distress and disturbance in the churches. To a certain extent they have also created a stronger sense of church identity. It could be expected that as church members faced the competition of these new religious movements they would, if they did not fall into the new enthusiasm, develop a stronger sense of identification with the church as distinct from the general community and would be pressed to a more serious acceptance of Christian beliefs. To a limited extent this has taken place. Those who know the Methodist Church in the Solomons, which is now part of the United Church of Papua New Guinea and the Solomon Islands, maintain that it is the most vital part of that entire united body and attribute this vitality to the challenge that came through Silas Eto. It is also reported that the Yali movement around Madang has caused some Christians to recognize the committed body of the faithful as distinct from the mass of conventional believers. But it cannot be maintained that this effect has been widespread or powerful. Too often the decision to reject the new movement and stay with the church was based on old animosities and divisions, which had existed between clans and villages, rather than being based on strong Christian convictions. This was the case in many of the decisions regarding Eto and regarding Yali.[21] Even those few who remained faithful to the Presbyterians on Tanna seem often to have been more isolated than deepened by the decision. A great increase in the sense of church identity has not been a common result of the adjustment movements as they have affected the ordinary church members.

For the pastors and catechists, however, the case has been different. They usually stood by the church, and held aloof from or even opposed the adjustment movements. Many of them suffered as a result. They saw this as a testing of their faith. A Presbyterian pastor in the New Hebrides, speaking of the John Frum movement, said, "I think this thing came to Tanna, not because the Tanna people were stupid, but to test us New Hebrideans to see if our church is strong and can stand out against it."[22] The Anglican priests in the Solomons who stood almost to a man against Marching Rule—perhaps because Marching Rule was anti-English and their church was so identified with England—believed that their church should be strengthened from this trial. They started Church Associations as a result, which were local associations formed to provide stronger financial support for the church and make it more independent of foreign funds.

Alongside this it must be remembered that not all the pastors stayed out of the adjustment movements. Most of the SSEM teachers, as opposed to the Anglican priests, entered vigorously into Marching Rule and were in fact its mainstay. When the Johnson cult swept New Hanover, six of the thirty Methodist ministers were captivated by it and believed and preached its great expectations. Elsewhere there were occasionally pastors who combined their Christianity with the new cults. Yet they were exceptional, and in the more normal cases there can be no doubt that the encounter with the new movements strengthened the Christian identity of the pastors.

The missionaries, as might be expected, set themselves in opposition to these movements. In their first contacts with them they were mystified and condemnatory.[23] Many a movement was nipped in the bud because of missionary intervention at its first sign. On at least two occasions all the Lutheran churches of two areas in New Guinea were put under discipline, with an end to all baptisms, communions, and collections, because they had been infected with cargo excitement.[24]

As the missionaries gained more experience, however, their opposition tended to soften. They learned that little could be accomplished by condemnation and that preaching against a movement only magnified its importance in the eyes of the people and enhanced the suspicion that it contained some truth that the white people did not want others to learn. It was better to stand by the people and to wait than to try to stem the tidal wave. So missionary policy usually became one of watchful waiting and keeping contacts open. Furthermore, some of the positive values of the adjustment movements were recognized. At the time of the beginning of the John Frum excitement one of the Presbyterian missionaries noted that the illusory ideas of the movement were nevertheless based on worthy national pride and a humble desire for respect,[25] and while the movements were still seriously disrupting the Lutheran area the missionary bishop of the Lutherans said it was incumbent upon the missionaries to do more by way of showing sympathy for these efforts by the people to stand up and to help themselves.[26] In more recent years this recognition of values has increased and missionaries have tried to learn what cargo cults have to teach traditional Christianity.[27] Also there has been more attempt by the missionaries to provide training in new types of economic production to satisfy some of the pressing needs of the people. The Presbyterians, for example, began a Christian Institute of Technology on Tanna, and the Catholics inaugurated a similar program on Buka.[28] The Lutherans carried on a massive development program in New Guinea, as we shall see in a later chapter.[29]

In sum, it may be said that the churches of the western Pacific did make some steps toward greater independence, indigeneity, and self-identity as a result of their encounter with the adjustment movements, but, as in the case of the war experience, these were not as great as might have been expected.

NOTES

1. E.g., Keesing 1945: 78. Kahn 1965: 275. Koskinen 1953: 101–4. Freeman 1959. Mühlmann 1968.

2. For standard treatments of these movements, see Wallace 1956, Worsley 1957, and Lanternari 1963.

3. Margull 1962. Guiart 1962: 123–26. Guiart also stresses other factors in the work of the missionaries, such as the size of the gifts they gave, as productive of cargo cults. He shows how in cases of mass conversion to Christianity the people often expected a total transformation.

4. Christiansen 1969: 73–74. Brunton 1971.

5. Vidich, n.d.: 84–93.

6. *Missionary Review*, Feb. 4, 1919: 8–9; Nov. 4, 1919. A. D. Lelean to Chairman, Fiji District, March 31, 1930. Methodist Archives, Suva.

7. Ratu Emosi of Daku long had a collective economy for his village and kept good relations with the Methodist church. He began the movement in 1937. The Dra ni Lami, or Blood of the Lamb, group was begun in 1949 and reorganized outside the Methodist church in 1962, but did not prosper. The Congregation of the Poor was set up about 1950 and still continues, as reported in Rokotuiviwa 1975.

8. Later movements among Catholics in Papua are described in Trompf 1977: 20–107, 147–73.

9. Pilhofer 1963: vol. 2: 178–81. Wagner 1964: 7–11.

10. Burridge 1960. Lawrence 1956 and 1964. Inselmann 1944.

11. Bigault 1947: 122–28. O'Reilly and Sédès 1949: 193–97. Laracy 1969: 185–93.

12. Lawrence 1964. Ahrens and Hollenweger 1977: 23ff.

13. Keysser 1950: 294–95.

14. Mead 1956: 231–41, 322–42. Schwartz 1962. Rowley 1966: 157–58.

15. Scharmach 1960:235–39. Counts 1978. Janssen 1974.

16. O'Reilly and Sédès 1949: 198–99. Laracy 1969: 193. Knoebel 1974: 64–65. New Zealand Methodist Church, Overseas Missions Board, Minutes, Oct. 16, 1963. Methodist Mission Archives, Auckland. Tuza 1977.

17. The earlier movement in Santo, that of Rongofuro, resulted in the death of a planter, and there were fears on at least two occasions that it or something like it was being revived. The postwar Santo movement was known as the Naked Cult and spread widely over the island. On Malekula there was a Cargo Cooperative and on Ambrym a typical cargo cult. Worsley 1957: 148–70. Guiart 1958: 198–212.

18. On two other movements of lesser importance, the Chair and Rule movement and the Moro movement, see Worsley 1957: 171–72, and Davenport and Coker 1967.

19. Laracy 1971.

20. Harwood 1978. Scheffler 1971. Tuza 1977.

21. Scheffler 1971: 15. Ahrens and Hollenweger 1977: 30–31.

22. Presbyterian Church of the New Hebrides General Assembly, 1963: 42.

23. J. Wagner 1964: 30–37. Dupreyat 1935: 497–98.

24. American Lutheran Church, *Official Reports*, 1940: 210, on the Madang district. H. Wagner and H. Fontius, interviews, on the Kalasa Circuit in 1961.

25. Nottage 1940: 26.

26. Kuder 1964: 8.

27. E.g., *Point*, no. 1 (1974): 93–193. Ahrens and Hollenweger 1977: 81–105. Oosterwal 1967.

28. Laracy 1969: 327.

29. Hueter 1974 questions the usefulness of economic projects in dealing with cargo cults, believing that the problem lies in concepts and in the sense of history and that these matters must first be dealt with or else the economic projects will only perpetuate old cargo expectations.

10
The Completion of Church Independence

The years immediately following World War II were not years of rapid decolonization in the Pacific, as they were elsewhere. Oceania was the last part of the world to see national independence for its territories, moving about two decades behind Asia and a decade behind Africa. Yet in the history of the churches, the immediate postwar years were the time when independence took hold vigorously and began to spread throughout the islands. Church independence here, as in Asia and Africa, moved well ahead of national independence.

The chief reason for this, apart from the general changes brought on by the war and its aftermath, was a new outlook among the missionaries. Whereas in earlier years they had been grudging in their recognition of the need for independence and had often had to be prodded by their sending boards, in the postwar years they were strongly committed to independence as soon as possible. The islands saw a new generation of missionaries trained to think in terms of working with independent churches and putting an end to the paternalism of the past. These people proceeded to press for independence and to hand it, ready-made, to churches that were by no means asking for it and perhaps not even ready for it. The dynamics of independence were, therefore, very different in the postwar scene from what they had been in the prewar days when Tonga, Samoa, and Fiji were moving to independence (see chap. 7). There was little or no local agitation, such as had been seen in Tonga's early breakaway or in Samoa's Mau-related crises and Fiji's Toko Farmers. There was little need, on the other hand, for the sending boards in Europe or Australia to press their views on independence. They could now work easily with the missionaries. The change was harmoniously achieved by missionaries and mission boards working in cooperation with interested, but often hesitant, islanders.

Presbyterians

The New Hebrides Presbyterians were the first to move toward independence. It is strange that they came first because the Presbyterian mission in the New Hebrides had been the most domineering of all the island missions. Its missionaries had held more power over the people and had repressed more of their local culture than any other major mission in the South Pacific. They

164

were also unusually slow in developing an indigenous ministry. As late as 1943 after nearly a century of mission work there were only ten pastors and even they were regarded more as assistants to the missionaries than as pastors of churches.[1] There was no national church organization but only a meeting of the missionaries to handle interisland questions. On each island the local missionary controlled all church life. What a contrast this picture presents to Samoa where by 1943 the Congregationalists had over four hundred pastors and a fully self-governing national church, which had been developing its organs of self-government for sixty years.

But 1943 was about the time when things began to change in the New Hebrides. The world war had introduced masses of foreign troops and economic prosperity and many new experiences to the people. There were also some young missionaries from New Zealand, particularly J. Graham Miller, who arrived at that time and pressed for the creation of an independent national church. The mission boards in Australia and New Zealand who supported the work were cautious, but willing to move in this way. So it was that the 1945 meeting of the missionaries took action to draw up a constitution for the new church and in 1948 the Presbyterian Church of the New Hebrides was inaugurated. The New Hebrideans had little to do with all this. The newer missionaries were convinced that independence should be given before it was requested. This would forestall any possible discontent and antimissionary sentiment among the people and would implement a long-standing mission policy that had been ignored.[2]

Action like this by the missionaries was in some ways obviously premature. One of the principal authorities on younger-church development has said that the creation of organs of self-government in the church must come out of the life of the people and cannot be created artificially.[3] The creation of the governing bodies for this new church was artificial in these terms. One historian of the area thought that the action was too hasty and would likely lead to trouble.[4] The missionaries realized that they had a major assignment ahead of them in educating the church leaders and they set themselves to that task. The governing body of the new church was to be the General Assembly and each meeting of that body for a period of years revealed the missionaries doing most of the talking but always urging the local leaders to greater participation, sometimes waiting through long and embarrassing silences for them to begin to speak, and gradually finding a greater and greater participation and then leadership from among the New Hebrideans. The missionaries had their own continuing organization, known as the Mission Council, which acted as advisor to the General Assembly, giving most people the impression that the major power was still lodged there. But after a decade the mission boards in New Zealand and Australia began to put mounting pressure on the mission to abolish the Mission Council. This was finally done.[5] The real test of the success of the missionary venture came in the early 1970s when New Hebrideans were chosen as moderator and as executive officer of the synod, and the church was challenged to take a formative part in the new national life of the islands. Presbyterians met these challenges vigorously and used the imported church structures as if they were their own. They proved that a vital church could be created even when its independence had been an imposition by the foreign missionaries.

Lutherans

Soon after the Presbyterian missionaries began their independent church in the New Hebrides the Lutherans in New Guinea took the same step. They had more of a foundation to build on because the local congregations had been more independent from the beginning. The Lutheran philosophy, related to the folk-church pattern in Germany, had emphasized church leadership by the natural local leaders of the community and thus a stronger corps of community/church lay leaders had developed than the Presbyterians had ever seen. But the number of local ordained ministers was even smaller than among the Presbyterians, and at the national level there were only mission organizations with no national church body to which the mission could turn over responsibilities. In fact the heavy emphasis on the local congregation and its lay leaders, with no outside support, meant that there were no church members with a wider vision or broader experience to enable them to think in terms of a national church or to develop the qualities of statesmanship needed in national leadership. The New Guinea Lutheran experience was in this respect very much like that of the Korean Presbyterians. In Korea, under the so-called Nevius Method, the emphasis was on developing a church leadership that was very close to the level of the village congregation both in training and in lifestyle. The result was that the Korean Presbyterian church suffered from a dearth of leaders with wider vision, and its many splits may be traced in part to this lack.

Christian Keysser, as the Lutheran missionary most closely associated with the folk-church pattern, recognized the difficulty of creating a wider consciousness and tried to work on it. In 1914 his local congregation arranged for a meeting with the coastal peoples and suggested that they strengthen each other. But nothing came of it because the other missionaries thought there was no urgency in moving toward a national church and because the coastal people, who were a minority, began to fear that they would be robbed of their language in any united body.[6] Since there were different languages each of which had been adopted in different parts of the church as a *lingua franca*, and there were different Lutheran missions, the problem of unity was a difficult one.

But there were forces making for unity and church development. Within the language districts, district-wide conferences began to be held in 1914. When village congregations began sending islander missionaries into the highlands, after the first exploratory trips among the eastern highland peoples in 1920, they realized that they could not do this in the entirely independent fashion in which they had carried on their missions to their own neighbors. So they began to hold conferences to plan cooperative work in the highlands. Then came World War II during which the internal strength of the New Guinea church was made evident. When the foreign missionaries returned, they recognized this and felt that it justified the immediate creation of a national church even though the broader leadership had not yet appeared. The American Lutheran Mission, which was the newest of the Lutheran missions working in New Guinea, was the one most dissatisfied with the separations between the mission organizations. It called for a single, united mission, "one Lutheran mission working toward one Lutheran church."[7] The Australian government forwarded this view by initially turning over the whole operation to the American mission, because it did not want any German organization to have a voice in the controls.[8]

The desire for unity prevailed, and the missions coalesced in 1953. Then, at a meeting of the united mission, it was agreed that a single church should be formed. In 1956 a gathering was held of church representatives from all the districts and the Evangelical Lutheran Church of New Guinea (later of Papua New Guinea) was launched. The decision to form an independent national church was then, among the New Guinea Lutherans as among the New Hebrides Presbyterians, a decision made by the foreign missionaries without any great pressure for it coming from the indigenous people. A former missionary, Georg Vicedom, who had become a professor of missions in Germany, did most of the work on producing the church constitution, though it was then discussed and amended by the congregations. It was a structure based on Western models that he proposed, but as there had never been any indigenous structures above the local level in any aspect of life, no other models were available to him.[9] It was a pyramidal structure that was created, based on the congregations and the district conferences with indirect elections to higher bodies culminating in a General Synod. Foreign missionaries were given special positions in the structure. They were the leaders of the groups of congregations, called circuits; they were members of the next higher bodies, the District Councils; and they were members of the highest body, the General Synod. The separate organization of the mission also continued in existence and it continued to operate the medical, educational, and commercial institutions that it had created. The man elected to be the bishop of the church in every election from its inception till 1973 was a foreign missionary, John Kuder from America.[10]

Some maintained that the church was only a façade and that the decisions were still made by the missionaries. Yet there was, as in the New Hebrides, a gradual moving into the mission-built house behind that façade by the indigenous people. They had a large majority in the membership of all the church bodies, and the missionaries were under instructions not to speak in those bodies unless true doctrine and the well-being of the church were at stake. Discussions in those bodies were often patterned on the slow, deliberative method of village gatherings where no decision is made until there is effective unanimity, rather than using the Western method of majority votes.

The delegates elected by the congregations to the governing bodies were usually the most respected elders, conservative men who were not eager to see the church expand at the expense of the mission. Missionaries had to press them to accept the leadership of the District Councils. When missionaries began to talk about abolishing the separate mission organization, the General Synod pointed out that many were not ready for this.[11] Nevertheless, in 1976 the mission was dissolved by the missionaries and from then on missionaries took their place simply as members of the church, serving under the church and its first indigenous bishop, Zurewe Zurenuo.[12]

By the time the Lutheran Church was established the currents toward church independence were flowing strong throughout the Pacific. Missionaries everywhere were pressing for the implementation of the long-established policies in favor of the creation of independent churches. So one independent church followed another, springing up in the island world in rapid succession. Since the forms of church government determined the procedures through which independence came, this succession is best examined according to the denominational groupings of the churches: first, the Congregationalists, then the French Reformed, the Methodists, the Anglicans, and finally the Roman Catholics.

Congregationalists

The first grouping, the Congregationalists, were nearly all related to the London Missionary Society, and that society had already been moving in the direction of church independence, as has been seen in their dealings with Samoa. The Commission of 1916 which started the self-supporting church in Samoa and urged greater self-government there, also suggested the first step toward local self-government in the churches of the Cook Islands, the Gilbert Islands, and Papua. That first step was the creation of local councils made up of the representatives of all the churches of a single island, or, in Papua, of a district. This suggestion was carried out during the following years, sometimes after considerable prodding and reminders from London.[13] In the period after World War II, London was determined to move rapidly to the establishment of independent national churches, each with a central assembly carrying responsibility for the entire life of the church. This transformation was achieved in the Cooks in 1945, in Papua in 1962, in Kiribati (the Gilberts) and Tuvalu (the Ellice) in 1968, and in Niue in 1972. Papua actually began with a preparatory church assembly somewhat earlier, in 1950, but that assembly could only discuss matters, not decide them. Full power was turned over to it in 1962 and in the new constitution it was specified that at least three-fourths of the members of the assembly must be Papuans. Their church was called the Papua Ekalesia.[14] The LMS missionaries, following instructions from London, were the prime agents of these changes. They had not pressed the churches toward independence during the first half of the twentieth century.[15] But in the second half they were the ones who took responsibility for carrying through the change and were the ones who consulted with local church leaders and drew up the blueprints for the new church structures.

A lesser group of Congregationalists were those, located in Micronesia, who were connected with the American Board. They were more strictly congregational in operation than were the LMS churches. During the nineteenth and first quarter of the twentieth centuries nothing was done to develop church structures above the local congregation, though locally the churches managed their own affairs. Then some change came, but only because of an unusual combination of events. When Japanese rule came to the islands after World War I, firm controls were maintained over church life by Japanese government regulations.[16] Japanese missionaries, for all their helpfulness in maintaining and developing churches and schools, weakened church independence. In the Caroline Islands, where they worked, they made all the decisions, paid the pastors with Japanese funds, and handled all the money given in collections.[17] They wished to extend their work also into the Marshall Islands, where there were still two or three American missionaries. But the Marshallese churches expressed themselves as strongly opposed to such a move.[18] To ward off possible Japanese mission interference, they enlarged the scope of their own independence. Conferences of the Marshall Islands teachers and pastors were held in 1926, 1929, and 1932 at the call of the American missionary, and, in order to avoid Japanese church control, these conferences voted to establish the Association of Marshall Islands Churches to handle the affairs of the church in their territory. The constitution of the association was approved by the American Board and came into effect in 1933.[19]

When World War II descended upon the area, church life beyond the local level fell largely into abeyance, but after the war was over the Marshall Islands church resumed its independent operation. In the Carolines, the churches in each district at last came together as the Japanese left. The churches of Ponape, for example, formed their own association and eventually, with the help of an American missionary, drew up their own constitution, which went into effect in 1963.[20] The churches related to the Liebenzell Mission did the same thing in their districts. No overall governing body for the Carolines or for Micronesian Protestantism was established, but conferences were held by representatives of the different area churches and in each area the churches were self-governing. The independence of the churches related to the American Board (now known as the United Church Board) was fully completed by the decision of that board finally to withdraw all its missionaries and its support for educational institutions in 1972. This was not the kind of completion for independence that the churches had wanted and they would have been happier if they had been able to prevent it.[21] But the Board had heavy commitments elsewhere and believed that it should not continue its missions in areas where the people had already become Christians.

French Reformed

Of the two French areas, New Caledonia moved first to independence. It had reason for making haste because it was confronted in the 1950s with the revolt of the Free Church under the leadership of the missionary Raymond Charlemagne. To a certain extent this revolt and subsequent separation of the Free Church can be seen as an expression of indigenous dissatisfaction with the subordinate position of the people under missionary leadership. There had been some discontent in earlier years among local leaders who had been stimulated, by Leenhardt and Rey Leseure, to take greater responsibility and develop indigenous ways of church life. They had been unhappy with the eventual exclusion of these two missionaries from work in New Caledonia. The Free Church denounced its parent body as being missionary-controlled and drew people away on the basis of this complaint. But this does not seem to have been the main cause of the difficulty. After all, the Free Church was itself missionary-led. Its formation was more the consequence of a revolt of the young, better-educated teachers of the church against the domination of the older, tradition-loving pastors than it was an expression of opposition to missionary domination.

Yet the attacks of the Free Church were in some measure justified. The General Synod, which had been organized at the end of the 1920s as a result of Maurice Leenhardt's vision, drew together pastors from all of New Caledonia and the Loyalties, but it had no power of decision. It could only discuss. The yearly meeting or *Yunian* of the churches on each island, which, as its name suggests, had been in operation since the days of the English missionaries, was presided over by a foreigner, though now he was a Frenchman. Most important, the decisions about the church as a whole were made by the council of missionaries, a small body with heavy responsibilities.

Starting in 1948 Paris began to put on pressure for the creation of an autonomous church. Immediately after the Charlemagne secession, on initiatives from Paris, the council of missionaries was dissolved and in its place was created the Superior Council, on which missionaries had seats but the islanders had a majority. This began to function in 1959. A New Caledonian was made secretary of the new council. Local pastors were chosen to preside over the *Yunians*. On the basis of these changes, on April 24, 1960, the autonomy of the church was proclaimed. Some islanders expressed fears about the change, but those in charge were confident.[22]

Tahiti and the Leeward Islands followed soon after. They had no constitutional organ of missionary control; hence the change was simpler. In 1950 all the regional councils of the church were still presided over by missionaries. The Superior Council, which united the churches of the islands, had an islander majority but its top leadership was French. In the days when the church had been officially established, the government had insisted that the top leaders be French. Now there was no such government requirement and it was only necessary to elect local people to the top positions in the regions and the center and to declare the church independent. The mission society in Paris was eager that these two things be done and pressed this on the missionaries.[23] The missionaries had some fears and the Tahitians seemed indifferent, but finally in the year 1963 both changes were accomplished. The Tahitian church, which has always been very self-reliant, has since then also been fully independent.

Methodists

The Methodist churches, aside from those in Fiji, Tonga, and Samoa, moved very slowly for a long time and then came quite suddenly to independence. These were the churches in the area around New Britain, in the islands off eastern Papua, and in the Western Solomons. As in Fiji, each church was governed by a synod and its chairman. Growing autonomy could come as the indigenous ministers and laity took their places beside the European ministers in that synod and gradually outnumbered them. But the numbers of indigenous ministers were pitifully small in some of these islands and nonexistent in others. So synod control meant mission control.

Things began to change when the New Britain District, where the oldest, largest, and wealthiest churches were located, adopted a program of self-support covering all its budget except the cost of Australian missionaries. This was in 1925 at the time of the district's golden jubilee. In response the Australian church in 1926 gave the district full control of its own finances and also gave it a new constitution, which brought lay representatives into the synod. The local people had not been asking for an independent church, but they were concerned about the way their money was spent and the new constitution was designed to meet that concern, since the lay people would now have a voice in financial decisions.[24] The work of ministers continued to be controlled by only ministerial votes in the synod, so an indigenous voice did not become strong in that area until a significant number of local candidates for the ministry had been accepted—fifteen in the years between 1915 and 1960, seventy-eight in the years between 1961 and 1974. These figures and dates indicate that foreigners were all too slow about ordaining people in a church that had been in operation since 1875. Even those who were ordained were not allowed to celebrate Communion alone until 1961. It was also in 1961 that every minister was put in full charge of his own area, a change that had been suggested by the mission board in Sydney in 1918. As a next step, in 1966, indigenous men began to be appointed as superintendents of circuits in considerable numbers.[25] The foreign missionaries who had once been inordinately slow about entrusting responsibilities to local people were now pressing forward as rapidly as possible.

The other Methodist districts, those of the Papuan Islands and the Solomon Islands, lagged far behind New Britain. This can be partly ascribed to the fact that the New Britain church began about a quarter-century earlier and was located in a center of concentrated population with vigorous economic development. But the lag was also due to lack of foresight. The mission board in Sydney was pressing the missionaries in the Papuan Islands from 1910 on to turn over leadership, including some of the most responsible positions, to the local people, but the missionaries only replied that the Papuans did not make good leaders and that their efforts to get them to take charge even of local meetings had not been successful. It was not until 1962 that lay people came into the synod (the step taken by Fiji in 1908), and not until after that that Papuan Methodists had a sense of sharing significantly in the decisions of their church.[26]

The Solomons District was equally slow or slower. It was extremely laggard in developing a local ordained ministry,[27] the delay being due largely to the autocratic and paternalistic policies of John Goldie who founded the mission.[28] After Goldie left, his successors were faced with the large secession of Silas Eto (see pp. 159–60). That movement may also be seen as expressing a strong indigenous demand for an independent church, quite the opposite of the usual situation where the demand for independence came from the foreign mission. But if this is what Eto's movement represents, it was certainly not clear at the time. A careful inquiry just a few years before had discovered no islander demand for more independent church government, though complaints had been found regarding the amount of money given to the mission when so little was received in return.[29] It may be that even if the church had been long independent with its own leaders, those leaders would have been no more able to control or contain the revolt. However, the mission believed that localization of leadership was one of the main needs revealed by the revolt and proceeded to move strongly in that direction.[30]

Independence came fast and from an unexpected quarter. In 1963 the parent churches in Australia and New Zealand, responding to initiatives from the leading missionaries, agreed to set up a United Synod for the Districts in New Britain, the Papuan Islands, the Solomon Islands, and also including the new district in the New Guinea Highlands. This United Synod had limited powers, but the intention was that it should move forward to become an independent conference such as was being established just at that time in Fiji.[31] At the same time, however, the four districts agreed to send representatives to discuss church union with the Papua Ekalesia. Union would mean not only severing the ties with the parent churches and with Methodism as a separate movement, but would also involve complete independence. Union had been something that people expected to consider after independence had been achieved. Instead the representatives who discussed the matter—mostly expatriates—proposed that union be entered at once and that independence be achieved thereby. All four district synods, somewhat to their own surprise and with a strong sense of divine leading, voted to do this. In the synods it was islanders rather than expatriates who were in the majority and thus making the decision. The parent churches were entirely supportive of this new step. Thus in 1968 Methodism in the western Pacific became independent as part of the United Church in Papua New Guinea and the Solomon Islands.[32] The majority of the bishops elected for the new church were islanders, and in 1973 one of those bishops, Leslie Boseto, a Methodist from the Solomon Islands, became the first indigenous head of this church of over 300,000 people.

Anglicans

Anglican churches in the Pacific, next in our view, had a well-defined road to follow toward independence. In the beginning the bishop was all-powerful, the bishop was a European, and the bishop was appointed by a foreign body in Australia or New Zealand. This was dependency. There were three stages, then, to pass through in achieving independence. First it was necessary to have the power of the bishop shared with a local synod and gradually to increase the proportion of indigenous people. Next it was necessary to have an indigenous man chosen as bishop. Finally it was necessary to establish an independent province of the Anglican communion so that no foreign bodies would have a hand in the selection of the bishop.

The diocese of Melanesia, that is, the Solomons, northern New Hebrides, and intervening islands, naturally took the lead in this process, since it had a fifty-year head-start over the other major Anglican area, eastern Papua. Both areas at the beginning of the twentieth century had a clearly expressed commitment to the creation of an indigenous church with an indigenous ministry.[33] The first step for Melanesia was taken in 1921 when a synod was established to consult with the bishop, though at that time the priests who made up its membership were mostly Europeans. The bishop retained a veto power over its action.[34] It led a fitful existence. Bishop Baddeley, who was in office during World War II, did not believe in synodical government. But it was revived after the war by Bishop Caulton, and in 1965 laity were added to the clergy members.[35] By then the clergy were predominantly indigenous and the earlier tendencies to accept foreign guidance were beginning to disappear. In 1963 the first islander bishops were consecrated, two outstanding men who then gave fine service as assistant bishops for Ysabel and Malaita. Melanesia was emerging as an independent force in the Anglican church.

The only remaining steps were taken in 1975. Melanesia was still a diocese of the Province of New Zealand and its bishops were chosen by the bishops in New Zealand, after consultation with people from Melanesia. In 1975 the New Zealand province gave its hearty approval to the separation of Melanesia as a new province in its own right, having an archbishop and three bishops, two of whom were the indigenous assistant bishops already mentioned. The archbishop was still a foreigner, but by a strange turn of events, he died that same year, though only fifty-two years of age, and a Solomon islander was elected as the new archbishop. The process was complete and it was clearly an achievement of the foreign bishops and missionaries who had labored for this end. The supporting missionary society in England and New

Zealand had little role in all this because, unlike the mission boards and societies of the Protestants, its role was largely confined to money raising. But the bishops and missionaries had kept the goal of indigenizing before them with rather unusual steadiness, and although somewhat behind the Protestants they did reach it before any strong local demand developed and before the country became independent.

New Guinea Anglicanism followed the same path but on a later schedule. The delay was due not only to the later start but also to the fact that New Guinea bishops more often had a monarchical bent, which fitted with the general tendency of that mission to exalt the early and medieval church as its model. Then too, New Guinea suffered a grievous blow to its plans for creating an indigenous priesthood when Mount Lamington erupted in 1951 and killed nearly all the young men who were in priestly training. It is not often that natural disasters play a significant role in the course of human history, which is why we have had no occasion to mention the various hurricanes with their wakes of devastation, which figure prominently in most reports from the Pacific islands. But Mount Lamington was a natural disaster that delayed the advance of the Anglican church by a decade or more.

Synodical government came very slowly in New Guinea. The bishops for the most part did not want a synod that would share in the power of decision making. They were willing to consult with the people, however, and at the very beginning of the twentieth century they began to hold informal councils of representatives of the church. The people at first were too divided for this and some of the councils were marred by physical fighting between groups, but in later years they were revived and improved.[36] More important were the conferences of foreign clergy, meeting first in 1905, to advise the bishop. Native clergy were added to that group in 1938 and they gradually increased in number.[37] Because of the setback caused by Mount Lamington it was not until 1964 that an islander majority was reached.[38] One indigenous priest, George Ambo, became an assistant bishop in 1960, the first Pacific islander to enter the episcopate of any church. But there was still no constitutionally established synod and Anglicans had to admit that they were far behind the New Guinea Lutherans and the United Church in indigenous leadership.[39]

They have moved rapidly in recent years, however. A synod was finally constituted in 1971, fifty years behind Melanesia, and an independent province was established in 1977 when the ties with the Province of Queensland were broken. At that time four bishops, including two Papuans, were established along with one archbishop, a European. The major power in governing the new province was given to five diocesan synods and a provincial council where the indigenous voices were in the majority.[40]

There was, we must not forget, the third, much smaller Anglican diocese in Polynesia. Its original membership was made up mostly of the Europeans settled in that area, though there were also the small group of Tongans who were instrumental in its establishment and the Solomon islanders who came from Melanesia to work on the Fiji plantations. The last group, being poor and depressed, had little influence. There was a synod, which was filled with Europeans. Priests and bishops were imported from abroad. As a whole the church was decidedly foreign in its orientation. The very idea of indigenization seemed not to occur in its thinking until the 1960s.

At that time there came from Australia a new bishop, J. C. Vockler, who turned the direction of the church sharply around. He was determined to make it a part of the island scene and abandoned the thought of its being primarily for expatriate white people. He pressed for the training of clergy from among the limited number of Tongans, Samoans, Fijians, and Indians who had come into the communion. He met with a surprisingly enthusiastic response from these groups and by 1971 the majority of the priests were islanders. The synod by then already had a non-European majority.[41] The new bishop elected in 1975, Jabez Bryce, was himself part-Samoan. So, even though the diocese remained in the Province of New Zealand, it was establishing itself as one of the independent, indigenous churches of the Pacific.

Roman Catholics

When we come finally to the Roman Catholic church, the consideration of independence seems out of place. There was never any thought of independent Catholic churches being created in the Pacific as there were independent Protestant churches. All Catholics were to be part of the one church centered in Rome and subject to the pope. Nevertheless, independence was not a meaningless concept for Pacific Catholics. Varying degrees of autonomy were possible within the single church structure and some of the Catholics' international ties were bonds that could be loosened if not severed.

First of all, there was the fact that the dioceses in the Pacific were classified not as normal dioceses but as vicariates apostolic, having a missionary status under the supervision of the Congregation for the Propagation of the Faith in Rome. Their bishops were subject to transfer as normal bishops were not, and, what is more, the appointment of bishops was made after nomination by the missionary order rather than by the diocese. This whole arrangement could be changed by the stroke of a pen in the Vatican and in fact on several occasions Rome considered changing it, but decided that the vicariates were not yet sufficiently developed.[42] Rome's interest in moving in this direction was evident in other parts of the world in the 1950s as vicariates apostolic in Africa and Asia were rapidly being changed into dioceses.[43] An increasing interest in a local emphasis was also evident in Rome's canonization in 1954 of Pierre Chanel, the early missionary martyr in Futuna who became the first person connected with the South Pacific islands to receive canonization. Vatican Council II produced a greater momentum for change with its emphasis on regional episcopal structures to deal with regional problems. Finally in 1966 Pope Paul VI decreed the establishment of the regular hierarchy throughout the Pacific. The only area left as a vicariate was the Caroline and Marshall Islands, where the American Jesuits were working and which at that time was related to the American hierarchy. Not till 1979 was it raised to the rank of a diocese and fitted into the Pacific rather than American structures. In the 1966 action six archbishoprics were created and with them twenty-two other bishoprics. The missionary orders, whose local structures had served as the diocesan structures, now had to separate themselves and create their own structures and identities. They no longer were to operate the dioceses but were to serve them. Regional episcopal structures, that is, regular conferences of the bishops to deal with their common problems, now came into being, one for Papua New Guinea and the Solomon Islands and another for the remaining South Pacific islands.

The bishops up to this time were always foreigners from Europe, Australia, or America and herein lay an even more important need for independence. Bishops had autocratic control in their dioceses and did not have to share their power any more than they wished. Therefore as long as the bishops were foreigners the churches could well be seen as under foreign rule. This situation was not so readily susceptible to change, as was the missionary status of the dioceses. No simple order from the Vatican could alter it. Rome could and did urge a rapid indigenization of the episcopate, as it had urged a rapid indigenization of the priesthood from about 1920. But each diocese had to find and nominate the indigenous person who was qualified for the episcopate and this was not easily done when indigenous priests were so few. In the earlier years the missionaries had been slow and reluctant about training and ordaining priests.[44] At midcentury only about one-twentieth of the Pacific priests were indigenous, as compared to one-fourth of the Asian and African priests. Of the few indigenous men, most were serving as assistants to foreigners rather than carrying independent responsibilities. Out of these few the new bishops would have to be found. The remarkable thing is that after Vatican II this was done. Indigenous priests were given consistent preferment over their far more numerous foreign colleagues. Starting in Samoa in 1968 and then in the Marianas, Tonga, Bougainville, Wallis, Fiji, Papua New Guinea, and Kiribati in the 1970s indigenous men were made bishops of their dioceses. Tahiti also received a bishop whose ancestry was one-eighth Tahitian. The first of these bishops, Pio Taofinu'u of Samoa, was made a cardinal in 1973, the first Pacific islander to reach this position. Samoa seemed to take the lead among Catholics, as among Protestants, in creating a more independent church life in the Pacific.

On the local level Catholics did not develop self-government as most Protestants had known it from the beginning. The priest ran the parish, and since most of the priests, unlike the Protestant pastors, were foreign, this meant foreign control in the parish. Some steps were taken, however, to ameliorate this situation before the time when priests would all be indigenous, a time that seemed infinitely far in the future. In some parishes, particularly in Papua New Guinea and in the Vicariate of the Caroline–Marshall Islands, there began to develop councils of lay people to advise and assist the priests. This modified the foreign controls. At the same time (1968) the Micronesian

Vicariate began to train permanent deacons, married men from the island populations who would function as priests, except for the celebration of the Eucharist and hearing confessions. Through them the indigenous voice could increasingly become the major voice in clerical matters.[45]

Another kind of advance toward local control appeared in an enormous self-study project in Papua New Guinea in 1972–75. Two hundred thousand Catholics took part in discussions on the life of their church and made reports that were carried to a National Catholic Assembly consisting mostly of lay people. The Assembly gave first priority to the development of the self-consciousness of the church.[46] This study process and the spirit of discussion and involvement that it engendered everywhere may have done more to create a sense of independent responsibility in the church than could ever come from the creation of indigenous priests or bishops.

The Papua New Guinea self-study led to a National Catholic Council composed chiefly of lay persons. In other parts of the Pacific, diocesan synods began to be formed, again made up largely from the laity.[47] These bodies gave indigenous advice and assistance to the bishop, whether he was foreign or local.

The Roman Catholicism of the Pacific has thus been overcoming to a considerable extent the dependency that has characterized its life. The moving forces in this have not, on the whole, been the islanders. The island priests were too few in number to have much effect. But some foreign missionaries have been vigorous forces for change, even though in earlier generations missionaries had been resistant. The strongest long-continuing force for indigenous leadership has come from the most nonindigenous body, the Vatican itself. In this respect the Catholics were much like the Protestants whose missionary headquarters outside the Pacific islands were the strongest factors in developing independence within the islands.

Other Churches

We have looked now at all the major churches of the Pacific; there are in addition to these the many lesser churches that are found in the islands. Most of these are of recent appearance and therefore have not had a long time of dependency to grow out of. A few are older and have developed significantly.

The South Sea Evangelical Mission has had a long history in the Solomon Islands and out of its work has emerged the independent South Sea Evangelical Church, inaugurated in 1964. It had no long history of gradual development as a national church, but it had strong local foundations. The mission had always believed in self-governing and self-supporting congregations at the local level and these had existed from the beginning. There had also been, since the 1930s, gatherings of the pastor-teachers from the areas around the major mission centers.[48] But at the national level there was no organization or organized activity except what was carried on by the missionaries. It was they who gave the congregations whatever wider contact and vision they might enjoy. Only after World War II did one of the missionaries start organizing associations of neighboring congregations that could develop some common life of their own, and then in 1964 it was a group of missionaries again who traveled about the local churches suggesting that now was the time for creating a national church. This idea was well accepted by the people at a representative assembly held that year and the church was launched forthwith. The first president, chosen by the islanders, was, as in the case of the Lutherans, a foreign missionary. But the rest of the leadership was local and the church had enough strong men to take over all the leadership.[49]

The other long-established churches of smaller size are the Seventh-day Adventists, the Mormons, and the Reorganized Mormons, or Sanitos. All of these groups, like the Roman Catholics, have operated on the principle of appointment of their chief officers by church headquarters that are located outside the Pacific islands. Unlike the Catholics, they do not all allow for local nominations to these offices and their outside headquarters have not been as determined as the Vatican to put local people in power. They have each had a uniform pattern of organization wherever they might be established. Full independence, then, and the opportunity to erect locally conceived structures are not expected in these churches. Yet, as with the Catholics, indigenous leaders can be chosen to take over the top positions, and there have been movements in this direction in all three of these churches. The Seventh-day Adventists in the 1920s and 1930s were already giving local people oversight over considerable areas of their work in the Solomons.[50] And in the 1970s both groups of Mormons put indigenous presidents in charge of their long-established areas of work.

The new missions that poured into the New Guinea highlands after the war were for the most part imbued with the postwar missionary philosophy in favor of the rapid establishment of an independent indigenous church and they proceeded to do this much faster than the old missions had. The Wabag Lutheran Church, for example, was established in 1961, only twelve years after the large Missiouri Synod Lutheran Mission came from America, and the Baptists from Australia created an independent church at the very start of their work.[51] By the 1970s the day of the independent church had evidently come to the Pacific and "the mission" was finally replaced by "the church" as the center of attention and influence.

NOTES

1. Anderson 1943: 34–35. Miller 1978: 118–24.

2. J. Graham Miller, "How Has the Presbyterian Church of the New Hebrides Progressed. . . ," 1949. Archives of Overseas Missions Committee, Presbyterian Church of New Zealand, Auckland. Mrs. E. Holmes, "Report on a Visit to the New Hebrides," 1948. Archives of Overseas Missions Committee, Presbyterian Church of New Zealand, Auckland. Murray 1969: 54–55, 59. South Pacific Missionary Con-

ference, Morpeth, New South Wales, 1948. Report of Commission 10. Archives of Australian Council of Churches, Sydney.

3. Beyerhaus 1959: 104.

4. Parsonson 1954: 12.

5. *Constitution of the New Hebrides Mission Council.* General Secretaries of the Australian and New Zealand Mission Boards to the Secretary of the New Hebrides Mission Council, April 3, 1959, Archives of Overseas Missions Committee of the Presbyterian Church of New Zealand, Auckland. Presbyterian Church of New Zealand, Overseas Missions Committee, "Report of the Assistant Secretary on Visit to the New Hebrides, June-July 1960." Archives, Auckland. Australian Presbyterian Board of Missions, "Visit of the Treasurer to the New Hebrides, June-July 1963." Archives of the Presbyterian Board of Missions, Sydney. Presbyterian Church of New Zealand, Overseas Missions Committee, "Draft of Proposal for the Early Establishment of Responsible Partnership between Presbyterian Churches of the New Hebrides, Australia and New Zealand," April 27, 1965, Archives, Auckland.

6. Keysser 1929: 213-15.

7. American Lutheran Church, Board of Foreign Missions, Executive Committee, Minutes, March 27, 1950. Board Archives, Minneapolis. Kuder 1952: 322.

8. Reitz 1975: 47. Board of Foreign Missions, American Lutheran Church, Minutes, Jan. 8-9, 1946. Board Archives, Minneapolis.

9. Frerichs 1957: 99.

10. Kuder 1974: 158.

11. Minutes, 1966, p. 4. Grosart 1970: 378.

12. *Lutheran World* 24 (1977): 191, 193. The same source reports the formation of the Wabag Lutheran Church as an independent church in 1961, only twelve years after the start of the Missouri Synod Lutheran Mission in the New Guinea highlands.

13. Viner et al. 1916: 29, 33-37, 143, 166. Barradale 1927: 15. Lenwood to H. B. James, March 5, 1918, July 9, 1919; Council for World Mission Archives, London.

14. Williams 1972: 63-64. Cocks 1950: 69. The first assembly of all LMS pastors in the Cook Islands came in 1937, although the organization of the church came later. R. L. Challis, "Report for 1937." Council for World Mission Archives, London.

15. E.g., Challis 1940: 13-16. Challis to Goodall, Sept. 11, 1941; Council for World Mission Archives, London.

16. "Rules Concerning the Propagation of Religion," Japan 1934: 76-78.

17. Jimmy 1972: 101. Report of Delegation to Micronesia 1947, ABC new series 2, vol. 1:7. American Board Archives, Harvard University.

18. ABC 19.4, vol 19, document 27. American Board Archives, Harvard University.

19. George Lockwood to Wm. Strong, June 11, 1929, ABC: 19.4, vol. 19. Third Conference of Marshall Islands Teachers, April 1932; Carl Heine to Mrs. L. O. Lee, May 30, 1933; document 4 and document 5, ABC 19.4, vol. 20, American Board Archives, Harvard University. The name of the church is now the United Church of the Marshall Islands.

20. H. Hanlin, "Brief Report on the . . . Work in Micronesia, 1952," ABC new series 2, vol. 1:4. Jimmy 1972: 112. The churches related to Liebenzell took the name Evangelical, e.g., the Palauan Evangelical Church.

21. United Church Board for World Ministries Annual Report, 1973: 28.

22. E. Thidjine, "Rapport de l'Eglise Evangélique en Nouvelle Calédonie . . .," Dec. 4, 1960, Church Archives, Noumea. Pastor Kicine Buama in *La Vie Protestante,*

July 3, 1960. Evidence of dissatisfaction in the 1920s may be seen in Nerhon 1969: 73.

23. Schloesing 1952: 25.

24. *Missionary Review* 35, no. 10 (April 5, 1926): 3.

25. Threlfall 1975: 198-99.

26. Wetherell 1974: 384-89, 393. Methodist Church of Australasia 1923: 17. Williams 1972: 222.

27. Williams 1972: 270. Hilliard 1966: 338. The first indigenous ordination was in 1938, the second in 1942. The mission board in New Zealand suggested discussion of training ministers, but no discussion took place.

28. Tippett 1967: 91, 360. Hilliard 1966: 338-40. Carter 1973: 136-37.

29. New Zealand Methodist Church, Foreign Mission Department, Report of General Secretary's Visit to the Solomons, 1952, pp. 9-10. Methodist Mission Archives, Auckland.

30. Williams 1972: 270-72.

31. Methodist Church of New Zealand, Overseas Missions Board Minutes, Oct. 16, 1962. Methodist Mission Archives, Auckland. Williams 1972: 3.

32. Threlfall 1975: 214-15.

33. Morrell 1973: 154, 196. Wetherell 1974: 395.

34. Hilliard 1966: 177-78.

35. Morrell 1973: 200, 243. *Southern Cross Log,* November 1965: 105. *Melanesian Mission Broadsheet,* no. 1. Dunstan 1962: 74-75 gives 1958 as the date for adding laity, but this does not accord with the more contemporary evidence in the two previous references.

36. Wetherell 1974: 397-98. Sharp 1917: 34-35. Henslowe 1949: 33.

37. *Historical Sketches. New Guinea* 14. Strong 1947: 164-67. Tomlin 1951: 148. Bishop Strong points out, 1958:6, that it was his decision, two years after assuming office in 1936, to enlarge the conference by including the indigenous priests.

38. Hughes and Tomkins 1969: 132-33.

39. *Pacific Islands Monthly,* December 1972: 25. Gill 1973. Two New Zealand Maoris had been made bishops before Ambo, but he was the first from the islands covered in this study. *Melanesian Messenger,* Easter 1961: 5.

40. Anglican Church of Papua New Guinea 1977: 11-14. *Family,* no. 4: 11, 20-23.

41. Morrell 1973: 251.

42. *Horizons Blancs,* January 1967: 400.

43. Welling 1958: 5.

44. Forman 1974: 427-28. Only the island of Wallis departed from the usual Catholic pattern and, as was noted in chap. 4, had a high proportion of indigenous priests. This was due to the fact that in the nineteenth century Bishop Bataillon had departed from the usual Catholic standards of priestly training and had created a seminary at a fairly elementary level, such as the Protestants developed in most islands. Huonder 1909: 252-56. The Wallis priests, however, were usually stationed alongside Europeans who took the lead in the work. (*Kreuz und Charitas* 32 [1923-24]: 7. Dubois 1927: 82). They were regarded as faithful men, dependable in the daily routine; but not as vigorous leaders and certainly not as innovators.

45. Curran 1978. Caroline and Marshall Islands Mission 1968: 88. A training program for permanent deacons was begun in 1971, but their numbers remained small. The reforms in Micronesia were not followed widely in the Pacific. *Outpost. A Fiji Forum* questioned in 1974 the seriousness of the commitment of the Pacific church to the creation of parish and diocesan councils (July 1974: 24-25). Micronesia's perma-

nent deacons were older men. In 1969 Samoa sent a missionary to Rome to request permission to invite and to train for the permanent diaconate younger men who would expect to marry. On this matter the permission from Rome was not forthcoming and the minimum age of thirty-five for permanent deacons was maintained. At this point, therefore, Rome did not fulfill its usual role of pressing the missions toward more indigenous leadership.

46. Janssen 1975. *Self-Study. . . Newsletter,* nos. 1–7, March 1973–February 1975. *Self-Study Seminar Handbook*, 1972. Self-Study, *Church: Material and Questions for Discussion*, 1973. The self-study was modeled on one made by the Catholics in Tanzania and the man who had organized the effort in Tanzania was brought to New Guinea to help. *Catalyst* 3, no. 1 (1973): 72–73. A similar, smaller self-study was undertaken by the Catholics in the Solomons. *Catalyst* 7, no. 1 (1977): 68.

47. Janssen 1975: 237–38. Coppenrath 1976: 29.

48. Hilliard 1966: 396.

49. *Not in Vain,* June 1964: 2–3.

50. Hilliard 1966: 459–60.

51. *Lutheran World* 24 (1977): 191, 193. The new Baptist church was named the Enga Baptist Union.

11
The Postwar Role of the Church in Education and Medicine

The end of the war saw a new enlightenment appearing in the colonial governments of the Pacific. They now, much more than before, saw themselves as responsible for the welfare of their subjects. They were convinced that it was the duty of government to provide educational, medical, and other social services on a scale that had not been even considered previously, and they were willing to pour in money from their home countries to bring this about. The new attitude was partly the result of the concept of the welfare state, which was spreading throughout the world at that time. It was also in part the result of the retreat from imperialism, which followed the war. Imperialist governments were under international pressures and local pressures to divest themselves of their colonies and, if not immediately divesting, to develop these colonies to the point where divestment would be a realistic possibility. Thus the colonial powers in the Pacific felt themselves pressed to justify their continuing rule by improving their social services.

Education

Education was the principal field where the churches were affected by the change. The education that the church had provided in the Pacific prior to government involvement had been of a fairly simple sort. The village schools conducted by the pastors and catechists had taught literacy and religious knowledge, but usually little more. Sometimes even this was done in seriously garbled and inadequate ways.[1] Any education beyond the elementary level had ordinarily been directed toward the Christian ministry and had also been fairly simple.[2] But through this fairly simple program the churches had produced populations which, in the eastern and central islands, had literacy rates that were among the highest of any countries in the world.[3] They had also maintained fairly homogeneous populations educated in local languages, in touch with much of their traditional heritage, and without an alienated elite such as tended to appear when the government drive for advancement began.[4]

The government's appearance on the stage meant that the church's role would inevitably be reduced. As government schools spread through the islands, church schools would gradually be replaced. We have already seen how this happened in relation to the primary schools in most of the eastern and central islands. There the village schools under church auspices had already disappeared or were beginning to disappear by the time of World War II. The churches in consequence had begun to concentrate on central schools and secondary education. Gradually the governments were moving into secondary education too, although in some territories—Fiji, Samoa, and Tahiti—they provided help for the churches' secondary schools at the same time that they were building up their own. Church contributions to secondary education remained important everywhere except in the Cook Islands. Yet the trend toward displacement of the church from primary education and from part of secondary education was clearly established by 1942 in most of the eastern and central Pacific.

In the western Pacific, government involvement had a different effect at first. It led to a great increase in church activity. The prewar period had not seen any significant growth of government education in that part of Oceania. The church still operated almost all the primary education and there was no secondary education for indigenous people. Therefore, when, immediately after the war, the governments awoke to their responsibilities, the first effect was that they tried to increase what the churches were doing rather than to replace it. The governments were so far behind in educational endeavor that they needed all the help they could get, and the churches with their already established system of schools were the readiest source for help. So in the western Pacific the governments asked the churches—or, more strictly speaking, the missions, since it was the missionary organizations that they dealt with—to join them in a common effort to advance education and they offered large funds for this task. They also established new standards and made the grant of any funds contingent upon the meeting of their standards.

Nearly all the missions accepted this challenge and joined in the governments' efforts. They had certain qualms about the introduction of educational standards that recognized only intellectual, not moral, goals and about the possible deleterious effects of government syllabi and government examinations dominating the life of the classroom. But they went ahead nonetheless. Some of them recognized the likelihood that after this time of increased church activity the governments would move in and take over. Eventually the same pattern that had been followed in the east would emerge in the west. When the government programs were stronger and no longer in such need of church help, they would begin to displace the church and to take over more and more of education.

Different points of view struggled within the churches in regard to this eventual retreat from the educational field. The foreign missionaries were divided in their outlook. Some of them, particularly the Protestants who came from countries where secular government schools had long been the common form of education, believed that the action of the Pacific governments was the right one and was even to be encouraged. They believed that the church should gradually withdraw from education, or at least withdraw to a few specially supported schools where a strong program could be maintained. The leaders of the Methodist missions from Australia had been expressing this point of view as early as the mid-1930s.[5] The representatives of the London Missionary Society were also sympathetic to it, as was evident in the Cook Islands by 1915. More missions came to this position as government standards and pressures increased and as the deleterious effects on church life of heavy concentration on education became more apparent.[6]

On the other hand, many missionaries believed that the church should hold on to education as much as possible, using whatever government help might be available, and retreating from the field only under the greatest pressure. They believed that church-related education would be necessary if future generations were to receive adequate character training with a desire for service to the community and were to have developed religious convictions and knowledge. This outlook was practically universal among Roman Catholic missionaries before Vatican Council II. It corresponded to their background in Catholic schools in their home countries and to the official Catholic position as expressed in the 1929 papal encyclical on education.[7] It was shared also by many Protestant missionaries, especially Anglicans and Lutherans.[8]

The indigenous Christians generally supported this latter view. They were accustomed to a unified society with religion at its core, not to a secularized society with religion as one compartment. Therefore they were happy with schools that had a church connection and stressed religious knowledge. They were usually proud of their schools of this type, which they had developed and, in most cases, paid for. To many of them the church was identified primarily in terms of its schools. In the New Hebrides the very word used for church and for Christian worship was "school." In the postwar years education was the focus of the islanders' hopes for advancement. People trusted thereby to gain many of the advantages enjoyed in the more technologically advanced countries. Therefore they were eager to keep the church schools and to improve them with government aid and mission contributions. Whenever missionary leadership moved in the direction of reducing church commitments in this field it was sure to encounter opposition from the local Christians.[9] The churches of Africa, it may be noted, were having this same problem with the same attitudes represented among missionaries and indigenous Christians during these years.[10]

The specific territorial developments of the churches in education have already been noted for the territories in most of the eastern and central Pacific because they took place in large part before the war. At this point, therefore, attention needs to be directed to the western Pacific where the major changes came after the war. American Samoa and the Gilbert and Ellice Islands also developed late and therefore need to be included with the western islands in this regard.

American Samoa

American Samoa saw the most rapid and total change. The transformation there was from a government that did almost nothing to a government that did almost everything. After the war a complete school system, free and compulsory, from the first grade through high school, and eventually even including a noncompulsory junior college, was established in those islands. Protestant education faded before this. The LMS, which had been the chief educational agency before the war, tried operating some secondary schools when primary education had been taken over, and the Mormons built a large high school. But none of these could compete with the government facilities and they were eventually abandoned. Catholics, on the other hand, came in with new resources. They established and maintained elementary and high schools both for boys and for girls that were able to survive despite the government competition and the almost exclusively Congregational nature of the population. In the 1970s the Seventh-day Adventists and—as a new group in the Pacific—the Southern Baptists began elementary schools.

Gilbert and Ellice Islands (Kiribati and Tuvalu)

The Gilbert and Ellice Islands followed the more usual and gradual pattern of development. The government before the war had done little in education. It had maintained a single central school where for a time some mission teachers could receive a year's supplementary training, and it had given small grants to help the missions.[11] Now, after the war, it gradually raised the standards of the central school to secondary level. It also began to found government primary schools on the various islands. Grants were made to church schools wherever satisfactory standards were maintained. But the grants were small, whereas the standards were ever more exacting.

Under these circumstances the LMS missionaries came to the conclusion that they did not have the resources to continue meeting government expectations, and since they believed that education was a state responsibility in any case, they informed the government in 1965 that they would gradually withdraw from their primary schools over a ten-year period and asked the government to take over their work.[12] As they moved to implement this policy they encountered much reluctance from Protestants in the villages. These people, for whom religion permeated all of life, were not ready to give up church schools for government ones. At a number of places where the government school did not materialize in adequate form, the local Protestants succeeded in securing the continuation of their old LMS schools.[13] The Catholics, on the other hand, proved well able to maintain an educational system supplementary to the government one. They had sufficient foreign personnel to develop their own teacher training college and through it to raise the level of their local schools. Where their schools were strong and the majority of the people were Catholic, the government did not even try to create a competing school. Protestants in these cases had to send their children to the Catholic schools, although the bishop gave permission for them to have separate religious teaching given by their pastors.[14] Catholics also expanded their schools into some of the more strongly Protestant islands, including the entirely Protestant Ellice Islands, now named Tuvalu.[15]

New Hebrides (Vanuatu)

In the New Hebrides, likewise, Protestants and Catholics both joined the government—or, more precisely, the governments, French and British—in advancing the educational system. New Hebrides schools were regarded as the most backward in the Pacific. There were at the end of the war nineteen Roman Catholic schools, usually with European Sisters teaching, and some two hundred Protestant schools, usually with untrained New Hebrideans teaching. The Protestant teachers were part of the system of church workers in the villages and usually served also as pastors. Their salaries and the school costs were paid by the villagers who sometimes put 60 to 80 percent of their total cash income into the maintenance of their schools. Immediately after the war the Presbyterian missionaries, as we have seen, conferred independence on their New Hebridean church, and they therefore had to begin rapid improvements in their education to ready the church for its new responsibilities. They began several district schools and, in 1953, the first secondary school in the islands.[16] In that same year the intergovernmental South Pacific Conference called attention to the New Hebrides' backwardness, and both governments began at last to assume some responsibilities for education. The French administration began to open schools and to pay subsidies to indigenous teachers in French mission schools. The British did something of the same and there was not a little rivalry between the two powers and consequently between the missions, the Catholics associated with the French regime and the Protestants with the British, as each tried to win the people as well as to educate them.[17] The British government in 1959 appointed its first education officer and called a conference of the Protestant missions to consider education. There it was decided to create a teacher training college operated jointly by missions and government.[18] Once it was in operation, however, the government gradually pushed the missions out of the joint enterprise. The Presbyterian missions were also gradually displaced from all primary education, but in this case with their ready concurrence. The Presbyterians, as the largest mission, took the lead in 1965 in calling on the government to take over in this field and announced their intention to turn over their primary schools to it.[19] During the 1970s this was gradually accomplished. Catholic schools, however, continued with French subsidies, alongside the French administration schools. And both Catholics and Protestants continued to operate the secondary schools they had begun.

New Caledonia

New Caledonia followed a course in some ways similar to that of the New Hebrides. There, too, it was only in the postwar years that the French government began to give significant support to the church schools for indigenous people. In this case both Catholic and Protestant schools were supported, by payment of teachers' salaries, purchase of equipment, and subsidies for buildings. This was a marked change from earlier years of the twentieth century, when there had been so much hostility between government and church that Catholic religious had been driven out of government schools and had had to begin their own establishments. The new policy, like the old, was simply a reflection of changing attitudes in France. The government also built up its own system of education rapidly—much more rapidly than the churches could build up theirs.[20] In comparison to the prewar years, the government by 1962 was teaching ten times as many pupils as it had earlier, the Catholics four times as many, and the Protestants 50 percent more. It was clear that the government was outdistancing the churches and the Catholics were far outdistancing the Protestants.[21]

The cost of church education was far below that of government education, partly because the churches' teachers were paid less and were often not so highly trained as their governmental counterparts. The goverment was pushing for improvements in these respects and in the 1970s offered to provide the full cost of higher salaries for teachers provided that it had the right to place its own teachers in schools that did not have enough properly qualified staff, and also provided that French was made the dominant language and a French education was given. The churches bridled at the conditions attached to the help. The Catholic archbishop and priests made a declaration against any education that would be unsuitable to the culture and would make people dependent, and the Protestants sent a letter of protest to the territorial assembly.[22] That assembly finally voted to make the help available without any such stringent conditions. Church education was preserved more fully in New Caledonia and the Loyalties than in almost any other territory, except for solidly Catholic Wallis and Futuna where the church continued to provide all the schools, and the government continued to pay all the costs.

Solomon Islands

In the Solomons, as we have seen, nothing came of the hesitant government efforts at educational improvement before the war. Immediately after the war the picture began to change. The government appointed an education officer and held a conference (in 1947) with all the missions. The missions were ready for cooperation but not for the control that the government wanted to impose. They resisted the proposal that no school could operate without government approval. The Roman Catholics were most strongly opposed, but the Anglicans too were in opposition and even the Methodists, who had the most open attitude to government advances, felt that the proposed penalties were premature in light of the small contribution the government was prepared to make. It was not until 1954 that official regulations, which granted the missions the desired freedom to have additional, unapproved schools, were finally agreed on and promulgated.[23] It was also not until about that time that government began to make significant grants to approved mission schools. These gradually increased until they covered the major part of the salaries of trained teachers.

The missions strained to do all they could for the advancement of education. Schools were soon eating up about half the foreign personnel and half the budget of most of the missions. Following the government's lead all of them, except the South Sea Evangelical Mission, developed secondary schools. The SSEM improved its schools, but was not as financially capable, nor did it have as great a devotion to education as did the other missions—a fact that caused some disaffection among its Melanesian adherents, who shared the usual enthusiasm of this period for education. The Methodists also, strangely enough, lagged behind the other missions, although they did make a start in the secondary education field. The leadership that they had had in more advanced schooling before the war disappeared. The Anglicans and the Catholics were the leaders now, although the Seventh-day Adventists advanced remarkably for their small size.[24]

Eventually, however, it became clear that the missions could not keep up with the necessary pace of educational advance. As the schools improved in accordance with government demands, they also became more expensive. At the same time there was need for more informal adult education to enrich the lives of village people, and the churches felt called to help in this. Some of them also felt that the cause of national unity required a unified school system operated by the government. The Methodists already in the 1950s were calling on the government to take over all primary education, and the SSEM was assuming that development. The Anglicans and the Catholics continued to believe strongly in church schools supported by government grants, but by 1974, because of the several reasons mentioned here, the Anglicans changed their minds. At the end of that year they and the other two major Protestant missions announced that they were withdrawing from primary education. Financial pressures forced the Catholics to follow suit. The government proceeded, then, to set up area school boards to continue the work. Only the Adventists and Silas Eto's followers in the small Christian Fellowship Church continued their own systems of primary education.

Among secondary schools, however, the majority remained under church control, while the government proceeded to build up its own secondary system. Churches also pressed forward with the creation of about a dozen rural training centers which tried to help those many people for whom there were no places in the few secondary schools and no opportunities in urban-industrial life. The churches thus had a special role to play even though they no longer dominated education.[25]

The Solomons provide the clearest example of what has happened and is happening to the widespread system of church-sponsored education that once characterized the Pacific. The simple and limited village education that was found at the beginning of the twentieth century in most of the Pacific was found in the Solomons, although not as widely as in most island groups. The great expansion of educational work by missions that came in the postwar years was very much in evidence in the Solomons. And then the retreat from educational involvement, in favor of government operations and a more limited, specialized role for the church, took place in the Solomons as completely as anywhere else and more rapidly than in almost any other territory.

Papua New Guinea

Papua New Guinea followed the same road as the Solomons, but not so far. The experiences of the war awoke Australians to the tremendous importance of that island for them and the necessity of paying attention to and providing funds for the development of this previously neglected area. The fact that the northern half of the island was held under mandate from the United Nations was a further reason to make Australia move, because the United Nations would be pressing it to prepare the territory for eventual independence. At the close of the war, therefore, the Australian government began to give new attention and fresh resources to Papua New Guinea.

One of the first things done was to call all the missions together for a conference with the government on educational plans and policies. Such conferences continued to be held biennially. At the first of them the government indicated its new interest in the rapid advancement of education, its desire to bring the missions into partnership in this task and its readiness to make large grants to the missions to help them in their educational efforts. There were problems in this for the missions. They saw that in the long run this would mean government control, for if they expanded their efforts using government funds they would become dependent on government. The villages, which in many areas of the country had built up self-reliant church schools, would also become dependent on government. A secular rather than religious basis would be established for education. The government's desire to make English the language of the schools would divorce people further from their indigenous culture than had been true in the mission schools. Mission schools all used indigenous languages, albeit selected languages that were not the mother tongues of many of the people in the schools.[26] Certain negative actions of the government also led some of the missions to see the plan as primarily an effort to enhance government influence at the expense of the churches.[27]

But for the same reasons that applied elsewhere in the Pacific islands, the missions were ready to accept the government's plan and to plunge into the new endeavor. They were given four representatives, chosen by the government from mission personnel, to sit on the Educational Advisory Board and, along with five other members, to advise the administration on educational policy. They were given rapidly increasing grants for their work even though the government was also beginning its own school system. They also threw larger and larger resources of their own into education. In eleven years (1953–64) the mission funds put into education increased from $222,000 to $907,000, while the government's grants to them increased from $81,000 to $489,000.[28]

At first the administration did not press its school regulations strictly and did not insist on the teaching of English. But with the Education Ordinance of 1957 it made the teaching of English a requirement for any recognized school and started closing the unrecognized schools. This brought a crisis, for many mission schools did not have English-speaking teachers and could not qualify for the grants they had been receiving, and many schools were told to close down. There were demonstrations in the villages and protests from the missions with the result that the government finally relented and allowed the continuation of unrecognized schools as long as they were primarily for religious instruction, the so-called Bible Schools. It also relented temporarily on the English requirement, allowing noncompliance in recognized schools until the beginning of 1959.[29] The pressure for English and for better-trained teachers, however, did force the missions to separate their "teacher training" from their "preacher training," and some sixteen teachers' colleges were established by them. For a time the government talked of having a central government college to which all the missions would send their future teachers, as was done in the New Hebrides.[30] But adamant opposition by the Catholics and the Anglicans, who feared the loss of religious concerns in such a college, led to the dropping of that proposal, and the church-operated teachers' colleges have continued.

The missions had difficulty getting the best teachers and attracting the best pupils because they paid much lower salaries and usually had poorer facilities than the government schools. The difference was apparent in the much lower cost of a mission education. A pupil in a mission school cost the government only one-sixth the cost of a pupil in a government school.[31] Because of the difficulties, the number of schools operated by some of the major Protestant missions began to decrease sharply in the late 1960s. Some were closed because the government proceeded to build its own schools almost alongside them. The Catholic bishops saw the increasing weakness of their position as they found it difficult to recruit teachers, and they called on the government to provide the same salaries for mission teachers that it gave to government teachers.[32]

The government was in a position now, both because of the strength of its own educational enterprise and because of the difficulties of the missions, to bring about agreement on the establishment of a single national system of education. The missions were also readier for a government system. The Protestant groups, except for the Seventh-day Adventists, felt that academic improvements and better salaries would justify government operation of the

school system. The Roman Catholics, as a result of the transformations following Vatican Council II, were also more ready to merge their efforts in a
larger whole and not to try to cling to what had been their own.[33] Accordingly
a national system, incorporating all churches but the Adventist, was begun in
1970. All teachers, including foreign missionaries, were placed under government appointment with a common salary scale, and all could be moved to any
school in the system. Local and district boards managed primary education
and a small number of church representatives were allowed on these and on
the National Education Board, much smaller proportionately than on the old
Educational Advisory Board. Boards of control of church-sponsored secondary schools, however, could still be made up mostly of church representatives. At the time the churches entered into the national system they were still
educating 70 percent of the pupils of the country.[34]

Micronesia

Finally, in the field of education, we come to Micronesia. Before the war,
mission schools had already been greatly limited by the Japanese, who built
up their own much better system of education. At times new buildings had
not been allowed for mission schools and pupils had been required to leave
the mission schools to fill up government schools.[35] The American government, which took over from the Japanese, was oriented toward universal
public education as found in the United States, and it began a system of
schools at elementary level for a number of islands. At the same time the
Protestant and Catholic missions revived schools they had operated in earlier
days or began new ones. The Catholics, who soon had over forty teaching
Sisters as well as a number of priests in education, were especially noted for
the quality of their schools.[36] They began the first real high school in 1953,
and later developed four others. The Protestants followed with four high
schools, two established by the Liebenzell Mission in the west, one by the
American Board in Truk, and one by the Marshall Islands churches for their
own area. The government, in accordance with the American system of separation of church and state, did not give direct financial support to these
church schools, but it was interested in their progress and occasionally gave
help with materials or other needs.[37]

When President John F. Kennedy launched his new program to throw
enormous funds into Micronesia, especially for education, and thus to link
the people of the islands to the United States, the situation changed rapidly.
New schools went up all over the islands and scores of new teachers were
brought in from America. Government high schools, of which there had been
only one, were now started in all six districts. This was a program clearly
designed to give a full American education to the young people, and it was
eagerly accepted by the Micronesians even though there was little hope of
employment for academically educated people in large numbers.[38]

As the government program gained momentum the churches began to reduce their educational commitments. Numbers of elementary schools were closed and their pupils transferred to government schools. When a hurricane blew down many Catholic schools in the Marianas, they were not restored. The American Board—now known as the United Church Board—turned over its high school to the government in 1973, to the dismay of Micronesian Protestant leaders.[39] Micronesia was following in a limited way the pattern of educational developments in the rest of the Pacific, though it still had a number of strong church schools on Catholic and Liebenzell foundations, which operated without government support.

Medical Service

In the other common branch of Christian service, health care, developments were similar to those in education. As we have noted this was a much smaller service than education and was less common in the Pacific missions than in missions in other parts of the world. It was concentrated in three territories, the New Hebrides, the Solomons, and Papua New Guinea. The reason for this concentration is to be found in the fact that governmental health services began later in these territories and so there was more need for church-sponsored services.

Immediately after the war the governments of these three territories began ambitious plans for expanded medical service. In Papua New Guinea the great medical program carried out by the military authorities during the war set an example and spurred the government to plan an ambitious program.[40] The expanded government plans in the three territories included increased grants to missions for their medical work; in fact in the New Hebrides the British regime expanded chiefly by increasing its help to missions.

The missions likewise increased their efforts, quite apart from and beyond the increased aid that they received. New hospitals were established, and old ones were rebuilt and greatly enlarged. The Anglican mission in Papua, which had had three hospitals that were little more than dressing stations with a couple of beds, transformed these into larger structures with operating rooms and training programs and with trained European nurses in charge.[41] In the New Hebrides the Presbyterians started a system of training and stationing dressers around all the islands of the group in order to provide a broad program of simple medical care. The Seventh-day Adventists began new hospitals in all three territories. Thus despite the growth of government services the missions continued to play a large role in health care. In Papua New Guinea in the mid-1960s it was estimated that they provided one-half the medical care that was available.[42]

But this was an inordinately expensive service for any voluntary organization to maintain. Although most of the hospitals were simple affairs with nurses in charge rather than doctors, the bigger hospitals, which required doctors, were becoming more numerous. The cost of equipment was also a heavy burden. Some hospitals, such as the Missouri Synod Lutheran one in the western highlands of New Guinea, were most elaborate in their equipment. Governments established continually higher standards to emulate. It was estimated that the cost of establishing one government hospital in Papua New Guinea equaled the cost of all the mission hospitals in the country put together. The government grants to the missions, though increasing, did not come near to covering the increased costs. For Papua New Guinea in 1964 the missions were spending from their own funds for medical services something approaching twice the amount they were receiving in government grants.[43] In the Solomons the discrepancy was even greater, for the government there concentrated much more on its own services and gave very little to the missions.

One unexpected source of help appeared in the Lepers' Trust Board of New Zealand. This vigorous fund-raising organization developed by a buoyant and resourceful Catholic layman, P. J. Twomey, made major grants year after year to all types of missions in the Pacific for their medical work. Though its original interest was in serving lepers, it raised its sights to helping with all the health services, particularly for the building of hospitals and the provision of hospital boats to travel among the islands. The work for lepers also got special help from the governments. In all three territories as well as in New Caledonia, Fiji, and Tahiti, the mission-operated leper asylums were completely funded by governments as long as asylums were still used.

There were increasing questions as to whether the missions could continue to do what was required of them in the medical field and whether the government should not take full responsibility and pay the full costs. The Presbyterians in the New Hebrides pressed this question very strongly on the British administration there. In Papua New Guinea Roman Catholic and Lutheran leaders, whose churches carried the largest burdens of medical work, began to question whether they were not too heavily involved in this sphere, doing what the government should be doing. Lutherans were putting one-third of their mission funds into medical work.[44] The Catholics saw in the French regimes of New Caledonia, the New Hebrides, and Wallis an alternative arrangement. There the Catholic mission had all along provided nurses for government hospitals, and they continued to work in that way rather than trying to maintain hospitals themselves.

Some reduction in mission medical work began. In 1966 the British regime in the New Hebrides took over the system of local medical stations, operated by dressers, which the Prebyterians had created, and a few years later it took over the main Presbyterian hospital, the Paton Memorial Hospital at Port Vila, and some other hospitals. It continued, on the French regime's model, to employ some mission personnel in these institutions. In 1974 the Papua New Guinea government took the first steps toward the creation of a National Health Plan by assuming responsibility for the full payment of all medical workers associated with the churches. This meant a great increase in salaries for these workers. As in the schools, the workers associated with the churches had been working at much lower salaries than the government employees, and the churches could not possibly afford to raise those salaries to administration levels. The change thus brought a greater degree of justice to the workers and financial relief to the churches.

The reduction of church burdens in the medical field, as in the educational field, meant that the island churches were free to concentrate more on their own church life. They were also more able to stand on their own feet financially. The maintenance of large medical institutions, as of large educational institutions, had required the constant injection of foreign funds and so prevented the churches from reaching independence in their own financial life. Some island church leaders saw this very clearly. The first indigenous secretary of the Lutherans in Papua New Guinea spoke strongly against the dependence resulting from large institutions, and the General Assembly of the Presbyterian Church of the New Hebrides declared that that church "should not try to enter into medical work or take over in any way from the overseas churches."[45]

The churches without such heavy institutional commitments could now explore new avenues of service. In the educational field they began to explore adult education, nonformal education, and the provision of some useful training for the majority of people who could not reap the benefit of the advanced education available to a select few. They stressed again the values of village life and of the improvements possible within it.[46] The Roman Catholic church in Tonga decided in 1974 to close down all its primary schools, into which it had been pouring resources, and began instead a lively program of "Education in Christian Living," which included religious instruction, agricultural education, home improvement and family-life education for all ages, given by traveling teams.[47] Church conferences became centers for critical reflection on what was happening educationally in the society, questioning the growing alienation, dependency, materialism, and individualism that were built into educational and other social service programs.[48]

It is doubtful whether the members of the churches as a whole shared these new visions. They were more distressed at losing the central and dominating place that the church had had in education and medicine than they were excited at any new prospects that emerged. When the French Protestant Mission in New Caledonia, for example, closed the small dispensaries it had operated since the 1920s, because the government was now opening its own dispensaries nearby, it found resistance from local church people at each closing. The average pastor who no longer was allowed to operate the village school was more likely to feel deprived of his past role than to turn his attention forthwith to needed tasks in pastoral service to his congregation. Yet though it was not immediately recognized, there was clearly emerging a whole new life for independent churches in an ecumenical age.

NOTES

1. Hogbin 1939: 178–79. Hilliard 1966: 488. Dupeyrat 1935: 413. Groves 1936: 105.

2. Forman 1969: 151–55.

3. Keesing 1945: 255.

4. Hillas 1938 speaks of the loss of the traditional heritage through mission education in the northern Cooks, and certainly much of that heritage was lost through mission action. Yet it is also clear that the mission schools served to preserve important elements of traditional culture in places like Tahiti, Samoa, Tonga, and Fiji. Leymang 1969 criticizes the deracinating consequences of mission schools, but seems to be talking of the situation after rapid changes had been introduced with government assistance and prodding. R. Oliver 1952: 289 reports how in Africa, too, mission education maintained a unified society with modified tribal structures and something of a cultural renaissance without a deracinated elite before government came in.

5. Methodist Church of Australasia Board of Missions, Special Education Commission 1933–35, Report. Methodist Mission Archives, Sydney. McArthur 1933: 53. Burton 1949: 127.

6. Morpeth Conference, Commission 10 Report, p. 9. Early LMS support for this viewpoint is shown in Viner et al. 1916: 43–45. The Presbyterian missionaries in the New Hebrides requested government to enter education in 1938. New Hebrides Presbyterian Mission Synod, Minutes, Aug. 10, 1938.

7. *Divini Illius Magistri*. Cf. Dupeyrat 1935: 403f.

8. Fullerton 1969: 196. Hand 1966. Ahnne 1931: 48. Korn 1978: 410–11 shows how Catholics and Protestants alike took this attitude when it came to a question of holding the loyalty of their church members.

9. E.g., Methodist Church of Australasia Board of Missions, Report of Commission to Fiji. Board Minutes, Nov. 21, 1946. Methodist Archives, Sydney. At a later time the Methodist churches in New Britain were eager to start a new church high school even though they were denied funds by the Australian Methodist Mission Board, which doubtless saw that government operation of schools was coming. The churches voted, in the absence of foreign aid, to take money from the trust funds of the individual congregations, and thus the high school was built in 1967. Threlfall 1975: 206.

10. African developments were often looked to by Pacific leaders, particularly leaders in Melanesia. This was nowhere more the case than in relation to education and the church. Cf. McArthur 1933: 4. The African eagerness for education had developed a generation earlier than the Melanesian. Cf. Dupeyrat 1935: 403; R. Oliver 1952: 266–67; and *Missions des Iles* 1961: 26–27. In the 1940s the churches of Ghana experienced exactly the same disagreement, between Methodist missionaries who believed in limiting church education, Roman Catholic missionaries who believed in expanding it, and local congregations who believed in its maintenance, which we have noticed in the Pacific. Bartels 1965: 242–44. On the way in which the African governments and churches cooperated in this field and the churches were brought to a total concentration on it, see R. Oliver 1952: 263–84.

11. London Missionary Society 1931: 19–21. Goodall 1954: 390.

12. LMS Annual Report, 1965–66: 20. For a time, starting in 1952, they operated a teacher training college to provide teachers, as distinct from pastors, to be in charge of their schools.

13. Edwards 1971: 15–18.

14. The recognition of Protestant religious teaching in Catholic schools was a sign of the new ecumenical outlook among Catholics and a far cry from the earlier view, which saw schools as a main way of securing converts from a Protestant population.

Cf. Vicariate Apostolic of Samoa, "Report to Society for the Propagation of the Faith, 1911," S.P.F. Archives, Paris.

15. In Tuvalu, the first government schools began in the early 1960s and rapidly replaced the low-level pastors' schools. By 1971 there were only three pastors' schools left. Edwards 1971: 15–18, 22. However, when the country became independent it chose to work in partnership with the Protestant secondary school rather than starting one of its own. National Council of Churches 1979.

16. Duncan and Stuckey 1966. J. S. Murray to G. S. Parsonson, Aug. 13, 1954. Presbyterian Mission Archives, Auckland.

17. V. W. Coombes, Memorandum, June 15, 1953, Presbyterian Mission Archives, Sydney.

18. "Record of Educational Conference, Sept. 11–17, 1959." British Resident Commissioner's Office. Port Vila.

19. Presbyterian Church in the New Hebrides. General Assembly *Proceedings* 1968: 31.

20. The first stirrings of government interest in education of the indigenes had come earlier, in 1927. Martin 1960: 30.

21. Belshaw 1954: 56. Nouvelle Calédonie et Dépendances 1962. The actual figures in 1962 were: 10,424 pupils in government schools, 8,342 in Catholic schools, 885 in the schools of the Free Church of M. Charlemagne, and 634 in the schools of the Evangelical church. Seven years later the Catholic schools had grown only slightly. *Journal de la Société des Océanistes* 25 (1969): 29. By 1978 the Catholics had over 13,000 pupils, the Evangelicals had 1700, and the Free Church 1300. Kohler 1980: 18.

22. Apparently the Free Church of M. Charlemagne was willing to accept the proposals. This was in accord with its earlier attitude toward government and toward a more metropolitan type of education.

23. Laracy 1969: 353–66; 1976: 150–54. *Southern Cross Log,* April 1951: 9–11. New Zealand Methodist Church Annual Conference 1949: 107. New Zealand Methodist Overseas Missions Board, Report of General Secretary's Visit to the Solomons 1952: 8–9. Methodist Mission Archives, Auckland. *Pacific Islands Monthly* 18 (June 1948): 36.

24. British Solomon Islands Protectorate, *Report for the Year 1965:* 47. British Solomon Islands Protectorate, *Report for the Year 1974:* 68. *Not in Vain,* March 1965: 4. New Zealand Methodist Overseas Missions Board, General Secretary's Report to the Board, 1972, pt. 2, pp. 18–21, 23. Methodist Mission Archives, Auckland.

25. British Solomon Islands Protectorate, *Report for the Year 1974*: 66. Australian Board of Missions, Minutes, April 30–May 2, 1963, "Pacific Islands Church Development," p. 20. ABM Archives, Stanmore, New South Wales. New Zealand Methodist Overseas Missions Board, General Secretary's Report to the Board, 1972, pt. 2. pp. 18–21. Palmer 1979: 448–54.

26. Stanner 1953: 106, 152. Frerichs 1957: 155. Pilhofer 1963: vol. 2: 275.

27. Strong 1947: 134.

28. Territory of Papua, *Report for 1953–1954*: 171. Territory of New Guinea, *Report for 1953–1954*: 223. *Responsibility in New Guinea*: 15. Cf. Höhne 1962.

29. Stanner 1953: 153. American Lutheran Church *Official Report* 1956: 157f. Methodist Church of Australasia, Papua District, Report for 1953. Methodist Archives, Sydney. The Lutherans changed the name of Bible School to Tok Ples (i.e., Vernacular) School in 1973. These have continued to meet ordinary village needs in more relevant ways than the more advanced recognized schools. Jaeschke 1974: 269–73.

30. Strong 1947: 139.

31. *Responsibility in New Guinea*: 16. Hand 1966: 46–48.

32. Loy 1970: 5. "Statement of the Catholic Bishops" 1970. Threlfall 1975: 206.

33. Moira 1972: 9. Hellberg 1972: 5.

34. Jones 1972: 2. Threlfall 1975: 221, 230. Cf. Brammall and May 1975.

35. Heine to Strong, March 28, 1922, and Lockwood to Strong, June 11, 1929, ABC 19.4, vol. 19, American Board Archives. Jimmy 1972: 96. Mission schools were of less importance under the Japanese than they had been under the Germans, who left all education to them, but they were by no means as insignificant or nonexistent as stated by Clyde 1935: 109 or Dunstan 1962: 76–77. Cf. document 15, ABC 19.4, vol. 20, American Board Archives and Japan 1923: 10; 1933: 53; 1937: 63.

36. Feeney 1952: 156. Coulter 1957: 358. The teaching Sisters were divided between the newly arrived Maryknoll Sisters—about one-third—and the Mercedarian Sisters, who came originally from Spain and had been in Micronesia before and during the war, but now came also from America, where they had developed a branch.

37. Feeney 1952: 155.

38. Cf. Nevin 1977.

39. Jimmy 1972: 107, 109. *Micronesian Seminar Bulletin*, November 1964, p. 2. *PCC News*, April 1973, p. 5. Crocombe 1973: 13.

40. Territory of Papua and New Guinea 1946: 5–6.

41. Henslow 1958: 196.

42. *Responsibility in New Guinea*: 36. Eight years later missions were providing 60 percent of rural health services, 90 percent of leprosy and tuberculosis care, but only 9 percent of hospital beds. Strong 1974: 20–22.

43. *Responsibility in New Guinea*: 36. Government reports over the previous ten years show an increase in mission expenditure from $88,000 to $292,000 and an increase in government grants from $68,000 to $173,000. Territory of Papua, *Report for 1953–54*, p. 171; *Report for 1964–65*, p. 235. Territory of New Guinea, *Report for 1953–54*, p. 223; *Report for 1963–64*, p. 308. It was the missions in New Guinea Territory that gave so much more than the government. Papua missions contributed less than the amount added by government funds.

44. Moira 1972: 9. Schiotz 1950: 2. Reitz 1975: 27.

45. Zurenuo 1968: 4–5. Presbyterian Church of the New Hebrides, General Assembly 1968: 27.

46. E.g., Beevers 1972. Bugotu 1973. Leadley 1975. *Shaping Educational Ministry* 1977.

47. *PCC News*, December 1974. *Outpost. A Fiji Forum* 4, no. 6 (November 1976): 28.

48. Micronesian Seminar 1974. Jaeschke 1974: 258–60, 272. Spades 1973: 11–15. *Shaping Educational Ministry* 1977.

12
Independent Churches in an Ecumenical Age

During the decades of the 1960s and the 1970s a new kind of world broke in on the Pacific. In consequence a new kind of church began to appear. We have already seen how the churches' educational and medical work expanded and contracted because of the new interest and responsibility that governments took in those spheres. But this was only one example of the way in which the churches changed in response to a transformed environment.

Travel and Communication

The most noticeable change in the environment was the decrease in physical isolation of the islands as new methods of travel and communication appeared. The introduction of radio communication and then of air travel had begun to make an impact in the 1930s. But widespread air travel came later when large airports began to be constructed all over the Pacific. Tourism, which was only beginning as a major industry in the 1950s, grew by leaps and bounds in the following years. It brought swarms of consumption-oriented people from wealthy countries into contact with island people who had simpler wants and expectations. The churches, when they first took note of this development, were generally opposed to it. But later, when tourism was firmly established, they spoke only in terms of controlling its more demoralizing aspects and making sure that the profits from it would come to the island peoples and not to the international corporations.[1]

Not only did outsiders flow in, but islanders flowed out in increasing numbers. Educational opportunities in other parts of the world drew young people away from their homelands. Prospects for economic gain led young and old alike to emigrate. Samoan colonies grew up in Hawaii, California, and New Zealand. Tahitian, Wallisian, and New Hebridean colonies appeared in Noumea. Niue and the Cook Islands lost most of their more vigorous citizens to New Zealand. Within a five-year period one-third of Tonga's men spent time working in New Zealand. The Samoan churches were the only ones that tried to expand with their adherents to these new abodes. The Samoan Congregational church set up districts in the United States and a Samoan Methodist district was created in New Zealand. Other churches, less imperial than the Samoans, relinquished the emigrants to the churches of their new lands, but were still concerned for them. The Tongan churches made demands for fairer treatment and decent wages for their countrymen abroad.[2]

Urbanization

Another change of great significance was the growth of cities in the island world. Places like Suva, Papeete, Noumea, Apia, Port Moresby, and Lae grew at surprising speed and began to develop a cosmopolitan, urban environment. The Pacific churches were not prepared for this; they had always been designed for village life. The problem was most difficult in Melanesia because there each city brought together people of a great variety of languages and tribes. Newcomers to the city might find the language of worship and the congregational life in the city church entirely strange to them. It was to the village church that they really belonged. It was found in 1970 that over 70 percent of the people of Port Moresby had no connection with the church in the city, although many kept in touch with their home churches in the villages. Likewise in the first city church of the Lutherans, the one in Lae, no decisions were taken during the early years without first consulting the village churches from which the members had come.[3]

The churches made varied responses to the new problem. The first was to place foreign missionaries in the cities. Since the missionaries came from more urbanized societies they were more familiar with urban church tasks.[4] Some city congregations organized themselves to keep people of similar backgrounds together so they would feel more at home. The Evangelical church in Papeete divided its congregation into groups, each made up of immigrants from a particular island, and put three or four deacons in charge of the common life of a group. In all of the cities it was found necessary to make the ministry a full-time occupation instead of the half-ministry, half-gardening division of time that was usual in the villages.[5] The training for the ministry had to be radically revised to produce people who could handle the new conditions.

Sectarianism

One effect of the cities upon the church was the rapid rise of small sectarian groups. Just because people coming to the urban centers felt isolated and cut off from their village friends they responded more easily to the appeal of small, tightly knit, and mutually supportive religious groups that had strong convictions and strict standards. In Africa the indigenously established independent churches provided this kind of religious fellowship in the cities and grew greatly as a result. In the Pacific the corresponding indigenous movements—the so-called cargo cults—did not seem to have sufficient sophistication to reach the city people and they did not develop in the urban environment. People who had belonged to the Paliau movement in Manus, for example, abandoned that group when they came to Port Moresby because they felt it was incompatible with city life.[6] But sects from abroad were able to play something of the role of the African independent churches in the Pacific islands, and they grew considerably, though to nothing like the same extent as the independents in Africa.

Five new sectarian groups appeared in the Pacific and grew significantly, usually in the cities but also spreading into some village situations. Most noticeable were the Jehovah's Witnesses, who were spreading in many parts of the world and who made themselves conspicuous by their house-to-house visitation program. Because they attacked other churches vigorously, their literature was not allowed to be imported into several territories, including the first one they entered, Fiji, where they came as early as 1939. There were also restrictions placed on the entry of their personnel in the Solomons, Tonga, and other areas. But during the 1950s and 1960s they succeeded in gaining entry into practically every island group in Oceania. The only ones where they were able to gather more than single small congregations were Fiji, the Solomons, and Papua New Guinea.

Another group that proved popular in the new cities was the Pentecostal church from America known as the Assemblies of God. Its first efforts were also in Fiji, starting in 1926, but it attracted very little response until about 1960. Then it spread into Tonga, Samoa, New Caledonia, Vanuatu (the New Hebrides), and the Marshalls. Like all Pentecostal churches it allowed for a free and emotional type of worship, which appealed to many people who were not satisfied by the formality of most of the Pacific churches.

A surprising mission to find in this group is that of the Bahai. Stemming from a reformist movement in Islam and appealing mostly to intellectuals in the West, with a message of interreligious unity and international, interracial harmony, they seemed poorly adapted to growth among vigorously Christian, practical peoples with little cosmopolitan experience. Yet a certain amount of response was forthcoming from some youths of wider experience and education and from some village folk among whom their missionaries settled. They had some noticeable response in Fiji, Kiribati, the Solomons, Tonga, Samoa, and Vanuatu. Probably their greatest single increase came in 1966 when they won the adherence of Tommy Kabu, leader of an important modernizing movement in the Purari river area of Papua, along with many of his followers.[7]

There were numerous sectarian groups that were able to maintain work in only one area. Of these we should note two, the Brethren Mission— sometimes called Plymouth Brethren—in Suva and the Salvation Army in Port Moresby. The former began in 1935, the latter in 1956. The Brethren remained a small sect, but the Salvation Army, which was originally conceived for an urban proletariat, grew quite fast in its new urban environment, and spread into other parts of the country.

The fastest-growing body in Port Moresby was the Seventh-day Adventists. They may well be included in a listing of the urban sectarian growth, though their main numbers in the Pacific continued to be found in those rural areas where they had started early and where we have already encountered them—the Papuan coast east of Port Moresby, the eastern highlands of New Guinea, the Western Solomons, Aore in Vanuatu, and some villages in Fiji. They now began to spread much more widely in scattered groups. They became considerably more numerous in the Pacific islands than in Australia and New Zealand from where their missionaries came.[8]

It cannot be claimed that this sectarian growth altered the church scene of Oceania in any major statistical way. The bulk of the population continued to belong to the same churches they had always belonged to. But the variety of new, minority churches made people conscious of choices in the field of religion and introduced an element of uncertainty and relativity in many people's views on religion, which meant a great inner change, if not an outer one.

Theological Education

To deal with the urban population and the educated elite, a new kind of ministry was needed by the churches. The slow-moving, steady, and comfortable religious leader of a unified village needed to be replaced by a more alert, active person of higher education and broader experience.[9] The way to change the ministry was to change theological education.

Theological schools had been the first educational institutions above the primary level in the Pacific islands. The oldest of them, Takomoa College in the Cook Islands and Malua in Samoa, began before the middle of the nineteenth century. Each island group normally developed one major institution for the training of Protestant pastors, and these were, for their day, the most advanced and prestigious institutions of their islands. Catholic theological schools came later than the Protestant ones and led only a fitful existence prior to 1950. None of the schools, Catholic or Protestant, could make any great boast of their academic standards. In the Protestant schools the students were normally self-supporting, raising their own food crops and often building their own houses. Mornings might be spent in the classroom, but afternoons had to be devoted to food and housing. It was the kind of education that could be maintained within the economy of the country and it produced pastors who lived like their people, finding their own means of subsistence and espousing a rather practical religion, not given to intellectual profundities or scholarship. But it was not the kind of education that could meet the challenge of the new day when islanders were developing higher education and traveling abroad and acquiring many new ideas.[10]

In the 1950s and 1960s a general upgrading of theological education came about. Self-support efforts by students were reduced or abandoned and the young theologians for the first time gave their whole attention to their studies. While the language of teaching continued in most places to be a Pacific language, English or French became the language of the books that were used and in some places they became also the language of the classroom.

New schools with higher entrance requirements were established in several territories—Tahiti, Tonga, Kiribati, the Solomons, and Papua New Guinea—and where the older schools were maintained they were given much higher standards. Roman Catholic schools were established on a firmer footing.[11]

A further step up was taken with the creation of central schools to serve the entire region. The first of these was the Pacific Theological College in Suva, a joint establishment of the Protestant churches of all the islands except New Guinea. It opened its doors in 1966. This was the first educational institution in the South Pacific islands to grant degrees. The Catholics, who had been considering a central institution longer than the Protestants, delayed opening one until 1972 when the Pacific Regional Seminary was established in close proximity to and in close cooperation with the Protestant college.[12] Since Papua New Guinea was not involved in these institutions, advanced theological schools for that country were founded by the Catholics, the Lutherans, the United Church, and by a cooperating group of conservative evangelical bodies in the highlands.[13] To enable these rising institutions to help each other, two associations of schools were formed, the South Pacific Association of Theological Schools and the Melanesian Association of Theological Schools, the latter largely concentrated in Papua New Guinea. At the conferences of these associations it became apparent that theological education was moving onto new levels and embarking on bold experiments.[14] The central schools were producing people who could become the teachers of the territorial schools, thus replacing expatriate personnel. Foreign teachers gradually disappeared from work in the territorial schools in the 1970s, and by the end of that decade even the central Protestant school in Suva had a largely indigenous staff.

Ecumenicity

The cooperative relationships in theological education were one mark of an ecumenical revolution that swept through the islands from 1960 onward.

In earlier years isolation and hostility had characterized interchurch relations. The isolation resulted from the agreements between the first Protestant missions not to infringe on each other's areas of work. So the Congregationalists worked in Tahiti and Samoa, the Methodists in Fiji and Tonga, and the Presbyterians in Vanuatu. In the Solomons and Papua there were several churches, but in separate sections. These churches had little contact with each other because they were separated by hundreds of miles of ocean. Where this practice of comity was not followed, as in the existence of some Methodists along with the Congregationalists in Samoa or of some Anglicans in Vanuatu or of the South Sea Evangelical Mission along with the Anglicans on the island of Malaita, contacts did develop between them but relations were strained.[15]

The strain was greatest where Catholics and Protestants met. There were never any comity agreements between these two branches of Christianity. We have already seen examples of their rivalry and hostility in Kiribati, New Caledonia, and other islands. There had even been open warfare between them in the nineteenth century in Tonga, Wallis, Mare, and Rotuma, and warfare almost broke out again on Bougainville in 1930.[16] Catholic and Protestant magistrates often could not be trusted to deal fairly with members of the opposite faith, and in Kiribati the government preferred to appoint non-Christian magistrates, as long as there were any, because they stood outside these rivalries.[17] The Samoan high chief Mata'afa, a Catholic at the beginning of this century, had a Protestant minister tied up like a pig and exposed to the blazing sun all day because he had made fun of the Catholic church.[18] On the other side, a chief of Manu'a who tried to give land for a Catholic chapel was expelled from his island in 1946.[19]

The ecumenical revolution, although it burst out suddenly in its full strength, had adumbrations all through the first half of the present century. There was a gradual lessening of hostility, a greater tolerance, an increased mutual respect, which was noticed in island after island from 1900 on.[20] This must be attributed largely to the slowly improving ecumenical climate in the world as a whole. It became most noticeable after the worldwide ecumenical movement got under way in the 1920s with the formation of the International Missionary Council and the world conferences on questions of faith and order and on common social concerns.[21]

The fact that the new attitudes originated in other parts of the world meant that the foreign missionaries were more affected by them than the islanders were. Although the foreigners had originally introduced the church divisions, they now found, as they wanted to soften them, that these divisions were deeply entrenched in island life and were not easily susceptible to modification. Sometimes church lines had followed the lines of old clan or tribal hostilities and these made them doubly hard to modify. Missionaries from abroad were coming together amicably while their indigenous colleagues were still hostile to each other.[22] This was true not only of the rift between Catholics and Protestants but also of some of the inner Protestant tensions. Foreign missionaries in Samoa tried to bring the Congregational and Methodist churches together in the years from 1940 to 1942, but they were met by a firm refusal from the local pastors on both sides.[23]

The better relations between the missions were cemented by a series of conferences. These began among the Protestants. The first conferences of missions working in the Pacific were held in Australia[24] and New Zealand[25] in 1926, in connection with the visit of John R. Mott, the great ecumenical leader. After the Pacific war a more ambitious gathering was held in 1948 in Morpeth, Australia. The focus in these meetings was still on the missions rather than the churches; only one Pacific islander was present at Morpeth.[26] But with the rise of independent churches and the closer relationships between the island governments,[27] it was evident that the focus had to change. In 1961 the churches finally came together, though the missions cooperated closely with them in the process.[28] Their meeting was held at Malua in Western Samoa. The Catholics were not present yet, nor were the Mormons or the South Sea Evangelical Church, but all the other major churches sent representatives. There was a great sense of thankfulness and rejoicing as churches that had so long been neighbors in isolation finally came to know each other.[29] Out of this meeting came the culmination of ecumenical organization, the Pacific Conference of Churches, a continuing body, which held assemblies every five years and maintained a vigorous headquarters operation in Suva.[30]

Just at the time the Pacific Conference of Churches was beginning, a great new development occurred. The Roman Catholic church entered the field of cooperation. Vatican Council II revolutionized Catholic attitudes toward other churches. First cooperative efforts began in Bible translation and in the formation of syllabi for religious instruction in schools. In 1976 the Catholics joined the Pacific Conference of Churches.[31] In taking this step the Catholics of the Pacific moved out ahead of Catholics in all the rest of the world, for nowhere else were Catholics members of the regional councils of churches, though here and there they participated in local and national councils.

The next step in cooperation was the formation of national councils of churches. In all other parts of the world national councils had been formed before any wider regional bodies came into existence. The Pacific reversed this more logical order because of the peculiarities of its religious geography. In most of the territories one church was the major and dominant one, the traditional church of the majority of the people. This church naturally regarded the other, smaller churches, which had come on the scene at a later date, as interlopers. The other churches naturally feared domination by the major church. Church councils, then, might be seen by the major church as a way by which the smaller churches could claim equality and be accepted as part of a plural religious scene rather than being the exceptions in a uniform religious scene. At the same time councils might be seen by the minor churches as arenas where they could ill compete with the longer established and often better prepared leaders of the major church. The frequent result of these problems was that national councils of churches were not established, or if they were established they came late and were kept weak. The countries that established councils were, in the order of their establishment, Fiji, Vanuatu, Papua New Guinea, the Solomons, Samoa, and Tonga. In all these countries councils were created between 1964 and 1973. The most active of them tended to be the ones located in areas where there was no dominant church, that is, Papua New Guinea and the Solomons.[32] In all the councils Roman Catholics were active, but the new sectarian groups and conservative evangelical churches were absent.

The largest and most effective of the national councils was that of Papua New Guinea, named the Melanesian Council of Churches. Papua New Guinea tended to remain aloof from the Pacific Conference of Churches (PCC); only one of its religious bodies, the United Church, became a member of the PCC. New Guinea was so large compared to the other Pacific islands

and was located so far away from the center of the region that it found difficulties in cooperating with the others on an equal basis. The Melanesian
Council of Churches thus became in some respects a parallel body to the
Pacific Conference of Churches. It maintained a larger program than any of
the other national councils.[33] It also kept in close touch with another parallel
body, the Evangelical Alliance of the South Pacific, an organization made up
of those new conservative evangelical churches, located mostly in the New
Guinea highlands, who were opposed to the ecumenical movement. The ties
between this alliance and the Melanesian Council were as close or closer than
could be found between such bodies in any other part of the world.[34] Local
cooperation was deemed more important than international contacts.[35]

Papua New Guinea had not only the most effective national council, but
also the only example of interconfessional church union in the Pacific
islands. It will be remembered that Tonga had seen a church union in 1924,
but this was between Methodist bodies and thus was not interconfessional.[36]
Papua New Guinea's singular example was the United Church in Papua New
Guinea and the Solomon Islands, a body that we noted in connection with the
discussion of church independence. It was born of a merger in 1968 between
the Papua Ekalesia and the old Methodist mission areas.[37] Union was
achieved remarkably easily in four years of negotiations, with little of the
struggles and reverses that have marked the course of most interconfessional
unions in the world. This was partly because of a strong ecumenical orientation among the foreign missionaries and partly because of national sentiment
and practical considerations among the islanders.[38] The new church moved
toward indigenous leadership faster than any other church in the country and
it spoke vigorously to the missionary bodies abroad.[39]

Youth Work

Perhaps the most urgent challenge to the churches came from the new
generation of young people in the Pacific, those who were moving to the
cities, traveling abroad, or receiving a better education. People of this kind
were not attracted or held by the traditional life of the churches. Apart from
the education given to a fortunate few in postprimary schools, the churches
had done little or nothing to develop the interest or involvement of young
people. The usual way of the churches was to ignore the youth or to try to
restrict them. In most of Polynesia the churches expected the youth to run
free between the ages of about fifteen and thirty and young people were kept
on the periphery of the church during this time. Later they would settle down,
marry, and become useful church members. In Micronesia and Melanesia
they were usually kept under stricter controls but they still had no role to play
in the life of the church. They were more disciplined, but no more was done
for them. In all areas they were kept in awe of the church leadership; they
would not presume to go to the pastor's house or raise questions about the
church's teachings. Sunday schools were provided for them in most of the

central Pacific islands from the nineteenth century onward, but these were more a method of exerting control by the pastors than a method of helping the youth. There were no separate classes for young people, but only a single group of all ages lectured by the pastor, or sometimes the pastor's wife. When foreign missionaries pressed for graded groups and discussion there was strong resistance from the pastors. Even as late as 1970 it was reported from Papua that pastors and church leaders resisted the idea of any youth organization in the church because it might give a base for opposition to their rule.[40]

From time to time foreign missionaries started some activities for youth, but these operated only sporadically. Boy Scouts and Girl Guides were active in Papuan and Gilbertese churches in the 1920s and 1930s, and about 1940 there was a burst of activity when Boys Brigades and Girl Guides or Girls Life Brigades were begun in Samoa, the New Hebrides, the Solomons, the Cooks, and Niue. Christian Endeavor was already operative in Fiji, Samoa, and some other islands at the beginning of the century and spread to further areas such as the New Hebrides and Tonga in the 1930s. But whereas in other parts of the world this was primarily an organization for youth, in the Pacific islands it included all ages and was dominated by the older people.[41]

After World War II, however, things began to change.[42] As new influences came in, the youth refused to accept the rule of their elders and as the old society broke up they found their own roles harder to identify. Many became confused and rebellious. This was most true in the urban centers, but the urban influences also infected wider areas. A missionary in American Samoa in 1958 reported that throughout western Tutuila the influences of Pago Pago were felt so strongly that young people even in the villages now refused to obey the orders of the chiefs.[43] Faced with this situation the churches went through a complete volte-face in their attitude. They tried to develop a system of Christian education that would meet the needs of people who were asking questions and seeking their own answers. Starting in 1964 an ambitious new Sunday school curriculum covering seventeen years of classes, with study materials that could be translated into many languages, was developed cooperatively under the auspices of the Pacific Conference of Churches.[44] Relevance to the contemporary world and an increase in social and political awareness were central concerns in the new education.[45]

New organizations for youth also sprouted everywhere, providing opportunities for study and discussion, for social activities and sports, for camping and conferences. New Caledonia Catholics began a cluster of youth organizations under the umbrella of Catholic Action about 1950. Tahitian Protestants started church youth groups in 1951, church camps in 1953, and the YM-YWCA in 1954. The Presbyterians of the New Hebrides started youth fellowships about 1955. The Scout and Brigade groups from earlier times were greatly expanded and developed in these same years. Somewhat later, in 1970, a big organization, the Young Christians, was begun by the Catholics in New Guinea and it became the largest youth organization in the country. Its costs were largely borne by the government. New Guinea's United Church established a major youth leadership training center at Malmaluan near Rabaul, which had a wide influence in the western Pacific in advancing the interests of youth in the churches. Mormons, who, as we have seen earlier, had been challenging the other churches by their appeal to youth, continued to develop their many youth activities.[46]

The most influential of all these operations was one that started early in Fiji, the Methodist Youth Fellowship. It began in 1947, but its great growth dates from 1952 when Setareki Tuilovoni began his service as the first full-time director. Tuilovoni had been trained in America and many of the patterns for the work as well as the name came from America. A large annual camp for youth was begun and a big headquarters erected by the labors and contributions of the young people themselves. Some twenty thousand youth were claimed as members of the organization.[47] When the government in later years began to develop youth activities, it depended primarily on the local Methodist youth groups and the Methodist pastors to get its operations going.[48] The Fijian youth invited New Hebrideans, Tongans, Samoans, and others to attend their conferences, and they in turn traveled to other island conferences. These meetings were the forerunners of wider contacts which developed as the Pacific churches came closer together. Training sessions were offered for youth leaders from many areas, and in January 1980 a large Pacific Youth Convention was held by the Pacific Conference of Churches. In all these things the churches recognized at last that they had a ministry to the youth of the islands.[49]

Women's Work

As youth emerged, so did women. Local groups for women had been part of church life from the early days. The wives of foreign missionaries had initiated these, and after them the pastors' wives and other leading women had established groups in most villages. Eventually the local groups were brought together into national church women's organizations. The one in Samoa began in the late nineteenth century. Fiji's began in 1924. Further west they came later, mostly in the 1950s and 1960s in the New Hebrides, the Solomons, and Papua New Guinea. The strongest of these in the west was the United Church Women's Fellowship, which took responsibility for occasionally leading church services and was active in the national affairs of Papua New Guinea, even organizing a march on the National Assembly in 1974 to protest the high cost of living.

Moving beyond their own organizations women began to enter the governing bodies of local congregations and of national churches. Women became deacons in the Congregational churches, elders in the Presbyterian and Lutheran churches, and lay preachers in the Methodist churches. They were elected to the central governing bodies of some churches, for example, the Congregationalists of Samoa (1956) and Papua (1963), the Methodists of the Solomons (1953) and of Tonga (1966), and the Evangelical Church of New

Caledonia (1956). Such a thing had never been considered in earlier times. The United Church in Papua New Guinea and the Solomon Islands even voted to accept women for ordination to the ministry. In 1971 a woman was chosen as chairperson of the Pacific Conference of Churches, and in 1977 a woman became general secretary of that organization. Clearly women had moved into the center of church life in a way that had never been known before.

Roman Catholic women, it should be recognized, did not enjoy such opportunities for involvement in the whole operation of their church. However in their separate religious orders they made great strides. Before midcentury there were only a few indigenous women in orders, and they were given only menial tasks. In Fiji their subordinate status was implicit in the very name of their order, "Helpers of the Sisters." But after 1950 they grew in numbers, doubling their size in many countries, reaching to a hundred or 150 members in New Britain, Papua, and Fiji. The order in Papua was the first to choose an indigenous mother superior (in 1966). The women also broke into new fields of service, becoming trained as teachers and nurses. They did far more in these fields than was done by the Catholic men of the Pacific. Male orders for nonpriestly work never took hold in the Pacific. But the female orders became firmly established.[50]

Indigenization

Out of the new cosmopolitan experiences and the new type of theological schools the churches began to receive a new kind of leadership, one more intellectually oriented and able to speak to the modernized elements of the population, though also less in tune with village life and ways.[51] For the first time writing on theological matters began to appear from the pens of Pacific islanders, and the first essays of what might be called an indigenous Pacific theology began to appear.

One of the principal foci of attention for this new group of church leaders was the recovery of the traditional culture of the Pacific and the relating of Christian belief and Christian worship to that culture. Though these leaders were educated with a view to meeting the modern, urbanized, and secular world, they constantly spoke of the need to adapt to the old traditions. This was in part because the modernized people of the islands generally were showing a renewed interest in traditional culture in connection with their new national independence. Theological writing fell in with this interest. Esau Tuza, one of the most articulate Protestants of the Solomons, declared that Christianity should revive and develop the old culture and its power consciousness. Francis Misso of the Catholics of New Guinea and Gérard Leymang of the Catholics of Vanuatu endeavored to interpret Christianity according to the Melanesian way of thinking, and Sione Havea of Tonga wrote of the "Pacificness" of theology.[52] The report from the participants in the great self-study of the Catholic church in Papua New Guinea declared, "We want to build our church on our worthy traditional values."[53] There was in this thought little tendency to condemn the missionaries of an earlier generation for their attacks on the traditional culture. A gathering of indigenous Catholic priests in Papua New Guinea said that the mistakes of earlier times must be understood in terms of the thought of those times.[54]

The later missionaries supported this new tendency. Indeed they were often its main proponents. The new anthropological understanding that had been absorbed by the missionaries, combined with the new appreciation in the West of the importance of the Third World in general, made the foreigners eager to support indigenizing tendencies in the Pacific churches. Among the Catholics the stress of Vatican Council II on the need for the church to fit into the various cultures of the world gave a special stimulus in this direction. In Micronesia it was noticeable that the Catholic church, which was in the hands of foreigners, was far more concerned to explore the relationship of Christianity to the traditional culture than was the Protestant church, which was in indigenous hands.[55]

The results of this interest began to be seen in the worship of the churches. Here and there indigenous elements were used in the liturgy—a conch shell or a rattle instead of a bell, water poured over the hands of a bride and groom and their relatives at a marriage, the traditional orator's symbols carried by a preacher. A few church buildings were built according to indigenous styles, and traditional carving or painting was used in the decoration of others. Performers and composers of Pacific music were brought together to strengthen their role in the church. All of those who wrote or spoke on the subject called for the introduction of traditional elements into the liturgy and church structures and a reduction in the foreignness of Christian worship. But it must be recognized that what was actually done consisted mostly of experiments by a few of the better-educated Christian leaders. The usual forms of Christian worship used by the great majority of church people did not change. The indigenization maintained by the masses continued to be, as we have seen in chapter 5, an indigenization of content put into the Western forms, rather than the new indigenization of forms with an increasingly Westernized content.[56]

Nation Building

Besides indigenization, the other major interest of the new generation of church leaders was nation building. This included an interest in both the political activity of creating independent nations and the economic activity of national development.

The political change in the environment most obviously attracted attention. The colonial regimes came to an end in all but the French and American islands. Western Samoa became independent in 1962, then Fiji in 1964. The other territories followed in steady succession, Papua New Guinea, the largest of them, reaching statehood in 1975, the Solomons in 1978. The only group of islands outside the French and American connections that did not become completely independent were the Cook Islands, which chose to remain in free association with New Zealand, establishing internal self-government in 1965, but assigning their defense and foreign affairs to their former rulers.

There was a natural tendency for the churches to be involved with the political life of the new states. In the indigenous cultures of Oceania there had been no line of division between religion and the other parts of society. Religion, economics, politics, and personal and family life had all been viewed together in a single whole. When Christianity was first established in the region the missionaries, as leaders in religious life, were expected to play an active role in political and economic affairs, and they were soon involved in tasks that they had never expected.[57] It was only after the colonial powers took control, bringing with them their Western ideas of the limited place for religion, that the missionaries' role was reduced. Even so religious leaders were usually more important in the Pacific colonies than they were in Western lands, and at the village level the pastors and catechists continued to play a leading role. They sat in the village councils or were consulted by the chiefs on matters of importance.

It was no surprise, therefore, when the colonial regimes departed, that the indigenous church leaders took a strong interest in national affairs and that the new nations made a considerable place for religious perspectives in their national life. Western Samoa, the first Pacific country to emerge from colonial rule, took as the motto on its crest, "Samoa is founded on God," and it dedicated the monument in front of its new legislative assembly building "To God our Father. . . ruler of the universe . . . protector of Western Samoa. To Jesus Christ our Lord and Savior, the Light of the World." When the Solomons became independent, extensive religious services were held by the new government, and the new national anthem was filled with Christian references. Papua New Guinea put in the preamble to its constitution the assertion that the people work with God to establish the nation and that the nation is founded on the unshakable values of Christianity and the worthy, God-given customs of the ancients. There were frequent statements from the leaders that Papua New Guinea must be a Christian country.[58] The Melanesian Council of Churches was represented on half a dozen government committees and was not reluctant to press the government on matters that concerned it. Some of the important leaders were priests or one-time seminarians, such as Father John Momis of Bougainville, who led the drive for Bougainville's rights and became a minister in the government as well as the church.[59] The exceptionally high level of training that the Catholics had given to their few indigenous priests became evident in the way in which these men were used for leadership in public affairs and in ecumenical organizations.

Church independence, which had preceded national independence, and the experience of church self-government at various levels had provided some background for national self-rule. The Fono Tele in Samoa, which had acted as a kind of national assembly for the church, the Methodist synods for Fiji, the Solomons, and Papua New Guinea, the Lutheran and Anglican local councils that preceded the government local councils, and similar bodies throughout the islands built up experience in decisions of governing. In a few cases, such as among the Catholics and the Methodists in Papua New Guinea, there were study programs in the churches to train people for participation in the new national life.[60]

The churches also contributed significantly to the sense of national identity and national unity. Where one church embraced most of the population, its life provided a sense of continuing national identity during the colonial regime. This was true of the old LMS churches in Tahiti and Samoa and of the Methodists in Fiji. The Presbyterians in Vanuatu played an even more significant role in this respect because they brought together people throughout that island group who had not been otherwise united in any way. In the Solomons and Papua New Guinea the churches likewise brought together separate and often hostile peoples, but in those islands there was no predominant church that could serve as a vehicle for national identity as was true to an extent in Vanuatu. Therefore, in the Solomons and Papua New Guinea it was Christianity as a whole rather than any particular church that was referred to as a unifying factor.[61] The particular churches sometimes played a divisive role for the colonial territory while playing unifying roles within their own areas.

The country with the most tension between the unifying and the divisive role of the church in the nation was Fiji. The Methodist church provided a continuing bond among Fijians and was a focus of Fijian national identity and unity. But as the Indian population of Fiji grew and became the majority, the fact that Indians were mostly Hindus and Muslims while Fijians were Methodists became one of the marks of division between the two peoples. The Fijians clung to the church as the place where they could do things in their own way and did not have to compete with Indians. They even had a separate church government for the small group of Indians who became Methodists and some separate Methodist schools for Indian children. There was great resistance to missionary suggestions for making the schools interracial.[62] However, another point of view gradually prevailed. As a younger generation of Fijian pastors and deaconesses grew up their training was made to include work among the Indians, and a new generation of missionaries did not identify so completely with the traditional Fijian interests as their predecessors had done. In 1960 it was voted to make all the Methodists' Indian schools interracial.[63] In the same year the momentous decision was made to create an independent Methodist church in which Fijians and Indians would be one, though separate sessions for the two racial groups were kept for certain important tasks.[64] In 1977 the combined church elected an Indian minister as president despite the qualms of many of the older generation.[65] The difference in views between generations regarding the role of the church was seen most clearly when two women's groups met with British representatives who were planning the constitution for independent Fiji. The older, prestigious group, made up of the leading church women of the country, advocated separate electorates for the racial groups and maintainance of all special Fijian rights, while the younger group coming from the YWCA urged a single electorate and a gradual end to Fijian privileges.[66] Evidently with the change of generations the Methodists and other Christians of Fiji were becoming a force for national unity, but it was a slow process.

The churches were little involved in independence movements except in the territories where France ruled. This was because only in those territories was there much of an independence movement. British, Australian, and New Zealand colonies generally became independent without a struggle. But with France it was a different matter. French efforts to keep the colonial ties resulted, by way of reaction, in a number of movements for freedom, to which the churches were related in one way or another. The first relationship was largely a negative one. In Tahiti Marcel Pouvanaa organized a party that announced, in 1958, that its purpose was to secede from France. Pouvanaa had already been a representative of French Oceania in the French parliament and had been a member of the territorial assembly, but after his movement came out clearly for independence he and some of his followers were sent to jail for six to eight years and he was forbidden to return to Tahiti for a decade or more. The pastors of the Protestant church might have been expected to sympathize with such a movement since their church had been so long related to Tahitian national feeling, but Pouvanaa had been in disfavor with them for years. Many of them advised their people to vote in favor of continued association with France when the referendum was held in 1958. Some of them even claimed that Pouvanaa was the devil. At this time Pouvanaa broke away from the Protestant church and started his own church, called the Church of Jesus Christ, which continued as a small splinter group supporting his policies.[67]

In New Caledonia the relationship was more positive. When, immediately after the war, the Melanesians were released from the restrictions that had bound them to their reserves and subjected them to forced labor, both the Catholic and the Protestant churches proceeded to form associations for action on public affairs. In both cases this was done under the inspiration of missionaries although the members and leaders of the associations were Melanesians.[68] The two groups cooperated well together and when, in 1951, the indigenous people were given the vote, the two jointly formed the Union Calédonienne as their political party. This body gained and continued to hold the most seats in the legislative council. Gradually it came to favor independence for the territory.

But other political parties were eventually formed and the churches had to learn not to be too closely identified with any one of them but to allow freedom for their members to be in different parties. Some of the parties, such as the Multiracial Union and the Kanaka Liberation party, or PALIKA, were more radical than the Union Calédonienne and early came out in favor of independence for the territory. Both of these later parties looked to the churches for support. The leader of the first was a strong Protestant layman, and its statement on "The Churches and the Liberation Struggle of the Kanak People" declared that "Jesus Christ is the sole liberator."[69] The Catholic church leadership, which was largely French, refused to support the demands for independence although it favored more local autonomy and full scope for the development of Melanesian culture. A revolt against its more colonial mentality led, about 1970, to the resignation of a bishop and several young priests and the departure of a number of missionaries as well as the closing of the major seminary which was a hotbed of discontent. The Protestant church, with indigenous leadership, was more sympathetic to the radicals, and in 1979 its governing synod, in a radical move, voted unanimously to demand independence for the Melanesians.[70]

The greatest involvement of the churches in independence efforts came in Vanuatu, or the New Hebrides. During the early stages of the nationalist movement, in 1973, the Presbyterian church made a declaration in favor of independence for the country. It continually insisted that, though it would not align itself with any particular party and would be free to criticize all parties, it was committed to justice and freedom and would work in the traditional New Hebridean way where politics and religion were closely related. When the principal political party for independence, the Vanuaaku party, was organized in 1971, its president was an Anglican priest seconded by his church, Father Walter Lini, and its vice-president was a Presbyterian pastor, Reverend Fred Timakata. This party was closely related to the Protestant churches and to the English-speaking population.

On the other hand, the parties that favored a slower approach to independence with more ties to France and more power for French settlers were related to the Catholic church and the French-speaking population. These parties were combined in the Union des Communautés des Nouvelles Hébrides of which the secretary was an indigenous priest, Fr. Gérald Leymang. Thus the political divisions began to affect church life. The Catholic church, while sympathetic to the desire for independence, refused to support the actual independence movement, whereas the Presbyterians clearly did support it.

The New Hebrides Council of Churches, which represented all the major churches, became impotent in political matters because of the differences within it. The differences became dangerous by 1978 when the Vanuaaku party initiated nonviolent resistance to the government set up by the French parties. But the churches kept pressing for mutual understanding and cooperation and, partly because of this, at the end of 1978 an agreement was reached and a government of national unity was established in preparation for independence. Gérard Leymang was the prime minister and Walter Lini the deputy prime minister. Elections the following year gave the Vanuaaku party full control of the government. Independence came in 1980 with much recognition given, in the ensuing celebrations, to the important part that the churches had played in reaching that goal. With Lini and Timakata in the two highest positions in the new country it is clear that the churches had contributed more to the independence of Vanuatu than to that of any other colonial land in the world.[71]

In Micronesia, the only other remaining colonial territory, the Catholic and Protestant roles in relation to independence were almost the opposite of what they were in Vanuatu. Here the Catholics were more active in relation to the development of an independent national life. The Protestant pastors and their churches, though they were thoroughly indigenous, were not interested in wider political questions but only in village life and personal morality. The Catholic priests and church leaders, on the other hand, though they were nearly all foreigners, were very aware of the political and social issues and tried to educate and stimulate their lay members to think and act on these matters. They supported the national aspirations of the islands and deplored the growing dependency on the United States—even though they came from the United States.[72]

The most vigorous church action came from groups outside Micronesia itself. The Pacific Conference of Churches became greatly interested in the self-determination of the Micronesian peoples. It called together a conference of independence movements from all the colonial territories of the Pacific and held this conference in Micronesia. Its quinquennial assembly, held in 1976, after endorsing self-government for the New Hebrides, went on to express its opposition to the ways the United States was impeding self-determination in Micronesia and it appealed to the American churches to intervene. The National Council of Churches in the United States responded by creating a coalition of religious and academic groups in support of greater Micronesian independence, which made representations to the American government and appeared before the United Nations to appeal to that body to exercise fully its rights of oversight in the Trust Territory. The American Catholics, though they were not part of the National Council, cooperated vigorously through their Jesuit mission organization in this coalition.[73] Despite the concern of outsiders, however, the Micronesians wanted to keep their American connection, along with autonomy in local affairs.

Economic Development

The other element of nation building was economic development. The churches were no strangers to this side of national life. Some of the early missions had introduced new crops to advance the economic well-being of the people. The Catholics in Papua introduced rice cultivation to the area where they worked. The Presbyterians long maintained a small arrowroot industry in the New Hebrides, the product of which was sold through mission societies in New Zealand. The Lutheran mission gave each teacher graduating from its training college some coffee seedlings to take home, and thus coffee growing spread over a wide area in New Guinea, with the first consignment of coffee being exported by the mission in 1938.[74]

The plantations and building operations of the missions were also a source of some economic development over the years. Mission plantations were largely confined to Papua New Guinea and the Solomons where government policy was more favorable to mission acquisition of land. In Papua New Guinea all the original missions, except the Anglicans, had large coconut plantations to help pay their operating costs, the Catholics being especially large landholders. Other business operations such as boat building, printing presses, and sawmills were also maintained. Roads were constructed and coastal shipping provided so commerce could develop. In the Western Solomons, as we have seen, the Methodists acquired considerable land. After these two countries became independent the mission lands and businesses were seen less as a form of national economic development and more as a national problem, for many people did not approve of religious organizations being financed by commercial ventures and there was increasing need for land. Eventually among the Protestants the mission holdings were all transferred from the missions to the newly independent churches. Among both Catholics and Protestants the continuation of the holdings was justified on the grounds that the income was used for educational and social service work, which benefited the whole country.[75]

Technical and agricultural schools had flourished among the missions as a contribution to economic development from early in the century. The main ones were located in Papua New Guinea and Fiji. On the technical side the usual subjects of instruction were boat building, carpentry, and house building, and the graduates of such schools were readily employed in the islands. The Catholic Brothers and Protestant artisans who came from abroad usually taught their skills to young men, while they were themselves engaged in construction or printing for the mission.[76] The two most influential missionaries in industrial education were C. W. Abel of Papua and R. A. Derrick of Fiji. Abel's work we have already considered, since he started a separate mission in Papua conceived in terms of modern industrial and agricultural operations. Derrick was a leader of the Fiji Methodists who, starting in 1919, developed their industrial school till it had over three hundred students. He later became the supervisor of technical education for the Fiji government, and the main technical school of Fiji has since been named for him.[77] The Fiji government became interested also in the Methodist Agricultural College, which was located at Navuso. It was begun in 1924 and became the largest agricultural school in the South Pacific islands. Eventually the funding for it was largely provided by Britain.[78]

After World War II technical and agricultural training increased. The most notable new development was that of Father Hugh Costigan in Micronesia. This American Jesuit developed the Ponape Agricultural and Trade School and also a cooperative housing construction company that was a great success, and a cooperative store. Those who were critical of American academic education in the Micronesian environment regarded Costigan's school as the only useful one in the territory.[79] Cooperatives were increasingly popular among the missions after the war. One Anglican missionary in Papua,

James Benson, developed them widely in his church. The Presbyterians took the initiative about 1950 in starting them in the New Hebrides and maintained a full-time cooperatives officer until such time—1964—that the government appointed a man for that work. The cause of credit unions received a great boost from Reverend Michael Ganey, a Jesuit authority on their operation, who was brought in by the government of Fiji in 1953 and by Western Samoa immediately thereafter. In three years in Fiji he had 109 credit unions in operation. The cooperatives and credit unions were not always successful. At times the generosity of their managers spelled their ruin. But taken as a whole they contributed significantly to the economic advancement of the people.[80]

The biggest business enterprise ever undertaken by the islanders was Namasu (Native Marketing and Supply Service), set up by the Lutheran mission in New Guinea in 1959, not as a cooperative but as a joint stock company in which New Guineans could buy shares and the mission provide the balance of the capital. Europeans were allowed to buy some shares but very soon New Guineans formed the majority of shareholders and of the Board of Directors and the higher staff. The company was enormously successful, paying good dividends at the start and expanding all through the areas of Lutheran work. It became the largest indigenously owned business in the country. Its main business was the operation of small stores or the supplying of goods to the stores operated by Lutheran congregations. These congregational stores were sometimes so successful that the church members came to rely entirely on them to provide for the expenses of the church.

Cargo-like expectations were often attached to the stores and to Namasu, one village even building a special house in which to keep its Namasu shares surrounded by flowers and provided regularly with food. These exaggerated expectations later led to disappointment and rebellion when the capital needs of rapid expansion forced a stoppage of dividends. The hiring of more hard-headed businessmen to strengthen the business at that point produced disaffection among the many shareholders who were church members and who did not like the conduct of these men. So a return to closer church ties became necessary in 1973. But despite these problems, Namasu provided a startling example of what islanders could do in a business. The example was soon followed by others, notably the Missouri Synod Lutherans and the Baptists.[81]

During the 1960s and 1970s development efforts became the major new interest of the churches. Projects for improvement of livestock, better water supplies, cottage industries, and the like sprang up under church auspices in many of the countries. Development funds came from church groups in Europe, Australasia, and America. The Pacific Conference of Churches and the Melanesian Council of Churches both mounted projects of their own and served as a conduit for financing the projects of others. The Melanesian Council's *Liklik Buk, a Rural Development Handbook* stimulated the creation of an information center for village people and was even used in Swahili translation by the government of Tanzania. New training centers for village people were established, such as the Tutu Rural Education Center of the Marists in Fiji and the Hango Agricultural College of the Methodists in Tonga. The Lutheran Economic Service carried on a dozen development projects in New Guinea, and Catholic priests initiated a number of important ones in Bougainville, western New Britain, and the Sepik River area.[82] This work was done in most cases in friendly and fruitful cooperation with government efforts, which were moving along the same lines.

The constant concern of the churches was for a style of development which would stay close to the present life of the people rather than uprooting and disorganizing them, which would arise from the expressed wishes of the people rather than being imposed by elitist leaders, which would emphasize self-reliance rather than foreign support, which would be on a small scale and labor-intensive rather than using large and expensive equipment, and which would be as concerned for justice, spiritual values, and human dignity as for economic growth.[83] In advocating this kind of economic development the church leaders were ready to challenge the new national governments and to take them to task when they adopted more elitist and exploitative plans of development.[84]

There were also some who were beginning to question the whole economic order and to demand fundamental changes in the name of justice.[85] The most notable case of this was a conference on land tenure sponsored by the Tonga Council of Churches in 1975. Though the king was present to give the opening address, there were other speakers present who attacked the operations of Tongan society, saying that many nobles were enriching themselves at the expense of the common people, that some who wanted land to work on could not get it and that those who worked the best were least rewarded, while nobles who did not work at all were best rewarded.[86] The churches that had long been intertwined with the traditional order of Pacific society were cautiously untying some of their connections and looking in new directions.

The 1960s and 1970s were clearly times of profound transformation in the churches and the societies around them. There are elements of continuity between the new church life and the old, but it is the newness that is most striking. In urban work, youth work, theological education and ecumenicity, in the concern for indigenization, national independence and a humane form of development, radically new directions were being adopted.

NOTES

1. International Missionary Council 1961: 94. Mauer 1961. Spades 1973: 18.

2. Tamaali'i 1975: 38, 57, 65. Constitution of the Congregational Christian Church of Samoa 1962: 17–18. De Bres and Campbell 1975: 1, 43. Finau 1975. Tonga Council of Churches, 1975, Appendix C. An exception to the usual pattern of the non-Samoan churches was the establishment by the Tahitian Evangelical church of a congregation of its adherents in Noumea. The Cook Islands Christian church felt so

closely related to New Zealand that in 1959 it joined the National Council of Churches there. However, it was never an active member.

3. Parratt 1970: 113. Schuster 1974: 279. Theile 1975: 20, 25 reports that in Lae 80 percent of the Lutherans did not attend church. Cf. Knoebel 1974b: 174; Parratt 1975.

4. *Catalyst* 3, no. 3, pp. 25 and 34 mentions this use of missionaries by the Anglicans and Roman Catholics. The first time the Lutherans placed a missionary in a city was 1956. Schuster 1974: 279.

5. Schneider 1976: 148–49, 154.

6. Parratt 1970: 107.

7. Maher 1961: 58–59. Parratt 1970: 106, 111–12.

8. Official figures of the church headquarters in Australasia in 1974 showed 60,874 members in the South Pacific Islands mission field and 43,202 in Australia and New Zealand.

9. For a description of the older type of ministry and the beginnings of change, see Forman 1974.

10. In the more developed territories such as Fiji there was a demand even before the war for a more highly educated ministry. Methodist Church of Australasia, Dept. of Overseas Missions, Report 1938, pp. 11–13. Methodist Mission Archives, Sydney.

11. For a fuller statement of this "quiet revolution," see Forman 1969 and *Theological Education in the Pacific*.

12. The first proposal for the central Protestant school seems to have come from Norman Goodall, secretary of the LMS, in an article in the *International Review of Missions* in 1943: 399. In that same year Backmann 1943: 37 stated that efforts for a central Roman Catholic seminary had been going on for a long time. Darnand wrote of such efforts in 1934: 190.

13. The central Catholic school was a union, made in 1968 near Port Moresby, of two major seminaries founded in 1963 near Rabaul and Madang. The United Church institution was likewise a union of a Methodist school founded near Rabaul in 1964 and an older LMS school in Papua, which had originally been designed to train pastor-teachers but had been concentrating on ministerial as distinct from teacher training since 1962. The higher theological institution of the Lutherans was located near Lae, and began in 1967. The conservative group had their school, the Christian Leaders Training College, which did not reach to the academic levels of the others, at Banz in the highlands beginning in 1965.

14. Cf. *Point*, no. 1 (1976): 146–83.

15. Cf. Keesing 1956: 17, 89. Godden 1967: 85. Ross 1978. Hogbin 1939: 206.

16. Koskinen 1953: 122. D. Oliver 1955: 313–14.

17. Viner et al. 1916: 155.

18. Darnand 1934: 100.

19. Holmes 1958: 36–37.

20. Lewis 1935: 5 notes that as early as 1892 Methodist missionaries in New Britain declared their belief that they and the Catholic missionaries each wished the other success in their efforts. For other examples of good relations in the nineteenth century, see Garrett 1977: 60–67.

21. Cf. Australian Missionary Conference, 1926: 41. Courtais and Bigault 1936: 42–44. *LMS Chronicle* 89 (1924): 118. Sabatier 1939: 282. Jepson 1945: 4. Strong 1947: 133. Threlfall 1975: 193. These sources speak of good relations after the ecumenical movement was organized, but good relations earlier in the century are evidenced in *Cyclopedia . . .* 1907: 74, and Kraft 1964: 35–36.

22. E.g., Darnand 1934: 154–55. Bigault 1947: 83. Leymang 1969: 253–54. These three references deal with the Catholic-Protestant relations in Samoa, the Solomons and the New Hebrides, respectively. The division of churches according to traditional rivalries was most noticeable in Samoa. Davidson 1967: 34.

23. Burton 1949: 85. LMS Islands Committee, Minutes, Oct. 21, 1940; April 21, 1941: Sept. 21, 1942. Council for World Mission Archives, London. At the annual meeting of the Samoan Congregational pastors in 1902, there were proposals from the pastors for retaliation against the Methodists for moving into Tutuila, which was a purely LMS island. The missionaries had to resist these proposals vigorously. Samoa District Committee, May 1902: 294–96, 302; June 1903: 409. Congregational Church Archives, Apia.

24. At the Australian conference the National Missionary Council, which had been begun in 1920, was given new strength, and plans for cooperation in the Pacific islands were advanced. Australian Missionary Conference 1926: 3, 39, 69–71. *International Review of Missions* 15 (1926): 675–91.

25. The National Missionary Council for New Zealand was formed out of this conference. New Zealand Missionary Conference 1926: 73, 78–79, 96, 98.

26. First plans had called for Suva to be the venue of this conference and for one-third, and then one-half, of the delegates to be from the "native churches." New Zealand Methodist Board of Missions, Jan. 26, 1944; July 19, 1945. Methodist Mission Archives, Auckland. South Pacific Missionary Conference 1948b. The French-speaking areas were also neglected in the membership of the conference, only one missionary from those areas being present. Roman Catholics and Seventh-day Adventists were consciously omitted, not without some complaint from the latter, and the South Sea Evangelical Mission declined to attend. Morpeth Conference Committee Minutes, Sept. 17, 1945; Feb. 18, 1946; Feb. 24, 1947; Jan. 19, 1948. The failure to include islanders as originally planned was because this conference was seen as preliminary to a larger one to be held in the Pacific two years later. But the second conference did not materialize.

27. Closer relationships between the governments were organized by the South Pacific Commission, a body established by the colonial powers of the Pacific in 1947. The commission held triennial conferences of representatives of the islands, the first one being in 1950, and included mission representatives as observers at these meetings. Gribble 1950. *South Pacific Bulletin* 6 (1956): no. 2: 40; no. 3: 8.

28. The activating proposal for this conference was made by Stuart Craig, general secretary of the LMS, in letters to the various churches, addressed through their related missions, in 1957. All but one of the churches responded positively and the International Missionary Council in London was then asked to make the arrangements for the meeting. Craig 1961: 6. The first suggestions for such a conference had been made as early as 1943 by Norman Goodall, secretary of the LMS, and then in 1955 by Cecil Gribble, secretary of the Australian Methodist Mission Board. Goodall, "The Church in the South Seas," p. 8. Council for World Mission Archives, London. Australian Methodist Mission Board, Minutes, July 15, 1955, p. 81. Methodist Mission Archives, Sydney.

29. International Missionary Council 1961. Initial members of the Pacific Conference of Churches were seventeen churches located in every island group in the Pacific. The churches of Australia and New Zealand were not made members. They had previously been included in the regional council set up by the churches of Asia. But in Oceania there was fear that their much larger size and resources might lead to

their domination of the other churches if they were included.

30. The assemblies after Malua were held in Lifou (1966), Davuilevu, Fiji (1971), Port Moresby (1976), Nuku'alofa (1981). For reports of these assemblies, see *Pacific Journal of Theology*, June–September 1966, and Pacific Conference of Churches 1972, 1976.

31. The joining body was the Episcopal Conference of the Pacific, which was made up of all the Catholic dioceses east of the Solomons. Catholics of the Solomons were represented through their membership in the Solomon Islands Christian Association, which was a member of the Pacific Conference of Churches. The only Catholic dioceses in the Pacific that were not in the PCC were those of Papua New Guinea, though these did join the Melanesian Council of Churches (made up of the churches of their country) and the dioceses in American Micronesia, which were part of the United States bishops' conference. After 1979 Micronesian Catholics moved from the American to the Pacific connection.

32. Senerivi 1974: 58–66 reports that in the Fellowship of Christian Churches in Samoa, the Roman Catholics usually had the largest number at meetings, and the Methodists were second, suggesting the aloofness of the largest church in the country.

33. A full list of these agencies is given in Knoebel 1974b: 177–79.

34. Loeliger 1974: 212.

35. Melanesian Council of Churches, Minutes, Sept. 6–8, 1966, Archives of Australian Council of Churches, Sydney.

36. There was also a union within one confessional group in 1976 when the small Siassi Lutheran Church joined with the large Evangelical Lutheran Church in Papua New Guinea. The Siassi mission, located in the Rooke–Siassi Islands, had originally been part of the larger Lutheran mission but had been turned over in 1936 to the mission of the Australian Lutherans, who had developed a separate, small church. *Lutheran World* 24 (1977): 193–94.

37. It also included a single congregation made up largely of expatriates, known as the United Church of Port Moresby.

38. Reasons for the union that were given by church leaders were the prayer of Christ for unity among his followers, the need for cooperation in the new cities, the common experience during the war, and the need for a united stance before the rushing in of new sects. Reasons given by some village people were: a larger body for mutual support in the faith, more church boats, a step toward the unity and independence of Papua New Guinea, and a single church for people with the same skin. *Missionary Review* 76, no. 1 (1968): 2–11. R. Perry, Annual Report for 1964, Council for World Mission Archives, London. F. Kemp, "Change and the Church," 1965, document in personal files of F. Kemp. "The Basis of Union," report of the Joint Standing Committee on Church Union, document in personal files of F. Kemp.

39. B. Turner 1976: 99. "Consultation" 1974.

40. Grosart 1970b: 651. For earlier examples of the indifference of the church to youth and opposition to giving them a program which woud develop their interest and involvement, see Delord 1905: 5; Gunn 1924: 60; South Pacific Missionary Conference, 1948, Report of Commission IV; United Church Board of World Ministries, Report for 1968, p. 19; London Missionary Society, Annual Report, 1962–63, p. 57; Schneider 1976: 155–57; *Journal des Missions Evangéliques*, 138 (1963): 229; *O le Sulu Samoa*, January 1966, p. 4; Samoan Church 1958: 19–20. Similar indifference in the Methodist church in Ghana is reported in Bartels 1965: 228–32.

41. Fiske 1966: 180–81. London Missionary Society, 1941: 13. Falatoese 1961:

49–250. New Hebrides Presbyterian Mission Synod, Minutes, 1944, action 61. Challis 1940: 26–27. C. Beharell, "Report for 1945," Council for World Mission Archives, London. W. G. Murphy, Report for 1958, Council for World Mission Archives. Tippett 1967: 182–83. J. G. Miller, "Christian Endeavor on Nguna," New Zealand Presbyterian Archives, Auckland. McHugh 1965: 17. Samoa District Committee Minutes, May 1904, tell of the first coming together of Christian Endeavor representatives from all Samoa. *Missionary Review* 45, no. 11 (May 5, 1937) tells of the beginnings of Christian Endeavor in Fiji, though McHugh 1965: 17 reveals that it was already operative in the 1880s. Catholic priests in New Caledonia and Tahiti sometimes had weekly game periods for parish children, starting in 1903 in Tahiti and about 1905 in New Caledonia, according to present informants in those areas, but the practice was dropped in Tahiti in 1914.

42. In more cosmopolitan areas like Fiji, the change in attitudes among the youth was noticed ten or fifteen years before the war, e.g, Methodist Church, Fiji District Chairman's Report for 1933. Methodist Archives, Sydney.

43. L. H. B. Neems, "Report of Sept. 1958," Council for World Mission Archives, London. Cf. Micronesian Seminar, 1977: 32–33. For a discussion of the problems of youth, this entire seminar report is helpful.

44. Evaluation Conference 1972: 31–32. Coop 1977: 128–29. Trautmann 1974.

45. Evaluation Conference 1972: 31–32. Trautmann 1974. Coop 1977. *Sharing Educational Ministries* 1977.

46. Other youth movements should be noted. The earliest was the Torchbearers, organized in the LMS churches of Papua immediately after the war. Cocks 1950: 120. Later came the Catholic youth clubs under the Legion of Mary in Samoa starting in the early 1960s. Pearce 1963: 19. About the same time a youth movement began among Protestants in Mare and spread to other parts of the Loyalties and New Caledonia. *La Vie Protestante*, March 13, 1966. By the early 1970s the Lutherans in New Guinea had many popular rural youth clubs with trained agricultural advisors. Ruthenberg 1974: 62.

47. *Souvenir of the First Fiji Methodist Conference* 1964: 9. *Journal de la Société des Océanistes* 25 (1969): 6

48. Waqa 1977: 52 and passim.

49. For an example of the early interisland exchanges, see *La Vie Protestante*, Oct. 1, 1961. Later ecumenical activity can be seen in Pacific Conference of Churches 1976: 45 and *CWM Newshare*, June 1979: 6.

50. For fuller information on the changing place of church women, see Forman n.d.

51. Cf. Raapoto 1974: 15.

52. Tuza 1977: 119–20. Misso 1977. Leymang 1969. Havea 1977. Cf. *Melanesian Culture and Christian Faith*.

53. Janssen 1975: 229. John Guise, the first governor-general of independent Papua New Guinea, made the same emphasis. Guise 1977: 210–14.

54. *Catalyst* 1, no. 2: 83. Cf. Liu 1976: 98–99.

55. Hezel 1978: 251–52, 266–67. For important examples of foreign missionaries working in the indigenization of Christianity, see: *Christ in Melanesia*; *Pacific Journal of Theology*, June–September 1966, pp. 50–63; Nilles 1977.

56. A Pacific-wide conference on indigenous church music is reported in *Point*, no. 1 (1973). Various experiments in indigenizing Christian worship are reported in Garrett and Mavor 1973; Williams 1970: 674–75; and *Das Wort in der Welt*, 1976, no. 5. Calls for greater indigenization may be found in *The Word in the World*, 1969, p. 60;

Catalyst 1, no. 2, p. 84; *Dialogue* 1, no. 2, pp. 15–16; Self-Study. . . *Seminar Handbook*, 1972, article nos. 12–15; Ete 1972; Hagesi 1972; and Nabetari 1970.

57. Koskinen 1953.

58. *PCC News*, December 1974, pp. 4–5. *Catalyst* 6, no. 1, p. 56. Fisk 1966: 118. The wife of a leading Papua New Guinea politician maintained that in order to be elected any politican must be seen as closely associated with a church. *Point*, no. 2 (1975): 65–67.

59. *PCC News,* June–September 1978, p. 19. Bürkle 1978: 316–17. *Pacific Perspective* 3, no. 1, p. 91. Momis 1975. *Catalyst* 8, no. 1, p. 58. Another priest, Cherubin Dambui, was the premier of the East Sepik Province. *Kibung* 1, no. 2 (November 1976): 61–63.

60. Lawrence 1956: 81. Tomlin 1951: 95, 103. Hogbin 1951:164–66. Threlfall 1975: 201. "A Statement by the Catholic Bishops of Papua New Guinea." Reitz 1975: 47–48. Italiaander 1974 is evidence of the interest of the mission bodies in Germany in these political developments. *Responsibility in New Guinea* 1965: 11–12 shows the concern of outside mission bodies that the churches do more political discussion. The Catholics in New Britain were accused of being reluctant to see local government councils developed just because they had already developed their own local councils and were unhappy to see rival bodies appear. Rowley 1966: 153. *Pacific Islands Monthly,* March 1966, pp. 65–69. Harrison 1975: 242–43.

61. In Kiribati and Tuvalu there were some attempts by the Protestant church to hold together the peoples of those two island groups as they approached independence. Both groups had a common church background coming out of the Samoan LMS. Joint worship services using both languages were held in the capital on Tarawa, and discussion groups to consider the problems between the areas were held. But in the end it was found better for the two areas to form separate countries.

62. E.g., the Fijian rejection of the proposal that the Lelean Memorial School include Indians. William Green to John Burton, Dec. 7, 1942. Methodist Archives, Suva. The school did, in fact, become interracial.

63. D. Fullerton to C. Gribble, Aug. 19, 1960. Methodist Archives, Suva.

64. Thornley 1979: 284–86.

65. *PCC News*, June 1977, p. 2. The choice of an Indian, Daniel Mastapha, was reported to be in considerable measure the result of support from Setariki Tuilovoni, the first Fijian president of the church.

66. *Fiji Times*, April 29, 1965. Baro 1975: 38. The older group came from the long-established women's organization, the Soqosoqo Vakamarama. These older leaders were shocked two months later when a group of Methodist missionaries, including two who worked in the Fijian side of the church, urged in a public letter that there be a common electorate for some seats and separate electorates for others. Public meetings were organized to protest the missionaries' statement.

67. Langdon 1968. Henri Vernier, interview, 1975.

68. The move to form the associations was in large measure an effort to combat communism, which seemed to have come forward as the political force among the people as soon as they were released for participation in the national life. The name of the Catholic association was "Union des Indigènes Calédoniens Amis de la Liberté dans l'Ordre," and the name of the Protestant association was "Association des Calédoniens et Loyaltiens Français." When the Protestant church split in 1958 its association was dominated by the separating Free Church, and therefore in 1961 the principal Protestant church organized the Association Autochtone de Calédonie et des Iles

Loyauté. The Catholic association was much more influential than the Protestant ones. Both the Catholic group and the main Protestant one were quite conservative in their orientation, trying to preserve the structure of the traditional tribes and the power of their chiefs. O'Reilly 1948. Guiart 1959: 49–60. Saussol 1969: 123. *La Vie Protestante*, Dec. 17, 1961.

69. It attacked the churches for not giving the full, liberating message of Christ and for presenting a white God. The statement can be found in the files of the Pacific Council of Churches, Suva, and the National Council of Churches, New York.

70. Martin 1975: 44. *PCC News*, October 1979, p. 1. Kohler 1980: 26.The Protestant Church made a statement in 1974 calling attention to the imprisonment of some of its young men and the "deep sense of discontent" among the people, and in 1977 it made an appeal to the Protestant Federation in France to fight the proposed reapportionment of the legislature, which would reduce the power of the Melanesians. Pacific Conference of Churches Archives, Suva. Trautmann 1976: 65–66.

71. Plant 1977: 59–66. *New Hebridean Viewpoints*: June–July 1973: 1,3. Dyt 1978: 2. *PCC News*, November 1976, pp. 3, 5–6. Lini 1974: 12. *Catalyst* 6, no. 2: 136.

72. Caroline and Marshall Islands Mission 1968: 88. Micronesian Seminar 1974: 20–21, 27. Hezel 1975.

73. The Pacific Conference of Churches was specifically opposed to the separate agreement made between the United States and the Marianas Islands, creating there a commonwealth attached to the U.S. *PCC News*, June 1976, pp. 2–3. National Council of Churches, news release, May 22, 1979. "Petition to the 46th Session of the UN Trusteeship Council." Murphy 1977. The particular issue on which the National Council of Churches made representations to the American government was the desire of the Congress of Micronesia to preserve the right to make treaties with other governments and to change any defense arrangements made with the United States. Roxanna Coop, Memorandum, Nov. 14, 1978. Archives of National Council of Churches, New York.

74. McAuley 1956. Nottage 1940: 32–33. Fairbairn 1969: 1–2. Cf. Rowley 1966: 136. J. King 1905: 29–36. Hurst 1937. A special development was the creation in 1904 of Papuan Industries, Ltd. by a former LMS missionary. All profits beyond 5 percent per annum were to go to help the Papuans. This venture continued fairly prosperously until the depression of the 1930s forced it out of business. G. Martin 1908: 82ff. Goodall 1964: 15–17.

75. Some effort was made by the churches to transfer unused portions of their land to local people, but the efforts were frustrated by lack of effective cooperation by those people and by the government. Threlfall 1975: 235–36. Cf. J.King 1905: 29–36. Hurst 1937: 16–17. Loeliger 1975: 37. Both the Lutheran Church and the United Church created large holding companies to manage the lands and businesses that they received from the missions. Ruthenberg 1974: 46–47. *CWM Newshare*, June 1979: 9. Reitz 1975: 16–21.

76. On the Catholic technical school established in Papua in 1919 see Dupeyrat 1935: 427–32 and Goyau 1938: 106–7. The Catholics also had two technical schools in New Caledonia. *Missions des Iles* 1961: 41–42. On the Protestant schools in Papua New Guinea, see Rich 1937: 16; Bromilow 1929: 305; Pilhofer 1963: vol. 2: 86–91, 100–101.

77. Burton and Deane 1936: 113–15. Thornley 1979: 242. An additional technical high school was established in Fiji in 1976 by the Mormons.

78. Wood 1978: vol. 2: 338. A much smaller industrial and agricultural school, but

one of unusual significance, was that established by Pastor Abraham at Havila on Lifou in 1918. Pastor Abraham was trying to recreate some of the practical education combined with a communal life and strict discipline that had been characteristic of the life of young men in pre-Christian society. The school passed through many vicissitudes but was still operating in 1967. Allégret 1928: Part 2: 22. Schloesing 1952: 10.

79. Nevin 1977: 179–83. Kahn 1965: 271–72. The New Guinea Lutherans established after the war their important technical school, agricultural school, and commercial school. Pilhofer 1963: vol. 2: 283. Frerichs 1957: 89ff., 202, and 1969: 151. Anglicans and the United Church also had new technical schools in Papua.

80. Tomlin 1951: 209–11. Presbyterian Church of the New Hebrides, General Assembly *Proceedings*, 1952, minutes 40–41; 1960: p. 14; 1964; pp. 20–21. *Mission des Iles* 1961: 111. Arbuckle 1965: 284–87. Kent 1966. Schneider 1976: 151. Roman Catholic missionaries were also strongly involved in developing cooperatives in Bougainville, the Marshall Islands, Tonga, and the outer islands of French Polynesia. Laracy 1969: 326–31. Feeney 1952: 178–81. These were postwar developments. An earlier missionary effort to establish a cooperative existed among the Protestants of Lifou prior to 1928. Allégret 1928: Part 2: 22.

81. Fairbairn 1969. Ruthenberg 1974: 47–54. The first group to follow Namasu's example was the Wabag Lutheran Church established by the Missouri Synod Lutheran Mission in the New Guinea highlands. It set up Waso, an equally successful, if smaller, operation. The Australian Baptist Mission and its associated church, also in the highlands, began Enga Products, Ltd., which maintained a large marketing program for the numerous cash crops the mission had introduced.

82. Murphy 1970: 698, 700. Murphy 1977: 77. *Education for Rural Development* 1977. Wood 1975: 236. Ruthenberg 1974: 54–58. Laracy 1969: 326–31. F. Wagner 1960. Wilson and Menzies 1967: 56. *PCC News*, Dec. 1974. Arbuckle 1978: 284 states that only 35 percent of the Marist missionaries regarded development work as essential to mission, but over 50 percent saw it as either essential or useful.

83. Murphy 1977: 75–77. Spades 1973. *Pacifique '77. Catalyst* 3, no. 2: 64–73; 6, no. 1: 53; 6, no. 2: 136. Micronesian Seminar 1975: 16. Finau 1974: 1–6. Momis 1974. McCarthy 1973: 31. Ratuvili 1974. Vusoniwailala 1977. Mavor 1973.

84. E.g., Turner 1976: 99–100 on Papua New Guinea. *Outpost. A Fiji Forum* 4, no. 5 (September 1976): 27 on Fiji. Finau 1974: 1–7.

85. E.g., Spades 1973: 16

86. Tonga Council of Churches 1975: 23–25, 116, Appendix B.

13
Conclusion

The three-quarters of a century traversed in these pages began with mission organizations and foreign missionaries at the center of the scene, operating the main religious structures of the islands. Under them were vigorous village congregations deeply involved in the traditional culture, led by local pastors and catechists, and quite different from the churches found in other parts of the world. By the end of the period foreign missionaries were no longer the center of the scene. National churches had emerged as independent, recognizable entities, governing themselves and taking their place on the stage of the world-wide church. They were being transformed through closer contacts with other cultures, and were no longer so different from the churches in the rest of the world. The village congregations were less vigorous and less traditional than they had been, but still reflected much of the old village life and played an important role in village affairs.

The establishment of the national churches had taken place with remarkably little struggle. The only areas where there had been any major difficulties over church independence were the three areas which took the lead in the process: Tonga, Samoa and Fiji. Tonga's struggles had come in the late nineteenth century, involving the one large-scale ecclesiastical revolution in Pacific history. It was an odd revolution since it was led by a king and a prime minister, but it was a revolution nevertheless since its aim was to throw off the power of the missionaries. Samoa's experience was somewhat less traumatic; yet the struggles and controversies of the Mau period destroyed the whole operation of the church and only the pacifying intervention of the delegation from London turned that turmoil into a constructive movement toward church independence. Fiji had its times of tension and uncertainty in connection with the drive to put laymen on the synod and the effort to unify the separate racial synods into a single independent church, but the transition there was smoother than in either Tonga or Samoa.

Once these three leaders had made the change, the churches of all the other islands reached independence almost effortlessly. The mission boards and societies in Europe and Australasia were determined to make independence a gift, even in places where it was not particularly desired. The missionaries whom they sent out to the Pacific Islands after World War II were fully indoctrinated by them to carry out this policy. These missionaries urged the islanders forward and cooperated with them in moving toward self-government.

The missionaries of the first half of this century had been very different. They had been the major obstacles to greater church independence. It was they who had resisted the revolution in Tonga, had fought the Mau influences in Samoa and had tried to block lay representation in Fiji. After mid-century, however, the policy of the mission boards prevailed among their own missionaries. The mission boards and the Vatican throughout the twentieth century were a constant force in favor of greater church independence and bore the major responsibility for its achievement.

The creation of independent churches involved a change from foreign to national leadership. By the end of the 1970s this change was accomplished in all the churches except some Roman Catholic dioceses and a few smaller Protestant churches. As the national leaders took over, the style of operation of the churches sometimes changed to fit with traditional Pacific ways: the church assemblies moved more slowly in their debates and waited for consensus in their decisions, rather than taking quick votes; loans to friends of church officials and other financial irregularities sometimes produced financial crises; more personalized styles of leadership appeared within some inherited democratic church structures, especially in areas where self-made "big men" had traditionally dominated the society. Some outside observers wondered whether the imported church structures were too foreign and too cumbersome to survive, but, while there may have been some loss of initiative, it soon became clear that the local leaders were quite capable of handling the imported structures in their own way.[1]

Foreign missionaries adopted a less important role as the national leaders took charge. They served as advisors, technical specialists or educators and were increasingly removed from the centers of decision making. It was not an easy transition for them. Some people still saw them in their traditional roles. Some looked to them to take initiatives, yet did not desire them to take leadership. In a few of the churches their numbers were reduced by the end of this period to the vanishing point. This was true in the Samoan Congregational Church, the Marshall Islands Church, the Cook Islands Church and of course the small churches of Niue, Nauru and Tuvalu. The major Protestant churches of Tonga, Kiribati, Vanuatu and New Caledonia each had only four or five missionaries. Fiji and Tahiti each had about ten. In most churches of Papua New Guinea and the Solomons, missionaries continued at close to their previous numbers, but for shorter periods of service which meant that they had less influence.[2] The reductions in every area applied only to the older Protestant churches. The large Catholic numbers continued and the new sectarian groups may even have had increasing personnel. Foreign funds continued to give significant but not essential help to most churches.

As the churches changed in the receiving, so also they changed in the sending of missionaries. At the beginning of the century the Protestants of Fiji, Samoa, Tonga and Rarotonga were sending hundreds of missionaries to Papua New Guinea and the Solomons. These numbers declined as the churches of those new territories came to greater size and maturity. The Samoan Congregationalists kept a few workers in Papua till the 1970s, when, after some difficulties in connection with the arrangements, they finally withdrew. Tongan Methodists still had eight missionaries in Papua New Guinea at the end of the '70s, mostly in the highlands. But essentially the great work in the western islands was now completed and their missionary role there had come to an end.

In its place a new and more widely scattered missionary activity was appearing. Pacific islanders began helping churches in other parts of the world. Twenty or more, primarily Fiji Methodists, were working, in cooperation with Australians, among the Australian aborigines and also, to a smaller extent, among the white population of Australia. A few were in Europe, in France and Britain, assisting the churches which had so long assisted the Pacific. Four or five others were in Africa.

Much of the structure for this new outreach was provided by two new world-wide organizations binding together two groups of churches, those with an LMS background and those with a French Protestant background. Churches in every part of the world that had once received LMS missionaries now joined together to exchange funds and personnel in mutual aid through the Council for World Mission which replaced the old LMS. Those which had been linked to the Paris Evangelical Mission did the same thing through the Communauté Evangélique d'Action Apostolique. This new form of mission implied a radical change in the relationship of the Pacific to the wider world. At least in the case of the major Protestant churches the Pacific was becoming a sending as well as a receiving area in relation to the world as a whole.[3]

The Pacific Islands were now, in all probability, the most solidly Christian part of the world. At the beginning of the century many island people had still not heard the Christian message. Seventy-five years later that situation had changed completely. Practically all of the islanders, except for the Indian people in Fiji, were Christians. The people were more devoted in Christian belief and gave to the churches a larger place in their life than did the people of any other region. Christianity was more important here than in Europe, America or Australasia, the lands from which Pacific missionaries had first come.

In the structures of world wide Christianity the Pacific churches now had a recognized place. Many of them were members of the World Council of Churches, and on global committees it was now assumed that one or more Pacific islanders would have seats. The Pacific Conference of Churches was recognized everywhere as one of the important regional councils, along with those of other areas such as the Caribbean or Africa. Its secretary travelled constantly to committee meetings and conferences in other parts of the world. Similarly among Catholics the two bishops' conferences were recognized as part of the structure of bishops' conferences covering the world. One Pacific islander, from Samoa, sat in the College of Cardinals at Rome.

Ideas as well as people were travelling back and forth between the Pacific and the rest of the world. In some circles in Europe and America it began to be recognized that the Pacific churches had lessons to teach their brothers and sisters in other regions, lessons, for example, on the solidarity of the Christian congregation, on the need for a sense of myth in human understanding, and on the reality of demonic forces in human life.[4] But the much greater flow of ideas was into the Pacific from the rest of the world. The new forms of Christian education and youth work which flourished in the Pacific churches in the 1960s and 1970s were all patterned on Western models. The major forms of national development and the alternative forms which the churches championed were both equally drawn from other parts of the world. The ecumenical organizations, such as the Pacific Conference of Churches and the Melanesian Council of Churches, and the advanced central theological schools, depended for their existence on foreign funds. Programs of family planning, though they were doubtlessly needed with the sudden growth of Pacific populations, were brought in by imported experts and taught in foreign-financed conferences. Even new conceptions of Christian life and faith, though they might have strong Biblical roots, were foreign in their actual introduction. This was true of the effort to break away from the formalism and legalism which had characterized Pacific Christianity. It was also true of the more personal and spiritual emphases which began to replace the communitarian and materialist ways of thinking about the Christian faith. It is obvious that as these new emphases came in, the churches of the Pacific were becoming more like churches in other parts of the world and the distinctive qualities of Pacific Christianity as they have been described in earlier chapters were gradually disappearing.[5]

Though these changes originated in other parts of the world they were nonetheless necessary for the Pacific churches because Pacific life itself was becoming more like life in other parts of the world. It was impossible to keep up the old formalistic and communal style of church life as pluralism and secularization spread in the surrounding society. With the greater movement of people and the growth of sects, the islanders faced a plurality of churches among which personal decisions had to be made, rather than simply participating in a unified society with its single church. With the greater variety of outside contacts and of economic and recreational activities there was less time available for the activities of the church and secular attitudes increased. In the Cook Islands it was noticed that the number of people attending church dropped dramatically as soon as the new international airfield began construction. A pastor in New Guinea commented, "Formerly there was but one road. We did everything with prayer and according to the gospel. Now the road has split up into two: one is business work, one is living according to the gospel and mission."[6]

Even in the outlying and more isolated islands, attendance at the daily sessions of morning and evening prayer was declining. Many a time the village pastor would ring the church bell, or more likely strike the empty ammunition shell which since World War II served the purpose of a church bell, but few people assembled for prayer. Where there had once been a unified society possessing a religious core and religious underpinnings, there was now coming a more diversified society with no readily identifiable core or underpinnings. These tendencies were not carried as far in the Pacific as they were elsewhere. The old church life remained strong in many of its traditional ways. But the new tendencies were present everywhere.

In response to this new secularism and pluralism the churches saw a new vision of the direction they should go. They began to recognize themselves as distinct from, rather than coterminous with society. They saw their task as serving rather than leading the people around them. They began to feel a comprehensive interest in the entire Pacific region in relation to the world rather than seeing only their small village community. These at least were the visions which the new indigenous leaders held up before the churches as they entered into modern Pacific life. They were visions which implied difficult tasks in the years ahead. Though great changes had already occurred, greater still were in store.

NOTES

1. Jaeschke 1978: 194–198. Threlfall 1975: 224. Tamaali'i 1975: 45–50, 79–84, 93–95 reports financial irresponsibility and Jacobsen 1974: 11 speaks of modification of democratic processes. In Turner 1976: 96, Koschade 1967: 74–75, Heinsius 1976: 13, Gosart 1970b: 646–8 and Helm 1973: 33–37 it is maintained that the church structures were too costly and complex for the island people, yet there is no doubt that in general the island people kept them operating effectively. There was indeed a tendency for the structure to become increasingly complex and costly, but this was not inherent in the forms that had been taken over from the foreign missionaries. It was the consequence of the increasing complexity of Pacific life and world culture, and grew out of decisions by islanders, not foreigners. The Evangelical Church in Tahiti, for example, during the first decade of its independence reduced the number of its pastors by five but increased the number of its specialized workers and administrators by eight. Raapoto 1974: 11–14.

2. On the change in missionary life and work during this century cf. Forman 1978b.

3. Loeliger 1974: 214; 1975: 36. *Catalyst*, vol. 6, no. 3, p. 220. Pacific Conference of Churches 1976: 68. *Journal des Missions Evangéliques* 1974, 2nd quarter, p. 13; 1976, 2nd quarter, p. 58. A short-lived experiment in receiving Asian missionaries in the islands was the acceptance by the Papua Ekalesia of a missionary from the Church of South India when that church was first organized. This experiment did not prove successful, partly because of tensions with the Papuan workers on one side and the European workers on the other. The missionary, who had come in 1947, died in 1955 and was not replaced. But in 1980 the CWM had two Indians in Papua.

4. Bürkle 1978 is a collection of essays centering on what the Western churches could learn from the Pacific. Ahrens and Hollenweger 1977: 75–105 explores the meaning of a New Guinea myth for Western Christians.

5. The new ideas in Christian education as shown in Coop 1977: 123–129 are all those which were popular in ecumenical circles throughout the world. That the intro-

duction of new ideas in Christian communication was by people sent in from outside is clear in Evaluation Conference 1972. The presentation of family planning was in conferences and organizations paid for by outside bodies, both Protestant and Catholic, as is apparent in Thomson 1968; Pacific Conference of Churches Continuation Committee 1970: 2; and *Outpost. A Fiji Forum*, vol. 4, no. 2, p. 24.

    6. J. Wagner 1964: 24. Crocombe 1973: 10–11 notes the change in the Cook Islands. We should recognize that though these changes became most noticeable at the end of our period, they came about gradually and their beginnings were evident early in the century. The Catholic bishop of New Caledonia said as early as 1907 that there was religious indifference among the natives. Tahiti received its first cinema in 1912 and this was seen as a threat to religion. A mission delegation visiting the Cook Islands in 1915 told how secularization coming from the close contacts with New Zealand was hurting the church. And a Fiji missionary reported two years later how European influence was changing social customs and producing a general listlessness toward religion. It should be noted that the four island groups mentioned in these early changes—New Caledonia, Tahiti, the Cooks and Fiji—were the islands which had the most contact with the outside world. Vicariate Apostolic of New Caledonia, "Report to Society for the Propagation of the Faith," 1907, S.P.F. Archives, Paris. *Journal des Missions Évangéliques*, vol. 87, part 2, p. 353. Viner et al., 1916: 33, 36–37. Steadman 1917: 21–22.

Bibliography

Note on Location of Archives

The archives referred to in the endnotes to the various chapters are located in the headquarters of the mission societies or churches concerned, with the following exceptions: The Methodist Mission Archives in Sydney are located in the Mitchell Library. The Council for World Mission Archives in London are located in the University of London. The American Board Archives in Harvard University are located in the Houghton Library. The Methodist Archives in Suva are located in the National Archives of Fiji. The Society for the Propagation of the Faith Archives in Paris are located in the Centre de Recherche Théologique Missionnaire.

References

Abel, Russell W.
   1934   *Charles W. Abel of Kwato. Forty Years in Dark Papua.* New York: Fleming H. Revell.
Adams, Henry
   1930   *Letters of Henry Adams (1858-1891).* Edited by Worthington Chauncey Ford. Boston: Hougton Mifflin Co.
Ahnne, Edward
   1931   *Dans les Iles du Pacifique.* Paris: Société des Missions Evangéliques.
Ahrens, Theodor, and Hollenweger, Walter
   1977   *Volkschristentum und Volksreligion im Pazifik.* Frankfurt: Verlag Otto Lembeck.
Alazard, Ildetonse
   1905   *Réponse aux Calomnies de M. Dejeante.* Paris: Librairie Américaine.
Allégret, E.
   1928   *Rapport de M. Allégret sur son Voyage en Océanie Juillet 1926-Février 1928.* Paris: Société des Missions Evangéliques.
Allen, Michael R.
   1968   "The Establishment of Christianity and Cash Cropping in a New Hebridean Community." *Journal of Pacific History* 3:25-47.

American Board of Commissioners for Foreign Missions
    Annual Report of the American Board of Commissioners for Foreign Missions. Boston: 1810–1960.
American Lutheran Church
    Official Reports of the President and the Various Boards and Committees. Columbus, Ohio and Minneapolis, Minn. Biennial, 1932.
Anderson, Efraim
    1968   *Churches at the Grass Roots. A Study in Congo-Brazzaville.* London: Lutterworth Press.
Andersson, George
    1943   *Tour of the New Hebrides.* Report of a Visit to Mission Stations Presented to a Combined Meeting of the Foreign Committee and the Presbyterian Women's Missionary Union on Tuesday, 30th, November. Presbyterian Church of Victoria.
Anglican Church of Papua New Guinea. Province of Papua New Guinea
    1977   *Provincial Constitution and Provincial Canons.* Madang: Anglican Centre.
Arbuckle, Gerald A.
    1965   "The Role of Education in the Economic and Social Development of the South Pacific Islands." *Acta Societatis Mariae*, n. 35 T. 7:265–88.

    1978   "The Impact of Vatican II on the Marists in Oceania." In *Mission, Church and Sect in Oceania*, edited by J. Boutilier, D. Hughes, and S. Tiffany; pp. 275–99. Ann Arbor: University of Michigan Press.
Artless, Stuart W. (ed.)
    1936   *The Church in Melanesia.* London: Melanesian Mission.

    1965   *The Story of the Melanesian Mission.* London: Melanesian Mission, 5th ed.
Australian Council of Churches
    1966   *Australian Missions. A Statistical Survey.* Mimeographed. Sydney: Division of Missions of Australian Council of Churches, 2nd ed.
Australian Missionary Conference, 1926
    1926   *Australia Facing the Non-Christian World.* Melbourne, Alpha Printing Co.
B.M.
    1901   *L'Oeuvre de la Mission Mariste en Nouvelle Calédonie.* Noumea: Imprimerie Calédonienne.
Baro, Eta
    1975   "Lolohea Akosita Waqairawai." In *Women's Role in Fiji*, by Jyoti Amratlal, Eta Baro, Vanessa Griffin, and Geet

Bala Singh. Suva: South Pacific Social Sciences Association.

Barradale, V. A.
1927   *Report of Rev. V. A. Barradale after Secretarial Visit to the South Seas, Papua, Australia and New Zealand August 1926–June 1927 (with the Rev. G. J. Williams in Papua).* London: London Missionary Society.

Bartels, F. L.
1965   *Roots of Ghana Methodism.* Cambridge, Eng.: Cambridge University Press.

Beaglehole, Ernest
1957   *Social Change in the South Pacific. Rarotonga and Aitutaki.* London: G. Allen and Unwin.

Becke, Louis
1899–1900 "Surrender of Samoa and How It will Affect Missionary Enterprise." *The Leisure Hour* 48: 218–21.

Becker, R.
1954   "L'oeuvre missionaire de M. Leenhardt en Nouvelle Calédonie." *Journal de la Société des Océanistes* 10: 11–27.

Beckmann, Johannes
1943   *Der Einheimische Klerus in den Missionsländern. Eine Übersicht.* Freiburg (Schweiz): Paulusdrucherei.

Beevers, R.
1972   "Non-formal education: The Role of the Churches." In *Fifth Waigani Seminar. Change and Development in Rural Melanesia.* Canberra: Research School of Pacific Studies, Australian National University.

Bell, Arthur
1946   *Among the Ruins. The Story of the New Guinea Martyrs.* Sydney: Australian Board of Missions.

Belshaw, Cyril S.
1954   *Changing Melanesia. Social Economics of Cultural Contact.* London: Oxford University Press.

Benson, James
1957   *Prisoners' Base and Home Again. The Story of a Missionary P.O.W.* London: Robert Hale.

Berganza, Higinio
1947   "Cinco años de guerra sobre la Mision de Marianas y Carolinas." *El Siglo de las Misiones* 34:68–72, 94–101.

Bergeret, E.
1935   "Paganisme Vivace." *Journal des Missions Evangéliques* 110:370–75.

Berkhofer, Robert F.
1965   *Salvation and the Savage. An Analysis of Protestant Missions and American Indian Response, 1787–1862.* Lexington: University of Kentucky Press.

Berndt, Ronald M.
  1965   "The Kamano, Usurufor, Jate and Fore of the Eastern
            Highlands." In *Gods, Ghosts and Men in Melanesia*, edited
            by Peter Lawrence and M. J. Meggitt. Melbourne: Oxford
            University Press.
Beyerhaus, Peter
  1959   *Die Selbständigkeit der Jungen Kirchen als missionarisches
            Problem*. Wuppertal-Barmen: Verlag der Rheinischen
            Missions-Gesellschaft.
Bigault, Guy de
  1939   "Les Soeurs Maristes dans les Missions d'Océanie." *Mis-
            sions Catholiques* 71:293–300.

  1943   "Une Mission sans Histoire." *Missions Catholiques* 75:
            163–66, 179–81.

  1944   "Premier Centenaire de la Mission de Nouvelle Calédonie."
            Missions Catholiques 76:6–8, 118–122.

  1946   "Les Missions d'Océanie pendant la Guerre." *Missions
            Catholiques* 78: 67–70.

  1946–47   "La pratique du dépaysement." *Bulletin Trimestriel de
            l'Oeuvre Pontifical de St. Pierre Apôtre* 1946: 27–29; 1947:
            10–12, 20–21.

  1947   *Drames de la Vie Salomonaise*. Namur: Grands Lacs.
Bitton, Nelson
  1947   *Alfred Sadd of the Gilberts, A Memoir*. London: Living-
            stone Press.
Black, Peter W.
  1978   "The Teachings of Father Marino: Christianity on Tobi
            Atoll." In *Mission, Church and Sect in Oceania*, edited by
            James A. Boutilier, D. Hughes, and S. Tiffany; pp. 307–54.
            Ann Arbor: University of Michigan Press.
Blackett, A. H.
  1948   "A Survey of Methods Suitable for the Future Evangeliza-
            tion of the Indian People of Fiji. Prepared for the Morpeth
            Conference." Mimeographed. Morpeth, Australia: South
            Pacific Missionary Conference.
Blakeslee, George H.
  1921   "Japan's New Island Possessions in the Pacific: History and
            Present Status." *Journal of International Relations*
            12:173–91.

Blanc, Joseph Félix
1914   *Les Iles Wallis; la dernière acquisition de la France dans le Pacifique.* Paris: Perrin.

1926   *Histoire religieuse de l'Archipel Fidjien.* Toulon: Impr. Sainte-Jeanne-d'Arc; 2 vols.

Boutilier, James A.
1975   "The Role of the Administration and the Missions in the Provision of Medical and Educational Services in the British Solomon Islands Protectorate, 1893–1942." Paper for Symposium of Association for Social Anthropology in Oceania.

1978   "Mission, Administration, and Education in the Solomon Islands, 1893–1942." In *Mission, Church, and Sect in Oceania,* edited by James A. Boutilier, Daniel Hughes, and Sharon Tiffany; pp. 139–62. Ann Arbor:University of Michigan Press.

Braam, Johann
1936   "Die Gestaltung der ozeanischen Kirche." *Zeitschrift fur Missionswissenschaft* 26:241–55.

Brammall, John, and May, R. J. (eds.)
1975   *Education in Melanesia. Papers Delivered at the Eighth Waigani Seminar. . . 5-10 May 1974.* Canberra: Australian National University Press.

Braun, F., and Sheatsley, C. V.
1937   *On Both Sides of the Equator. A History of the New Guinea and India Mission Fields of the American Lutheran Church.* Columbus, Ohio: Lutheran Book Concern.

de Bres, Joris, and Campbell, Rob
1975   *Worth Their Weight in Gold.* Auckland: Auckland Resource Centre for World Development.

Brewer, David L.
1968   "The Mormons." In *The Religious Situation: 1968,* pp. 518–46. Boston: Beacon Press.

British Solomon Islands Protectorate
        Report for the Year. Honiara: British Solomon Islands Protectorate.

Britsch, R. Lanier
1979   "Mormon Missions: An Introduction to the Latter-day Saints Missionary System." *Occasional Bulletin of Missionary Research* 3:22–27.

Bromilow, William
1929   *Twenty Years among Primitive Papuans.* London: Epworth Press.

Brown, Reverend G.
1903 "Fiji: A Statement Presented to the Board of Missions by the General Secretary." Methodist Overseas Missions Archives, Mitchell Library, Sydney.

Brunton, Ron
1971 "Cargo Cults and Systems of Exchange in Melanesia." *Mankind* 8:115–28.

Buck, Peter Henry
1939 *Anthropology and Religion.* New Haven: Yale University Press.

Bugotu, Francis
1973 "Decolonizing and Recolonizing: The Case of the Solomons." *Pacific Perspectives* 25:77–80.

Bürkle, Horst (ed.)
1978 *Theologische Beiträge aus Papua Neuguinea.* Erlangen: Verlag der Ev.-Luth. Mission.

Burnett, Frank
1911 *Through Polynesia and Papua. Wanderings with a Camera in the Southern Seas.* London: Francis Griffiths.

Burridge, Kenelm
1960 *Mambu. A Melanesian Millennium.* London: Methuen and Co.

Burton, John Wear
1909 *Our Indian Work in Fiji.* Suva: Methodist Mission Press.

1910 *The Fiji of Today.* London: C. H. Kelley

1930 *A Missionary Survey of the Pacific Islands.* London: World Dominion Press.

1949 *Modern Missions in the South Pacific.* London: Livingstone Press.

Burton, John W., and Dean, Wallace
1936 *A Hundred Years in Fiji.* London: Epworth Press.

Cadoux, Th.
1953 "Evolution de la Chrétienté papoue." *Missions Catholiques* 85:260–68.

Carmichael, David Kenneth
1967 "The Doctrine of the Church as Seen in Mission Work at the Middle of the Nineteenth Century (with particular reference to Mission work on Aneityum, the New Hebrides)." Typescript, Theological Hall of Presbyterian Church of New Zealand.

Caroline and Marshall Islands Mission of the New York Province of the Society of Jesus.
1968 "Position Papers and Consensus Statements. Plenary

Meeting of all Jesuit Missionaries. Held at Xavier High School, Truk. August 22–25, 1968." Mimeographed. Buffalo: The Jesuit Bureau.

Carter, George G.
1973   *A Family Affair: A Brief Survey of New Zealand Methodism's Involvement in Mission Overseas, 1822–1972.* Auckland: Wesley Historical Society of New Zealand.

Cato, A. C.
1947   "A New Religious Cult in Fiji." *Oceania* 18:146–56.

1956   "Disintegration, Syncretization and Change in Fijian Religion." *Mankind* 5:101–6.

Centenaire des Écoles Protestantes Françaises à Tahiti 1866–1966.
1966   Papeete: "La Dépêche."

Challis, R.L.
1940   *A Pacific Pastorate.* London: Livingstone Press.

Chatterton, Percy
1968   "The History of Delena." Mimeographed. London Missionary Society.

Christ in Melanesia. Exploring Theological Issues. Point 1977.
1977   Goroka: Melanesian Institute for Pastoral and Socio-Economic Service.

Christiansen, Palle
1969   *The Melanesian Cargo Cult. Millenarianism as a Factor in Cultural Change.* Copenhagen: Akademisk Forlag.

Clyde, Paul
1935   *Japan's Pacific Mandate.* New York: Macmillan.

Cocks, Norman F.
1950   *Report following a Secretarial Visit to Papua, August 20–December 18, 1949.* London: London Missionary Society.

The Constitution of the Congregational Christian Church in Samoa, 1962.
1962   Malua, Samoa.

Constitution of the Samoan Church, 1928.
1928   Malua, Samoa.

"Consultation, United Church of Papua New Guinea and the Solomon Islands with the Cooperating Churches. 25th to 27th November 1974"
1974   Typescript. In possession of Charles Forman.

Coop, Roxana
1977   "Which Way for Christian Education?" *Catalyst* 7, no. 2:127–38.

Coppenrath, Michel
1976   "Les Églises du Pacifique et l'Evangélisation." *Mission de l'Église*, no. 32:27–31.

Cormack, James E.
1944   *Isles of Solomon.* Washington: Review and Herald.

Cormack, Maribelle
    1956   *The Lady was a Skipper; the Story of Eleanor Wilson, Missionary Extraordinary to the Marshall and Caroline Islands.* New York: Hill & Wang.

Costantini, Celso
    1949   *L'Art Chrétien dans les Missions. Manuel d'Art pour les Missionaires.* Translated (from the Italian of 1938) by Edmond Leclef. Paris: Desclée de Brouwer.

Coulter, John Wesley
    1957   *The Pacific Dependencies of the Unites States.* New York: Macmillan.

Counts, Dorothy Ayers
    1978   "Christianity in Kaliai: Response to Missionization in Northwest New Britain." In *Mission, Church, and Sect in Oceania*, edited by James Boutilier, D. Hughes, and S. Tiffany; pp. 355–94. Ann Arbor: University of Michigan Press.

Courtais, E., and Bigault, Guy de
    1936   *Centenaire des Missions Maristes en Océanie.* Paris and Lyon: Emmanuel Vitte.

Craig, C. Stuart
    1961   "Notes on a Secretarial Visit to Samoa and Fiji 16 April–17 May, 1961." Mimeographed. London: London Missionary Society.

Crocombe, R. G.
    1972   "Protocole dans le Pacifique. Le roi de Tonga à l'église." *Journal de la Société des Océanistes* 28:169–72.

    1973   "The Future of Religion in Fiji." *Outpost. A Fiji Forum* 1, no. 3:9–20.

Cummings, David W.
    1961   *Mighty Missionary of the Pacific: the Building Program of the Church of Jesus Christ of Latter-Day Saints, Its History, Scope and Significance.* Salt Lake City: Bookcraft.

Curran, John F.
    1978   "Providing Permanent Church Leaders: The Diaconate Program in the Caroline and Marshall Islands." *Worldmission* 29:44–54.

Cyclopedia of Samoa, Tonga, Tahiti and the Cook Islands.
    1907   Sydney: McCarron, Stewart & Co.

Danks, Benjamin
    1933   *In Wild New Britain. The Story of Benjamin Danks, Pioneer Missionary, from His Diary.* Edited by Wallace Deane. Sydney: Angus & Robertson.

Darmancier, Michel
1965   "Relatio de Statu Vicariatus Apostolici de Wallis et Futuna
            A. D. 1965." Microfilm in Marist Secretariat, Rome.
Darnand, Joseph
1934   *Aux Iles Samoa: la forêt qui s'illumine.* Lyon & Paris: Em-
            manuel Vitte.
Davenport, W., and Coker, G.
1967   "The Moro Movement of Guadalcanal, B.S.I.P." *Journal
            of the Polynesian Society* 76:123–75.
David, Caroline Martha (Mrs. T. W. Edgeworth David)
1899   *Funafuti, or Three Months on a Coral Island: An Unscien-
            tific Account of a Scientific Expedition.* London: John
            Murray.
Davidson, James W.
1967   *Samoa mo Samoa. The Emergence of the Independent State
            of Western Samoa.* Melbourne: Oxford University Press.
Davis, Hassoldt
1935   "Auctioneers of Paradise." *American Mercury* 36:216–27.
Deane, W.
1910   "Girls' Boarding Schools. An Immediate Necessity in Fiji."
            Missionary Review 20, no. 7:9.

1921   *Fijian Society or the Sociology and Psychology of the Fi-
            jians.* London: Macmillan and Co.
Debrunner, Hans W.
1959   *Witchcraft in Ghana: A Study of the Belief in Destructive
            Witches and Its Effect on the Akan Tribes.* Kumasi: Presby-
            terian Book Depot.
Deeken, Richard
1901   "Schulinspektor auf Reisen." In *Manuia Samoa. Samoa-
            nische Reiseskizzen und Beobachtungen.* Berlin and Olden-
            burg: Gerhard Stalling.
Delord, Ph.
1905   *Sur les plages lointaines à marée.* Paris: Soc. des Missions
            Évangéliques.
Derrick, Ronald Albert
1952   *Vocational Training in the South Pacific.* London: Oxford.
Destable, Cyprien, and Sédès, J.M.
1944   *La Croix dans l'Archipel Fidji (de 1894 à nos jours).* Paris:
            Editions Spes.
Diocese of Melanesia
1961   *The Faith of the Church. Lessons in the Faith for Junior
            Schools in the Diocese of Melanesia.* Honiara: Melanesian
            Mission Press.

1962   *Canons of Discipline of the Diocese of Melanesia as Revised
              at the Synod of 1962.*

Diocese of New Guinea
n.d.   "Hearers and Catechumens." MS., n.p., n.d. Australian
              Board of Missions Archives, Stanmore, New South Wales.

Dobson, Denis
1963   "Not Their Fashion." MS. in Franciscan Headquarters,
              Waverly, New South Wales.

Don, Alexander (ed.)
1918   *Light in Dark Isles. A Jubilee Record and Study of the New
              Hebrides Mission of the Presbyterian Church of New
              Zealand.* Dunedin: Foreign Missions Committee of the
              Presbyterian Church of New Zealand.

Don, Alexander
1927   *Peter Milne (1834–1924). Missionary to Aguna, New
              Hebrides 1870–1924 from the Presbyterian Church of New
              Zealand.* Dunedin: Foreign Missions Committee of the
              Presbyterian Church of New Zealand.

Douceré, Victor
1934   *La mission Catholique aux Nouvelles-Hébrides; d'après des
              documents écrits et les vieux souvenirs de l'auteur.* Lyon: E.
              Vitte.

Douglas, Norman
1974   "Latter-Day Saints Missions and Missionaries in Polynesia,
              1844–1960." Ph.D. thesis, Australian National University.

Dubois, L.L.
1927   "Les origines du clergé indigène de l' Océanie Centrale." In
              *Les Elites en Pays de Mission. Compte Rendu de la cin-
              quième Semaine de Missiologie de Louvain.* Louvain: Edi-
              tions du Museum Lessianum.

1928   "Activité Protestante en Polynésie occidentale et Mélané-
              sie. Reactions et espoirs catholiques." *Revue d'Histoire des
              Missions* 5:369–406.

Duncan, D. E., and Stuckey, J. M.
1966   "Statement on Presbyterian Educational and Medical Work
              in the New Hebrides by the Australian Presbyterian Board
              of Missions and the Overseas Missions Committee, Presby-
              terian Church of New Zealand." Mimeographed. Presby-
              terian Mission Archives, Auckland.

Dunstan, J. Leslie
1962   "The Christian Mission Since 1938: The Pacific Islands." In
              Frontiers of the Christian World Mission Since 1938, edited
              by Wilber C. Harr; pp. 62–82. New York: Harper & Bros.

Dupeyrat, André
1935   *Papouasie, Histoire de la Mission (1885–1935)*. Paris: Editions Dillen.

1948   *Papuan Conquest*. Melbourne: Araluen Publishing Co.

1958   "La dévotion à la Sainte Vierge en Papouasie." *Annales de Notre Dame du Sacré-Coeur* 92:215–20.

Durrad, John Walter
1920   *The Attitudes of the Church to Suqe*. Melanesian Mission Occasional Papers, no. 1. Norfolk Island: Melanesian Mission.

Dyt, Adriane
1978   "Report on Visit to New Hebrides." Australian Council of Churches Executive Committee Meeting, November 15, 1978. Mimeographed.

Education for Rural Development. The Tutu Experiment and Its Relevance for the Pacific.
1977   Suva: Institute of Pacific Studies, University of the South Pacific.

Edwards, E. J.
1971   "Report by the Rev. E. J. Edwards of a Secretarial Visit to the Pacific 23 April to 23 June, 1971." Mimeographed. London: Congregational Council for World Mission.

Église Evangélique de Polynésie Française. 166 ans d'histoire. (1797–1963).
n.d.   Papeete: Eglise Evangélique.

Ellsworth, S. G.
1959   *Zion in Paradise*. Logan, Utah: Utah State University.

Englert, Sebastian
1964   *Primer Siglo Cristiano de la Isla de Pascua, 1864–1964*. Villarica, Chile: Escuela Lito-Tipografica Salesiana "La Gratitud Nacional."

Eppelein, Friedrich
1934   *Die Mission aussenpolitisch*. Neuendettelsau: Freimund Verlag.

Ete, Risatisone
1972   "The Present Worship of the Congretional Christian Church in Samoa in Light of the Liturgical Movement." B. D. thesis, Pacific Theological College, Suva.

Evaluation Conference on Christian Communication in the Pacific.
1972   *Market Basket Media. Report of the Evaluation Conference on Christian Communication in the Pacific, Suva, Fiji*. Suva: Lotu Pasifika Productions

Fairbairn, J.J.
1969   *Namasu: New Guinea's Largest Indigenous-owned Company.* New Guinea Research Bulletin no. 28. Canberra: Australian National University, New Guinea Research Unit.

Faletoese, K. T.
1961   *Tala Faasolopito o le Ekalesia Samoa (L.M.S.)* [A History of the Samoan Church (L.M.S.).] Malua: Malua Printing Press.

Feeney, Thomas J.
1952   *Letters from Likiep.* New York: Pandick Press.

Finau, Patelisio
1974   "Prayer, Persuasion and Politics." *Pacific Perspective* 3, no. 2:1–11.

1975   *Some Theological Reflections on Migration.* Auckland: Auckland Resource Centre for World Development.

Firth, Raymond
1970   *Rank and Religion in Tikopia.* London: George Allen and Unwin.

Fish, Ernest Kelvin (ed.)
1966   *New Guinea on the Threshold: Aspects of Social, Political and Economic Development.* Canberra: Australian National University.

Flierl, Leonhard
1931   *Eemasang. Die Erneuerungsbewegung in der Gemeinde Sattelberg (Neuguinea). Geschichtliches und Grundsätzliches.* Gütersloh: C. Bertelsmann.

Forman, Charles W.
1969a   "Theological Education in the South Pacific Islands: A Quiet Revolution." *Journal de la Société des Océanistes* 25:151–67.

1969b   "The Wanted Missionary—Pacific Island Style." *Frontier* 12:267–73.

1970   "The Missionary Force of the Pacific Island Churches." *International Review of Mission* 59: 215–26.

1972   "Missionaries and Colonialism: The Case of the New Hebrides in the Twentieth Century." *Journal of Church and State* 14:75–92.

1974   "The South Pacific Style in the Christian Ministry." *Missiology,* 2:421–35.

1978a   "Tonga's Tortured Venture in Church Unity." *Journal of Pacific History* 13:3–21.

1978b   "Foreign Missionaries in the Pacific Islands during the Twentieth Century." In *Mission, Church, and Sect in Oceania*, edited by J. Boutilier, D. Hughes, and S. Tiffany; pp. 35–64. Ann Arbor: University of Michigan Press.

n.d.   "Sing to the Lord a New Song: Women in the Churches of Oceania." *In Rethinking Women's Roles: Perspectives from the Pacific.* (Tentative title), edited by Denise O'Brien and Sharon Tiffany. Forthcoming

Freeman, J. D.
1959   "The Joe Gimlet or Siovili Cult; an Episode in the Religious History of Early Samoa." In *Anthropology in the South Seas*, edited by J. D. Freeman and W. R. Geddes. New Plymouth, New Zealand: Thomas Avery and Sons, Ltd.

Freitag, Anton
1952   "Das Mittelozeanische Missionsfeld der Maristen." *Zeitschrift für Missionswissenschaft* 36:144–52.

Frerichs, A. C.
1957   *Anutu Conquers in New Guinea. The Story of 70 Years of Mission Work in New Guinea.* Columbus: Wartburg Press.

1969   Revised edition by Albert and Sylvia Frerichs. Minneapolis: Augsburg Press.

Freytag, Walter
1940   *Spiritual Revolution in the East.* London: Lutterworth Press.

Fricke, Theodore
1947   *We Found Them Waiting.* Columbus, Ohio: Wartburg Press.

Fritz, George
1912   *Ad Maiorem Dei Gloriam! Die Vorgeschichte des Aufstandes 1910–11 in Ponape.* Leipzig: Dieterichsche Verlag.

Fullerton, Leslie Douglas
1969   "From Christendom to Pluralism in the South Seas. Church–State Relations in the Twentieth Century." Ph.D. dissertation. Drew University.

Garrett, John
1977   "Thunder and Rainbows." *Outpost, Fiji Forum* 5, no. 4: 46–74.

Garrett, John, and Mavor, John
1973   *Worship the Pacific Way.* Suva: Lotu Pasifika.

Gifford, Edward Winslow
    n.d.   *Tongan Society.* Honolulu: Bernice P. Bishop Museum Bul-
                letin 61.
Gilbert Islands Protestant Church
    1966   *Second Draft of the Constitution of the Church Prepared
                by the Executive Committee of the G.I.P.C.* n.p.
Gill, R. M.
    1973   "Localization Review. Sociology of Localization of the
                Churches in Papua New Guinea." *Catalyst* 3, no. 1:37–60.
Gill, Stephen R. M.
    1954   *Letters from the Papuan Bush, 1942–1946.* Liverpool:
                Eaton Press.
Gilson, R. P.
    1970   *Samoa 1830 to 1900. The Politics of a Multi-cultural Com-
                munity.* Melbourne: Oxford University Press.
Godden, Ruth
    1967   *Lolowai. The Story of Charles Godden and the Western Pa-
                cific.* Sydney: Wentworth Press.
Goodall, Norman
    1940   *Report . . . after a Secretarial Visit to the Pacific.* London:
                London Missionary Society.

    1954   *A History of the London Missionary Society 1895–1945.*
                London: Oxford University Press.

    1964   *Christian Missions and Social Ferment.* London: Epworth
                Press.
Goodsell, Fred Field
    1959   *"You Shall Be My Witnesses."* Boston: American Board of
                Commissioners for Foreign Missions.
Goward, W.
    1900–1902 "Report of Work in the Tokelau, Ellice and Gilbert Groups
                LMS. September 1900 to September 1902." Typewritten. In
                J. E. Newell Papers, box 5, Council for World Mission Ar-
                chives, London.
Goyau, Georges
    1938   *Le Christ chez les Papous.* Paris: Beauchesne et ses fils.
Gribble, C.F.
    1950   "A New Voice for the South Pacific." *International Review
                of Missions* 39:431–38.
Grimble, Arthur
    1952   *A Pattern of Islands.* London: John Murray.
Grimshaw, B.
    1915   *Adventures in Papua with the Catholic Mission.* Mel-
                bourne: Australian Catholic Truth Society.

Grosart, Ian
  1970a   "Disengagement in New Guinea: The Establishment of an
           Indigenous Church." *Public Administration* 29:368–79.

  1970b   "Disengagement in New Guinea: The Mission Paradigm."
           In *Fourth Waigani Seminar: The Politics of Melanesia.*
           Canberra: Australian National University Press.
Groves, William C.
  1935–36 "Tabar Today." *Oceania* 5:224–40,346–360; 6:147–57.

  1936   *Native Education and Culture Contact in New Guinea.* Mel-
           bourne: Melbourne University Press.
Guiart, Jean
  1958   *Espiritu Santo (Nouvelles-Hébrides).* Paris: Librairie Plon.

  1959   *Destin d'une Église et d'un Peuple. Nouvelle-Calédonie
           1909–1959. Étude monographique d'une oeuvre mis-
           sionaire protestante.* Paris: Mouvement du Christianisme
           Social.

  1962   "The Millenarian Aspect of Conversion to Christianity in
           the South Pacific." In *Millennial Dreams in Action. Essays
           in Comparative Study,* edited by Sylvia Thrupp; pp. 122–38.
           The Hague: Mouton and Co.

  1970   "Les évènements de 1917 en Nouvelle-Calédonie." *Journal
           de la Société des Océanistes* 26:265–80.
Guise, John
  1977   "The Role of the Churches in Independent Papua New
           Guinea." *Catalyst* 7, no. 3:210–14.
Gunn, William, and Mrs. Gunn
  1924   *Heralds of the Dawn. Early Converts in the New Hebrides.*
           London: Hodder and Stoughton.
Gunson, W. Niel
  1969   "The Theology of Imperialism and the Missionary History
           of the Pacific." *Journal of Religious History* 5:255–65.

  1973   "A Missionary Comity Agreement of 1880." *Journal of Pa-
           cific History* 8:191–95.
Hackett, Harold
  1947   "South Pacific." *Missionary Herald* 143, no. 8:48–51.
Hagesi, Robert
  1972   "Towards Localization of Anglican Worship in the Solo-
           mon Islands." B.D. thesis, Pacific Theological College,
           Suva.

Hand, David
  1966   "Education and the Missions." *New Guinea and Australia,
              the Pacific and S.E. Asia*, no. 6: 46-49.
Hannemann, E. F.
  1935   "Papuan Dances and Dancing." Mimeographed. Min-
              neapolis: American Lutheran Church.

  1942   "Village Life and Social Change in Madang Society."
              Mimeographed. Minneapolis: American Lutheran Church
Hare, Eric B.
  1969   *Fulton's Footsteps in Fiji*. Washington: Review and Herald
              Pub. Association.
Harris, Leonard
  n.d.   *Our Days Are in His Hands. A Short History of the Un-
              evangelized Fields Mission*. n.p.
Harris, W. T., and Parrinder, E. G.
  1960   The Christian Approach to the Animist. London: Edin-
              burgh House.
Harrison, Brian W.
  1975   "Christ and Culture in Northeast New Guinea. Social and
              Educational Policies and Attitudes of Lutheran Mission-
              aries in New Guinea: 1886-1942." M.A. thesis, University
              of Papua New Guinea.
Harwood, Frances
  1978   "Intercultural Communication in the Western Solomons:
              The Methodist Mission and the Emergence of the Christian
              Fellowship Church." In *Mission, Church, and Sect in
              Oceania*, edited by J. Boutilier, D. Hughes, and S. Tiffany;
              pp. 231-50. Ann Arbor: University of Michigan Press.
Hau'ofa, Isikeli
  1944   "Buliga, a Native of Seagaia, Misima Island," and "What
              Happend after the Evacuation of All Europeans on Misima
              Island." Manuscript notebook in Methodist Overseas Mis-
              sions Archives, Sydney.
Havea, Sione 'Amanaki
  1977   "The Pacificness of Theology." *Mission Review,* December
              1977:3-4.
Heighway Family
  1932   *Not as Men Build. The Story of William Aitken Heighway
              of Fiji*. Sydney: Methodist Women's Auxiliary of Foreign
              Missions.
Heine, Carl
  1974   *Micronesia at the Crossroads. A Reappraisal of the Mi-
              cronesian Political Dilemma*. Canberra: Australian Na-
              tional University Press.

Heinsius, Peter
 1976   "Die Zwanzig Jahre Junge Kirche." *Das Wort in der Welt*, no. 2:13.
Hellberg, J.
 1972   "The Need to Adjust Church Related Health Services to Papua New Guinea to the Needs of the Situation." Self-Study of the Catholic Church in Papua New Guinea, *Seminar Handbook*. Goroka: Self-Study Secretariate.
Hemphill, Robert F.
 1971   "Sunday on Saipan." *The Chaplain* 28, no. 4:13–20.
Henao, Ravu, and Perry, Raymond
 1964   "Let's Discuss These Things." Typescript. Port Moresby: Papua Ekalesia.
Henslowe, Dorothea
 1949   *Papuan Post, Being Letters from New Guinea*. Hobart, Tasmania: Mercury Press.

 1958   *Papua Calls*. Hobart, Tasmania: Mercury Press.
Hernandez, Faustino
 1955   "Missions in the Carolines and Marshall Islands." Mimeographed. Maldonado, Madrid.
Herrera, Luis
 1921–22 Letters in *Cartas de la Provincia de Leon,* vols. 3–4. Camillas, Spain: Jesuit Missions.
Hezel, Francis X.
 1970   "Catholic Missions in the Caroline and Marshall Islands. A Survey of Historical Materials." *Journal of Pacific History* 5:213–27.

 1975   "Micronesian Political Education. Micronesia's Education for Self-Government: Frolicking in the Backyard?" *Catalyst* 5, no. 4:23–35.

 1978   "Indigenization as a Missionary Goal in the Caroline and Marshall Islands." In *Mission, Church, and Sect in Oceania*, edited by J. Boutilier, D. Hughes, and S. Tiffany; pp. 251–74. Ann Arbor: University of Michigan Press.
Hillas, Julian
 1938   "The Value of Mission Work in Polynesia." *Pacific Islands Monthly*, Jan. 24, 1938:50–52.
Hilliard, David
 1966   "Protestant Missions in the Solomon Islands 1849–1942." Ph.D. thesis, Australian National University.

 1969   "The South Sea Evangelical Mission in the Solomon

Islands: The Foundation Years." *Journal of Pacific History* 4:41–64.

1973   "The Battle for Rennell Island: A Study in Missionary Politics." In *W. P. Morrell: a Tribute,* edited by G. A. Wood and P. S. O'Connor. Dunedin: University of Otago Press.

1974   "Colonialism and Christianity: The Melanesian Mission in the Solomon Islands." *Journal of Pacific History* 9:93–116.

1978   *God's Gentlemen: A History of the Melanesian Mission, 1849–1942.* St. Lucia: University of Queensland Press.

Historical Sketches. New Guinea.
1915   London: Society for the Propagation of the Gospel.

Hogbin, Herbert Ian
1939   *Experiments in Civilization: the Effects of European Culture on a Native Community of the Solomon Islands.* London: G. Routledge.

1947   "Native Christianity in a New Guinea Village." *Oceania* 18:1–35.

1951   *Transformation Scene. The Changing Culture of a New Guinea Village.* London: Routledge and Kegan Paul.

Höhne, Johannes
1962   "Die gegenwärtigen Schulprobleme in Papua-Neuguinea." *Neue Zeitschrift für Missionswissenschaft* 18:208–16.

Holmes, Lowell D.
1958   *Ta'u: Stability and Change in a Samoan Village.* Wellington: Polynesian Society.

Hölter, G.
1946   "Die Kleiderfrage in den beiden Vikariaten Ost- und Zentral-Neuguinea." *Neue Zeitschrift für Missionswissenschaft* 2:43–55.

Hopkins, Arthur I.
n.d.   "Autobiography." Manuscript. Melanesian Mission Archives, Auckland.

Horne, Shirley
1962   *Out of the Dark.* London: Oliphant, Ltd.

1968   *Them Also. First Mission Contact with the Primitive Biamis.* Port Moresby: Unevangelized Fields Mission.

Hough, A., and Parker, G.
1928   *Report of Rev. A. Hough and Rev. G. Parker Deputation to*

Samoa August–December 1928. London: London Missionary Society.

Hueter, Richard
1974   "The Battle for the Abundant Life." *Point* 1:123–40.

Hughes, Brian, and Tomkins, Dorothea
1969   *The Road from Gona.* Sydney: Angus and Robertson.

Huonder, Anton
1909   *Der Einheimische Klerus in den Heindenländern.* Freiburg im Breisgau: Herdersche Verlagshandlung.

Hurst, H. Leonard
1937   *Report by Rev. H. Leonard Hurst after Secretarial Visit to Papua, September 1936–January 1937.* Sydney: Australia and New Zealand Committee of London Missionary Society.

Hüskes, Josef (ed.)
1932   *Pioniere der Südsee. Werden und Wachsen der Herz-Jesu Mission von Rabaul zum Goldenen Jubiläum 1882–1932.* Hiltrup-Salzburg: Herz-Jesu Mission.

Inselmann, Rudolph
1944   "Letub, the Cult of the Secrets of Wealth." Thesis, Hartford Seminary Kennedy School of Missions, Hartford, Conn.

1948   "Changing Missionary Methods in Lutmis New Guinea." B.D. thesis, Wartburg Seminary, Dubuque, Iowa.

International Missionary Council
1961   *Beyond the Reef. Records of the Conference of Churches and Missions in the Pacific . . . 22 April–4 May, 1961.* London: International Missionary Council.

Italiaander, Rolf (ed.)
1974   *Heiszes Land Niugini.* Erlangen: Verlag der Ev.-Luth. Mission.

Jacobsen, Werner
1974   "Papua-Neuguinea: Erste Schritte auf dem Melanesischen Weg." *Das Wort in der Welt*, no. 3:10–11.

Jaeschke, Ernst
1974   "Kirchenschule und staatliche Schule." In *Heiszes Land Niugini,* edited by Rolf Italiaander; pp. 250–76. Erlangen: Verlag der Ev.-Luth. Mission.

1978   "Bedeutung und Einfluss des 'Big Man' Systems auf Gesellschaft und Kirchwerdung." In *Theologische Beiträge aus Papua Neuguinea,* edited by Horst Bürkle; pp. 154–221. Erlangen: Verlag der Ev.-Luth. Mission.

Janssen, Hermann
1974   "The Story Cult of Kaliai. A Cargo Cult in West New Bri-
            tain." *Point* 1:4–28.

1975   "From Mission to Church in Papua New Guinea." *Austra-
            lian Catholic Record* 52, no. 3:229–38.
Japan
1923,1925,1928,1933,1937
            *Annual Report to the League of Nations on the Administra-
            tion of the South Sea Islands under Japanese Mandate.*
            Tokyo: Nanyocho.
Jepson, C.
1945   "A Century of Progress toward a Catholic Samoa." Manu-
            script. Marist Archives, Rome.
Jimmy, Shem
1972   "The Influence of Christianity among the People of
            Papua." B.D. thesis, Pacific Theological College.
Jones, W.
1972   "The National Education System." Self Study of the Catho-
            lic Church in Papua New Guinea, *Seminar Handbook.*
            Goroka: Self-Study Secretariat.
Kahn, E. G.
1965   *A Reporter in Micronesia.* New York: W. W. Norton.
Käiser, Lothar
1972   *Und Bleibe am äussersten Meer. Mikronesisches Tagebuch.*
            Bad Liebenzell: Verlag der Liebenzeller Mission.
Keesing, Felix M.
1934   *Modern Samoa. Its Government and Changing Life.* Lon-
            don: George Allen and Unwin.

1945   *The South Seas in the Modern World.* Rev. ed. New York:
            John Day.
Keesing, Felix M. and Marie M.
1956   *Elite Communication in Samoa. A Study of Leadership.*
            Stanford: Stanford University Press.
Keesing, R.
1967   "Christians and Pagans In Kwaio, Malaita." *Journal of the
            Polynesian Society* 76:82–100.
Kennally, Vincent I.
1946   "Missions in the Pacific." *Woodstock Letters* 75:116–20.
Kent, Patricia
1966   "The Church in the Pacific." *Manna* 6:27–28.
Keysser, Christian
1921   *Was Die Braunen dawider zu Sagen Wussten.* Neuendettel-
            sau: Verlag des Missionhauses.

1929   *Anutu im Papualande.* 2nd ed. Kassel: Bärnreiter Verlag.

1934   *Altes Testament und heutige Zeit.* Neuendettelsau: Frei-
            mund Verlag.

1950   *Eine Papuagemeinde.* 2nd ed. rev. and enlarged. Neuendet-
            telsau: Freimund Verlag.

King, Joseph
1905   *Report by the Rev. Joseph King, organizing agent for Aus-
            tralia, of his visit . . . to the stations of the Society in New
            Guinea and Torres Straits, March–April, 1905.* London:
            London Missionary Society.

Knoebel, Joseph
1974a   "In Search of Tomorrow's New World. A History of Ad-
            justment Movements in Melanesia." *Point* 1:50–73.

1974b   "Der Aufbruch der ökumenischen Bewegung." In *Heiszes
            Land Niugini,* edited by Rolf Italiaander; pp. 168–82.
            Erlangen: Verlag der Ev.-Luth. Mission.

Kohler, Jean Marie
1980   *Le Christianisme en Nouvelle Calédonie et aux Iles Loy-
            auté.* Noumea: Office de la Recherche Scientifique et Tech-
            nique Outre-Mer.

Korn, Shulamit R. Dektor
1978   "After the Missionaries Came: Denominational Diversity
            in the Tonga Islands." In *Mission, Church, and Sect in
            Oceania,* edited by James A. Boutilier, D. Hughes, and S.
            Tiffany; pp. 395–422. Ann Arbor: University of Michigan
            Press.

Koschade, Alfred
1967   *New Branches on the Vine—From Mission Field to Church
            in New Guinea.* Minneapolis: Augsburg Publishing House.

Koskinen, Aarne
1953   *Missionary Influences as a Political Factor in the Pacific
            Islands.* Helsinki: Academia Scientiarum Fennica.

1957   "On the South Sea Islander View of Christianity." *Studia
            Missiologica Fennica* 1:7–16.

Kozaki, Hiromichi
1933   *Reminiscences of Seventy Years: the Autobiography of a
            Japanese Pastor.* Translated by Nariaki Kozaki. Tokyo:
            Christian Literature Society of Japan.

Kraft, Hermann
1964   *Morgenrot auf Manus. Vom Anfang unserer Missionsarbeit
            auf Manus vor 50 Jahren.* Bad Liebenzell: Liebenzeller Mis-
            sion.

Kuder, John
  1943   "New Guinea—End of a Mission or an Interlude." Manu-
            script. In American Lutheran Church archives, Minneapo-
            lis.

  1952   "The Lutheran Mission in New Guinea Today." *Interna-
            tional Review of Missions* 41:310-23.

  1964   "The Cargo Cult and Its Relation to the Task of the
            Church." Mimeographed. Minneapolis: American Luth-
            eran Church.

  1974   "From Mission to Church: the Story of ELCONG" *Luth-
            eran World* 21: 152-59.
Lambert, Sylvester M.
  1941   *A Yankee Doctor in Paradise.* Boston: Little, Brown and
            Company.
Landes, Albert
  1939   "Le soi-distant 'nationalisme missionaire' des Maristes en
            Océanie." *Missions Catholiques* 71: 340-46, 374-80.
Langdon, Robert
  1968   *Tahiti: Island of Love.* 3rd ed. Sydney: Pacific Publication.
Lanternari, Vittorio
  1963   *The Religions of the Oppressed. A Study of Modern Mes-
            sianic Cults.* New York: Alfred A. Knopf.
Laracy, Hugh M.
  1969   "Catholic Missions in the Solomon Islands 1845-1966."
            Ph.D. thesis, Australian National University.

  1971   "Marching Rule and the Missions." *Journal of Pacific His-
            tory* 6:96-114.

  1976   *Marists and Melanesians: A History of Catholic Missions in
            the Solomon Islands.* Canberra: Australian National Uni-
            versity Press.
Larkin, Fanaafi
  1966   "Education." *Pacific Journal of Theology,* June–
            September 1966:38-44.
Larranaga, Maria Dolores
  1961   "Twenty-five Years in Truk in the Central Carolines."
            Typescript translation of article in *Angeles de las Misiones,*
            no. 227:6-15. In Jesuit Archives, Fordham University.
Latukefu, Sione
  1969   "The Methodist Mission and Modernization in the Solo-
            mon Islands." In *The History of Melanesia: Papers de-*

livered at the Second Waigani Seminar. . . 1968. Canberra: Australian National University.

Laufer, Carl

1948   "Zur Katechistenfrage im Vikariat Rabaul." *Neue Zeitschrift für Missionswissenschaft* 4:121–28.

1949   "Die Stellung der Mission zum Geheimbundwesen auf New Britain." *Neue Zeitschrift für Missionswissenschaft* 5: 217–27.

1950   "Too much Christo-Zu viel Christ." *Die Katholischen Missionen* 69:106–9.

1957   "Christliche Gemeindefeiern in Neubritannien." *Neue Zeitschrift für Missionswissenschaft* 13:148–49.

1961   "Einheimisch bauen wir die Kirche." *Die Katholischen Missionen* 80:89–92.

1962   "Christliche Südseegemeinde in Aktion." *Priester und Mission* 1962:109–22.

1963   "Die Frau und Mutter im Melanesichen Raum." *Zeitschrift für Missionswissenschaft* 47:47–59, 111–18.

Laurent, Charles

1900   *Les Missionaires de la Nouvelle Calédonie au sujet de l'enquête administrative de Wagap. Réponse et défense de la mission.* Paris: Firmin-Didot.

Lawrence, Peter

1955   "Cargo Cult and Religious Beliefs among the Garia." *International Archives of Ethnography* 47:1–20.

1956   "Lutheran Mission Influences on Madang Societies." *Oceania* 27:73–89.

1964   *Road Belong Cargo. A Study of the Cargo Movement in the Southern Madang District of New Guinea.* Manchester University Press.

Lawrence, P., and Meggitt, M. J. (ed.)

1965   *Gods, Ghosts and Men in Melanesia: Some Religions of Australian New Guinea and the New Hebrides.* Melbourne: Oxford University Press.

Leadley, Alan

1975   "Emancipating Relevant Education. Adult Education." *Catalyst* 5, no. 1:4–15.

Lebeau, Henri
1911   "Le Christianisme et la musique populaire." In *Otaheiti, au pays de l'éternel été;* pp. 227–59. Paris: Librairie Armand Colin.
Leenhardt, Maurice
1922   *La Grande Terre. Mission de Nouvelle-Calédonie.* 2nd ed. Paris: Société des Missions Evangéliques.

1947   *Do Kamo. La personalité et le mythe dans le monde Mélanésien.* Paris: Gallimard.
Leenhardt, R. H.
1969   Review of *Vos Racines* by Philippe Rey Lescure. *Journal de la Société des Océanistes* 25:394–95.
Leeuwen, Arend Th.
1964   *Christianity in World History. The Meeting of the Faiths of East and West.* London: Edinburgh House Press.
Lehner, Stephen
1921   "Ein Kleiner Beitrag zum Verständnis des Evangeliums seitens der Melanesier." *Allgemeine Missions-zeitschrift* 48:214.

1922   "Die Anknüpfungen für die Predigt im Papuanischen Heidentum." *Allgemeine Missions-zeitschrift* 49:363–75.
Lenwood, Frank
1922   "The Missionary Significance of the Last Ten Years in the South Pacific. II. Seen from Great Britain." *International Review of Missions* 11:493–501.

1925   *Modern Problems in the South Seas.* London: London Missionary Society.
Lesourd, Paul
1931   *L'évangélisation des Colonies Françaises. Bulletin de l'Association Charles de Foucauld.* 7th year (1931) March–December Special issue. Paris: Association Charles de Foucauld.
Levy, Robert I.
1969   "Personal Forms and Meanings in Tahitian Protestantism." *Journal de la Société des Océanistes* 25:125–36.
Lewis, F. G.
1935   "Methodist Overseas Mission. New Guinea District. The First Sixty Years." Mimeographed. Rabaul: Methodist Mission.
Leymang, Gerard
1969   "Message Chrétien et mentalité néo-hébridaise." *Journal de la Société des Océanistes* 25:239–55.

Ligeremaluoga, Osea
1932   *An Account of the Life of Ligeremaluoga (Osea), An Auto-biography.* Translated by Ella Collins. Melbourne: F. W. Cheshire.
Linckens, Herbert
1911   *Auf den Marschall Inseln (Deutsche Südsee). Land und Leute Katholische Missionstätigkeit.* Hiltrup: Hertz-Jesu Missionshaus.
Lini, Walter
1974   *"Should the Church Play Politics?" Pacific Perspective* 3, no. 2:12–13.
Liu, John
1976   "Mission Imperatives for Churches of Christ in the New Hebrides." B. D. Project, Pacific Theological College.
Loeliger, Carl
1974   "The Church and National Life in Papua New Guinea—a Bibliographical Essay." *Lutheran World* 21:211–17.

1975   "State of the Churches." *Catalyst* 5, no. 1:31–39.
London Missionary Society
        [Annual] Report. London: 1795–1966.

1920   *A Day of Good Tidings. Being the Annual Report of the Gilbert Islands and Nauru Mission, South Seas, for the Year 1920, the Jubilee of the LMS Work in the Southern Gilberts. From Darkness to Light 1870–1920.* Roñoroño: London Mission Press.

1931   *Progress, Being the Decennial Report 1920–30 of the Gilbert Islands and Nauru Mission, Central Pacific.* Beru: Roñoroño Press.

1941   *In Times of Trial. Being the Decennial Report 1931–40 of the Gilbert Islands and Nauru Mission, Central Pacific.* Roñoroño: London Mission Press.
Lopinot, Callistus
1964   *Die Karolinenmission der spanischen und deutschen Kapuziner, 1886–1919. Zusammen gestellt nach den Jahresberichten.* Koblenz-Ehrenbreitstein: Provinzialat der Kapuziner.
Lovett, Richard
1899   *The History of the London Missionary Society 1795–1895.* 2 vols. London: Henry Frowde.
Loy, Allan W.
1954   "The Church among Indians in Fiji." *International Review of Missions* 43:82–87.

1970   "Impressions of the Second Assembly of the United Church of Papua New Guinea and the Solomon Islands." Mimeographed.

Lubach, Aurèle
1929   *L'alcoolisme et l'oeuvre des missions. Rapport présenté au VII Congrès de la Ligue Internationale Catholique contre l'alcoolisme . . . août 1928.* Berlin: Hoheneck Verlag.

Luke, Harry Charles Joseph
1962   *Islands of the South Pacific.* London: Harrap.

Lundsgaarde, Henry P.
1966   *Cultural Adaptation in the Southern Gilberts.* Eugene, Ore.: Department of Anthropology, University of Oregon.

1968   "Social Change in the Southern Gilbert Islands: 1938–1964." Mimeographed. University of Oregon Department of Anthropology.

Luxton, C. T. J.
1955   *Isles of Solomon. A Tale of Missionary Adventure.* Auckland: Methodist Foreign Missionary Society of New Zealand.

McArthur, L.A.
1933   "The Educational Problems of the Methodist Mission in New Britain with Special Reference to the Training of Teachers." Mimeographed. Methodist Archives, Sydney.

McAuley, James
n.d.   "Economic Development among the Mekeo." *South Pacific Bulletin* 6, no. 1:30.

McCall, Theodore B.
1957   *Challenge in New Guinea.* Sydney: Australian Board of Missions.

McCarthy, V.
1973   "The Catholic Church and the Development of the Peoples of the South Pacific." *Outpost, A Fiji Forum* 1, no. 2:31–35.

McHugh, Winifred
1965   "Memoir of Rev. A. J. Small." Mimeographed. Suva: Methodist Church.

Mafi, Tevita Feke
1978   "Sunday School in the Church of Tonga." B. D. thesis, Pacific Theological College, Suva.

Mager J. F.
1937   "Education and Social Change in a New Guinea Society." Mimeographed. St. Paul, Minn.: American Lutheran Church.

Maher, Robert Francis
1961   *New Men of Papua: A Study in Culture Change.* Madison: University of Wisconsin Press.

Malia, S.
    1910   *Chez les Méridionaux du Pacifique*. Lyon and Paris: Em-
                manuel Vitte.
Malinowski, Bronislaw
    1922   *Argonauts of the Western Pacific*. London: G. Routledge
                and Sons.

    1935   *Coral Gardens and Their Magic: A Study of Methods of
                Tilling the Soil and of Agricultural Rites in the Trobriand
                Islands*. London: G. Allen and Unwin.
Mann, C.W.
    1933   "Interim Report of the Special Educational Commission on
                Education in Fiji." Mimeographed. Suva: Government of
                Fiji.
Margull, Hans Jochen
    1962   *Aufbruch zur Zukunft; chiliastische Bewegungen in Afrika
                und Südostasien*. Gütersloh: Gütersloher Verlags-
                haus.
Martin, George Currie
    1908   *The New Guinea Mission*. London: London Missionary So-
                ciety.
Martin, Pierre
    1960   "Relatio de Statu Vicariatus Apostolici Novae Caledoniae.
                A.D. 1960". Microfilm in Marist Secretariat, Rome.

    1975   "New Caledonia." *Pacific Perspective* 4: 37–44.
Maude, H. E.
    1967   "The Swords of Gabriel: A Study in Participant History."
                Journal of Pacific History 2:113–36.
Mauer, Daniel
    1961   "Tahiti à vendre" and "Le tourisme à Tahiti." *Journal des
                Missions Evangéliques* 136:76–77, 262–65.
Mavor, John
    1973   *Development = Growth + Change*. Suva: Lotu Pasifika Pro
                ductions.
Maxwell, Arthur S.
    1966   *Under the Southern Cross: the Seventh-Day Adventist
                Story in Australia, New Zealand and the Islands of the
                South Pacific*. Nashville: Southern Publishing Co.
Mead, Margaret
    1956   *New Lives for Old. Cultural Transformation. Manus 1928–
                1953*. New York: William Morrow and Company.
Melanesian Culture and Christian Faith
    1978   Vila: Pacific Churches Research Centre.
Metais, Pierre
    1953   "Quelques Aspects de l'Evolution culturelle Neo-

Calédonienne." *Journal de la Société des Océanistes* 9:171–201.

Metcalf, J. R.
n.d.   "How the Lauruans Met the Japanese." MS. In possession of J. R. Metcalf.

Methodist Church of Australasia
1907   *The Fiji Mission. Report of Commission Appointed by the Board of Missions to Visit Fiji and Report on Matters Connected Therewith. January 1907.* Sydney.

1912   New Britain District "Recommendations of the New Britain Synod *re* the Transfer of the New Britain Mission to the German Methodist Church." In George Brown papers, Mitchell Library, Sydney.

1917   *Report and Recommendations of the Commission appointed by the Mission Board to Visit the Fiji District, 1917. Also the Resolution of the Mission Board.* Sydney: Epworth Printing and Publishing House.

1923a   Methodist Missionary Society. *Commission* re *Native Church 1922. Copy of Memorandum.* Sydney: Printed for Private Circulation. In Methodist Archives, Sydney.

1923b   Methodist Missionary Society. *Commission* re *Native Church: Information Collected for the Consideration of the Commission.* Melbourne: Spectator Publishing Co.

"Michael"
1957   *75 Glorious Years: 1882–1957. This is the story of 75 years since the First Catholic Missionaries landed in New Britain.* Vunapope: Catholic Mission.

Michelsen, Oscar
1934?   *Misi.* London and Edinburgh: Marshall, Morgan & Scott.

Michener, James A.
1950   *Return to Paradise.* New York: Random House.

Micronesian Seminar
1974   "Education for What? Conference on Micronesian Education Held in Kolonia, Ponape. Sponsored by Micronesian Seminar." Mimeographed. Ponape: Catholic Mission.

1975   "Developing Micronesia's People. Conference on Human Development Held in Kolonia, Ponape, March 4–8, 1975." Mimeographed. Ponape: Catholic Mission.

1977   "Micronesia's Youth Today. A Report on the Conference on

Youth Held in Kolonia, Ponape. April 20–24, 1977." Mimeographed. Ponape: Catholic Mission.

Miller, J. Graham
    1978   *Live. A History of Church Planting in the New Hebrides to 1880*. Book One. Sydney: Christian Education Committee, General Assembly of Australia.

Missionsleiden und Missionsfreuden. Hiltrup-Shihtsien-Rabaul 1941–45.
    1947   Hamm, Westfalen: Herz-Jesu Kloster.

Misso, Francis
    1977   "An Ecclesial Theology for Melanesia." *Kibung* 2, no. 2:72–80.

    1978   "Signs, Symbols and a Child's Religious Experience." *Kibung* 3, no. 1:9–22.

Moira, Sister
    1972   "The Proposed National Health Plan: What Are the Advantages and Disadvantages for the Catholic Missions?" Self Study of the Catholic Church in Papua New Guinea, *Seminar Handbook*. Goroka: Self-Study Secretariat.

Momis, John
    1974   "Unity in Diversity." *Pacific Perspective* 3, no. 1:1–3.

    1975   "Values for Involvement. Theology and Politics." *Catalyst* 5, no. 3: 3–18.

Monberg, T.
    1967   "An Island Changes Its Religion: Some Social Implications of the Conversion to Christianity on Bellona Island." In *Polynesian Culture History: Essays in Honor of Kenneth P. Emory*, edited by G. A. Highland et al. Honolulu: Bishop Museum Press.

    1962   "Crisis and Mass Conversion on Rennell Island in 1938." *Journal of the Polynesian Society* 71:145–50.

Montauban, Paul
    1948   "En marche vers une famille chrétienne (à Buka, îles Salomons)." *Missions des Iles* 2:10–19.

Moritzen, Niels-Peter
    1974   "Tok bilip bilong yumi, Eine Darlegung des Glaubens in Neuguinea." *Evangelische Missions-zeitschrift* 31:80–92.

Morpeth
    1948   *See* South Pacific Missionary Conference.

Morrell, William P.
    1960   *Britain in the Pacific Islands*. Oxford: Oxford University Press.

1973 *The Anglican Church in New Zealand: A History.* Dunedin: Anglican Church of the Province of New Zealand.

Mouly, Delmas

1939 *De la guillotine aux îles du Pacifique. Le père Marie-Joseph Condrin fondateur de la Congrégation des Sacrés-Coeurs (Picpus) 1768–1837.* Paris: Tolra.

Mühlmann, W. E.

1968 "Les Mouvements Polynésiens." In *Messianismes Révolutionnaires du Tiers Monde,* edited by W. E. Mühlmann. n.p.: Editions Gallimard.

Müller, Kilian

1912 *Ponape "im Sonnenlicht der Offentlichkeit." Eine Erwiderung.* Cologne: Y. P. Bachem.

Murphy, Patrick

1970 "From Mission in New Guinea to Church of New Guinea." In *Fourth Waigani Seminar: The Politics of Melanesia.* Canberra: Australian National University Press.

1977 *A Report about Captivity, Liberation and Total Human Development in the Trust Territory of the Pacific Islands.* Pacific Conference of Churches, Church and Society Program.

Murray, John Stanley

1969 *A Century of Growth: Presbyterian Overseas Mission Work 1869–1969.* Christchurch, New Zealand: Presbyterian Bookroom.

Nabetari, Baiteke

1970 "Indigenization of Worship in the Gilbert Islands." B. D. thesis, Pacific Theological College, Suva.

National Council of the Churches of Christ in the U.S.A.

1979 Pacific Joint Action Group. Preparatory Papers for meeting, June 1979. Mimeographed. New York: NCCC Committee for East Asia and the Pacific.

Neill, J. S.

1955 *Ten years in Tonga.* London: Hutchison.

Neill, S.; Anderson, G.; and Goodwin, J. (eds.)

1971 *Concise Dictionary of the Christian World Mission.* Nashville: Abingdon.

Nerhon, Acoma

1969 "Histoire de ma vie." *Le Monde non-Chrétien* 89–90: 38–78.

Nevin, David

1977 *The American Touch in Micronesia.* New York: W. W. Norton & Co.

New Hebrides Presbyterian Mission Synod

1839–1947 *Minutes.*

New Zealand Missionary Conference, 1926
    1926   [Report of the] *New Zealand Missionary Conference Held at Dunedin, April 27–29, 1926*. Dunedin: New Zealand Missionary Conference Committee.

Nilles, John
    1977   "Simbu Ancestors and Christian Worship." *Catalyst* 7, no. 3:163–90.

Nix, B. J.
    1967   "Mission History of the French Polynesian Mission of the Church of Latter-day Saints." Typewritten. Latter-day Saints Archives, Papeete.

Nordhoff, Charles, and Hall, James N.
    1934   *Pitcairn Island*. Boston: Little, Brown and Co.

Nos Champs de Mission
    1922   Paris: Société des Missions Evangéliques.

Nottage, Basil R. C.
    1940   *New Hebrides Calling*. Auckland: Presbyterian Church of New Zealand.

Nouvelle Calédonie et Dépendence. Secteur Education.
    1962   *L'activité du Service de l'Enseignement en 1962*. Noumea.

Oliver, Douglas L.
    1955   *A Solomon Island Society. Kinship and Leadership among the Siuai of Bougainville*. Cambridge: Harvard University Press.

Oliver, Roland
    1952   *The Missionary Factor in East Africa*. London: Longmans, Green and Co.

Oosterwal, Gottfried
    1967   "Cargo Cults as a Missionary Challenge." *International Review of Missions* 56:469–77.

O'Reilly, Patrick
    1931   "La Léproserie de Makogai." *Missions Catholiques* 63: 464–68.

    1948   "Voteront-ils? Le statut des indigènes de Nouvelle Calédonie." *Missions des Iles* 2: 132–34.

    1962   *Tahitiens; répertoire bio-bibliographique de la Polynésie française*. Paris: Musée de l'homme.

    1963   "Chronologie de Wallis et Futuna." *Journal de la Société des Océanistes* 19:12–45.

O'Reilly, Patrick, and Sédès, Jean-Marie
    1949   *Jaunes, Noirs et Blancs, Trois Années de Guerre aux Iles Salomon*. Paris: Editions du Monde Nouveau.

Pacific Conference of Churches
    1970   Continuation Committee. "Minutes of the Continuation
              Committee, Vila, New Hebrides, April 6–10, 1970." Mime-
              ographed. Suva.

    1972   *The Fourth World Meets, PCC Assembly, Davuilevu, Fiji,
              1971.* Suva: Pacific Conference of Churches.

    1976   *Report of the Third Assembly.* Suva: Lotu Pasifika Produc-
              tions.
Pacifique '77. Ecumenical Planning for Development.
    1977   *An International Meeting August 22–September 2, 1977.*
              Suva: Pacific Conference of Churches, Church and Society
              Program.
Palma, Rafael
    1946   "Flores de Matiro. En la Mision de Carolinas." *España Mis-
              ionera* 3: 281–92.
Palmer, Bruce Stewart
    1979   "Options for the Development of Education in the Solo-
              mon Islands. A Critical Analysis." Ph.D. thesis, University
              of New England, Armidale, New South Wales.
Panoff, Michel
    1963   "Situation présente de la société futuniènne." *Journal de la
              Société de Océanistes* 19: 149–56.
Parratt, J. K.
    1970   "Religious Change in Port Moresby." *Oceania* 41:106–13.

    1975   "Religion and the Migrant to Port Moresby." *Missiology*
              3:177–89.
Parsonson, G. S.
    1954   "Report Made to the Overseas Missions Committee of the
              Presbyterian Church of New Zealand," June 17, 1954. Ar-
              chives of Overseas Missions Committee of the Presbyterian
              Church of New Zealand.

    1956   "La mission Presbytérienne des Nouvelles-Hébrides. Son
              histoire et son rôle politique et social." *Journal de la Société
              des Océanistes* 12:107–37.
Paton, Frank H. L.
    1913   *The Kingdom in the Pacific.* London: London Missionary
              Society.
Paton, W. F.
    1945   *Fred Paton of Malekula. The Story of Rev. F. J. Paton, of
              Malekula, New Hebrides.* Melbourne: Board of Missions of
              Presbyterian Church of Australia.

Patrick, John
  1966   *His Praise in the Islands.* Christchurch: Presbyterian Book-
            room.
Pearce, George H.
  1963   "Quinquennial Report of the Vicariate Apostolic of Samoa
            and Tokelau to the Sacred Congregation for the Propaga-
            tion of the Faith." Typewritten. Catholic Archives, Apia.
Pedley, Hilton
  1925   "Japan's Missions in the South Seas." *Missionary Review of
            the World* 48:861–64.
Pierson, Delavan L.
  1906   *The Pacific Islanders, from Savages to Saints: Chapters in
            the Life Stories of Famous Missionaries and Native Con-
            verts.* New York and London: Funk and Wagnalls.
Pilhofer, Georg
  1961–63   *Die Geschichte der Neuendettelsauer Mission in Neuguinea.*
            3 vols. Neuendettelsau: Freimund Verlag.
Plant, Chris (ed.)
  1977   *New Hebrides, the Road to Independence.* Suva: Institute
            of Pacific Studies, University of the South Pacific.
Preiss, G.
  1957   "The Church in Tahiti." *International Review of Missions*
            46:401–9.
Presbyterian Church of the New Hebrides.
  1948–   General Assembly. *Proceedings . . .*
Raapoto, Samuel
  1974   "Église Evangélique de Polynésie Française." *Journal des
            Missions Evangéliques* 149:9–15.
Radford, Robin
  1977   "Burning the Spears, a 'Peace Movement' in the Eastern
            Highlands of New Guinea 1936-37." *Journal of Pacific His-
            tory* 12:40–54.
Ratuvili, Sitiveni
  1974   "The Ethics of Economic Planning." *Pacific Perspective* 3,
            no. 1:17–18.

  1979   *Spiritual Bases for Rural Development in the Pacific.* Suva:
            Lotu Pasifika.
Reed, Stephen W.
  1943   *The Making of Modern New Guinea (with special reference
            to culture contact in the Mandated Territory).* Philadelphia:
            American Philosophical Society.
Reitz, G. O.
  1975   "The Contribution of the Evangelical Lutheran Church of
            New Guinea to Development in Papua New Guinea."
            Mimeographed. Minneapolis: American Lutheran Church.

Responsibility in New Guinea
1965   *Report of an Australian Ecumenical Visit to Papua and New Guinea. June 1965.* Sydney: Australian Council of Churches.

Rey Lescure, Philippe
1967   *Vos racines: Essai d'histoire des débuts de l'évangélisation de la Nouvelle-Calédonie.* Paris: Chez l'auteur.

Rich, C. F.
1937   *A Lighthouse in Papua.* London: Livingstone Press.

Rivers, W. H. R.
1914   *The History of Melanesian Society.* 2 Vols. Cambridge, Eng.: Cambridge University Press.

Rokotuiviwa, Paula
1975   *The Congregation of the Poor.* Suva: South Pacific Social Sciences Association.

Ross, Harold M.
1978   "Competition for Baegu Souls: Mission Rivalry on Malaita Solomon Islands." In *Mission, Church, and Sect in Oceania,* edited by J. Boutilier, D. Hughes, and S. Tiffany; pp. 163–200. Ann Arbor: University of Michigan Press.

Ross, W. A.
1969   "The Catholic Mission in the Western Highlands." In *Second Waigani Seminar: The History of Melanesia.* Canberra: Australian National University.

Rowley, Charles D.
1966   *The New Guinea Villager: The Impact of Colonial Rule on Primitive Society and Economy.* New York: Praeger.

Russell, James
1969   "The Methodist Mission to the Indians in Fiji during the Period of Indenture." Manuscript. Term paper, Yale Divinity School.

Ruthenberg, Donald
1974   "Lutheran Economic Service." *Catalyst* 4, no. 1:41–62.

Sabatier, Ernest
1939   *Sous l'Equateur du Pacifique. Les Iles Gilbert et la Mission Catholique (1888–1938).* Paris: Editions Dillen.

1946   "L'île de Apemama pendant la guerre." *Annales de Notre-Dame du Sacré-Coeur* 80:61–64, 121–23.

Samoan Church (LMS).
1958   "The Commission. Duplicated report of the Commission appointed in 1952 to review the life and work of the church." Apia.

Saussol, Alain
    1969   "La mission mariste et la colonisation européenne en
                Nouvelle-Calédonie." *Journal de la Société des Océanistes*
                25:112–24.

Scarr, Deryck
    1967   *Fragments of Empire. A History of the Western Pacific
                High Commission 1877–1914*. Canberra: Australian Na-
                tional University.

Schäfer, Alfons
    1940   "Die Stellung der Mission zur Polygamie in Mingende."
                Zeitschrift für Missionswissenschaft 40:52–59.

Scharmach, Leo
    1960   *This Crowd Beats Us All*. Surrey Hills: The Catholic Press
                Newspaper Co.

Scheffler, Harold W.
    1971   "Final Report. Revitalization Movements in the British
                Solomons." Multigraphed. New Haven: Yale University,
                Dept. of Anthropology.

Schiotz, F. A.
    1950   "Dr. F. A. Schiotz's Visit to New Guinea, February 1950. A
                Summary of Dr. Schiotz's Report to the Executive Commit-
                tee of The Board of Foreign Missions." Mimeographed.
                Minneapolis: American Lutheran Church.

Schloesing, E.
    1952   "Rapport de M. E. Schloesing sur son Voyage en Océanie
                (Nov. 1951–Mar. 1952)." Mimeographed. Société de Mis-
                sions Evangéliques de Paris.

Schneider, Albert
    1976   "Tahiti: Membres de l'Eglise, Diacres, Pasteurs." *Journal
                des Missions Evangéliques* 151:141–57.

Schuster, Adolf
    1974   "Stadtarbeit der Kirche." In *Heiszes Land Niugini,* edited
                by Rolf Italiaander; pp. 277–83. Erlangen: Verlag der Ev.-
                Luth. Mission.

Schwartz, Theodore
    1962   *The Paliau Movement in the Admiralty Islands, 1946–1954*.
                Anthropological Papers of the American Museum of Natu-
                ral History, 49, part 2. New York: American Museum of
                Natural History.

Self Study of the Catholic Church in Papua New Guinea.
    1972   *Seminar Handbook*. Mimeographed. Goroka: Self-Study
                Secretariate.

    1973   *Church. Material and Questions for Discussion*. Goroka:
                Self-Study Secretariate.

1973-75   *Newsletter.* Goroka: Self-Study Secretariate.
Senerivi, Akerei A.
1974   "An Examination of the Unity of the Church in the New Testament with Reference to the Pacific and Especially to Samoa." B.D. thesis, Pacific Theological College.
Sex, Marriage and the Family in the Pacific.
1969   *Report of a Seminar on Christian Marriage and Family Life, Suva, Fiji Islands. Jan. 6–Feb. 7, 1969.* Geneva: World Council of Churches.
Shaping Educational Ministry. A Consultation Organized by Christian Education Programme January 1977.
1977   Suva: Lotu Pasifika Productions.
Sharp, Gerald (Bishop of New Guinea)
1917   *Diocese of New Guinea. Its Rules and Methods.* n.p.
Shotton, Hedley
1947   "Rebuilding at Kiriwina." *The Missionary Review* 56, no. 1:12–14.
Snijders, John
1971   "A Review. Catholic Catechists of the South-west Pacific." *Catalyst* 1, no. 4:21–30.
South Pacific Missionary Conference, 1948.
1948   *The Cross across the Pacific. Report of Conference of Missionary Leaders Held at Morpeth, N.S.W. from Feb. 23 to 28, 1948.* Sydney: National Missionary Council of Australia.

Committee Minutes. Reports of Commissions 1–10. Conference Resolutions. Questionnaire on Commission Subjects and Replies to Same from Each Area. Manuscripts. In Archives of Australian Council of Churches, Sydney.
Souvenir of the First Fiji Methodist Conference, July 1964.
1964   Suva: Methodist Church in Fiji.
Spades (South Pacific Action for Development Strategy)
1973   *A Report of the Conference on Development Held in Vila, New Hebrides in January 1973.* Suva: Pacific Conference of Churches.
Stanner, W. E. H.
1953   *The South Seas in Transition: A Study of Post-war Rehabilitation and Reconstruction in Three British Pacific Dependencies.* Sydney: Australasian Publishing Co.
The Statement of Doctrine of the Samoan Church (LMS)
1958   Malua.
"A Statement of the Catholic Bishops of Papua New Guinea"
1970   *Zeitschrift für Missionswissenschaft und Religionswissenschaft* 54:211–16.

Steadman, W. R.
1917   "On the Field: Fiji District." *Missionary Review* 26, no. 10:21–22.
Stephen, P. J., and Hulme, J.
1904   *The Morals and Manners of Cardinal Moran: The Examination of a Recent Controversy.* Sydney and Melbourne: Christian World Publishing House.
Sterr, Joseph (ed.)
1950   *Zwischen Geisterhaus und Kathedrale; unter Steinzeitmenschen der Südsee.* Mödling bei Wien: St. Gabriel Verlag.
Steward, John M.
1926   *A Melanesian Use, together with Notes on Ceremonial, etc.* (Melanesian Mission Occasional Papers, no. 3). Maravovo: Melanesian Mission.

1939   *John Steward's Memories. Papers written by the late Bishop Steward of Melanesia;* edited with an introduction by M. R. Newbolt. Chester, England: Phillipson and Golder.
Stewart, Andrew G.
1956   *Trophies from Cannibal Isles.* Washington: Review & Herald Publishing Association.
Strong, P. N. W.
1947   *"Out of Great Tribulation." The Presidential Address and Charge of the Rt. Rev. P. N. W. Strong, M.A., Bishop of New Guinea, to his Diocesan Conference at Dogura, Papua, on Monday, July 30, 1947.* Printed by Methodist Mission, East Cape, Papua.

1958   "Presidential Address and Charge of the Rt. Rev. Philip N.W. Strong, Bishop of New Guinea. Conference and Sacred Synod at Dogura, Jan. 16, 1958." Manuscript. Australian Board of Mission archives. Stanmore, New South Wales.
Suárez, J. R.
1921–22 Letters in *Cartas de la Provincia de León.* Vols. 3–4. Camillas, Spain: Jesuit Missions.
Sullivan, Julius
1957   *The Phoenix Rises. A Mission History of Guam.* New York: Seraphic Mass Assocation.
Sutton, John
1963   "Education in Tonga: Church and State. An Appraisal of the Functions of Church in Education." Diploma thesis, University of Auckland.

Tamaali'i, Sione Uesile
  1975   "Church Administration and Finance in the Methodist
            Church in Samoa." B.D. project, Pacific Theological Col-
            lege.
Territory of Papua and New Guinea
  1946   *Proceedings of the Conference between Representatives of
            Government and Missions on Educational, Health and
            Agricultural Aspects of Native Welfare and Development
            Held at Port Moresby, Papua, 9–14 October 1946.* Port
            Moresby.

  1947   *Conference of Representatives of Administration and Mis-
            sions, May 1947.* Port Moresby.
Theile, Kenneth
  1975   "Mandate for Renewal. Lutheran Witness in Lae, New
            Guinea." *Point* 1:20–42.
Theological Education in the Pacific. Consultation ... Fiji, May 7–13, 1961.
  1961   New York: Theological Education Fund of the Interna-
            tional Missionary Council.
Therriault, H.
  1965   "Island Mission. The Story of the Beginning of Catholicism
            in Niue Island, South Pacific 1955–1965." Mimeographed.
            Niue: Catholic Mission.
Thomson, Claire
  1968   *A Christian Approach to Family Planning.* Suva: Pacific
            Christian Literature Society.
Thornley, A. W.
  1979   "Fijian Methodism, 1874–1945. The Emergence of a Na-
            tional Church." Ph.D. thesis, Australian National Univer-
            sity.
Thorogood, Bernard
  1960   *Not Quite Paradise.* London: London Missionary Society.
Threlfall, Neville
  1975   *One Hundred Years in the Islands. The Methodist/United
            Church in the New Guinea Islands Region 1875–1975.* Ra-
            baul: United Church.
Tippett, Alan R.
  1964   "It Becometh a Tree." In *Souvenir of the First Fiji Metho-
            dist Conference July 1964.* Suva: Methodist Church in Fiji.

  1965   "Shifting Attitudes to Sex and Marriage in Fiji." *Practical
            Anthropology* 12:85–91.

  1967   *Solomon Islands Christianity. A Study in Growth and Ob-
            struction.* London: Lutterworth Press.

Tomlin, J. W. S.
1951   *Awakening. A History of the New Guinea Mission.* London: New Guinea Mission.

Tonga Council of Churches
1975   "Land and Migration. Papers Presented at Seminar Sponsored by the Tonga Council of Churches in Nuku'alofa on September 22 to 26." Mimeographed. Nuku'alofa: Tonga Council of Churches.

Trautmann, Frédéric
1974   "Une Expérience d'animation biblique et théologique en Nouvelle-Calédonie." *Journal des Missions Evangéliques* 149, 2nd quarter: 2–8.

1976   "Où en est la Nouvelle-Calédonie." *Journal des Missions Evangéliques* 151:51–71.

Tremblay, Edouard
1929   *Under the Southern Cross in Tonga-Tabu.* Melbourne: Advocate Press.

Trompf, Garry
1977   *Prophets of Melanesia.* Port Moresby: Institute of Papua New Guinea Studies.

Trumbull, Robert
1959   *Paradise in Trust: a Report on Americans in Micronesia, 1946-1958.* New York: W. Sloane Associates.

Tuilovoni, S. A.
1948   "The Effects of the War on the Church in Fiji." *International Review of Missions* 37:76–79.

Ture Haapaoraa na te mau Ekalesia Tahiti
1882   [Discipline of the Church of Tahiti] Papeete: Imprimerie du Gouvernement.

Turner, Brian
1976   "A Nation of Beggars?" *Catalyst* 6, no. 2:92–101.

Turner, Charles V.
1964   "The Socio-religious Significance of Baptism in Sinasina." *Practical Anthropology* 11:179–80.

Tuza, Esau
1977   "Cultural Suppression? Not Quite." *Catalyst* 7, no. 2: 106–26.

1978   "A Melanesian Cosmological Process." *Catalyst* 8, no. 4:244–62.

UCBWM (United Church Board for World Ministries)
    [*Annual*] *Report.* New York: 1962–

United States Catholics Overseas in Missionary Service, January 1, 1970: A Statistical Directory.

1968   New York: Society for the Propagation of the Faith.
Utt, Richard H.
1963   *A Century of Miracles.* Mountain View, Calif.: Pacific
            Press Publishing Company.
Valentine, Charles A.
1958   "An Introduction to the History of Changing Ways of Life
            on the Island of New Britain." Ph.D. thesis, University of
            Pennsylvania.
Van Dusen, Henry Pitney
1940   *For the Healing of the Nations: Impressions of Christianity
            around the World.* New York: Charles Scribner's Sons.

1945   *They Found the Church There: The Armed Forces Discover
            Christian Missions.* New York: Charles Scribner's Sons.
Vicariate Apostolic of the Caroline and Marshall Islands.
1955   *United States Trust Territory of the Pacific.* n.p.
Vicedom, Georg
1957   "Von der Theologie einer jungen Kirche. Beispiel Neu-
            guinea." In *Das Wort gottes in Geschichte und Gegenwart,*
            edited by Wilhelm Anderson; pp. 103–16. Munich: C.
            Kaiser.

1961   *Church and People in New Guinea.* London: Lutterworth.
Vidich, Arthur J.
n.d.   "Political Factionalism in Palau. Its Rise and Develop-
            ment." Report #23. Mimeographed. Washington: Pacific
            Science Board of the National Research Council.
Viner, A. J.; Williams, G. J.; and Lenwood, Frank
1916   *Report of . . . Deputation to the South Seas and Papua (with
            a chapter on the organization in Australia) June 1915–June
            1916.* London: London Missionary Society.
Vusoniwailala, Lasarusa
1977   "Communicating a 'Pacific Model' for Human Develop-
            ment." *Pacific Perspective* 6, no. 1:64–71.
Wagner, Franz
1960   "Ein Beispiel missionarischen Sozialarbeit in der Südsee."
            Neue Zeitschrift für Missionswissenschaft 16:55–64.
Wagner, J. F.
1964   "The Outgrowth and Development of the Cargo Cult. A
            paper prepared by assignment of the Lutheran Mission New
            Guinea for the 18th Field Conference, 1964." Mimeo-
            graphed. Lutheran Mission New Guinea.
Wallace, Anthony
1956   "Revitalization Movements." *American Anthropologist*
            58:264–81.

Waqa, Meli
1977   *The Youth of Fiji.* Suva: South Pacific Social Sciences Association.

Welling, B.
1958   *Episcopal Hierarchy: A Study of Its Erection in Mission Countries (1946-1956).* Tilburg: A. Reijnen.

West, F. J.
1961   *Political Advancement in the South Pacific.* Melbourne: Oxford University Press.

Wetherell, David
1973   "Monument to a Missionary: C. W. Abel and the Keveri of Papua." *Journal of Pacific History* 8:30-48.

1974   "Christian Missions in Eastern New Guinea: A Study of European, South Sea Island and Papuan Influences, 1877-1942." Ph.D. thesis, Australian National University.

White, Geoffrey
1979   "War, Peace and Piety on Santa Isabel, Solomon Islands." In *The Pacification of Melanesia* edited by Margaret Rodman and Matthew Cooper, pp. 109-140. Ann Arbor: University of Michigan Press.

Wigg, Montague J. Stone-
1912   *Papuans: A People of the South Pacific.* Melbourne: The Shipping Newspapers, Ltd.

Williams, Francis Edgar
1944-1945 "Mission Influence among the Keveri of Southeast Papua." *Oceania* 15:89-141.

Williams, R.G.
1970   "From Mission to Church: A Study of the United Church." In *Fourth Waigani Seminar: The Politics of Melanesia.* Canberra: Australian National University.

1972   *The United Church in Papua, New Guinea and the Solomon Islands.* Rabaul: Trinity Press.

Williamson, Robert W.
1937   *Religion and Social Organization in Central Polynesia.* Edited by Ralph Piddington. Cambridge, Eng.: Cambridge University Press.

Wilson, R. K., and Menzies, K.
1967   "Production and Marketing of Artifacts in the Sepik District and the Trobriand Islands." In *New Guinea People in Business and Industry. Papers from the First Waigani Seminar.* Canberra: Australian National University.

Wiltgen, Ralph M.
1965   "The Death of Bishop Loerks and His Companions." *Verbum* 6:363-97; 7:14-44.

1969   "Catholic Mission Plantations in Mainland New Guinea:
            Their Origin and Purpose." In *Second Waigani Seminar:
            The History of Melanesia.* Canberra: Australian National
            University.

Winthuis, J.
1929   *Zur Psychologie und Methode der religiös-sittlichen
            Heidenunterweisung. Auf Grunde eigener Erfahrungen in
            der Südsee-mission.* Feldkirch: L. Sausgruber.

Wood, A. Harold
1975–1978   *Overseas Missions of the Australian Methodist Church.*
            Vol. 1, Tonga and Samoa, 1975; Vol. 2, Fiji, 1978. Mel-
            bourne: Aldersgate Press.

Worsley, Peter
1957   *The Trumpet Shall Sound. A Study of 'Cargo' Cults in Me-
            lanesia.* London: Macgibbon and Kee.

Wyllie, Mabel G.
1951   "A Study of Polygynous Marriage with Special Reference
            to North Australia and Papua-New Guinea and the Attitude
            thereto of Administration and Christian Missions." M.A.
            thesis. University of Sydney.

Yanaihara, Tadao
1939   *Pacific Islands under Japanese Mandate.* Shanghai: Kelly
            and Walsh, Ltd.

Young, Michael W.
1977   "Dr. Bromilow and the Bwaidoka Wars." *Journal of Pacific
            History* 12:130–53.

Zurenuo, Z. K.
1968   "How Can the Church Carry Its Responsibility?" In M.
            Sorenson, "Report of a New Guinea Field Trip. 1968."
            American Lutheran Church Archives, Minneapolis.

Periodicals

*Periodicals referred to only in connection with articles by particular
authors are listed only under the names of those authors, in the preced-
ing list of references.*

Annales de Notre-Dame du Sacré-Coeur
1865–   Issoudun: Société de Marie.
Annales des Sacrés-Coeurs
1885–   Braine-le-Comte and Evreux: Congrégation des
               Sacrés-Coeurs de Jésus et de Marie.

CWM Newshare
   1977–   London: Council for World Mission.
Caroline and Marshall Islands Mission Bulletin
   1949–   Jesuit Mission. Mimeographed.
Catalyst
   1971–   Goroka: Melanesian Institute for Pastoral and Social Studies.
The Christian Movement in Japan, Korea and Formosa
   1921–26   Tokyo: Christian Literature Society.
Christianisme au XXe Siècle
   1872–   Paris.
Chronicle of the London Missionary Society
   1836–1966   London.
Dialogue. Organ of the S.R.C. of the Holy Spirit Seminary, Madang
   1966–   Mimeographed.
España Misionera
   1944–1958   Madrid: Consejo Superior de Misiones.
Family. News of the Anglican Church of Papua New Guinea
   1977–   Port Moresby.
Fiji Times
   1874–   Suva.
Horizons Blancs
   1959–   Paris: Congrégation des Sacrés-Coeurs de Jésus et de Marie.
Improvement Era
   1898–   Salt Lake City: Church of Jesus Christ of Latter-Day Saints.
International Review of Missions
   1912–   London and Geneva: World Council of Churches.
J M E
                See *Journal des Missions Evangéliques.*
Japan Christian Yearbook
   1905–70   Tokyo: Christian Literature Society.
Jesuit Missions. National Magazine of the American Jesuits in the Mission Fields.
   1926–   New York.
Journal des Missions Evangéliques
   1826–   Paris: Société des Missions Evangéliques.
Journal de la Société des Océanistes
   1944–   Paris.
Kibung: Melanesian Priests' Forum
   1976–   Boroko, Papua New Guinea: Holy Spirit Seminary.

Kreuz und Karitas
1892–   Missionshaus St. Josef, Meppen, Hannover: Mis-
                sionsgesellschaft Mariens.
LMS Chronicle
                See *Chronicle of the London Missionary Society.*
Light and Life
                Bimonthly. Melbourne: Unevangelized Fields Mis-
                sion.
Lutheran World
1954–   Hamburg: Sonntagsblatt.
Micronesian Seminar Bulletin
                Turk: Micronesian Seminar.
Missionary Herald
1805–1951   Boston: American Board of Commissioners for For-
                eign Missions.
Missionary Review
1892–1977   Sydney: Methodist Church of Australia.
Missions Catholiques
1868–1964   Lyon and Paris.
Missions des Îles
1945–1966   Paris: Société de Marie.
New Hebridean Viewpoints
1972–   Aoba and Efate. Mimeographed.
Not in Vain
1896–   Sydney: South Sea Evangelical Mission.
O Le Sulu Samoa
1839–   Apia: Congregational Christian Church of Samoa.
Outpost. A Fiji Forum
1972–77   Suva: Quarterly and bimonthly.
P C C News
1966–   Suva: Pacific Council of Churches.
Pacific Islands Monthly
1929–   Sydney.
Pacific Journal of Theology
1961–69   Suva: Pacific Conference of Churches.
Pacific Perspective
1972–   Suva: South Pacific Social Sciences Association.
Point. Forum for Melanesian Affairs
1972–   Goroka: Melanesian Institute for Pastoral and Socio-
                Economic Services.
Samoa Bulletin
                Apia.
Le Semeur Calédonien. Journal Catholique Calédonien
1954–   Weekly: Noumea.
                Also entitled *Le Semeur.* Continuing the former
                Vie Catholique.

South Pacific Bulletin
1950–   Sydney: South Pacific Commission.
Southern Cross Log
1896–   Auckland and London: Melanesian Mission.
Steyler Missionsbote
1872–   Steyl: Society of the Divine Word.
La Vie Protestante. Journal Mensuel de l'Eglise Evangélique en Nouvelle Calédonie et aux Iles Loyauté.
1960–   Noumea.
Weltmission der Katholischen Kirche
1919–   Munich: Gesellschaft zur Verbreitung des Glaubens.
Woodstock Letters
1872–   Woodstock, Md.: Society of Jesus.
The Word in the World
1959–   Techny, Illinois: Divine Word Publications.
Das Wort in der Welt
1958–   Hamburg:Deutsche Evangelische Missionshilfe.

Index

Index

Finances, church, 82, 124-25, 130-32, 138, 144, 161
Flierl, Johann, 90
Free Church of New Caledonia and the Loyalty Islands, 45, 170
Free Church of Tonga, 125-29
Free Wesleyan Church of Tonga, 126
French Reformed Missions, 14-17, 43-45, 170-71

Gambier Islands, 9, 18
Ganey, Michael, 216
German Missions, 8, 20, 58, 61-63, 174
Gilbert Islands, *see* Kiribati
Goldie, John F., 51, 160, 172
Goward, W.E., 27, 107

Hauofa, Isikeli, 143-44
Havea, Sione 'Amanaki, 126, 208
Hawaii, 4, 9, 11, 18, 27, 29, 82, 128-29
Hawaiian Evangelical Association, 6, 19, 26, 42
Heine, Carl, 62, 142
Hermel, Athanase, 18, 22

Indians in Fiji, 33-35, 132-33, 211-12, 227
Industrial and agricultural schools, 51, 55, 215-16; *see also* Economic development

Japanese missions, 63-64, 125, 169
Jehovah's Witnesses, 200
Jesuit Missions, American, 175, 214-16; Spanish, 63, 145
John Frum Movement, 159, 160, 161
Johnson, Lyndon, 158

Kabu, Tommy, 200
Kava, 114
Kennedy, John F., 143, 191
Keysser, Christian, 59, 60, 103, 105, 111, 166
Kiribati, 6, 26-28, 38, 42, 71, 78, 102, 104, 107-8, 112, 139, 142, 168, 176, 202
Kopuria, Ini, 50
Kozaki, H., 63
Kuder, John, 167
Kwato Extension Association, 56

Labor conditions, 33-35
Lauaki, Chief of Savaii, 24
Laval, Honoré, 18
Lawes, W.G., 8, 107
Leahy, Michael, 146
Leenhardt, Maurice, 44, 45, 115, 116, 170
Leeward Islands, 3, 16, 18, 80, 103, 138
Lelean, A.D., 133
Lelean, C.O., 132
Leray, Joseph, 27

Pouvanaa, Marcel, 212
Presbyterians, 6, 10, 46-48, 74, 81, 106, 110, 114; and adjustment movements, 162; and church independence, 164-66; and education, 186; and medicine, 192-93; and national independence, 213

Reorganized Mormons (Sanitos), 18, 22, 23; and church independence, 178
Rey Lescure, Philippe, 170
Rhenish Mission, 59, 60
Roman Catholics, 4-8, 14-15, 17-19, 22-23, 27, 31, 37, 42, 47-48, 50, 54, 58, 61-63, 71, 75-76, 81-82, 93, 96, 117, 139, 147, 214, 226; and church independence, 175-77; and ecumenical relations, 202-4; and education, 184, 187, 191; and ethics, 103, 105, 107-8; and finances, 124; and medicine, 54, 193; and women's work, 208; and youth work, 206; *see also* names of missionary orders

Sacred Heart Missions, 26, 58-60, 62
Sacred Hearts Missions, 5-6, 17-20, 22
Sadd, Alfred, 139
Sailosi, 156
St. Joseph of Cluny, Sisters of, 17, 22
Salvation Army, 200
Samoa, 4-6, 9, 23-26, 71-72, 76-78, 80-81, 138, 149, 201, 206-7; and church independence, 125, 127-31, 165, 176, 225; education in, 26, 183-85; and national independence, 209-11
Scharmach, Leo, 141
Seventh-Day Adventists, 20, 22, 36, 46, 47, 52-54, 117, 147; and church independence, 178; and education, 188, 190; and ethics, 109, 113, 116, 200; and finances, 124; and medicine, 48, 54, 192, 200
Sharp, Gerald, 72
Sibree, J.W., 23
Society Islands, *see* Tahiti
Solomon Islands, 7, 10, 49-54, 71-72, 89, 113, 147, 200, 202-3, 206, 215; adjustment movements in, 159, 161; church independence in, 171-74; education in, 53-54, 187-88; medical work in, 54, 192; national independence in, 209
Sorcery, 95-96
South Sea Evangelical Mission, 52, 53, 59, 139, 159, 177, 188; and ethics, 109, 113; and finance, 124
Spanish missions, 61-63, 139, 145
Stewart, John, 72
Sunday observance, 116-18

Taboo, 93
Tahiti, 3-4, 6, 9-11, 14-19, 71-72, 76, 79-80, 93, 95, 105, 107, 149, 202; education in, 16-17, 183; medical work in, 47, 193; nationalism in, 211-12; *see also* Leeward Islands
Taofinuu, Pio, 176
Thakombau, 4
Theological education, 201-2
Thompson, L.M., 30
Timakata, Fred, 213